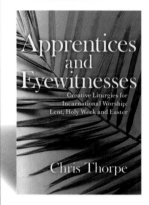
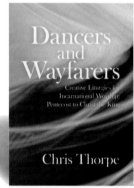
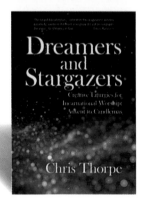

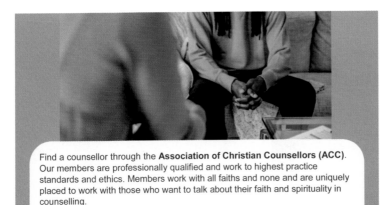

Round-the-Year Resources

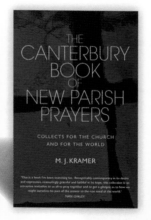

The Canterbury Book of New Parish Prayers
M. J. Kramer

This collection of 500 original collect-style prayers and biddings covers the life of the Church and the world. Contemporary in focus and language, they are written in a concise style that makes them ideal for public worship but will also appeal to anyone struggling to find the words when they pray.

978 1 78622 303 6 £19.99

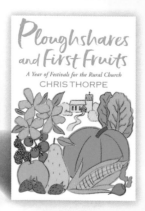

Ploughshares and First Fruits
Chris Thorpe

Plough Sunday, Rogation and Harvest are hugely important for churches serving rural communities. *Ploughshares and First Fruits* provides fresh ideas for keeping the established festivals, with ready-to-use, participative liturgies that engage all the senses, appeal to all ages and give small churches a round-the-year resource.

978 1 78622 290 9 £16.99

CANTERBURY PRESS

www.canterburypress.co.uk

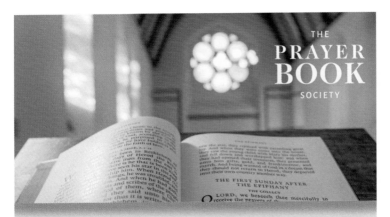

The Prayer Book Society

For half a century the Prayer Book Society has been working to keep the Book of Common Prayer at the heart of the worshipping life of the Church of England.

New generations are discovering the beauty, depth and majesty of the BCP, which remains the standard text for most churches in the Anglican Communion.

In addition to promoting Prayer Book services across the country, the Society runs many national and local events, including the annual Cranmer Awards for young people.

Join us and help keep this wonderful tradition thriving in our churches.

www.pbs.org.uk

Follow us on social media

@prayerbooksociety   @prayerbook_soc   @prayerbooksociety

Registered Charity No. 1099295

Saint Columba's House

t: 01483 766498
www.stcolumbashouse.org.uk
Maybury Hill, Woking, Surrey GU22 8AB

Situated in beautiful wooded gardens, our urban retreat house offers conference spaces, accommodation, quiet days and retreats.

- 9 flexible, well equipped meeting rooms
- Overnight accommodation for 31 guests
- On site Chapel and Oratory
- Home cooked food
- Easy access from London by rail and road

Contact us:

call: 01483 766498
email: admin@stcolumbashouse.org.uk
web: www.stcolumbashouse.org.uk

The Canterbury Preacher's Companion 2023

The Canterbury Preacher's Companion 2023

Sermons for Sundays, Holy Days,
Festivals and Special Occasions
Year A

Edited by Catherine Williams

CANTERBURY
PRESS
Norwich

First published in 2022 by the Canterbury Press Norwich
Editorial office
3rd Floor, Invicta House
108–114 Golden Lane
London EC1Y OTG, UK
www.canterburypress.co.uk

Canterbury Press is an imprint of Hymns Ancient & Modern Ltd
(a registered charity)

Hymns Ancient & Modern® is a registered trademark of
Hymns Ancient & Modern Ltd
13A Hellesdon Park Road, Norwich,
Norfolk NR6 5DR, UK

British Library Cataloguing in Publication data

A catalogue record for this book is available
from the British Library

978 1-78622-362-3

Typeset by Regent Typesetting
Printed and bound in Great Britain by
Ashford Colour Press Ltd.

Contents

SUNDAYS AND MAJOR FESTIVALS

Unless otherwise stated, the readings and the verse numbers of the psalms are taken from *Common Worship: Services and Prayers for the Church of England* (Church House Publishing, 2000), with revisions, and are for Year A.

2022

v

ix

Preface

Welcome to the 2023 edition of *The Canterbury Preacher's Companion*. In this second year of my time as Editor, the three-year lectionary cycle begins again. Year A brings the Gospel of Matthew into focus, and the majority of the Principal Service sermons in this edition are based on passages from Matthew's Gospel. Sermons for the Second Service draw on one of the set lectionary readings or the psalm. In addition, a third of the book is dedicated to sermons for the Red Letter Days in the lectionary: saints' days, festivals and various special occasions.

There has been some lively discussion recently about sermons and plagiarism. Is it right to preach a sermon that someone else has written? Surely, sermons are to be constructed for a particular time and place and therefore not transferable. Preachers are called to develop their particular voice and discern, with the guidance of the Holy Spirit, Jesus the Word's message for their context. Using another's voice may seem to lack integrity.

Bearing this in mind, the sermons in this resource book are not for preaching verbatim, but are given as examples of good practice. This is how a particular preacher has tackled the set scriptures on a given day in their context and from their particular theological, political, spiritual and cultural background. Though some of the sermons are newly commissioned, most have been preached to real congregations on a specific occasion. The writers, ordained and lay, come from a variety of settings and denominations, and their sermons have been preached in churches, chapels, cathedrals and online across the UK, and beyond. In offering these examples to you, we do so hoping that they will spark inspiration for your own preaching within the body of Christ, in the place where you are called to minister.

Working with such a dedicated, creative and passionate group of preachers to produce this book has been inspirational. I pay tribute to their commitment to preaching the Word of God during the particularly challenging time of the Covid-19 global pandemic, and to their ability to keep producing helpful and imaginative sermons while under considerable duress. Whether you are preaching every week or not, I encourage you to read the two sermons offered each Sunday in this book as part of your ongoing walk with God and your engagement with the Scriptures.

This year the article on preaching which follows has been written by Kate Bruce, a seasoned writer and teacher on the subject of preaching, and now also an RAF chaplain. Her excellent article focuses on preaching hope in times of trouble and draws on her experience of preaching during the pandemic. I am grateful for Kate's lively wisdom, and strongly commend her words to you.

As you continue in your vocation to preach, may Jesus walk with you as you prepare and deliver sermons, the Spirit fill you with her inspiring and inventive fire, and God the Creator bless your preaching endeavours in the months and years to come.

Catherine Williams

Understanding Pollyanna and Helping Eeyore: Facing Trouble and Preaching Hope

Kate Bruce

Pollyanna: a person characterized by irrepressible optimism and a tendency to find good in everything.[1]

Eeyore: a fictional grey stuffed donkey who lives in the thistle patch and is depressed, gloomy and pessimistic.[2]

Background

Against the backdrop of the pandemic, I preached regularly in a Zoom church, made up of friends, old and new, who gathered every Sunday evening from various locations (Durham, Cyprus, Cambridge, Lincoln and Suffolk). This small community has faced and is facing many difficulties: cancer, stressed work situations, chronic fatigue, depression, family challenges, dislocation from home contexts, isolation, and a myriad of major and minor demands. This is to say nothing of the questions raised by the wider context of all our lives: the suffering of millions due to displacement, conflict, war, hunger, environmental catastrophe, abuse, racism, rank inequality, unstable political contexts, volatile economic scenarios, and a deep sense of unpredictability. All this sharpened the challenge for me, as a preacher, of facing trouble and preaching hope. How to eyeball trouble without ducking it, yet see within and beyond such instability and suffering to the redemptive hope of God? In preaching hope the preacher's bind is this: too much Pollyanna and we all deny; too much Eeyore and we all despair.

The following chapter explores how we can preach hope with integrity, respecting the reality of profound trouble and deep suffering, without being smothered by it. I seek to understand Pollyanna and invite Eeyore to look up from the thistle patch. I consider the nature of Christian hope, looking at the themes of the Magnificat, Good Friday, Easter Sunday and Ascension as key foundations. I invite Pollyanna and Eeyore to explore the riches of lament and make the penitential walk through the Valley of Achor to the 'door of hope' (Hos. 2.14–16).

Understanding Pollyanna

For those who have suffered deep trauma, it does immense damage when Pollyanna dances on stage and offers statements like: 'God won't give us more than we can handle', or 'We know that our experiences are a blip in the great scheme of things; God is so much bigger' (I heard that one just the other day). Such unnuanced statements are starkly unhelpful. To the parents who lost their baby, the woman raped, the masses facing the tanks, such words are dehumanizing, flattening and silencing.

Am I being a bit hard on Pollyanna? Isn't it a positive thing to be 'a person characterized by irrepressible optimism and a tendency to find good in everything'? But is relentless optimism really a virtue? Does it help? Is optimism the same as Christian hope? I don't think so. Relentless optimism is exhausting, but so is unmitigated despair.

Pollyanna's easy answers are temporary, addictive and false. It is not true that God will give us no more than we can handle. The point is that we are not made to handle everything *alone*. We need others to help us, and here hope in God is earthed. We become vulnerable and dependent – which is part of learning the lessons of hope. The journey towards hope is a shared enterprise, not an individual quest. Hope is breathed in community, 'where two or three are gathered' in Christ's name (Matt. 18.20).

The sermon is formed in the context of the worshipping community, large or small; preaching hope is a shared event. Even though it may involve only one spoken voice, it requires active listeners. The preacher acknowledges implicitly the hearers' many experiences by using invitational phrases and creating spaces for the congregation to internally name their own troubles, questions and longings, drawing Pollyanna and Eeyore, and all the rest, into the event of the sermon, seeking hope together.

Pity Pollyanna

The Pollyanna posture is an expression of a felt loss of control, a sense of the world being out of kilter with all the doubt and fear this generates. If Pollyanna says often enough 'all is well' perhaps it will be well. Maybe she can batten down the hatches, live in her little space and cultivate a closed viewpoint that doesn't engage with the calamitous situations faced by the world today, or the internal ache of her own pain. Preaching which conforms to this stance is speaking from and into an echo chamber – a closed shop for the pious. It is comfortably deluded.

It is worth adding here that when Julian of Norwich uttered her famous dictum, 'All shall be well and all shall be well and all manner of thing shall be well',[3] she was speaking from the other side of profound suffering through illness that nearly took her life. Hers was not a deluded hope based on denial, but profound hope hammered out through her experience as she faced into her pain and struggle *with* God.

The Pollyanna dynamic is driven by factors like the need to control, to hide from fear and anxiety, or to distract from pain. It seeks to manage fear and anxiety by masking these drivers behind vacuous statements. It speaks 'Peace, peace, when there is no peace' (Jer. 6.14). Ultimately, this dynamic prevents us from acknowledging and exploring the felt sense of God's absence. It overlooks the riches of the lament tradition and circumvents the penitence called for in the Valley of Achor (explored below). It inhibits deep exploration of the story of Jesus, his suffering, his resurrection and ascension, and how these resources offer us genuine grounds for hope.

Christian hope: from the Magnificat to the Ascension

We cannot preach Christian hope aside from deep exploration of the narrative of Jesus; preachers need to dwell deeply in this, wrestling with its connections to the plethora of stories of suffering and struggle encountered within and without the walls of the Church.

The Magnificat, that song of Mary when Jesus was *in utero*, epitomizes Christian hope. Startlingly, a young woman, culturally of no significance, articulates a song reverberating with hope. Here the little people are remembered, in the powerful words of one disregarded for her gender. Here is a promise that the proud, the rich and mighty will be brought low, and the poor, downtrodden and unnoticed lifted high. This is good news for those who are in awe of God, for those who cry for mercy and know their need of God. However, Christian hope is not obviously good news for the rich and self-satisfied, for those whose grasp is so full of that which is not God there is no room to receive from God. There is still hope here for any who will drop the burden of idolatry and turn to God; no one is beyond the scope of God's hope – unless they choose to be.

Good Friday to resurrection and beyond

Preachers must resist the temptation to make a flat sprint from Good Friday to Easter Sunday, a dash that assumes that resurrection undoes the fact of Jesus' suffering and death. There is no erasing this. The resurrection is not a reverse step; it is an expression of forward momentum into something utterly new. We must face the appalling suffering of Jesus before we look at where the forward momentum of his resurrection takes us. If we skim over the Passion, we end up with an anaemic version of Christian hope, a flimsy bridge that will bear no weight.

Ponder the Passion: emotional wounds are ripped into Jesus through the betrayal and denial of his friends.[4] Loneliness must surely bite him as he wrestles in the garden while his friends slumber on oblivious.[5] Jesus is abused verbally and physically in the presence of religious, political and military powers. He is exposed, beaten, spat on and humiliated (Matt. 27.27–31). Then crucifixion – the oppressors' vicious tactic, calculated to shame and degrade, and warn. A humiliating murder cashed out with political expediency in mind.

Mugged by trauma at all they had witnessed, his friends and followers experienced the snuffing out of their hopes against a final soundtrack of stone grating against stone as the boulder sealed the tomb's entrance. Despair.

Hope's journey is not a straight line

The gospel accounts of the resurrection demonstrate that there is a mixed and complex shift from despair to resurrection hope. In Matthew's Gospel, the women and the men experience a mixture of fear and joy (28.8–10).

Mark's shorter ending reveals the women fleeing the tomb 'in terror and amazement', and silenced (16.8). In the longer ending Jesus appears to Mary Magdalene, but when she tells her story, we are specifically told that her hearers lack belief (16.11). This is repeated when Jesus appears to two disciples who are subsequently not believed (16.13).

Luke shows us the women at the tomb in a state of fear as they encounter the two shining men who remind them of Jesus' teaching about being raised on the third day (24.5). The women's story is dismissed as 'an idle tale' (24.11) by the other disciples. The two on the Emmaus road fail to recognize the risen Jesus right up until the moment he breaks bread (24.13–35). When Jesus appears to the disciples their reaction is fear; they think he is a ghost (24.37).

In John's Gospel, after a journey of anguish, grief and confusion, Mary Magdalene responds with surprise and joy to Jesus speaking her name (20.16). Similarly, the disciples shift from their story of grief and fear to joy in a sudden movement, as Jesus appears among them (20.19–20). But this is not the case for Thomas, who must wait another week before encountering the risen Christ (20.26). Thomas' encounter with Jesus is crucial for the preacher exploring how to face trouble and preach hope. Thomas is invited to touch Jesus' scars and put his hand into Jesus' side (20.27). The physical wounds and scars of abuse are not erased from Christ's risen body. It's fair to assume that the emotional scars are similarly not airbrushed out.

The experience of suffering etched into Jesus' body and mind is taken up in the ascension (Luke 24.50). The depths of human anguish are known intimately to God; there is no need to deny or suppress the effects of despair. It can be brought honestly in lament to the God who knows intimately and loves infinitely.

Lament: preaching hope from the thistle patch

Preaching hope calls for the preacher to sit with Eeyore without becoming stuck in the mire of despair. The lament tradition gives us language and a theological structure that is foundational for the articulation of hope. The lament psalms are addressed to God. Herein lies their hope. Rather than denying the truth of human suffering in a hasty leap to Easter triumph, lament calls for honesty to go deep into the experience of suffering and enter the paradox of wrestling with the God who seems absent. This was Jesus' own experience, captured in the anguished cry of dereliction: 'My God, my God, why have you forsaken me?' (Matt. 27.46; Mark 15.34). This is a crucial part of the journey into hope, facing into suffering and despair honestly, *with* God. The preacher who leapfrogs this will offer a nebulous hope that mutes the sufferer's cry.

Walter Brueggemann's three modes of orientation, disorientation and reorientation[6] are useful at this juncture. Orientation relates to life in a steady state, where the world seems predictable, reliable and consistent. The pandemic tipped us all out of this mode, upending us in a state of disorientation: a catastrophe marked by dislocation, fear and uncertainty. Preachers need to address disorientation to help people find hope, moving towards the mode of reorientation. This is a state marked by deeper grounding in God and a renewed experience of God's grace and sufficiency. This is the simplicity found on the other side of complexity, arguably where Julian of Norwich uttered her 'All shall be well'. Here we are more able to live with ambiguity and contradiction. *But how do we get there?* It's a journey, not a jump. It's instructive to examine the structure of the lament psalms to see how disorientation and reorientation are connected and how this might inform the preacher's quest to face trouble and preach hope.

Example: Psalm 13

Psalm 13 begins with a cry from the thistle patch. While Eeyore's temptation is always to turn inwards, the Psalmist turns to God, making the primary movement of the journey of hope. Anguish is expressed in accusatory terms: 'How long, O LORD? Will you forget me for ever? ... hide your face from me?' ... leave me wresting and in sorrow, defeated by my enemy?' (vv. 1–3). The triple 'how long' communicates clearly, the Psalmist has had a gutful.

Following this pattern, the preacher need not be squeamish about approaching God with such words and tone. In articulating pain and anguish openly, the preacher (like the Psalmist) can draw a lamenting community together. The underlying cadence of the lament is a cry of need, an act of trust in the defiant search for hope.

Despair expressed, the Psalmist calls for divine help (vv. 3–4), returning to the bass line of faith, the specific articulation of trust in the nature of God who is unfailingly loving, the bringer of salvation, and the source of all goodness (vv. 5–6). Such credal rehearsal reorientates the sufferer to the character of God. It is essential that the preacher gives voice to the love of God. We may feel flat, spent, despondent, and yet still we must name the truth of God's nature and remind ourselves of all God has done for us. Frequently in the psalms, we see the recitation of the faithfulness of God in the past to help people hold on in the storm of the present and hope for calmer days.

Theologically weighting the sermon

The movement from disorientation to reorientation is a useful structure for sermons seeking to name trouble and preach hope. When the preacher articulates disorientation and gives specific instances of such human experience, we communicate to the sufferer, 'You are heard and seen.' However, the preacher needs to ensure that the sermon doesn't stay in the thistle patch. Too much emphasis on disorientation and Eeyore will dominate, too much emphasis on reorientation and Pollyanna merely places a plaster on a blast wound. Theological weighting calls the preacher to give expression to the truth of disorientation and link this to the theological implications of resurrection power and hope, ensuring that the language used is strong enough to gather and reorientate the hearer before the transforming power and possibility of God.

It is right and good to cry to God in disorientation from the thistle patch, but we must also own our part in arriving (and remaining) in that place. Confession is an important part of preaching hope.

The Valley of Achor: a dead end becomes a doorway

The Valley of Achor is mentioned in Joshua (7.25–26) as the place where Achan and his family are stoned to death and buried. Captivated by the value of items taken from the fall of Jericho, Achan steals and hides some, having explicitly been told to keep away from them to avoid falling prey to covetous thoughts (6.18). The Valley of Achor is a place of failure, disobedience, greed, judgement and death – a place of profound sorrow. It's the dead end of sinful stupidity; no hope here, humanly speaking.

The Valley of Achor crops up again in Hosea, in a passage that speaks of God's judgement against faithless, forgetful Israel (2.1–13). God declares in a gift of sheer grace: 'I will make the Valley of Achor a door of hope.' In Isaiah, we see a similar motif when the Valley of Achor is described as 'a place for herds to lie down, for my people *who have sought me*' (65.10). Jesus' redemptive action through his life, death, resurrection and ascension creates a route from Achor, the place of death, into new life. He is 'the gate for the sheep' (John 10.7), leading all who follow to new pastures beyond 'the valley of the shadow of death' (Ps. 23.4 AV).

In preaching hope, the preacher must remember that people find themselves in the place of disorientation for a range of reasons: as a direct result of someone's actions, through no personal fault, through poor decision-making, or a mixture of factors: the failure to live in right relationship to God, others, the environment and self. The preacher should not be shy of speaking of sin, though the term needs earthing in contemporary examples to avoid being tuned out as an old-fashioned religious category. The seven deadly sins (pride, covetousness, lust, gluttony, envy, anger and sloth) seem remarkably contemporary. The pay-out from these things is severe, causing human disorientation. The movement from disorientation to reorientation is through the Valley of Achor, a place where the redemptive love of God stirs penitential searching and draws people to the forgiving and restorative work of Christ.

The doorway of hope in the Valley of Achor points to Jesus as the gateway (John 10.7), which points on to the open doorway of Revelation 4.1; a doorway through which we catch a glimpse of a future beyond death spent in the presence of God. This future does not erase the experience of the thistle patch – it gathers it up and transcends it. In the face of this wonder, Pollyanna's platitudes fall silent and Eeyore's despair is transfigured. Preaching hope calls for the preacher to paint with language to capture a glimpse of the future God invites us into where God 'will wipe every tear from their eyes. Death will be no more; mourning and crying and pain will be no more, for the first things have passed away' (Rev. 21.4). Pollyanna. Eeyore. This is hope. You are both invited.

Bringing hope into the now

I have long wrestled with the question of how to hold together trouble and hope and how to speak of this credibly and with integrity as a preacher. The answer is not to learn new turns of phrase, better ways of delivery, or new sermon structures – as important as these things can be. At heart, the answer is about relationship with God. If we stay in the shallows of faith, we will preach shallow sermons, platitudes for the pious. God is calling us to wrestle with life's ambiguities and contradictions; to eyeball trouble and pray with honesty; to lament loud and long, and own our part in the world's troubles. God invites us to meet the risen Jesus afresh and to seek him in the Scriptures, in the troubled places of our spirits, and the broken places of our communities. He invites us to meet Christ's gaze and know that we are known – all our mess, muddle, gift and glory. God calls us to face trouble and hold tight to love. Through her suffering, Mother Julian discovered the mystery that divine love makes all manner of things well. When you trust that for the future, it shapes the way you handle the present, bringing hope into the now.

Contributors

Mark Amos is head of philosophy and theology at The Abbey School, Reading, and part of the leadership team at Reading Family Church. He is the author of *God for Now: Theology through Evangelical and Charismatic Experience* (Wipf and Stock, 2020).

The Revd Dr Kate Bruce is an RAF Chaplain. She has spent many years teaching preachers, running training events and writing books and articles on preaching. Her latest book is co-authored with Liz Shercliff, *Out of the Shadows: Preaching the Women of the Bible* (SCM Press, 2021). She preaches regularly in a wide range of contexts. Alongside her love of preaching, she has an interest in performing stand-up comedy.

The Revd Kat Campion-Spall is an Anglican parish priest currently serving as Associate Vicar at St Mary Redcliffe in Bristol, and Dean of Women's Ministry for Bristol Diocese. Kat, influenced by feminist biblical interpretation, tries to listen carefully for, and bring to light, the voices that have been silenced by received interpretations of the Scriptures.

The Revd Canon Dr Tom Clammer OC ministered in the diocese of Gloucester before serving as Precentor of Salisbury Cathedral. He is now a freelance theologian, educator and spiritual director, and a novice brother of the Anglican Order of Cistercians. Used to full cathedrals, or half a dozen in a rural church, Tom preaches regularly, mostly in the dioceses of Salisbury and Gloucester.

The Revd Dr Mary Cotes is a Baptist minister. Having served in a number of ecumenical roles, she now works for the French association Servir Ensemble and exercises an itinerant ministry through preaching, teaching and writing. She is author of *Women Without Walls* (Graceworks, 2020).

Dr Esther Elliott is a workplace and community chaplain in Edinburgh and therefore has lots of opportunities to hear how all sorts of people think and talk about spirituality. She preaches in a Church of Scotland parish. Previously she preached regularly in an Anglican parish in Nottingham as a lay Reader and taught preaching for ministers in Derby Diocese.

The Venerable Tricia Hillas is Chaplain to the Speaker of the House of Commons, Canon Steward and Archdeacon of Westminster. Tricia treasures Scripture as a means to encounter God, while also looking for God's presence made manifest in the world. Preaching in various settings, for a range of people and situations, is an honour and responsibility which challenges and stimulates her faith.

The Revd Dr Wendy Kilworth-Mason is a Methodist presbyter, mission partner and theological tutor who has served in the UK, USA, Zambia, Kenya and Sierra Leone. She is to serve at the Theological College of Lanka. Wendy has an interest in teaching church history and preaching the Old Testament.

The Revd Jonathan Lawson is Vicar of St Gabriel's Church in Newcastle upon Tyne. He has served and preached in many different contexts from retreat houses to cathedrals, and ministered for ten years as a university chaplain. He has a particular interest in vocation and spiritual direction.

The Revd Canon Dr Rachel Mann is a parish priest, poet, novelist and broadcaster. Author of 12 books, she is passionate about literature, every aspect of culture, as well as ensuring that those traditionally excluded from the life of the Church have an honoured place. Her preaching reflects these passions and commitments.

The Revd Canon Dr Sandra Millar, former Head of Life Events for the Church of England, preaches in a wide range of contexts from cathedral to country church. She is interested in making Scripture connect to the realities of contemporary culture and everyday life.

The Revd Canon Peter Moger is a priest in the Scottish Episcopal Church at St Peter's Stornoway on the Isle of Lewis. Prior to this he has served as a parish priest in the Church of England, as Secretary of the Liturgical Commission, and as Precentor of York Minster.

The Rt Revd Lusa Nsenga Ngoy is the Bishop of Willesden. Prior to consecration, he was the Black, Asian and Minority Ethnic Mission and Ministry Enabler in Leicester Diocese. He is originally from the DR Congo and is a Belgian citizen. He is committed to amplifying global voices in theological discourse and ministry. He shares a particular interest in storytelling, with a commitment to racial equity.

The Revd Dr Catherine Okoronkwo is Vicar of All Saints and St Barnabas churches in Swindon and is the Bishop of Bristol's Adviser on Racial Justice. As a poet and writer, she has a particular interest in the use of creative arts in mission. Her debut collection of poetry, *Blood and Water / ọbara na mmiri* is published by Waterloo Press (2020).

Andrew Rudd is a lay Reader in Frodsham, Cheshire, in the diocese of Chester. He leads retreats and quiet days and teaches spirituality and New Testament to ordinands, trainee Readers and pastoral workers. He is Poet-in-Residence at Manchester Cathedral, and also offers spiritual accompaniment.

The Revd Carey Saleh is a parish priest in Worcester Diocese and preaches regularly. Her published writings include liturgy for Wild Goose, and a play addressing dementia and memory. She has a strong interest in Celtic spirituality, and in the use of metaphor and story to help in understanding God.

The Revd Canon Liz Shercliff is a writer, speaker, researcher and preacher. She is author of *Preaching Women* (SCM Press, 2019), and co-author with Kate Bruce of *Out of the Shadows* (SCM Press, 2021) and with Matt Allen, *The Present Preacher* (Canterbury Press, 2021), founder of an annual conference for women, Women's Voices, and of the North West Preaching Conference.

The Very Revd Dr Frances Ward was Dean of St Edmundsbury during 2010–17 and now serves as a parish priest in West Cumbria, preaching frequently there and in many different contexts, alongside teaching, leading retreats and writing. She is the co-editor (with Richard Sudworth) of *Holy Attention: Preaching in Today's Church* (Canterbury Press, 2019).

The Revd Catherine Williams is a spiritual director and writer. She contributes to spirituality resources such as *Pray As You Go*, *Daily Reflections* and *Fresh from the Word*, and is the lead voice on the Church of England's *Daily Prayer* app. Licensed to the Bishop of Gloucester as a Public Preacher, Catherine preaches regularly in a variety of contexts.

The Revd Canon Dr Paul Rhys Williams is Vicar of Tewkesbury and regularly preaches in and around Tewkesbury Abbey. Paul is a Commander of the Order of St John and Vice Dean of the Priory of England and the Islands. He is one of Her Majesty's Deputy Lieutenants of Gloucestershire. These and other settings provide stimulating contexts in which to minister.

Year A, the Year of Matthew

*(Year A begins on Advent Sunday
in 2022, 2025, 2028, etc.)*

Advent

First Sunday of Advent   27 November
Principal Service   **Be Prepared!**
Isa. 2.1–5; Ps. 122; Rom. 13.11–end; **Matt. 24.36–44**

Be prepared

The Cub Scout motto is 'Be prepared'. It's a good motto for anyone, I suppose, and it is the resounding, consistent message of Advent, which begins today. And actually, it's the golden thread running through everything we do on Advent Sunday, and the whole of this season if we let it speak to us.

This Sunday we launch into the reading of Matthew's Gospel. We'll read it for the whole of this year, up to and including the Sunday before Advent 2023, and, as odd as this might sound, I'd like to talk about what we will read in 51 weeks' time, just for a moment. When we get to the end of this year and we celebrate the feast of Christ the King, the Gospel reading we will read is Matthew 25 – the parable of the sheep and the goats. 'I was hungry', we will hear our Lord say to us, 'and you gave me no food. I was thirsty and you gave me nothing to drink … I was sick and in prison and you did not visit me.' We are starting this new church year with the end in mind. Our destination is that terrifying and illuminating parable where Christ makes it absolutely clear that when we make decisions about whether or not to act towards the needy in our world, we are making decisions about whether or not to ignore him.

The call to justice

The call, throughout Matthew's Gospel, is to justice. Advent is about justice. It is about listening, being ready, hearing that cry which wells up from the bone and the marrow of creation; that cry, that yearning, for a world that is fair, and just, and honest. Advent,

2

and indeed Jesus Christ, is about integrity. How is it that this baby in the manger, this shabby itinerant preacher, this crucified criminal, has something to say to me, to you, about how the world could be different, gentler and transformed?

So we begin, on Advent Sunday, holding in our minds the sheep and the goats, and we start with Isaiah. Isaiah the prophet is like a loudhailer with a conscience. It's as if someone is sitting on the shoulder of the people and shouting into their ears – 'Will you please look around you at what's going on? Look at your society, look at your religion, look at your heart. Can you not see the inconsistency? The hypocrisy? The double standards?'

Decommissioning our weapons

And what does Isaiah want to talk about? He wants to talk about what is going to happen to weapons. He wants to talk about swords being so entirely put beyond use that they can be used to furrow the ground instead. About spears so decommissioned that you can use them for your gardening. He wants to talk about justice. About a God who is coming to exact fair judgement upon the world. Weapons – swords, spears and so on – are only ever responses to imperfect judgement, unjust rule, bias, criminality, corruption, jealously, covetousness. It is these things that result in a need for weapons.

Injustice breeds mistrust and hatred, and that pollutes society. Isaiah is crying out to the people, a people who have drifted and relapsed and forgotten the principles on which their nation was founded. He is crying out to them to walk in the light. To make a radical decision to move into a new mode of being, a new set of assumptions about how we do business one with another. A society of faith and trust, where it is only God who gets to judge.

But that is not a world which has yet appeared. The kingdom is coming but is not yet here. And don't we know it?! And so, we do need to be prepared; to keep awake. 'Do not be taken by surprise' is the message of today's Gospel reading. The new order is coming, and it is not going to look very much like what you recognize now.

The unexpected King

Just as, of course, at Christmas, we recall that when the King entered his kingdom he did not look very much like a king. And, as we heard last week, when the King was enthroned, that throne

3

looked rather like a cross. And as we will hear in 51 weeks' time, when we meet our King in the street, he probably won't look much like a king either. He will look like a sick friend, or a homeless beggar, or the problematic and irritating person we most want to avoid.

Be prepared. Keep awake. Look for the arrival of the kingdom. These are the messages of Advent. That is why we light, slowly, one candle after the next, because the kingdom comes gradually. The light grows gradually. But it does grow. And, yes, we are counting down to Christmas, and all that means to us, but we are also counting down to the time when everything will be transformed: when weapons will be garden forks; when tears will turn to laughter, and unexpectedly the King will be in his kingdom. The Advent challenge is to live, as much as possible, as if all five candles were already burning. As if the kingdom were already here.

Tom Clammer

Hymn suggestions

O come, o come, Emmanuel; When I needed a neighbour; People, look east; Thy kingdom come, on bended knee.

First Sunday of Advent   27 November
Second Service   **Visitors Welcome!**
Ps. 9 [*or* 9.1–8]; **Isa. 52.1–12**; Matt. 24.15–28

Telling the story again

Apparently, it's really unusual to reread novels, especially if you reread not just once, but ten or twenty times or more down the years. I read for the joy and for the comfort of knowing the story and recognizing once more the skill of the other in shaping it. It's lovely to know the ending. Perhaps that's why I like the church year: today we simply begin telling the same story all over again.

At one level, we are beginning once more the story of waiting for a child, a child who will grow up, teach, heal and renew, before he dies and then lives again. It's safe and reassuring, this well-known comfortable story that starts again with every Advent Sunday. It's the story that informs a million Advent calendars, and the season that gets some excited and others anxious, as we prepare for the coming of the Christ-child at Christmas. But Advent is also about the unknown story, about waiting for Christ to return and for all things to be transformed and restored. The Advent readings make us tremble as they tell us of a world that will be full of fear, anxiety, danger and disaster even as we wait for the Lord to return, not knowing, when or where or how.

Advice for getting ready

The prophet Isaiah was speaking to a people who were anxious and afraid, exiled from their homeland, clinging on to the promise that the God of their songs and stories is faithful. Isaiah speaks words of hope and comfort, using language that has inspired countless songwriters ever since. He also uses some very homely metaphors, metaphors that speak to our Advent and Christmas preparation, as he talks of garments and buildings and visitors. These days we often don't have to wait for good news. It's a world of instant communication where short messages update us on new arrivals, new romances and new purchases. Good news comes quickly. Yet in this season of 'getting ready for Christmas', the media still tells us about what to cook, what to wear and how to be ready to receive visitors. In the next few weeks, people will travel far and wide, arriving at homes and hotels, attending lavish parties or simple suppers, perhaps bearing gifts and changing lives, even if just for a day or two. There is an excitement in the air at the idea of 'driving home', as we become or receive feet on the move.

Good news brings hope

The feet of those who bring good news are welcome. Isaiah paints a picture of a runner coming over the mountain, full of urgency, but with a smile and shout as they bring the news of victory. It is no coincidence that one of the world's most well-known brand identities, placed on running shoes, represents the idea of a winged messenger announcing victory. When a city was under siege, or a battle being fought far away, then messengers would be sent to those waiting to bring them the news they needed to hear of hope and future. Because victory is the news the people were waiting for. It was news that would give them hope and enable them to keep waiting, and trusting that God would be faithful.

No wonder Isaiah calls people to be ready, to put on their finest clothes, shake off the dust and start singing. As we prepare to welcome Christ again, we are also reminded of God's desire to restore us as we hear the good news. For even though the circumstances we live in, whether in our world or in our personal lives, are hard and demanding, there will always be a moment to be ready, and a moment to help others be ready. We can put on the garments of righteousness and praise that God has provided for us, and continue with the task of making ready as we repair and rebuild the lives of those around us. In Ephesians, St Paul suggests that we put on the shoes of the gospel of peace, ready to be those running with the good news that Christ is coming. Salvation is at hand as we start to tell again the great story of God's engagement with the world he loves. Listen for the sound of the messenger once more.

Sandra Millar

Hymn suggestions

How lovely on the mountains; Come, thou long-expected Jesus; We have a gospel to proclaim; Forth in thy name, O Lord, I go.

Second Sunday of Advent   4 December
Principal Service   **The Ultimate Prophet?**
Isa. 11.1–10; Ps. 72.1–7, 18–19 [*or* 72.1–7]; Rom. 15.4–13;
Matt. 3.1–12

All of us carry stereotypes around in our heads and hearts. They're usually acquired in childhood and they can become as fixed in the mind as a physical photograph or film. Once settled, these stereotypes can be difficult to displace. Thus, while cultural expectations have shifted over time, if you were asked to conjure up an image of a doctor or a nurse, it's reasonably likely that your first image would cast nurses as female and doctors as male.

The stereotypical prophet?

Perhaps these biases and prejudices apply also to prophets. In my head, when I picture a prophet, I see a man who is a little on the edge of normal behaviour, with wild eyes and bad personal hygiene; who dresses strangely and has angry, but righteous words to deliver to the masses. In short, I think I turn all prophets into a version of

6

John the Baptist. So deep does this image run in our society that I think the leaders of many of those cults and movements which flourished in the 1960s drew their personal style code from John.

On this Second Sunday of Advent, when according to one tradition the people of God are invited to reflect on the place of the prophets in directing us towards Jesus, I want to take a look behind the stereotyped image of a prophet. This isn't easy because the way Matthew presents John the Baptist – the final prophet God sends before Jesus arrives – is so rich in classic imagery.

Matthew's John wears camel-hair clothing and lives off bugs and honey. He has tough words for some, calling both religious leaders and the social elite 'you brood of vipers'. His message is uncompromising: 'Repent, for the kingdom of heaven has come near.' I suspect that as soon as any of us read these lines about 'broods of vipers' or 'repentance' we no longer need to be told any more details about John. Our brains do the rest: he is wild-eyed, long-haired and more than a little scary. I, for one, would be inclined to walk away.

Directing us towards God

However, the people of God in Matthew's Gospel walk towards him, even if they find his message difficult. It is not just the excluded and undervalued who are drawn to John. It is people from the 'centre': Pharisees and Sadducees. Jesus himself goes to John. If John is, like many of the faithful prophets of Israel, including Elijah, 'of the edge', he reminds us that those of us who like to occupy the centre can't always afford to stay there. We have to be prepared to go where God wants us. For example, I was once asked if I was more of a pastor or a prophet. I said I saw myself as more of a pastor because I liked to be seen as safe, approachable, an honest broker from the centre of things. The edge voice of a prophet like John reminds those of us who like the centre that truth is often most clearly spoken from the uncomfortable edge. Sometimes we need to be prepared to speak from there.

Most of all, as a prophet who points towards Jesus ('but one who is more powerful than I is coming after me; I am not worthy to carry his sandals. He will baptize you with the Holy Spirit and fire'), John invites us both to be faithful to our faith's historic truth and also know that it is fulfilled in Jesus. That is, John subverts the popular image of the prophet as one who makes predictions or is some sort of soothsayer who sees the future. Rather, in calling his hearers and indeed us to repentance he asks us to 'turn around'

7

and face God. He calls his hearers back to faithfulness. This is one reason why he gripped the attention of the people of his day: he had a message that was as old as the covenant that God made with Moses and the patriarchs (and, indeed, matriarchs) of Israel: be faithful to God as he is faithful to you.

The prophet's task

John, then, is a classic prophet. He does not seek to look into the future to make predictions. He calls the people of God to account. Where he truly shocks and stuns me is in the depth of his honesty and humility. He knows that one is coming after him who is the very presence of God; the one who will baptize with fire and the Holy Spirit: Jesus the Christ. He knows this not because he is making wild speculation about the future. He knows this because he is so grounded in the mystery and truth of the covenant. He knows who he is and glimpses as fully as any prophet ever has what God's love, justice and mercy requires. It requires nothing more or less than the very presence of God in his Son. He points us towards a truth that even now, two thousand years after Jesus walked the earth, stuns as it startles, excites and inspires.

Rachel Mann

Hymn suggestions

On Jordan's bank, the Baptist's cry; Christmas is coming, the Church is glad to sing; All my hope on God is founded.

Second Sunday of Advent 4 December
Second Service YHWH, He is God! YHWH, He is God!
Ps. 11 [28]; **1 Kings 18.17–39**; John 1.19–28

What a dramatic story. Surely it lends itself to the Hollywood treatment, with lots of special effects? Those of us whose imaginations have been nurtured by the film industry can see it in our minds' eyes. It's a confrontation story of the battle between Elijah, who stands alone as the prophet of YHWH, and 450 prophets of Baal: what an uneven contest. On a human level, Elijah evidently faces impossible odds, so only with divine intervention could he hope to win. He needs his God to authorize and vindicate him. On the divine level, the combatants are not these puny human prophets but YHWH and Baal, vying for the commitment of a people whose loyalty is wavering.

Our story, probably from an earlier tradition, sits oddly amid the drought stories that surround it (in which Ahab's apostasy features as the cause of the drought). The tension between the prophet and the king is coming to a head, as Elijah orders the king to have all Israel assemble at Mount Carmel, with the prophets of Asherah and those of Baal. Elijah is a prophet of YHWH, a jealous god who will not share the people's allegiance. To settle the question as to who is God, Elijah takes the initiative in arranging a contest at Carmel.

Showdown at Carmel!

Is the choice of Carmel as the venue significant? There's no tradition elsewhere in the Bible about there being a YHWH shrine there. It's more likely that it was a centre for Baal worship (there is archaeological evidence for Canaanite or Phoenician worship in that area). Why would Elijah single out this shrine for his demonstration of God's favour? It's a mystery. Perhaps we should set aside such questions about the location and historicity of the event and regard it as holy legend that has truths to convey.

Elijah explains the rules. The contestants are simply to prepare a sacrifice and then call upon their god to consume it. The god who acts, who brings down fire, will be proved to be the true God. Elijah allows the prophets of Baal to go first. It should be easy for Baal, a storm god, to strike with lightning! The prophets don't seem to give much attention to preparation for a ritual, and yet they take virtually the whole day, they cry out and then cry still more loudly, they cut themselves (perhaps in the belief that their blood will revive Baal who, in the tradition, entered a death sleep in the dry season) and doubtless they become increasingly frenzied. This is not polite religion; it's raw and dramatic, it demands blood and sweat. You can feel the tension rising.

The times for the two daily sacrifices pass, Baal does not answer and Elijah begins to mock the prophets and their god. He suggests that Baal is sleeping, or journeying or busy (a targum interprets the mockery to mean that Baal is in the toilet).

With the day drawing to a close, Elijah summons the people closer. Then he prepares a 'stage' for the final denouement. His arrangements are carried out efficiently and meticulously, as he builds a new altar and digs a trench that is then filled with grain.

The wood and the slaughtered bull are put in place. Next, Elijah gets 12 large barrels of water (which would be difficult in normal times, let alone in a time of drought. The river Kishon was the nearest source of water, some distance away at the foot of the mountain). He makes the challenge still more difficult by drenching the sacrifice with water and filling the trench. With the preparations complete, at the time of the evening sacrifice, Elijah prays to YHWH, the God of Israel's ancestors.

Down comes the fire from heaven!

The winner is ...

YHWH is victorious, Elijah is vindicated (as the true prophet of the true God), Baal is defeated, Baal's prophets are discredited. Having witnessed the awe-inspiring, breath-taking spectacle, the people fall on their faces, not daring to seek the face of God, as they declare, with certitude, 'YHWH, he is God! YHWH, he is God!' Elijah's actions have brought about the outcome he desired: he has convinced the wavering people to pledge their allegiance to YHWH.

Perhaps, therefore, the real 'winners' are the people of Israel who, following this demonstration, repent and return to God. The drought ends and, for a time, all is well.

What of ourselves? Do we waver and question the supremacy of God? Are we prone to split our allegiance between God and false gods? How do we convince ourselves, let alone those who profess no faith, that God alone is God?

It may be that we will see no extravagant spectacle but, perhaps in our familiar worship, we can be reminded that our God does not sleep, he does not go away. So, draw close to God and worship him alone.

Wendy Kilworth-Mason

Hymn suggestions

Lord, dismiss us with your blessing; The God of Abraham, praise; Sing praise to God who reigns above; My God, I know, I feel thee mine.

Third Sunday of Advent   11 December
Principal Service   **Waiting in the Wilderness**
Isa. 35.1–10; Ps. 146.4–10, *or Canticle*: Magnificat;
James 5.7–10; Matt. 11.2–11

From the depths

Stirring in the garden at this time of year there may already be daffodil shoots poking through, tiny little points of green. Although they are easily trampled or overlooked, they are there, the promise of spring even in the depths of winter. All we need to do is wait. Advent is all about waiting. Not really waiting for Christmas, although that's what our Advent calendars make us think. Christmas has, after all, already happened – two thousand times. No. It's not a sitting in a waiting room reading a magazine kind of waiting, not a crossing the days off kind of waiting. It's a heart-rending, gut-wrenching yearning, the kind of longing that makes us groan, a cry from the depths. Do you feel it? Is there a place of wilderness, a place of dryness, a place of weak hands and feeble knees, of fearful hearts, a place where eyes are blind and ears are deaf and legs are lame and tongues are made speechless? Do you know that place – in your life, in our city, in our nation, in the world? The place where we cry to God: 'O come!'

Two thousand Christmases

Year after year, we celebrate the coming of Christ at Christmas. He has already come, he is already here. When John the Baptist sends his disciples to ask Jesus, 'Are you the one who is to come, or are we to wait for another?' Jesus draws on imagery from Isaiah to say the time of rejoicing has come, the time of flourishing and freedom and abundance is here. The waiting is over. God is with us, Emmanuel has come, the Word is made flesh, God is incarnate, Jesus is born. And yet, even after the rejoicing of two thousand Christmases, we come back, again and again, to the place of wilderness, the place of as yet unfulfilled promise, the place of yearning and waiting. We are in the 'now and not yet' times between the incarnation and the second coming. Our Advent waiting, on the surface, looks forward to Christmas, but more profoundly it helps us find a language, an expression, for that deeper, aching longing, the yearning for the coming of Christ that is promised but that we don't really understand.

A place of potential

The wilderness isn't a place of death, nor, really, a place of hopelessness or despair. Isaiah sees it as a place ready for transformation, a place of unimaginable potential; it is a place where what seems lifeless and broken and constrained is allowed to come to life, to find fulfilment and flourishing and freedom beyond any hope or expectation. The wilderness is where the yearning, the deep longing, is fulfilled by a kind of abundance that bursts into life with joy and ferocity and power. The wilderness is where people go to see John the Baptist. And, as Jesus establishes, they go to see him not because they are looking for someone who will be swayed by changing influences; not because they are looking for someone whose life has been cushioned by power, wealth and privilege; but because they want to see a prophet. Someone who sees the world as God does, who looks at the dry earth and understands what will grow.

Through the eyes of a prophet

John prepares the way for God by calling for repentance. This requires us to look at ourselves and see if we are living and loving in a way that welcomes God, or in a way that rejects God. It requires us to change. But if we truly welcome God, then we can wait in the wilderness places, in places of brokenness, captivity and silence, and we can rejoice. We can stand in the place of now and not yet, knowing that God is both truly here and yet to come. We can look with the eyes of a prophet at a world that is crying out for healing and redemption, and imagine the unimaginable potential of the dull, dead soil; we can witness the tiny shoots of hope and know they are a sign of more to come. While our eyes see wilderness, our hearts can see rivers and blossoming and rejoicing.

Waiting in hope

Advent teaches us that our heart-breaking longing is not in vain, that God's promises will be fulfilled. It teaches us to look for the dawn on the horizon, to fix our eyes on the dawning brightness, and to walk towards the light, even as we dwell in darkness. We only know that the tiny green points are daffodil shoots if we have seen the daffodils. And because we know the beauty of the daffodils, we can rejoice at the appearance of the shoots, and wait for the fulfilment of their promise. Because, again, we wait for Christmas, when God came to us in a place of poverty, oppression and rejection, we know how to wait for something more, something better, something that transforms the wilderness into a place of rejoicing.

Kat Campion-Spall

Hymn suggestions

O come, O come, Emmanuel; Christ be our light; In a world where people walk in darkness; On Jordan's bank the Baptist's cry.

Third Sunday of Advent 11 December
Second Service **What Are We Waiting For?**
Ps. 12 [14]; Isa. 5.8–end; **Acts 13.13–41**;
Gospel at Holy Communion: John 5.31–40

Imagine

Imagine if we had no Scriptures; if the only copies of those holy scrolls – all the Law and the Prophets – hadn't survived. If we knew nothing of the histories and poetry and wisdom and prophetic writings, no psalms of praise and lament; if there were no gospel accounts recorded; if Paul had visited in person and not written to the early churches. If the only part of the story we knew was from a physician's travelogue called Acts and from that only a fragment had survived: Acts 13 from which we read today. Imagine!

Despite the huge loss of sacred literature, we would nonetheless have here a summary of the story. A summary of the history of the people of God. Not quite from the beginning but certainly an outline from the time of Exodus to the resurrection. All from this one reading.

Only connect

This day in the synagogue in Antioch, when Paul is invited to preach, he tells the people their story, their history. He reminds them what it means to be the people of God, a pilgrim people, delivered from slavery and brought into life. In these few verses, we travel with them through the wilderness, the Promised Land, the days of judges and monarchy. We meet Saul and then David, the great King of Israel, the one from whom another would come. Paul reminds his listeners, these descendants of Abraham's family, that the story continues in their own times, in their midst. Paul is interpreting, through the tumultuous times in which they are living, the next part of God's story.

Here and now, God is fulfilling the promise given to your ancestors. This is it. Right here, right now. And you almost missed it. This is the good news, for you. God was here, in Jesus.

Of course, they might not believe it. Neither did many people through the centuries. Prophets had come and gone and said: 'Here in your day God is doing something you wouldn't believe.' And they didn't believe. Not at the time.

Hindsight is a wonderful thing, but it does mean that sometimes we miss what is right here and now. Miss the wonder, miss the new thing in our midst, even miss the invitation to be part of it; the new work that God is always doing. We can be too set in our ways, assuming that we know all we need to know.

But when we hear the whole story, like a vast jigsaw puzzle coming together before us, a tapestry revealed in all its artistic glory and creative splendour instead of just the tangled knots at the back – then do our hearts not burn within us for a while?

What next?

Imagine then for a moment that we have heard the story – that the Scriptures did survive. But that the story isn't finished. At the end of the book of Revelation, there is a single instruction – *to be continued*. And then a series of blank pages.

Imagine that those pages wait for a mysterious sequel – a letter perhaps to the churches of today, or a travelogue of a pilgrimage that is still unfolding. What would it say?

What would the story be? What new thing is God to do in our midst in our time; today's world, now: to a people who have come through Covid and the breaking apart of the European Union, looking towards changes of administrations and governments in East and West, North and South with hope and fear, longing and terror?

A world that feels as though the sand is running too fast through the timer as creation groans amid the damage we have done to it in plundering its resources, refusing to listen to its cries of pain. We only grumble that the river – which was simply being a river – had broken its boundaries again due to the excessive rainfall while soaring temperatures have melted the ice caps and the oceans groan with plastic waste that has darkened and stifled the once vibrant life of the deep. While the stories of community and relationship are lost amid political power games and hate crimes. Is it only with hindsight that we will listen to the words Paul quotes, 'Look you, scoffers! Be amazed and perish'?

Or will we hear with all our hearts and minds and souls and bodies, 'I will give you the holy promises made to David ... In your days I am doing a work, a work that you will never believe'? Will we become a part of that work of life as pilgrim people?

Will we fully grasp the call because we want to live in a world where the good news is true for all? Because his holy one, brought into being, must not suffer corruption but find fullness of life? Whether we see the new thing that God is now doing may depend on how we choose to live the next part of the story.

Carey Saleh

Hymn suggestions

Come, thou long-expected Jesus; Here is love vast as the ocean; Lord, we turn to you for mercy; Here on the threshold of a new beginning.

Fourth Sunday of Advent   18 December
Principal Service   **Listening for Angels**
Isa. 7.10–16; Ps. 80.1–8, 18–end [*or* 80.1–8]; Rom. 1.1–7;
Matt. 1.18–end

Have you ever wondered what angels sound like? During this season our Scriptures are littered with angelic visits. Gabriel visits Mary, the angels tell the shepherds to go to Bethlehem, and in today's Gospel from Matthew Joseph meets with the angel of the Lord in a dream. Look for mention of angels and archangels in our Scriptures, liturgy and carols over the next week and beyond. Angels are a potent presence among us.

What did the angel sound like in Joseph's dream? Does one angel sound like the whole host of heaven? What is sound like when it's charged with the energy of God's love? Does every word contain rich harmonies or discords beyond our conscious hearing, yet completely understood by our spiritual heart, where Jesus dwells? Would we be moved to tears, or astonished, scared or crackling with excitement? Would we be dazzled? What would it be like to meet with or hear an angel?

Beyond honour

Joseph is in a tight spot. Mary, his fiancée, is pregnant and Joseph knows he isn't the father. This is always a difficult situation – even in today's liberal western society. In first-century Judaism, people were promised in marriage to each other from an early age, and then a year before the wedding they became betrothed, entering into a formal, legal contract. For someone in Mary's situation, she could, under the law, be brought to public trial and if found guilty be stoned to death. Mary's position is potentially very dangerous. Joseph is a good man and his solution is honourable. He decides to quietly dismiss Mary, brushing this embarrassment under the carpet to keep Mary safe. It's a good way forward that protects her from public disgrace.

But human honour and civility is not God's way. In a dream, the angel of the Lord tells Joseph to rise above convention, to go beyond being honourable and righteous, and to do the even harder thing – the braver thing, to take the more difficult and demanding path – to marry Mary and to take on this child and raise him as his own.

Beyond convention

Mary's child is not just any child, but *the* child – the one prophesied throughout Jewish history – the Messiah. Mary with child is the sign that Isaiah looked for, the sign that all will be well, that all can be reconciled between heaven and earth. It's a sign as 'deep as Sheol' (the underworld) and as 'high as heaven'. It's a sign for everyone, everywhere. For Joseph to hear God's message and act in an incredibly courageous way, the angel of the Lord must have been very persuasive, utterly convincing and compelling – like nothing Joseph had ever heard before.

Joseph is called to do something new, something risky and un-conventional. It requires courage, strength, imagination and sheer guts – no wonder the angel tells him not to be afraid. Imagine the pressure Joseph would have been under to follow social and religious conventions. But with the intersection of the angel and Joseph's deep faith he can look beyond the surface disaster to the adventure within and respond with courage to the mystery of God. At the very heart of God is mystery. To be made in the image of God is to encounter mystery within ourselves and those around us. To be made in the image of God is to be capable of going beyond our natural human responses, transcending convention.

Beyond boundaries

God breaks natural and social conventions and constructions all the time. God will not be contained. God in Jesus moves between heaven and earth. God in Jesus breaks the laws of nature: being born to a virgin, walking on the water, stilling storms, creating banquets from meagre lunches, turning water into wine, healing and raising the dead – even breaking through the finality of human death into new resurrected life.

And all of us – made in God's image, called to follow Christ and filled with God's Spirit today – should not be surprised if God calls us to go beyond human convention, to take risks, be more than honourable, go somewhere completely unexpected. We're part of the new creation that God is doing in our midst. We're called to be co-creators with God who is constantly in the process of creating a new heaven and a new earth.

Just days away from Christmas, our rehearsal of the Christmas story in the Gospel today reminds us that God acts and loves in fresh, divine ways, beyond honour, beyond convention, beyond boundaries. There is always more to Jesus than we can discern, and when we try to fit God into our small, safe boxes, then we close down possibilities – we're no longer open to God's adventures. We forget to listen for angels.

With God, anything is possible. With God, there is always hope whatever chaos, mess or disaster is upon us. Let the courage of Joseph and Mary inspire you to new adventures in your faith. Listen for angels calling you to meet with the Child of Bethlehem, and be ready to be changed, renewed and blessed this Christmas, by God with you and for you.

Catherine Williams

Hymn suggestions

Ye holy angels bright; Christ, be our light; Long ago, prophets knew; People, look East.

Fourth Sunday of Advent 18 December
Second Service **Advent Imaginings**
Ps. 113 [126]; 1 Sam. 1.1–20; **Rev. 22.6–end**;
Gospel at Holy Communion: Luke 1.39–45

Holy imagination

As Christmas draws near in our household, boxes of decorations have been rooted out of cupboards. Among them, lifted with care from scrunched-up tissue paper have come, in various sizes, crib or nativity scenes. Made of fabric, wood and pottery, there is one from Peru, another from Ecuador, one from South Africa and one made in Northampton, here in England. Each of these and countless other nativity scenes displayed on every continent can trace their ancestry back to a famous celebration of Christmas at Greccio and the holy imagination of St Francis of Assisi.

Greccio is a small town in Umbria, Italy. Set among oak woods more than 2,000 feet above sea level its monastery remains a modest, simple place, typifying the qualities that drew Francis to the region. This was the place which, in his imagination, would become Bethlehem.

The birth of Jesus was a source of great wonderment to this humble friar of Assisi. Francis never lost the overwhelming sense of joy at God coming to share the life of creation, becoming our kin.

So it was that around 800 years ago a cave near Greccio became the place in which Francis resolved to recreate the manger he had seen on a visit to Bethlehem many years before. Francis would find a baby, gather hay upon which to lay him, along with an ox and an ass to stand beside the manger. At the appointed time the people of the town arrived carrying torches and candles. One of the friars began celebrating Mass, while Francis gave the sermon. His biographer, Thomas of Celano, recalls that Francis stood before the manger, overwhelmed with love and filled with wonderful happiness.

For Francis, the simple celebration was meant to recall the hardships Jesus suffered even as an infant, a Saviour who chose to become poor for our sake. This was not some sentimental whimsy but a profound reflection on the generosity and poverty of the self-emptying God we know in Jesus Christ.

The self-giving which began long before any of our cribs in home, church or cathedral were crafted, before Francis knelt in the hills of Umbria, even long before the first Christmas itself. It began in the imagination and heart of God.

Human imagination is a great thing: it sees what is and dreams about what could be. It leads us to reach out and draws us forward. It is what lies behind and gives impetus to the great developments of science, engineering; it inspires the painter, sculpture, choreographer and composer, the baker, draftsman, writer and carver of wood.

The tragedy of a failure of imagination

The paucity – the lack of imagination – is our tragedy. As individuals, families, churches, nations and as a global community we sometimes lack the imagination to find new ways of relating, forgiving or working for the good of all. Sadly we often lack the imagination – or will – to see the world through the eyes of others, to experience it as they do before rushing to judgement or drifting into indifference.

It is our tragedy as individuals that we lack the imagination to find ways of reconciling ourselves with those from whom we are alienated. It is our tragedy as a society that we lack the imagination to ensure that the homeless are housed, that the lonely are embraced and that people young and older can use and develop their gifts. It is our tragedy that as a world we rush to war rather than to more creative solutions. We also lack the imagination to see what our continued demand for the earth's resources means for our planet.

On this last Sunday of Advent, let us be captivated again by the divine imagination. Captivated as we retell the creative plan of God, whispered to the ancient prophets who foretold his arrival. Captivated as we recall the imaginative 'yes' of Mary in accepting the divine invitation. Captivated by the divine imagination as we prepare to celebrate once again the coming of God to a small Middle Eastern hill town. Captivated by an audacious plan, brought to birth in the imaginative heart of God. This is not some sentimental whimsy but the profound generosity and poverty of the self-emptying God we know in Jesus Christ.

As we anticipate our celebrations of his first coming and watch with longing for his coming again, may the spirit of God ignite in *us* a holy imagination. An imagination that sees what is *and* what could be. That imagines what we might be called to be, for and with God. A holy imagination that prepares us to receive the good news with wonder.

'Come, Lord Jesus, Emmanuel, God-with-us.'

Tricia Hillas

Hymn suggestions

Of the Father's heart begotten; Come, thou long expected Jesus; Go tell it on the mountain; What child is this?

Christmas and Epiphany

Christmas Day   25 December
Set I   Presents
Isa. 9.2–7; Ps. 96; Titus 2.11–14; **Luke 2.1–14** [15–20]

Present and present

For many (not only children), Christmas is all about presents. The word 'present', of course, has several meanings. Today, let's talk about two that relate to Christmas:

1   a present (as in 'a gift');
2   the present (as in 'now').

To explain – at Christmas, we celebrate Jesus being born among us. His birth is (1), a present (gift), and (2), for the present (now).

Let's talk about the first meaning – the 'gift' kind of present. The present is Jesus. The birth of Jesus is the best gift ever! This child, wrapped up in the manger with people gathered around him, is God's Christmas present for the world. And Jesus is God – right up close and personal – in human form, no less. Jesus gives himself! When we see Jesus, we see, just as the shepherds saw, and we know, just as the angels knew, a most wonderful gift has arrived.

Who is the present for? Us! Everyone! Christmas is of course a Christian festival, but it's really for everyone. That's why the angel says to the shepherds that the coming of Jesus is 'good news for all the people'. Jesus came so that *all* might see and know the goodness of God. And, the second meaning – the 'now' kind of present. When is Christmas for? The present; now!

Some of us may have exchanged gifts last night; some, first thing this morning (just after the stockings, perhaps); others will wait until later when extended family arrive (worth the wait? You decide!). But Christmas is for *now*. It is for the present. Why? Because Jesus,

God's son, has entered earth's time zone. God is said to be outside of time, but in Jesus, God has come inside time. Jesus has come for this very moment, for every moment.

I have a mug with 'Jesus is for life, not just for Christmas' written on it. It's true. The Christian message is that Jesus has not only come to be with us on 25 December but every day. Christmas is as much for July as it is for December!

Receiving and giving

There are a few things I think all this talk of presents can mean for us. For one, when we think about Christmas as a present, we can enjoy the birth of Jesus for all that it is – an unprecedented, unwarranted, gratuitous gift. We can receive the love of God by receiving this infant Jesus into our lives. We receive from other people too: presents, food, pampering. Christmas is about receiving.

As much as we receive, we also give. We don't give so that we receive, but there is a connection. It's good to give, and it's good to receive. By giving to each other, we all gain.

We can also see how we might live as a present to others. We can be a blessing to other people, whoever they might be. Sometimes, we bless others just by being there for them: being a companion through life, a shoulder to cry on, a faithful friend.

What we give doesn't have to be fancy. The nativity scene, however we interpret it, is not glamorous. We only need to give as we are and what we can, with what we have. In the stable, the gift of God to the world comes in very simple terms, wrapped up (like every good present) and placed in a manger. But to us, it is the most wonderful gift of all. Likewise, what we give to others and receive from them can be very simple, but no less significant because of it.

Living for the present

Finally, we don't always need to live for the future: for the next holiday, for the new item we've spotted online, for that promotion. The shepherds are told, 'to you is born *this* day'. Jesus has come for the here and now. God loves us enough to become like us, to enter all the joys, complexities and challenges that life offers this day and every day. That means we can know the joy of God, the friendship of God, the hope of God, even today.

Take that in for a moment. You may do many things over the next few days, but in this place, at this time, think about everything that Jesus brings to you, to us, to the world. Let that rest with you now. It is for this moment that Christ has come, and even for us, in this place. Receive him, as you have and will receive everything else that is given today.

Mark Amos

Hymn suggestions

Joy to the world; Of the Father's love begotten; O little town of Bethlehem; O holy night.

Christmas Day   25 December
Set II   God with Us
Isa. 62.6–end; Ps. 97; Titus 3.4–7; **Luke 2.[1–7] 8–20**

It was a shame about Joe, especially at Christmas.

They had worried about all sorts of things, but not that.

The whole family, the grown-ups and all the cousins, were going to spend Christmas together at Grandma and Grandad's house. 'Yes, they said there'll be room for everyone. It will be lovely to have all our children and grandchildren together for Christmas.'

The children – all grown up now – hoped it would be lovely. But you know what families are like! The grandchildren hoped it would be lovely, and they all liked each other – mostly – but they worried that Father Christmas might not know that they would all be at Grandma and Grandad's this year and not in their own homes, and would their Christmas presents arrive at the right house on Christmas morning? Grandma and Grandpa knew it would be lovely but worried whether they had got enough food in or at least the sort of food the grandchildren would like. Grandad bought extra sprouts because he knew the children would enjoy those! Hopefully, the weather would be kind so everyone could travel safely.

Yes, there was lots to worry about at Christmas.

Everyone arrived safely and unpacked while Grandad assured everyone there were enough sprouts – and mince pies – and would they like tea soon. And Joe said, 'No thank you' – which was unusual because Joe liked his tea. Then he asked, 'Is it nearly bedtime?' – which was unheard of. Grandma saw that he was a bit pale curled up there on the sofa, not joining in while the other children ran around screaming with glee. Then he started to cough.

The next day Joe wasn't pale – he was rather red, and spotty, all over! The doctor was called and said it could be measles. Joe should be put to bed away from the other children. Keep an eye on them in case anyone else goes down with it.

So, Joe was put to bed in a room on his own and dosed with medicine to bring his temperature down, and left to rest while they all got on with all their other plans for Christmas. There was a lot to do and much excitement and chatter while reminding each other to keep things quiet because of poor Joe. But during the morning it began to dawn on Grandma that Christopher was a bit quieter than the others. And had he had that mince pie at elevenses – or had Billy had two? And did she really hear him coughing? O dear!

The doctor said they'd know when the rash appeared, but meanwhile they'd assume the worst. There wasn't another room, so Christopher was put to bed in the same room as Joe. Measles at Christmas! What a shame.

But by Christmas Day – although they were still upstairs on their own – it wasn't all bad. They had the TV up there, a bit of lunch on a tray, although Joe didn't eat anything. Christopher ate quite well except for the sprouts. 'He must be feeling rough,' said Grandad!

And all the presents arrived at the right house, so the boys could open theirs upstairs. The doctor checked on the boys and the other children again a few days after Christmas. No signs of anyone else going down with anything, so that was good. Joe shouldn't travel yet, he said, but Christopher? No rash had appeared and his cough hadn't developed. Whatever Christopher had, said the doctor, it wasn't measles. Just deep sympathy perhaps? He winked at Christopher who went a bit red. The doctor just smiled.

Later, when it was time for his family to leave, Christopher went up to say goodbye to Joe who was still in bed.

'I'm really sorry you had it too, Chris,' Joe said. 'But if I'm honest it would have been very lonely and miserable up here on my own. It was so much easier that you were with me, someone else who understood what it was like to be feeling ill at Christmas.'

Afterwards, when everyone had gone home and it was just Grandma and Grandpa again, they were talking about how lovely it had been and hoping everyone had had a happy time. It was a shame about Joe, though, said Grandpa. And poor old Chris! He seems to have missed out on it all!

'You know,' said Grandma, who had seen Christopher go rather red when the doctor had said he hadn't had measles, 'I think our Chris understood exactly what Christmas is about and entered into it better than any of us. He did what he could to make sure Joe wasn't left alone.' Well done, Chris! That was a splendid thing you did for Joe!

Rather like God who understood the needs of our world; chose to enter into our experience by coming as one of us in Bethlehem to make all the difference.

Christmas is so much more than sprouts and presents! It's about deep, life-transforming Love! Because of Christ!

Happy Christmas!

Carey Saleh

(adapted from an original story by my father, Donald Howell)

Hymn suggestions

Hark! the herald angels sing; Thou didst leave thy throne; See him lying on a bed of straw; Joy to the world.

Christmas Day   25 December
Set III   Gazing at the Crib
Isa. 52.7–10; Ps. 98; Heb. 1.1–4 [5–12]; **John 1.1–14**

Gazing at the crib

Christmas cribs, or manger scenes, are everywhere today. There is one here in church. You may have one at home. There are dozens on the fronts of Christmas cards, Advent calendars just completed today, and even in some public spaces. It's such a familiar scene: Mary and Joseph, the baby, the ox and the ass, maybe a shepherd or two, an angel as well.

In the Christmas crib, we see the truth of what today is all about. We see deep truth in this scene which is at once so simple and yet so extraordinary.

Seeing the reality

What we see is all the reality of what it means to be human people, and especially the reality of those who at this Christmas season are away from home: maybe homeless, or in prison, or hospital, or separated from their loved ones by an ocean. We see the kindness of strangers: an innkeeper lending his barn to some travellers. We see, in the animals, the natural world that it is our duty to care for. We see poverty: a baby who doesn't have a cot, or a room specially prepared. All he has is the food trough of some animals who have lent him that space to take his first few moments of sleep. There is human reality in this scene. There is the best and the worst of us in it. A young family, an unmarried mother, forced by government legislation to be on the road when they really should have been at home surrounded by familiar things at the time of giving birth. There's the kindness of strangers, hospitality, and people being totally surprised by the scene that they encounter. On one level it is the story of humanity.

And yet. And yet. What we also see is God. We see God Almighty, the Creator of Everything, the Author of the World, the King of the Universe, coming to meet his people. And not just coming to meet them, but coming to be with them, as one of them. To be with us, as one of us.

Christmas commitment

God is so interested in you, God is so interested in me, God is so committed to this relationship, that he empties himself of everything that would seem to be important about being a God – crowns and thrones and power and all that kind of thing – he empties himself of all of that and comes to meet us exactly as we are. One of the givens of every one of our lives is that it began as a baby. That is where we begin. So that is where God begins as well. And because human life is fragile, and some of it is marked with sadness, loneliness, poverty, and all the being shoved about that life often visits upon us, that is how God begins his life as well. In a borrowed manger, in an unfamiliar place, in the dark, dependent on the kindness of strangers. In one sense it is so familiar, and in another it is absolutely extraordinary.

Christmas presents

But it shows us how much God loves us. Christmas is of course about gifts. Christmas is about something that we don't deserve, and don't earn, being given to us anyway. You know, if later on this morning I hand over my Christmas presents to someone I love and, as they open them, I sit opposite them looking hard at the receipt, that's not going to feel very much like a gift, is it? If someone you love is opening the gift that you've bought for them, but they can see you examining how much it cost you, how much money you were willing to exchange for this present, that's going to make them feel pretty awful. That isn't how you and I give gifts to each other. Gifts are freely given. They are not earned. Or they shouldn't be.

Just so the gift of Christmas. There's nothing transactional about this. This isn't God saying, 'OK, well, if you promise to do this, this and this, then I will maybe love you a little bit. But I'll be checking all the time that you can remember how much it cost me to do this.'

Mangers don't look like that to me. Neither do shepherds. Neither do homeless families. And neither does a newborn baby.

Our story, God's story

When we look at the Christmas crib, we see our story in the story of the holy family. We see the story of our culture, of our nation, of our world in this mishmash of people, refugees, the poorest, the richest, people who own their own inn and people who have to sleep on the floor of the barn.

And in the middle of it, we see God. Coming among us as a baby. Loving us enough to begin at the beginning with us. Trusting us not to drop him. Saying to us, 'I would love to take the journey of life with you. Would you like to take the journey with me?'

Tom Clammer

Hymn suggestions

Once in royal David's city; Like a candle flame; Away in a manger; Child of the manger.

Christmas Day   25 December
Second Service   **Found!**
Morning Ps. 110, 117; Evening Ps. 8; Isa. 65.17–25; **Phil. 2.5–11**, or Luke 2.1–20 (*if it has not been used at the Principal Service of the Day*)

Found!

It's very early in the morning but the children are very much awake – they're already excited at all the things they are going to find in their stockings and under the tree. All the excitement of Christmas morning! And in all of our familiar Christmas stories that excitement of *finding* is already there.

We see the excitement of the shepherds as the angels tell them, 'You will find a baby lying in a manger ...' And, says Luke, 'they went and found'. They had found what they were looking for. They were overflowing with joy and praise for all the things they had heard and seen.

And in Matthew's account, we see the excitement of the Magi who travel great distances to find the object of their search. It's another story of discovery, of finding.

Shepherds and wise men received extraordinary news – and found that God had arrived among them. And it wasn't at all what they had expected. This God they found turned out to be the hidden, humble, unexpected God, the one who puts in an appearance in the least expected place.

We are often very aware of ourselves as *seekers,* as those who are full of questions. Brother Roger of Taizé used to say that if we are seeking, it may be that already there is a *finding.* Already the God we seek is at work in our hearts, already God is present – and maybe that is why we seek in the first place? God can be found. God is already found.

Found in human form

The apostle Paul, in his letter to the church in Philippi, breaks into this great song of praise. It's a great reading for Christmas! And at the very heart of this song is the idea of *finding.* Perhaps this text is the nearest Paul gets to offering us a Christmas story. Christ, he declares, is found, here and now, in human form.

Paul presents a very different account from the vivid narratives of Matthew and Luke. For Paul, there is no backdrop of angels, shepherds or kings. There is no Bethlehem, no busy inn, no star. For Paul, there is rather the familiar problem of how to get on with other Christians. There is only the very ordinary, challenging *everyday*, the question of how to relate to other people in the community where we live.

But to Paul, this is the central point. This ordinary world is the very place where the incarnation takes place, as we learn to discover Christ – in the place where we are. *Here* we can seek and find. *Here* we can discover, with great joy, the presence of Jesus.

And so Paul sketches out for us the extraordinary trajectory of God entering into God's world.

[Christ] emptied himself,
taking the form of a slave,
being born in human likeness.
And being found in human form,
he humbled himself
and became obedient to the point of death –
even death on a cross.

This is the essence of the Christmas story, certainly, seen as the story of God who lets go, who descends, who empties himself. And in so doing God leads the way for his followers to begin their own letting go. God reveals this *self-emptying* as a way of life, a way to bring the mind of Christ, and the body of Christ, into our world.

So now, Paul is saying, from this day forward, God is to be discovered, recognized, *found*. And this is happening not as a result of heroic effort on our part, or profound knowledge, but in human form. After this Christmas story, nothing is the same.

The humble place

God is found lying 'in a manger because there is no room in the inn'. God is found in the humblest place. And the humblest place – if we can find our way there – is precisely where the mind of Christ awaits us. As Paul says: 'Let this mind be in you that was in Christ Jesus.' The incarnation of Christ takes place in our relationships with one another, in our ordinary life – at home, in our places of work, in the church.

We looked and looked, we searched and searched, but when we emptied ourselves – there he was.

Christ was found in human form. Christ is found walking among us, Christ is found within us. And our call is now to express that human form of Christ in the life that we build together.

'Let us go and see this great sight.'

Andrew Rudd

Hymn suggestions

O little town of Bethlehem; In the bleak midwinter; You laid aside your majesty; Meekness and majesty.

Second Sunday of Christmas 1 January
(For Naming and Circumcision of Jesus, see p. 287.)
Principal Service   **God's Promises in His Unfolding Love**
Isa. 63.7–9; Ps. 148 [*or* 148.7–end]; Heb. 2.10–end;
Matt. 2.13–end

A new season

The Covid-19 pandemic highlighted many things about our human condition and behaviour. Although change and transition is an inevitable part of being alive, many people struggle to engage positively with change. We are creatures of habit and comfort. Yet, at some point in our lives, we've all experienced a situation that has upturned our world. This can happen at a local or global level. And when confronted by such, a key question is, how do we move forward through seasons of the unexpected and uncertain? As we press into a new year, how will we hold on to God's promise in its unfolding?

Unfolding love

Many of us might be entering this new year with a mix of emotions – excitement, anxiety, trepidation. Perhaps this isn't surprising in light of the last few years living through a pandemic. The world filled with darkness and evil has groaned with injustices of all kinds. The passage from Matthew's Gospel, known as the feast of the Holy Innocents within many Christian traditions, tells of Mary and Joseph's flight to Egypt. It is not an accident that this day follows soon after Christmas. The two events are interconnected. A full reading of both the story of Christ's birth and then this story challenges us with not only the triumph and promise of Christmas but its cost and redemptive sacrifice.

The birth of Jesus was an immense challenge to Herod. He was unnerved and undermined by this potential opponent. In our Christmas readings, we are reminded of how Herod tricked the magi into revealing where baby Jesus could be found. However, an angel guides them not to tell Herod about the birth. Thus Mary and Joseph, after revelling in the joy and wonder of the birth of Jesus, are now consumed with fear as they seek to protect their precious child. Their lives have been turned upside down.

Throughout the existence of humanity, we are confronted by the question: how can a just and loving God allow evil to exist? How can God let innocent people suffer?

But Jesus was a man who experienced fear and uncertainty. Throughout his life and ministry, he experienced pressures and evils of all kinds. He was tempted, accused and persecuted. If we deny Jesus this, we deny him his identification with us as humans. This is one of the wonders of the incarnation. Jesus took on human flesh and lived among us. This goes so far beyond our comprehension that we struggle to grasp the magnitude of God's sacrificial love. Every fear is temptation, every sense of uncertainty is temptation. Mary and Joseph would have been afraid of Herod's threats, but they chose to trust God. Jesus never acted or spoke out of fear, but in the power and authority of his Father. Jesus always chose to lean into the full-flowing life of the indwelling Father. Yet, as one who is entirely with us in his humanity, he fully understands our fears and anxieties.

God's promises

The faithfulness of God in the past, and the promise of God's future, shape our present. God's mercy is new every morning and, as we embrace this new year, there is always a fresh start. It is because of who God is that we can join the Psalmist and 'praise the name of the LORD'. Despite the challenges and pitfalls of this evil world, we can with Isaiah 'recount the gracious deeds of the LORD, the praiseworthy acts of the LORD'. With the writer to the Hebrews, we can put our trust in God and proclaim his name.

In 2023, may we be encouraged to journey through the Gospel of Matthew and remember God's promise to us. May we be blessed and be a blessing to others who perhaps need the touch of Christ in their lives. God is at work fulfilling and preserving the reality of Emmanuel, God with us.

Catherine Okoronkwo

Hymn suggestions

Unto us is born a son; When came in flesh the incarnate Word; Jesus comes with all his grace; Amazing grace.

Second Sunday of Christmas 1 January
Second Service **It All Depends on Where You Stand**
Ps. 132; Isa. 49.7–13; **Phil. 2.1–11**; *Gospel at Holy Communion*:
Luke 2.41–52

Vulnerability

How you see humility depends on where you are standing. If you are a powerful person with lots of resources, it's possible to choose to make yourself vulnerable and respond to the world with an attitude of humility. Perhaps this is a lifestyle choice, perhaps a choice of style of leadership. If you are a person with few external resources, vulnerability is something often forced upon you, something you have little choice over. Being humble is not really a choice open to you either, but your acquiescence, submission or compliance can be mistaken for it.

Recently, some theologians have pointed out that the Christian Church has been magnificent at using Philippians 2 in ways that assume we are all starting from a position of power and therefore can, and should, humble ourselves. We are not. And loud has been the call for us to stop using it to put unbearable psychological heaviness and socio/behavioural burdens on those of us who have little or no power.

Humility

In my mind, the lynchpin phrase in Philippians 2 is Christ 'humbled himself and became obedient to the point of death – even death on a cross'. The poetry of the language builds to it. Moreover, if this is a hymn about the uniqueness of Christ, as many would suggest, the flow of the language builds to a huge flashing arrow pointing right at this phrase. This is not a proverb or an instruction about humility as an individual attitude or as a practice. It is an invitation to reflect on Christ's death on the cross using the specific theme or idea of humility and all in the context of worship.

Solidarity

Son of Man is a 2006 film that dramatizes the life and death of Jesus. It is set in modern South Africa and the dialogue is in Xhosa. In it, Jesus is portrayed as a community and political activist with some supernatural powers. He is arrested, disappeared, privately executed and his body dumped in a shallow grave by the oppressive controlling regime. Mary his mother searches for him and when she finally finds his body she hangs it on a crude cross in the middle of the marketplace for all to see as evidence of the oppression her community faces. She makes violence, cruelty and victimization visible. It is a powerful interpretation of the story of the life of Christ and one which explores an awareness that many modern theologians have come to. Christ died in solidarity with all those who are powerless victims, victims of powerful oppressors who use violence, threats, secrecy and silence to control. Christ died in solidarity with all those who have little or no power, who do not have the choice to be humble. And Christ lifted high on the cross made violence, cruelty and victimization visible for all to see. The Christ who lived on earth, somehow in absolute relationship with God, knew that was God's desire and did it.

Clear light

Using this focus opens up the instruction to 'let the same mind be in you that was in Christ Jesus' so that it takes on distinctive and non-traditional hues and tones. Most straightforwardly it provides us with the understanding that one fundamental specific thing that God desires is to stand in solidarity with the powerless, with victims, using methods by which oppression is brought to light. That, if this language helps, is a goal, or a series of goals, to pursue to achieve the vision of the complete realization of the kingdom of God on earth. Less straightforwardly perhaps it provides us with the knowledge that being of the same mind as Jesus involves having a moral compass, a value if that helps too, of understanding what God desires, what's important to God and being willing, being obedient (if you want to use that word) to create that in our own lives. Of course, that is all messy, tricky, long-haul stuff, and how each of us might create and recreate that in our own lives will have different shapes and consequences.

We live in muddled and muddling times. Times when the powerful seem to be able to use the old oppressive tools in new ways and to find new ways of burdening and tyrannizing the powerless. Times when we are not quite sure who the oppressors and the victims actually are. Times when we are not quite sure we understand what is happening, or what we can do about what is happening. Evaluating the world by using a 'humility to death' gage isn't helpful – it increases the muddle. But perhaps a focus on the God who stands in solidarity with the powerless and brings oppression into clear light and view will provide us all with clues about how to be Christ-like in mind and action at the start of a new year.

Esther Elliott

Hymn suggestions

Tell out my soul; Let love be real in giving and receiving; My Lord, you wore no royal crown; What child is this?

Baptism of Christ (First Sunday of Epiphany)
8 January
(*For* Epiphany, see p. 290.)
Principal Service **Speaking Sustenance**
Isa. 42.1–9; Ps. 29; Acts 10.34–43; **Matt. 3.13–end**

Food for the wilderness

I picture Jesus, jostled by the crowds, approaching John for baptism, seeing his surprise, and knowing that this public identification with the people is the right way to begin. How did he feel as he waded into the water to make this public beginning to his ministry, taking the first step on a road that would lead through the brightness of transfiguration to the night of crucifixion and on to the dawn beyond? Like all of us at a key moment, he must surely have felt a mixture of excitement, maybe nervousness – after all, he was fully human and subject to human emotions. How important that at this moment he receives this affirmation from God: 'This is my Son, the Beloved, with whom I am well pleased.' He is claimed by God, named as Beloved and affirmed in that wonderful phrase *'well pleased'*. Put another way, Jesus hears God say he is in his corner, has his back, supports him, loves him and delights in him. What comfort these words must have brought him on difficult days as his journey unfolded, 'You are my Son, the Beloved, with whom I am well pleased.' Here is food for the wilderness.

Speaking sustenance

At a particularly bleak moment, a friend said to me, 'I've got you tucked into my prayers.' It was such a lovely affirmation, which I've long drawn strength from. *'I've got you tucked in.'* Words have such potential for holding and healing. In a world where language is so often used to wound, how important it is to speak sustenance. A thoughtful word can offer a banquet of sustenance in a desert experience. I wonder how often Jesus went back in his mind to savour God's words to him at his baptism? 'You are my Son, the Beloved, with whom I am well pleased.' I wonder how often he drew strength here? I suspect he chewed these words over, especially on the rough days, drawing the marrow out from the words. We are called to use language to heal, encourage, build up, support and love, after the pattern of God the Father.

Words of lament: crumbs of hope

Jump further into Matthew's Gospel, as Jesus hangs on the cross he cries out: 'My God, my God, why have you forsaken me?' Not – 'Have you forsaken me?' But, *'why* have you forsaken me?' For Jesus, in that moment God has backed off, done one, disappeared. The earlier expression of love is eclipsed by the darkness of Jesus' reality, which might make us question the worth of the words. How many people have raged at God because in their moment of greatest need God seemed silent? Suffering in whatever form can shrink our horizon till all there is is pain. The fact is, Jesus experiences the absence of God, the silence of his Father. This pleasing, beloved son experiences abandonment. Yet, amid his experience of horrendous abuse, Jesus still has enough of a sense of relationship with God to cry out in words of lament: 'My God, my God, why have you abandoned me?' From these crumbs of hope expressed to God, a banquet will be served, in time. The relationship between the Father and the Son, cemented in affirmation and trust, enables Jesus to cling on in his words of lament. There is nothing cheap or easy here.

Fast-food phrases

It doesn't much help for the onlooker to step into the story, look up at Jesus in his vulnerability and agony and say:

'Well, actually, God is here, you know.'
'If you had a bit more faith, you'd know God is with you.'
'It will be all right. Sunday's coming.'

These are fast-food phrases, empty-calorie words, lacking nourishment. At this point, Jesus is simply in too much physical, emotional and spiritual distress to connect easily with God. This is not failure. It's human. This is not faithlessness – since only the faithful rage at God's absence. The divine truth is that God's goodness is always here. The human truth is that *in extremis*, unaided, we can't easily connect with it.

But ...

The bread of God

As we heard in John's Gospel, 'The bread of God is that which comes down from heaven and brings life to the world.' This is Jesus. The human experience of pain, loneliness, abuse, fear, isolation and abandonment is intimately known to Christ; his deep experiences of suffering are life bringing. We have a high priest well able to draw alongside us in the experience of our struggles, of whatever magnitude.

We are known by the loving Father who affirms us; the empathetic Christ who feeds us from his experience, and the Comforter who holds our hands in the darkness.

Whatever you face today, hear God's words *for you*: 'You are my child. You are beloved. With you, I am well pleased.'

Know that the Christ who plumbed the depths of the chasm of abandonment is with *you*.

Sense the words of the Spirit *for you*: 'I've got you tucked in.'

Remember – those words of sustaining hope might be prompted from you to another. Speaking sustenance; it matters.

Kate Bruce

Hymn suggestions

On Jordan's bank; What a friend we have in Jesus; Christ's is the world (A touching place); From heaven you came.

Baptism of Christ (First Sunday of Epiphany)
8 January
Second Service   **Crossing the Jordan**
Ps. 46, 47; **Josh. 3.1–8, 14–end**; Heb. 1.1–12;
Gospel at Holy Communion: Luke 3.15–22

Echoing down the years, in my head I hear 'Joshua fought the battle of Jericho' and I realize that that song encapsulates much of what I can recall of the story of Joshua. Of course, that campaign incident is recorded in the book of Joshua later than our passage.

If we want to explore our passage in its context, we could begin by asking about the book. 'Joshua' is the sixth book in our Old Testament. It takes up the story of the children of Israel from where Deuteronomy ended, forming a continuous narrative. Since it brings to conclusion certain themes of the Torah (for example, that of the possession of the Land, in fulfilment of the promise to the Patriarchs), there was once a trend to seek evidence that it was compiled from the same major 'source document' strands (J, E, D and P). There may be as many as six fragmented texts woven into our particular story.

There's a strong consensus of Christian scholarship that sees Joshua as the first of the historical books, probably redacted (edited) by the so-called Deuteronomic-Historian during the period of the exile in the sixth century BC.

In Jewish tradition, it is a transitional book, the first of the former prophets. Hence, it's not 'history' as we understand it, nor does it seem to us to be a book of prophecy. It's about the interim period between the life and work of Moses and the time when Israel fully possessed and truly inhabited the Land.

What of Joshua? Moses, that towering figure, is dead. Joshua is no Moses, at times he comes across as an interim leader, the lesser after the greater, but maybe that's an unfair assessment. This son of Nun was a seasoned warrior who had served under Moses. He had been one of Moses' spies who scouted out the Land that they're to enter. Cometh the hour, cometh the man: they will need a strategist if they are to take possession of the Land. The conquest stories in the book reveal him to be an able and wily military tactician and commander (but that's later on).

Enough of the background, let's explore our passage.

Crossing the Jordan

It may be a short distance (they're encamped on the bank of the Jordan), and the river is very narrow at the point they're reputed to have crossed over, more a symbolic barrier than a challenging boundary, but crossing over is a big step for the people of Israel. After years in the wilderness, they're about to set foot in the Promised Land. All their dreams are about to be fulfilled (or are they?)! Can you imagine the hopes, the dreams and the trepidation? After three days, the officers tell the people to be ready, when they see the Ark, borne by the Levitical priests, they're to watch where it goes so that they can follow its route, but they're to maintain considerably more than 'social distance', staying at least 2,000 cubits back (around a kilometre). The Ark is to be their guide. (Incidentally, this is the only reference to the Ark in the conquest narratives.)

Joshua's in charge as he tells the people to sanctify themselves and tells the priests to take up the Ark. The people pull up their tent pegs and get ready. Sanctifying themselves in readiness to depart may have involved rituals of abstinence and cleansing. Aspects of the story are, perchance, recollections of liturgical and cultic practices at Gilgal which grew up to commemorate this event. The venue usually associated with this story is several kilometres north of Jericho. So, is this history or is it sacred drama?

The priests bearing their precious burden were ordered to halt in the shallows of the river. Then the waters parted, allowing the priests to move on dry ground to the centre of the riverbed, letting the people cross. Those who know the story of the crossing of the Re(e)d Sea will recognize the similarities between the two accounts: the ritual of departure from the land of slavery has become that of arrival in the land of blessing. Is this drying up of the riverbed a miracle, or the result of a (recurring) natural phenomenon? Our author certainly believes the crossing of the Jordan is due to the miraculous work of God (that is, not Israel's achievement).

What's this about?

Though details may be distorted by the mists of time, the final editor tells the story with intent. Joshua, Moses' successor, is identified as a charismatic leader, the intermediary between God and the people. God reassures Joshua that the people will recognize his leadership and promises him, 'I will be with you as I was with Moses.' When God's people obey his commands (keeping the covenant and obeying the law) and follow godly leaders the victory will be theirs.

Is this not true for us? Consider your discipleship. Are you ready to commit yourself to be of God's people, obedient to his will? Then, look around you and discern who it is that God has designated to lead you to the 'land' of the promise.

Wendy Kilworth-Mason

Hymn suggestions

Be bold, be strong; Guide me, O thou great Redeemer; Joshua fought the battle of Jericho; Thine be the glory.

Second Sunday of Epiphany   15 January
Principal Service   **Choices, Choices**
Isa. 49.1–7; Ps. 40.1–12; 1 Cor. 1.1–9; **John 1.29–42**

No easy answers, no easy choices

While white-water rafting in Peru, it became clear that the boat ahead was caught and buffeted by furious eddies around a large rock in the middle of the swollen river. Then the boat swept round the rock and was off again, but half its novice crew had jumped on to the rock – leaving their helpless crewmates at the mercy of the currents. This was not supposed to happen! A split-second choice and they were stranded. Eventually, with some difficulty, other boats plucked them off. A happy ending.

On other trips, I began to read about the choices that can face those attempting to summit the world's highest mountains. *In extremis*, these can include choosing whether to help or to leave behind others who get into difficulty.

Increasing numbers of people attempt these high peaks, sadly not all survive. One of around 200 bodies left on Everest is that of David Sharp. It's believed he made it to the summit in May 2006 but, descending fatigued and confused, he stopped unable to continue. It is said that around 40 climbers from several expeditions passed Sharp on their way up the mountain. Some mistook him for a known dead body, others thought him sufficiently experienced to make it back alone. No significant attempt was made to rescue him until climbers passed him again on the way down many hours later. By then it was too late.

On other occasions, climbers have abandoned summit attempts

for which they had worked long and hard to help others. Forty mountaineers passed David Sharp. In those high 'death zone' conditions, does 'normal morality' apply? Should they, could they, have stopped to help? What responsibility did they have, given his choice to be on the mountain? Does someone else's choice free us from the responsibility to help when it goes wrong? What if one's own condition is precarious? Can we expect someone to abandon their own hopes or interests to help a stranger? No easy answers.

What does this mean for us as a church and as a society – would we expect to sacrifice some of our own interests and preferences for others' benefit? Is it right for the money you earn to pay for my health care? And what about our individual life choices? Which career path will I pursue? How will I use my money? Whom will I entrust with my deepest self? Is the time right to try for another child?

Principles for choice-making

Many approaches can aid our choice-making, from the old chestnut, the list of pros and cons, to others which project outcomes for each option, asking:

- What is the probable outcome of this choice?
- What will/won't this option deliver?
- What are the likely outcomes of not choosing this option?

Behind such pragmatism, we might also do well to consider the principles guiding our choice-making. Whether overt and voiced, hidden and unreflected upon, they will be present.

Models of choice-making: Jesus, John and the disciples

In our passage from John's Gospel, we see choices taking shape.

Jesus' choice: 'Here is the Lamb of God, who takes away the sin of the world!' The weight of the sin of the world, every action, every evil intention, every word of hate and violence, is in truth impossible to comprehend. An almost unbearable burden. Save only for the one who chose to bear it for us.

John's choice: John has given everything to his calling and will soon give even more. His choices were always shaped by the desire that through his words and actions Jesus would be revealed. So much so that John sets the stage for his own disciples to leave him to follow Jesus.

The disciple's choice: on hearing John's exclamation, Andrew and an unnamed other follow Jesus. He asks a penetrating question, 'What are you looking for?' A guiding question for all our choices. Then he invites them to 'come and see'. Remaining with him for the rest of the day, they choose a lifelong journey of following him.

They followed *him*. It wasn't that Jesus called Andrew, his companion and then others to save the world through their own heroic performance. Rather, Jesus invited them to follow him. It meant being with him, sharing his life, his mission. It meant patterning their lives on his and taking his choices as the model for their choices, his guiding principles as theirs. His choices were sometimes risky and often costly. They would see him prioritizing compassion over pleasing others, as when he healed on the Sabbath; speaking to the realities of the human condition and divine grace when a woman was dragged before him by a baying mob, and choosing to exercise the kind of power baffling to hard-bitten rulers.

Always, Jesus' choices began with the Father's kingdom and its values. Not fear, condemnation or self-preservation but confidence in the One who liberates. May our choice-making be infused with his compassion, for ourselves as well as for others, his courage, determination and attentiveness to the realities of human hearts and divine grace.

Tricia Hillas

Hymn suggestions

Will you come and follow me? Father, hear the prayer we offer; Guide me, O thou great Redeemer; Blessed be your name.

Second Sunday of Epiphany   15 January
Second Service   **Nourished by the Word**
Ps. 96; **Ezek. 2.1—3.4;** Gal. 1.11–end;
Gospel at Holy Communion: John 1.43–end

We have such a lot of metaphors to help us describe understanding, and a surprising number of them have to do with consuming. We speak of 'taking it in', 'digesting the information', and even things being 'unpalatable' or 'hard to swallow'. Whether surprising or difficult, there is a process involved when words move from outside our heads to being nourishing and sustaining deep within our bodies. The physical food we eat literally forms our bones, our blood, our cells, and so it is with the words that we absorb as they shape our thinking and our actions.

Eat this scroll

Ezekiel is a prophet living in Babylon among the people of Israel who are exiled from their homeland. He has some extraordinary visions, does some extraordinarily odd things, and sometimes says some rather extreme things in his efforts to keep the people from losing sight of all that God has called them to become. The whole book of the prophet begins with an amazing vision of God – we might even call it mind-blowing – as he struggles to describe the indescribable using images and words that have influenced artists and poets down the centuries. The vision continues into chapter 2 when the messenger begins to let him know what it is that he has to say to the people, and then come these words: 'Eat this scroll.' So, he does.

It is not the only time in the Scriptures that someone is literally commanded to swallow the paper on which words are written. In the book of Revelation, John has the same experience, in many ways echoing some of the themes of Ezekiel as he too is transfixed by a vision of God and a message that will challenge all who listen. But the metaphor of digesting or swallowing the word is found throughout the New Testament. St Paul suggests that we let the word of Christ dwell in us richly, and also that Scripture should be read and digested.

Beyond the page

It is as if the things that are external need to go far beyond just being messages on a page. We can so often read things about God, or even the Bible itself, and the words don't become life-enhancing or life-changing. We carry on as if we had never been fed at all. The late Eugene Peterson, who was responsible for *The Message* Bible, and was a wonderful Bible scholar and pastor, writes that words – spoken, listened to, written or read – are intended to do something to us. They are meant to give health and wholeness, to bring us to wisdom, hope and holiness. Words are meant to change us.

This might mean that we need to approach reading the Bible, the word of God, with fresh enthusiasm. We may need to think about how we eat the words, or chew over them, letting them go deep into our inner being, so that they form who we are, just as the food we eat forms our bodies. Our world is full of tips and insights as to how what we physically eat affects our body condition and our mental well-being. Likewise, how we approach and digest the word of God will shape our spiritual lives, developing our relationship with God, God's people and the world around us. The letter of James writes memorably about how difficult it is to tame the tongue, reminding us that what comes out of our mouths is connected to what is within. So, for Ezekiel, it makes sense that, if you are going to fully grasp the mystery and purpose of a message God has for his people, you would eat the scroll.

Take time to eat

In this season of Epiphany, we think about how Christ is revealed to the world. He is revealed in baptism as the child of God; he is revealed as water turns into wine as the one who transforms lives and makes things new; and he is revealed as the one who is worthy of worship. As we journey through this season, perhaps we can take time to eat the word, not literally but in new and deeper ways so that we too may have a fresh revelation of just who Jesus is and the message he calls us to proclaim afresh to those around.

Sandra Millar

Hymn suggestions

Be thou my vision; Be still and know that I am God; My heart will sing to you; Forth in the peace of Christ, we go.

Third Sunday of Epiphany   22 January
Principal Service   **Kingdom Fishing**
Isa. 9.1–4; Ps. 27.1, 4–12 [or 27.1–11]; 1 Cor. 1.10–18;
Matt. 4.12–23

Jesus steps up a gear in his ministry. With the news of the arrest of his cousin John, Jesus leaves Nazareth and goes to Galilee, setting up home in Capernaum. In our Old Testament reading the prophet Isaiah foretells that Galilee of the nations, the territories of Zebulun and Naphtali will be made glorious by God. Those places, mainly

Gentile, were seen as lands of 'deep darkness'. Isaiah prophesies that on them the light will shine.

And here is Jesus, 'the light', beginning his ministry in that region. He picks up exactly the message of John the Baptist: 'Repent, for the kingdom of heaven has come near.' God's reign of justice and peace is upon you. Turn round and see.

The ideal ruler prophesied in Isaiah has come to release people from oppression, to increase the joy of the nations, and to help those who walk in deep darkness move into the light.

Calling disciples

Jesus begins by calling ordinary fishermen – not necessarily poor, since fishing was good trade around the sea of Galilee, but not particularly special either. Peter and Andrew, James and John are going about their everyday lives, working with their nets, casting and mending. Jesus comes by, calls them, and their lives change for ever.

Jesus calls them to follow him – the Greek here means 'Come after me'. Their skills are useful and needed, but the catch will now be different. Jesus promises they will fish for people. So compelling is Jesus that they all respond immediately. The rest we might say is history.

For us, as modern-day disciples, the call is the same: 'Come, follow me and I will make you fish for people.' So how do we fish for people? How do we catch people for the kingdom today?

Casting nets

Fishing for people takes time, patience and skill – just like fishing for fish. Catching people for God's kingdom is not about power, fear or subjugation. We don't frighten people into the kingdom by threatening them. This is something that Christians can be guilty of, but it isn't effective. Nor should we expect instant results when we try to tell people about God. That enormous 'net' – the World Wide Web – makes us think that anything can happen at the press of a button. Results to enquiries are instantaneous on the internet. But fishing requires patience.

We need to know our waters well. The good angler knows which side of the boat to fish from and in which seasons and conditions. Those who fish know their waters well, they know when something isn't quite right with the sea or the river.

When we're fishing for people, we need to know our community well too, to be wise about the context. We might identify particular groups or individuals who will respond well to the good news of Jesus. To do that we have to be with people, among them, networking, walking alongside as friends and neighbours – in clubs and pubs, schools, businesses and shops. Wherever you find yourself, that's the place God has called you to shine the light of Christ: to be Christ-like in your fishing.

Mending nets

James and John were mending nets. The nets were broken and needed attention. Perhaps our fishing nets require some attention too. We will not catch people for the kingdom unless our personal relationship with God is growing and blossoming; unless our prayers are regular and disciplined; unless our own lives reflect the love of God to all whom we meet.

If our church life is beset by quarrels, bickering and factions we won't attract anyone. St Paul knew that. He told the church at Corinth that they needed to mend their divisions and move forward together as the body of Christ, proclaiming the good news of Jesus.

We catch people for the kingdom by allowing the Holy Spirit we carry to work through us, directing us to the people that God is preparing to respond to the message of Jesus. Through the work of the Spirit, we can show attractive selfless lives to others, and invite them to share in the good news of God that helps people turn their lives around, rebuilding broken lives and relationships.

With the Spirit

Jesus calls his disciples to 'come after me', and he calls us too to come after, to imitate him in calling others. You may be thinking: 'I can't do that – I can't bring anyone into the kingdom.' But you can – we all can – if we allow the Spirit to direct us.

Begin by praying. Ask the Spirit to bring to mind five people you are alongside regularly who either aren't Christians or who used to come to church and have stopped. Commit to praying for them every day and see what happens. Never underestimate the power of faithful disciplined prayer. God does amazing work through our weakness, our fear and the very little we feel we can offer.

Together with the Spirit, through prayer, service, love and getting stuck deep into our community, let's make strong, faith-filled nets that will draw people into a loving and living relationship with Jesus Christ.

Catherine Williams

Hymn suggestions

Will you come and follow me? O Jesus, I have promised; Breathe on me, breath of God; Here I am to worship.

Third Sunday of Epiphany 22 January
Second Service **Possibilities Re-imagined**
Ps. 33 [*or* 33.1–12]; Eccles. 3.1–11; **1 Peter 1.3–12**;
Gospel at Holy Communion: Luke 4.14–21

New birth

I have an adopted daughter and I vividly remember the day she arrived into our family as a baby. It was incredible how this precious bundle wrapped in a colourful Nigerian wrapper offered so much promise and hope. In gifting me this child, God had birthed a re-imagined possibility for me, given me a much longed-for daughter of my own.

The idea of new birth is one that we encounter again and again in Scripture. In today's passage from 1 Peter, we are reminded that, 'By his great mercy he has given us a new birth into a living hope through the resurrection of Jesus Christ from the dead.' The idea of a birth has numerous meanings. To make a decision and commitment to be a follower of Christ, to be 'born again', speaks to our new state and reality. We are not only a new person but belong to a new family, having new relationships. In God's great mercy, we get a fresh start in life and this new birth has been achieved through the resurrection of Jesus.

Living hope

We live in a world filled with hopelessness where many are discouraged, fearful and despairing. And, even as a person of faith, it is easy to become overwhelmed by the difficulties of life's circumstances. However, as Christians, we are offered a living hope and 'an inheritance that is imperishable, undefiled, and unfading, kept in heaven' for us. Even in hard times, we have a living hope. We have a hope that is not based on the futile things of this world. In our suffering, we are called to fix our eyes on Jesus, on whom our hope is built – his life, death and resurrection.

Unlike Israel's inheritance which became spoiled and defiled by their disobedience, the inheritance promised us is one that does not perish, cannot be spoiled, cannot be defiled and cannot fade. It is an inheritance that can never be overcome by death, destroyed by evil or diminished by time. Ours is an eternal inheritance and cannot be taken away.

A new song

The perspective gifted to us here is that our lives, given the eternal inheritance and living hope we have, should offer us eternal joy because our faith is anchored in the timeless nature of Christ. Even though we find ourselves in seasons of sorrow and distress, a life of suffering only lasts a little while. For sure, Peter is not minimizing the fact that suffering is real and takes its toll on people's faith, but he is encouraging us to hold on to our hope in the risen Lord as we live through various trials. Faith must endure tough choices, difficult times and unimaginable suffering. But such suffering compels us to risk everything by trusting Jesus, even when it doesn't make sense. Because when all is said and done, our trials create opportunities for us to offer Jesus our worship and praise – as the Psalmist encourages us to 'Sing to him a new song' – bringing glory and honour to God who gives us strength and courage to keep pressing on. And as we continue to go on with God, despite the painful wounds in our lives, we receive the result of our faith through trials: the salvation of our souls.

Catherine Okoronkwo

Hymn suggestions

Great is thy faithfulness; O Jesus, I have promised; Be thou my vision; In Christ alone.

Fourth Sunday of Epiphany 29 January

(For Presentation of Christ in the Temple, see p. 297.)

Principal Service **The Wedding at Cana**

1 Kings 17.8–16; Ps. 36.5–10; 1 Cor. 1.18–end; **John 2.1–11**

In John's Gospel, Jesus' miracles are called 'signs'. Signs point beyond themselves, and John's 'signs' are designed to lead us to faith in Jesus. We miss the point if we get bogged down in asking what happened, and how, rather than asking why, and what the miracles signify about God. The Fourth Gospel is rich in symbol and layers of meaning; it is always worth digging deep.

On the third day

The first 'sign', at the wedding at Cana, is set 'on the third day'. The third day of, or after, what? We're not told. But to a post-Easter audience, 'the third day' carries an obvious resonance: it is the day of resurrection.

The sign at Cana speaks of the eternal life God offers in Jesus and the hope that this brings. It points beyond Jesus' earthly ministry: from this first minor miracle to the ultimate miracle of Jesus' resurrection. And beyond that, it signifies the consequences of that resurrection for all who come to believe and so have life in Jesus' name. 'The third day' has powerful resonances.

Numbers and completeness

John's Gospel is remarkable for its inclusion of detail, and a certain preoccupation with numbers – especially numbers one less than a prime number. At Cana there were six water jars – six being one less than the prime number seven. Later in the same chapter, the Jews stress that it took 46 years to build the Temple, 46 being one less than the prime number 47.

The inference seems to be that what is incomplete in the Jewish system of worship and sacrifice (one less than a prime number) is made complete – is made whole – in the person of Jesus. The water jars were for Jewish purification rites, but in the new life which Jesus brings, there is no need for ritual washing. The water in the jars may represent cleansing from sin but Jesus is the one through whom we are cleansed from sin. Likewise, the Temple is home to a sacrificial system in which powerful symbols speak of a forgiving

48

God. But in Jesus that forgiveness is embodied; he is himself the one through whom sin is forgiven.

Abundance and life

The miracle at Cana produced a remarkable quantity of wine – probably between 120 and 180 gallons! Why so much? Why did Jesus not give simply enough to avoid embarrassment on the part of the host?

If the sign is about God's offer of life, then the answer is straight-forward. God is a God of overflow (cf. Eph. 3.20) and gives not 'just enough' to get by but more than enough. The danger is that we settle for time-limited, earthbound existence rather than eternal life – life which begins in this world and continues beyond death into something far greater than we can imagine.

The best is yet to be

Finally, the Gospel tells us about the quality of the wine Jesus provided: the best was saved until last. This was unusual. Normally, as the steward of the feast pointed out, the best was served first, and the cheaper wine later, when people had drunk enough to be past caring about quality.

This points to the truth that what God provides for his people is the best. Jesus came that we might have life to the full. The quality of the wine reveals God's commitment to quality of life; the fullness of God's blessing is there for those who live in Christ. But there is another resonance too. Feasting is a powerful biblical image of the life of God's kingdom – the life of the world to come. The quality wine, provided by Jesus, and kept until last, is a sign that the best is yet to be.

And herein lies a challenge, to our attitude to death. Death has become the great no-go area of western culture. We can, it seems, speak freely about anything except death. We coin euphemisms – 'Fred has passed' – rather than talk positively about what, for the Christian, is not an end but the gateway to the best that is yet to be. As the wedding guests at Cana, we are sharers in the 'new wine' of the resurrection. In a culture that refuses to look death in the face, Christians have a positive gospel message to proclaim.

The account of the wedding at Cana is full of detail and layers of meaning. The miracle is a sign – which points away from itself to the God who, in Jesus Christ, leads us into everlasting life. May we know and enjoy that gift of life as much as the wedding guests enjoyed their wine, and may God use us to bring the hope of everlasting life to others.

Peter Moger

Hymn suggestions

Christ is our light! the bright and morning star; Jesus, come! for we invite you; Songs of thankfulness and praise; One shall tell another.

Fourth Sunday of Epiphany   29 January
Second Service   **From Flight to Faith**
Ps. 34 [*or* 34.1–10]; **Gen. 28.10–end**; Philemon 1–16;
Gospel at Holy Communion: Mark 1.21–28

There are many reasons why people flee their homes. It may be to escape violence, war or press gangs; it may be because drought, famine and poverty are destroying livelihoods. The Bible is as full of stories like these as is our current news coverage, and the character we meet today is one such example. But in Jacob's case, he's running from a deadly situation for which he bears much of the responsibility.

Running

Jacob the shepherd is fleeing from his older brother, the hunter Esau. Having grown up in a family with divided loyalties and favouritisms, Jacob has deceived his sight-impaired, dying father, overturned established patriarchal traditions by cunning and received the paternal blessing which should have passed to Esau, the older son. Furious at discovering Jacob's treachery, the hunter has vowed to kill Jacob. But when we meet Jacob today, there's a sense in which he's running not only from Esau: he's running also from God, from himself and from all the emotional baggage his action has burdened him with.

We too can find strategies for running away from the difficult situations and the parts of ourselves we cannot honestly face. We don't necessarily leave home, but we try blaming others for what's gone wrong or avoiding the person we've rowed with. We overindulge to soften the impact of stress or wear ourselves out trying to deny what deep down we know to be true. Yet Jacob's experience reminds us that fleeing need not be the end of the story.

Resting

Running away is exhausting. Jacob grows weary and finally comes to a halt. He has to live with the memory of what he has done. The encroaching darkness offers a chilling image of the depth of his fear, while the hard stone he has to use as a pillow speaks of the difficulty of his finding real rest, anywhere.

The hard stone also speaks powerfully of Jacob's poverty. Far from home, Jacob cannot enjoy the benefits of his treacherous action. As he lies on the ground with nothing to call his own, he dreams of a ladder which, like him, also rests on the ground. Yet it's also reaching to heaven. Angels are going up and down: a reminder of the dynamic relationship that exists between God and humanity, a vision of how heaven is reaching down to him and how he might be lifted to heaven. He hears God speak. It's an extraordinary moment of revelation and truth! Perhaps Jacob's poverty has stripped him of his usual defences and made him more open to God.

God's message to Jacob speaks to us too, and not only as individuals. When as continents and nations we cease running away from urgent realities, such as that of climate change, and stop to face our responsibility, God can bring us to a new understanding of who we are and who we might become. Jacob learns that the power of blessing is not something to be wrenched from others: it is offered freely by a generous, loving God. The earth's richness – corn and plentiful new wine – which Jacob thought he could own or control by stealing his father's blessing, is not to be captured through greed or possessed by treachery. The earth belongs to God who promises it to countless future generations. It's to be a source of life and goodness for them.

Trusting

When Jacob wakes, he has been changed by his encounter with God. Yes, as far as he is aware, his brother is still out to get him. But, sensing that he's at heaven's gate, he places his trust in God. His priorities have dramatically shifted. He's no longer craving power over his brother or greedily hoping to amass riches. On the contrary, he understands now that all he needs is simply to be clothed and fed and ultimately restored to the father he deceived. It's an extraordinary transformation. The purpose of the hard stone pillow is also transformed! Now a sacred memorial to the promise Jacob has received and to the place of his vow, it becomes the foundation stone of a future centre of worship.

Experiences of God aren't what happen only to other people. No matter what stage of life's journey we've reached, God promises to be faithful to each one of us, whoever we are, whatever we may be running from, and however painful our burdens may be. Like Jacob's, our own journey from terror to trust, or from rupture to reconciliation, may well take many years, and there may be twists and turns on the way. Yet when we dare to rest, even on the hard stone pillow of our fears, we can be surprised by the presence of God who promises to travel alongside us and bring us to the place we need to be. For us as for Jacob, trusting God will lead us towards the healing of the human family, and a just and rightful relationship with the earth. In God's eternal purposes, they belong inseparably together.

Mary Cotes

Hymn suggestions

O God, you search me and you know me; O God of Bethel, by whose hand; Oh, the life of the world is a joy and a treasure; All my hope on God is founded.

Ordinary Time

Third Sunday before Lent (Proper 1)   5 February
Principal Service   **Looking Towards Lent**
Isa. 58.1–9a [9b–12]; Ps. 112 [*or* Ps. 112.1–9];
1 Cor. 2.1–12 [13–end]; **Matt. 5.13–20**

We've waved goodbye to Christmas with the feast of Candlemas and now we turn to face Jerusalem. Lent begins on Ash Wednesday, 22 February. It's just a couple of weeks away. Our readings today help us to think about engaging with Lent, which is a time for fasting, for growing closer to God, for walking the road of suffering with Jesus.

The idea of giving something up – of fasting for 40 days – leading up to Easter is still part of our heritage in the UK. It's talked about jokingly in pubs, workplaces and schools. We can take it rather lightly, as a chance to save money, lose weight or get on top of a bad habit for a while.

The fasting acceptable to God

Isaiah tells us about the type of fasting that God longs for us to undertake. This fasting is to be taken seriously. Isaiah reminds the Israelites that fasting isn't just a tick-box activity, a way of trying to win God's favour. It isn't about drawing attention to ourselves. 'There is no point fasting', says the Lord, 'if you continue to oppress and cheat your workers, ignore the hungry, look after number one, quarrel and fight and hit out at others.'

Fasting acceptable to God contains within it desire and actions which bring liberation – freedom not just for ourselves, but for others, particularly the outcast and downtrodden. God calls us to feed the hungry, show hospitality to the homeless, clothe the naked and be reconciled to family members. 'Stop pointing the finger,' says God through Isaiah, 'stop gossiping and saying horrible things'

– then you will realize that God is satisfying your needs, helping you grow strong in faith and love for others. That's one of the reasons that many Christians take up something for Lent that brings them closer to God – Bible study, acts of service, prayer and so on.

Jesus began his ministry by undertaking a long period of fasting – 40 days – in the desert, ridding himself of everything so that he might be filled with God: entering fully into his calling as God's Son. Following his fasting, the oppressed, the poor and outsiders were very high on Jesus' agenda, as they should be on ours.

Salt and light

In the Gospel, Jesus reminds us that his disciples are salt. Salt is a preservative, a disinfectant and an enhancer. It stops meat from rotting, it cleans and heals our bodies, it brings out the flavour in food. Like salt, we can help those around us by seeking good, healing and restoring, and building up and bringing out the best in others.

Jesus says disciples are also light. Light helps us see, it banishes darkness and brings all that it touches into focus. A tiny candle flame can make a huge difference in a dark space. Shedding light on confusion, misunderstanding or fear helps to unite and liberate us.

Jesus, like Isaiah, has a warning for us. Salt is useless if it loses its taste, and a light that is covered up and hidden away isn't doing its job. To be true disciples, we must keep our relationship with Jesus alive and fresh. At our baptism, we were commissioned to shine with the light of Christ for our whole lives. All our words and actions should be illuminated with Christ's love and goodness, so that those around us experience something of God and find life in all its fullness. It's no use, says Isaiah, holding great rituals in our worship or undertaking spiritual discipline at home if they don't result in our turning outwards in acts of justice to relieve the poor, the hungry and the oppressed.

Looking towards Lent

So, these next weeks are a good time to be thinking and praying about how to engage with Lent this year. If you are going to give up alcohol, chocolate, crisps, social media or whatever, how will that impact the needy whom God calls you to serve? Can you make the connection between your fasting and justice in our society? You might perhaps give the money that you save to a charity working with those affected by addiction or homelessness.

And if your Lenten discipline is to take up study, prayer or action, how will it help those who are oppressed? Who is your Lenten discipline for? Yourself or others? Be creative – look at some of the charities like Christian Aid or Tearfund or Acts 435 for ideas, or think about how you could serve those in need locally. Ask the Holy Spirit to guide you. Be brave enough to go with the Spirit's suggestions, which you may sense as a nudge within yourself or an idea that just won't go away. Sometimes what the Spirit calls us to do is very small but significant, sometimes it's something huge. Whatever it is, go with it: God will be with you.

When we care for and serve others – especially those who are suffering or in need – we show the love of God in action. We are part of God's 'Here I am' for others, and others are part of God's 'Here I am' for us. God calls us to be salt and light – how will you respond?

Catherine Williams

Hymn suggestions

Brother, sister, let me serve you; O Jesus, I have promised; Build your kingdom here; Take my life and let it be.

Third Sunday before Lent (Proper 1)   5 February
Second Service Be Angry But Do Not Sin
Ps. [1, 3] 4; **Amos 2.4–end**; Eph. 4.17–end;
Gospel at Holy Communion: Matt. 1.29–39

Distant from God

How did you feel, hearing the litany of human depravity Amos recites to the people of Judah and Israel? The transgressions are numerous and grave – the people of Judah have rejected God and turned to idols; the people of Israel are greedy, exploiting the poor, needy and vulnerable; they are lustful and sexually abusive; they disregard God's law and corrupt God's servants. All this in the face of God's faithfulness over generations; in the face of God's generosity, giving them the land, their freedom, their particular callings and gifts. Whatever you felt about it, God's response speaks about punishment, devouring fire, crushing – God seems angry.

The behaviour that Amos is highlighting is also evident to Paul in Ephesian society. Just like the people of Israel and Judah, the picture Paul paints of the Gentiles' behaviour shows people who are distant from God, greedy, impure, senseless and dissolute. If you think about the world around us, does any of that resonate? Do you see, in our times, in our society, the behaviour of the Judaeans and Israelites, and the Ephesians? Paul's accusation of 'bitterness and wrath and anger and wrangling and slander' feels particularly relevant. More than ever, it feels that anger simmers just beneath the surface in our society, ready to burst out into a vitriolic tweet or other social media abuse, at the slightest provocation – or sometimes, it seems, entirely unprovoked.

Anger or grief?

Does this anger and vengefulness have anything to do with what God is doing in Amos? Is anger OK, and can God be angry? What we hear from Amos feels really raw. But is it raw anger or something else? Paul instructs his readers, 'Do not grieve the Holy Spirit of God.' Could this be about grief? Grief that the people are alienating themselves from God and from each other, grief that relationships are not right?

Rejecting God

In both these readings, rejecting God is linked to a way of living that is damaging to the people who practise it, to others around them, especially the most vulnerable, and to society in general. This theme runs right through the Bible. If we think of the Ten Commandments, the 'thou shalt nots' are preceded by what people *should* do – in a nutshell, put God first. Jesus echoes this when he says that the greatest commandment is to love the Lord your God with all your heart, and with all your soul, and with all your mind, and the next is to love your neighbour. There is a clear link between where we are with God and where we are with our neighbour. If you are right with God, this will shape your behaviour. It's hard to believe that people who are putting God first could or would do the things we heard about in our readings.

Longing for justice

But while there is clearly grief at the people turning away from God, we also see a burning passion for things to change. What is really clear in Amos is that God wants what has gone wrong to be made right – God wants justice. We see that in God, and we may also feel it in ourselves. When we are confronted with the kind of behaviours Amos and Paul condemn, we are right to want those things to stop, to change, for the world to be better than that.

Maybe we *can* call it anger. Paul writes, 'Be angry but do not sin; do not let the sun go down on your anger, and do not make room for the devil.' So, anger is an appropriate response when things go wrong that need to be put right, when people turn away from each other, and when people turn away from God. That is what grieves God. That is what stirs up that passion for justice. But it is anger without sin – anger that leads not to retribution, to violence, resentment, bitterness and other destructive behaviour, but to things being made right and good, to positive change.

It's not entirely clear what the punishment referred to in Amos is, but it does say that even the strongest warrior cannot save himself. We know that we can't save ourselves – salvation comes from God. If we reject God, we don't leave ourselves with many options. Separating ourselves from God is its own punishment, and it grieves God when we cut ourselves off. Perhaps that is a kind of anger. But if God is angry, God's anger is a force for justice, a force for good, fuelled by God's desire to be reunited with the sinner; and God is always ready to forgive when the sinner returns.

Kat Campion-Spall

Hymn suggestions

Inspired by love and anger; The kingdom of God is justice and peace (Taizé); Forgive us when our deeds ignore; Forth in the peace of Christ, we go.

Second Sunday before Lent 12 February
Principal Service **A Life Reoriented on Christ**
Gen. 1.1—2.3; Ps. 136 [*or* 136.1–9, 23–end]; Rom. 8.18–25;
Matt. 6.25–end

A most anxious generation?

We live in a generation where our anxieties and fears are propagated
and weaponized through mainstream and social media, fuelled by
the rhetoric of politicians. We are told if we don't vote in the right
prime minister, our economy might collapse. If we don't control
borders and human migration, we risk overwhelming our resources.
Identity politics and culture wars are being battled out second by
second on social media platforms. All these messages cause real
anxieties and pressures for people. Is it any surprise there seems to
be a rise in all manner of physical and mental health issues? Anxiety
and worry are natural human feelings; however, these emotions
can affect our outward look on life. They can shape our decision-
making, and ultimately the direction of our lives. In Romans 8, Paul
talks about our 'present sufferings', and this suggests our human
existence means we'll experience pain and suffering.

A life reoriented to the light

Jesus addresses this issue in the passage from Matthew's Gospel
we're looking at today. Jesus does not want us to be anxious and
full of worry. He wants us to live life differently. He doesn't want
us making decisions based on fear. He wants the direction of our
lives to be established on eternal truths and not the temporal and
hollow promises the world has to offer. But is this too simplistic?

Perhaps what Jesus is addressing here is the kind of destructive
anxiety that devours our souls, to the point that it causes anguish
and distress, even depriving us of sleep. That anxiety robs us of
peace and joy, but rather creates fear that paralyses us, to such an
extent we behave in ways that disadvantage and oppress others.
When we respond out of our fears and anxieties we so often do not
operate out of a spirit of love. Fear diminishes our capacity to live
a righteous life in Christ.

Today's gospel message is part of a larger message that Jesus
came to teach us. It's the message that the kingdom of God has
different values from a life that is rooted in this world.

Life in the kingdom of God includes the poor, the merciful, those who mourn, the persecuted, those who hunger and those who are willing to serve with a grateful heart. Life in the kingdom of God includes our privilege and calling to bring Jesus' light to those dark places of our world.

Outward looking

In Genesis, we are reminded of God's pleasure in creating all that was good. Jesus illustrates his Father's care for all he has created with the image of birds and wild flowers. He reminds us of God's love for each one of us through a series of questions: aren't you worth much more than birds? Won't he be all the more sure to clothe you? Can we add a single hour to our lives by worrying?

We cannot fully understand why God has chosen to weave the threads of suffering into our Christian experience. Sin and death, disease and suffering cause sorrow and misery. They make life so hard to bear, but our hope and strength are in Jesus. We know and trust that our present sufferings find their relief in the risen Christ. Thus, suffering is an extraordinary witnessing opportunity. Suffering points us to the reality of our human limitation and in turn points others to God as the source of comfort, healing and salvation amid suffering. Jesus, through his life, death and resurrection, restores humanity and all creation. And holding on to this eternal truth, we can 'give thanks to the LORD' because 'his steadfast love endures for ever'.

Catherine Okoronkwo

Hymn suggestions

All my hope on God is founded; There's a wideness in God's mercy; Alleluia, sing to Jesu; Christ triumphant, ever reigning.

Second Sunday before Lent   12 February
Second Service   **The Shapes and Sizes of Wisdom**
Ps. 148; **Prov. 8.1, 22–31;** Rev. 4;
Gospel at Holy Communion: Luke 12.16–31

Wise buildings

One of the things about old buildings is that they hold a lot of ideas
and opinions about what it means to live wisely. Being a Christian
community in such a building can be both comforting and quite
tricky. Sometimes it feels as though the very walls of the building
are telling you something of great significance for your journey of
faith. Sometimes it feels as though those same walls are being ever
so slightly judgemental.

The church community I work with has a building so old it has
the word 'old' in its title – the Old Parish, Corstorphine. Its current
foundations were laid in 1429 and, to use an effective Scots word,
you can have a good blether with it about wisdom. Naturally, it
contains the stories of people who gained wisdom from life experience; the Annas and the Simeons of the local community. It holds
its own versions of prophets, too; the stories of people with fore-
sight whose wisdom is to see things differently. And it has its own
version of Proverbs or pithy sayings. One of the tombstones, for
example, has this inscription: 'Death is a debt to nature deon. I paid
it and so must you' ('deon' is Old Scots slang for 'due').

And, if I were ever to forget that part of the role of a Christian
community is to lead people home, metaphorically as well as physically, there is a lamp on the outside east wall; there since medieval
times, to guide people across the marshes to safety. If I were ever
to think too highly of my theological and rhetorical skills, there
is an hourglass by the pulpit to remind me that a good sermon
is usually a short one. If I need a wise woman role model I need
only to look at the window dedicated to Jessie Chrystal Macmillan,
suffragist, peace activist, barrister, feminist and the first female
science graduate from the University of Edinburgh.

Building wisdom

Wisdom comes in many forms as well as shapes and sizes. At the
end of our reading from Proverbs, wisdom is quirkily described
as being right at God's side at the beginning of creation, like, our

translation has it, 'a master worker'. Actually, this is one of the most ambiguous verses in the Hebrew Bible. Depending on how you read it, you can also translate it as, 'I was beside God, like a little child.' The consensus is that both are good translations, so it is best to work with the ambiguity.

Wisdom is a master worker, an architect, working alongside God as God assigns limits to chaos and provides shape and structure to things that otherwise are shapeless, fluid and potentially overwhelming. This is a God who sets limits to the seas and establishes the foundations of the deep. The turmoil of waters is a powerful metaphor for the chaos and danger that threatens to overwhelm us. It's a place of monsters.

Inhabiting wisdom

We perhaps know this from our own life experience. When our lives are disrupted by things outside our control, and chaos threatens us, it is often wisdom that creates a way through, that makes our situation habitable again, that brings life and sees off the monsters. Perhaps it comes in the form of wise advice, perhaps in the form of seeing what is happening in a different light – reframing the experience, perhaps simply by the presence of someone walking alongside us who has depth and understanding.

Wisdom is also a little child who is at God's side delighting in the world and humanity. And honestly, how can you not laugh at a giraffe, or smile with complete joy when you look at the beauty of mountains and lakes or enjoy a proffered cup of tea from a friend, or delight in some of the things human beings create or imagine. Taking pleasure in things, delighting in each other without any need to control or define, or have power over, is built right into the foundations of the world.

Perhaps for those of us who are intentional about trying to understand God better and who are trying to follow Jesus' example wisdom is deeper than how we normally think about it. To be wise is to be someone who actively looks for ways to work alongside God to create life and a way through for people when chaos is looming large. To be wise is also to be someone who sits alongside God and delights in all of creation, including humanity in all our diversity, not to control but simply because delight, joy, gladness is what God is doing and we want to join in. In short, wisdom is not about pinning life down to what our ancestors can teach us or about gaining and containing knowledge and experience. It is about a way of life that opens up the world rather than closing it down.

Esther Elliott

Hymn suggestions

How shall I sing that majesty; Come and seek the ways of wisdom; Now thank we all our God; Seek ye first the kingdom of God.

Sunday next before Lent   19 February
Principal Service   **Special Meetings with God**
Ex. 24.12–end; Ps. 2, *or* Ps. 99; 2 Peter 1.16–end; **Matt. 17.1–9**

On this Sunday immediately before the beginning of Lent, the scriptures record special meetings where God is revealed in a new way – meetings that make a significant difference in the lives of ordinary people.

God calls Moses up Mount Sinai to give him the tablets of stone containing the law and the commandments. It's a very mysterious scene – cloud and fire – and the Lord speaks with Moses for many days.

In the Gospel – which is also referred to in the reading from 2 Peter – Jesus takes Peter, James and John up the mountain to pray. While there, something extraordinary happens – Jesus changes – and the disciples see the glory of God revealed within him. Just before this episode, Peter has proclaimed Jesus as the Messiah. Now he witnesses something dramatic, something inexplicable that confirms his declaration. Moses and Elijah appear alongside, symbolizing the Law and the Prophets, and a voice comes from heaven saying that this one – Jesus – is the Chosen One, God's Son, to whom we must listen.

Seeing God

Both these encounters give the participants a new vision of God, a new way of seeing and experiencing God. It's new ground – holy ground – and it leaves people feeling different. Moses is a changed man when he comes back down the mountain. Peter is excited and desperately wants to hold on to the moment.

But that isn't what happens. It's not possible to live at the height of spiritual experience. Peter has to continue with his everyday living. However, this spiritual moment changes Peter. He will never see Jesus in quite the same light again. Everything that subsequently happens is set against these moments of glory on the mountain. How much easier to accept the resurrection and to receive the Holy Spirit if you have already tasted a little of God's glory.

This episode on the mountain – the transfiguration – is recorded in all four Gospels. It was a vital piece of the puzzle when those early writers were getting their heads around who Jesus was. This incident would have helped the early Church to shape and form its doctrine of Jesus – very God and very man, two natures in one substance. God, who in Jesus is both immanent – alongside us, with us and one of us – and transcendent – far beyond us and totally other. Fully God and fully human.

Fully God and fully human

The idea of Jesus as fully God and fully human is very hard for us to grasp. It's a mystery, which we are called to live with and experience rather than try to solve. In practice, we tend to side with Jesus as human, or Jesus as divine, rather than relate equally to both. Some of us will be drawn more to the Jesus who walked on earth. We will find his teaching and his actions inspiring and a model for the way we live our lives. We will respond to his concern for the poor and oppressed – for justice and equality. Others of us will be drawn more to the risen Christ – who gives us his body and blood in the bread and wine of communion, who nourishes and feeds us in a mystical way, who informs our prayers and our spiritual practices.

What Peter came to experience was that Jesus was both the human being who inspired his daily living and the God whom he worshipped: the one informing the other.

Becoming Christ-like

As Christians, we are called to follow Jesus – to be Christ-like, to grow into the image of God in which we are made. Therefore, our understanding, knowledge and experience of Jesus needs to be as wide and encompassing as possible. Is your vision of Jesus big enough? Is Jesus, for you, both your earthly example and the God whom you worship? Does faith in Jesus inform your actions and your prayers?

This Lent might be the time when you grow more into Christ, learning more about the earthly Jesus as you follow him through the desert, on the way to the cross and beyond. It may be time to come closer to the risen Christ in your spiritual life. Read the Gospels again and listen to the words of Jesus. Take note of his actions and think about how you can emulate them. Make yourself familiar again with the extraordinary man Jesus. Then spend time meeting the risen Christ in worship. Pray to Jesus, sing to Jesus, ask him to reveal himself to you in new ways in your spiritual life. Ponder deeply the mystery of holy communion – that event that brings you together with other members of Christ's body, and fills you with Christ's new life.

Moses was being changed. Peter was being changed. We are being changed. This Lent, listen to Jesus and let him meet you in a new way, or a new place. May Jesus surprise you as he takes you deeper into himself, changing you more and more into the person you are called to be.

Catherine Williams

Hymn suggestions

Be thou my vision; Be still, for the presence of the Lord; All heaven declares; Open the eyes of my heart, Lord.

Sunday next before Lent   19 February
Second Service   **Taking Light into the Darkness**
Ps. 84; Ecclus. 48.1–10, *or* 2 Kings 2.1–12; **Matt. 17.[1–8] 9–23**

A journey to a deserted place

Why do we read the story of Jesus' transfiguration on the Sunday before Lent? The transfiguration has its own feast day in August, so it's not as if it won't get read in church otherwise. Of all the Gospel readings that the lectionary compilers could have chosen to send us on our way towards Lent, why this one? In our reading, we see Jesus with Peter, James and John going up a mountain. Next Sunday, once Lent has begun, we will hear the account of Jesus going into the wilderness. Although both accounts involve a journey to a deserted place, they are very different. The journey up the mountain takes them to a place where God is clearly present, a place that feels holy and special and saturated with light. Jesus is transfigured – his appearance is transformed, his clothes dazzling white, his face shining like the sun – and the disciples then see the great holy figures of Moses and Elijah, walking with him. It is a place where Peter says, 'Lord, it is good for us to be here', and they hear the voice of God the Father, declaring, 'This is my Son, the Beloved; with him, I am well pleased; listen to him!' The journey into the wilderness is altogether different. Jesus doesn't encounter God, but Satan. It is a place not of affirmation but of temptation, a place in which God feels hard to find, or even absent, in stark contrast to the overwhelming sense of the presence of God on the mountain.

Looking towards the cross

So why, as we are about to embark on our own journey into Lent, a season that mirrors Jesus' 40 days in the wilderness, that strips away the frivolities and fripperies of life, that pares down the glory and joy of our worship to a season of starker solemnity, why today are we going to the opposite extreme? The story of the transfiguration in Matthew's Gospel is sandwiched between two occasions on which Jesus foretells his death. As we start to look towards the cross, we are reminded most powerfully of God's glorious presence. Before the journey into the darkness, we see a dazzling light. The mountain is a holy place. We know God is to be found there. In Lent, we strip away our dependencies and comforts, those things that distract us and mask the truth, and try to see ourselves, and the world, more clearly. It's about going into the wilderness, a place that is not easy, a place that is wild and lonely, a place in which God feels hard to find, or even absent. And our Lenten journey ends at the cross, the place of ultimate darkness, where hope seems altogether lost. But we don't go in our own strength. We go bearing the light.

The light of Christ

At our baptism we are given a candle, symbolizing the light of Christ, to take out with us. To take out into the world. And where is light needed? In the darkness. That's where we find people who are marginalized, excluded, suffering. Walking into the darkness might mean walking alongside a homeless person or an addict, someone who is facing their own death or struggling with bereavement, someone who is weighed down with physical or mental illness, or someone who is lonely. Walking into the darkness might mean stepping into a part of the world that is not as good or kind or friendly as you want the world to be, discovering that things you take for granted are simply not true for someone else. Walking into the darkness might mean going somewhere you are afraid to go, and sometimes it might mean going on ahead of another so that when they get there, they won't be alone.

Resting in the light

You may know the tradition that Sundays don't count as Lent – they are not days of fasting, and if you count the period from Ash Wednesday to Holy Saturday, it is actually 46 days – the six Sundays during Lent aren't part of the 40-day fast. Because walking into the darkness is difficult, and frightening, and lonely. And so, we come back to the place of light to remind ourselves that not all the world is dark, that our little lights come from a greater light, the light that shines in the darkness and will never be overcome by it. We come to this holy place, where we expect to find God – we come to be fed, encouraged, strengthened; we meet with sisters and brothers and we seek the source of the light. Before we begin our Lenten journey, we are offered a reminder of the power of the light; and each week we are invited to return to rest in its brightness. It is good to be here. But it is our calling to walk into the darkness. May the light of Christ shine brightly in you as you go.

Kat Campion-Spall

Hymn suggestions

'Tis good, Lord, to be here; Kindle a flame; Christ is the world's light; In a world where people walk in darkness.

66

Lent

Ash Wednesday   22 February
Principal Service   The Greatest Treasure

Joel 2.1–2, 12–17, *or* Isa. 58.1–12; Ps. 51.1–18;
2 Cor. 5.20b—6.10; **Matt. 6.1–6, 16–21**, *or* John 8.1–11

Imagine you were asked to conjure in your mind a picture of
'treasure'. I suspect any number of standardized images would
appear. In my head, I get a vision of that enormous pile of gold,
jewels and precious stones that Smaug the dragon covets and rests
on in *The Hobbit*. Another part of my brain holds images derived
from *Treasure Island*.

Elusive treasure

The thing about treasure, though, is that in and of itself it doesn't
exist. It is not a thing like a table or a chair or even a pile of gold. To
appreciate this, imagine ringing up John Lewis or going on Amazon
and trying to buy some treasure. In no important sense can this be
done. Yes, you can buy gold or a ruby, but that is not the same as
buying treasure. Why? Because treasure is the kind of concept that
has transferable meaning. In principle, anything can be treasure.
For many that will be gold or jewels. These are things that society
says are valuable. For others, it could be any number of things. For
me, it is books. I have thousands of them. Anything can be treasure,
then, provided one attaches sufficient value to it. How much, then,
do I feel the chastening power of those words of Jesus we hear on
Ash Wednesday: 'where your treasure is, there your heart will be
also.'

The heart of the matter

If Ash Wednesday reminds us that each of us is mortal and limited – traditionally as people are marked with ashes the minister says, 'Remember that you are but dust and to dust you shall return' – it invites us to strip away all that gets in the way of the very fount of life itself, God. Jesus zeroes in on the very heart of the matter: where we locate our treasure will signal to what we have given our heart.

'Where your treasure is, there your heart will be also.' Part of the reason I think Jesus draws our attention to the power of desire is that he knows of what we are made – flesh and bone. Desire is simply part of us. One cannot live this enfleshed life without desire, nor should one. The heart will have its attachments. To be human is to long for things, whether they be material things – possessions, or for our bodies to be loved and cherished – through to more spiritual and abstract things like a longing for justice or a deeper communion with God. While we are called to centre our lives on God, we can only seriously do this if we are honest about what it means to be human. We daren't ignore the demands of the flesh.

This invitation to interrogate where we place our treasure is so helpful as we begin our Lenten journeys. All we have – at the most profound level – comes from God. It is all gift, and I believe God offers this gift freely. But pregnant in that gift is an invitation to thanksgiving. Equally, an invitation to ask, 'Have I mistaken *this* relationship or *that* thing for the Real Thing: God?'

Discerning the treasure

Such discernment requires tender, patient and, above all, rigorous and honest prayer. As humans, we have a genius for going 'off-course' and treating that which is temporary as the ultimate ground of meaning and life. Thus, in my own case, I do have a genuine love of books in their every aspect: I love the words and wonders they can contain; I love their covers and pages; I love their smell. I like to wonder who has held an old book before me. I like first editions, and sometimes (to my shame) because of their value to collectors, I like how much they are worth. I am ravished by libraries. I don't think there is a sin in enjoying and delighting in learning and the power of books per se. I do, however, see how my fascination might turn into obsession. Even without obsession, I regularly lose focus. As Jesus says, 'where your treasure is, there your heart will be also.'

A simple treasure

As we enter Lent I want to come back to Jesus Christ – his words, his life, all he reveals about the living God. I come back to the simplicity of the words of the Lord's Prayer and that line, 'Give us today our daily bread.' It might also be understood as, 'Give us today the bread we need for tomorrow.' That is where I want my treasure to be: in knowing not only that God is enough but that God gives us enough for today and tomorrow. In such simplicity is the deepest treasure.

Rachel Mann

Hymn suggestions

Be thou my vision; My song is love unknown; Lord Jesus Christ; Go forth, O people of God.

First Sunday of Lent   26 February
Principal Service   **Choices**
Gen. 2.15–17; 3.1–7; Ps. 32; Rom. 5.12–19; **Matt. 4.1–11**

I saw a motivational poster that read, 'Life is a matter of choices, and every choice you make makes you'. Some choices are small while others are life-changing. Some are trivial while others are fundamental to who we are or become. Even choosing not to do or say something can have devastating effects. Pastor Martin Niemöller's famous observation of choosing not to speak out when 'they' came for the other person meant that there was no one left to speak for him is an unwelcome lesson in the consequences of choosing not to choose.

The familiar gospel story of Jesus in the wilderness is a story about choices. It tells us first of all that Jesus chose to be led by the Spirit – to open himself completely to the gracious will and mighty power of God. Jesus chose to be led by the Spirit 'into the wilderness', to follow God into a place that was not at all like home, an uneasy place, a place of testing. He chose to be led by the Spirit into the wilderness 'to be tempted by the devil', to face up to the evil around him, to grapple with the demons, not ignore them. And he also chose to *fast* – something that Christian people, from time to time, have valued and embraced. The idea of fasting is to simplify our lives, to focus down on ourselves, to recognize our dependence on God, to more readily open ourselves to God. It's not an *easy* choice to fast. But Jesus made it.

Food, status and power

And then came the three temptations which offered Jesus three choices:

- a choice about food;
- a choice about status;
- a choice about power.

We have choices about food – well, if we are on a low income or have food intolerances our choices are limited. But we still do face them. For some people the hard and very limited choice will be, what can I afford to buy to make sure my children get fed right through the week? What should I not buy for myself to make sure that happens? For others it might be, can I afford to spend a little bit more on fair trade goods to help those who produce them? The choice for Christians is, do we give in to our dependence on food to keep us satisfied, or make the harder choice of holding on to our dependence on God? That's hard when you have very little – can we, will we, trust God to provide?

We have choices about status. Because status isn't just to do with well-to-do people or politicians or celebrities, we all have anxiety about what others think of us; about whether we're judged a success or a failure, a winner or a loser. The choice for Christians is, do we respond to that anxiety by trying to do dramatic or showy things to impress other people, or let ourselves simply rest in the grace of God, receiving our status from God's grace?

We have choices about power. Again, we might not think we're very powerful, compared to the landlord who can fix our leaking roof or keep us living in the damp, or the borough council who can decide to dig up the road outside our house or take our post office away. But we do have power, each of us. Personal power – power which gives us choices either to help someone in need or ignore them, to forgive someone who has hurt us or let them carry on suffering by ignoring or abusing them. We all know about the power games that go on in our churches – sadly, every church suffers these. They go on in our homes too. Each of us has power in relation to other people. The choice for Christians is, do we use that power as the world sometimes does, manipulatively, selfishly, greedily, or devote ourselves to the greater power of God?

Back to the beginning

All this about temptations and choices goes back to the very beginning, to the man and the woman in the garden of Eden, the tree, the apple, the serpent, the choice.

The difference between us and Adam and Eve is that we already know that we are naked; we know that we are flawed human beings, we know that we can choose good or evil, we even know what the consequences of our choices are likely to be before we choose.

In the end, I am sure that Lent is about asking God to help us keep our eyes open and keep the eyes of our hearts fixed on him who made the right choices.

'Worship the Lord your God, and serve only him.'

Paul Williams

Hymn suggestions

Forty days and forty nights; Lead us, heavenly Father, lead us; Take up thy cross; This is my prayer in the desert (Desert Song, Hillsong).

First Sunday of Lent 26 February
Second Service **Hear Ye, Israel**
Ps. 50.1–15; **Deut. 6.4–9, 16–end**; Luke 15.1–10

What's the story?

When did you last hear a sermon on the book of Deuteronomy? In Jewish tradition, Deuteronomy is given the name *debarim* (words): so, maybe it's neglected by preachers because it is 'wordy'. Perhaps you're trying to recall to mind what you've previously heard about this book!

A generation ago, the fashionable scholarly consensus was that the book was part of the work of the Deuteronomic historian who compiled the books of Joshua–2 Kings (with the omission of Ruth). Having consulted more recent scholarship, I gather that some fashions don't change.

While Jewish tradition regarded these books as the works of the 'former prophets', Christians have regarded them as historical books – a designation that is not without difficulties. The author/editor offers a sort of 'preached history'. A theological ordering of evidence from history.

The geographical context for our text is a liminal space, a border-crossing, as the people of Israel are about to cross over into the Promised Land. Moses, who is not going to be able to cross over with them, is taking his last opportunity to remind the people of what their God expects of them. It's a long 'sermon', wherein, after a brief introduction, the law is reiterated in chapters 5–26. Did Moses actually make such a speech? We might as well ask whether the opera's heroine, dying of consumption, could realistically sing a sublime aria (exhibiting excellent lung capacity).

Oy ...

It's the pivotal point in Deuteronomy. 'Hear,' (NRSV) is such a polite opening gambit. The (translated) word *Shema* is more forceful than that; it's more a case of, 'Oy, listen up, you lot.' In the previous chapter, we had the reiteration of the Decalogue (the Ten Commandments), God's words. Now Moses is commencing his own words to his people. It's his last chance to capture their attention and impress upon them the statutes and ordinances that are the foundation for their faith. (Think of Moses as a coach about to send his team out to play.)

The opening verse contains the fundamental truth about God: 'The LORD is our God, The LORD alone.' The meaning of the Hebrew is ambiguous: is it that the Lord alone is their God, the God for Israel? Or is the text going still further in a statement about the unity and the uniqueness of God (he is the One and only)? Surely these slightly differing interpretations complement each other.

The first law is: 'You shall love God.' This is the love that encompasses 'fear', reverence and awe: it's not about romantic feeling. It is absolute devotion, obedience and total commitment. They are to love God with their whole being: all that they are and all that they have is God's. It could be argued that the rest of the book of Deuteronomy is a commentary on this teaching!

The injunctions in verses 8–9 were later taken literally: devout Jews, to this day, bind phylacteries to their left arms and foreheads that contain the words of the Shema (and other foundational texts) and fix mezuzah to the doorposts of their homes. The words of the

Shema are recited in the morning and the evening. They are central to devotion and the faith of Israel.

The latter part of our passage contains a reminder of the centrality of the Exodus experience and God's promise to bless an obedient people who will experience prosperity in the land that God is giving to them. The people are exhorted to pass the faith on through the generations.

What can we learn from this text?

When Jesus was confronted by a question from some Pharisees about the greatest law, he stated that 'You shall love the Lord your God with all your heart, and with all your soul, and with all your mind' is the greatest and first commandment.

So, we might ask, how are we marked by this law? We may not, literally, tie it to our bodies or affix it to our doorposts, but do we keep it as the basis of our faith lives and our living? God's law calls us: it's a rule of life grounded in God's love. If you feel that you are not measuring up, remember, the amazing thing in the Deuteronomic historian's account of the relationship between YHWH-God and Israel is that despite their spirals into sin and disobedience, God does still, by his grace, keep on reminding, forgiving and restoring.

Do we put God first? Do we seek God's will? Are we endeavouring to become a righteous community? Let's fulfil the first and greatest commandment and then pass on our love of God to our children and our children's children.

Wendy Kilworth-Mason

Hymn suggestions

Fill thou my life, O Lord my God; God has spoken by his prophets; Great God, your love has called us here; What shall I do my God to love.

73

Second Sunday of Lent   5 March
Principal Service   ***Ecce Homo!***
Gen. 12.1–4a; Ps. 121; Rom. 4.1–5, 13–17; **John 3.1–17**

Travelling as pilgrims

We travel, pilgrims through Lent, seeking our way towards Good
Friday, in the hope of Easter Day. Good Friday always comes as
a day of reckoning. Am I ready for the light? Ready to come out
of the darkness, counted worthy to stand in the presence of the
resurrected Christ? Will the answer come: '*Ecce Homo!*' Look,
there she is! She stands firm in faith. She belongs to the glorious
company of those who have denied themselves, taken up their cross
and followed Christ. She is born of water and the Spirit.

The blessing of faith

Look, there is the man! says St Paul as he focuses on Abraham
to persuade the Christians in Rome that faith is an unconditional
response to God. It does not depend on external signs – Abraham's
faith preceded his circumcision, so it can't be that. It doesn't depend
on good works, either: you can't earn your way into heaven. To be
righteous in God's eyes is not to bargain, 'If I have faith, then God
will bless me.' No. Faith is not a contract, but a gift – freely given,
freely received. God desires our free response of worship and love.
So Paul looks back to the father of faith, the man who received the
promise of God, of greatness, of blessing, because he did not falter
in faith through all his wanderings in the desert, the mountain, the
valleys of death.

Light and darkness

Poor Nicodemus. Coming by night, not yet convinced, but curious
about this new birth from above. He needs a different imagination
to help him see what it means to be born of water and Spirit. To
leave behind the old man and become a new person. Nicodemas,
you need to believe, says Jesus. As with Abraham, faith comes first.
He needs that 'Yes!' to God. Then he will see – *Ecce!* 'The Son of
Man ... lifted up, that whoever believes in him may have eternal
life.'

Like Nicodemus, we come with questions, wondering about
Jesus; not sure if we want to go that far; not sure what it all means.

Life in Christ is spurred on by questions, by doubts, the dark night of the soul. Nicodemus is perhaps the first. Giving us all permission to ask the most difficult, challenging questions of our God. And when we do, and listen in openness and trust, we find we are not alone.

We might even find that our darkness is not the terrifying, dangerous place that we imagine. We find that God is there, as everywhere, keeping us in our going out and coming in from this time 'on and for evermore. That to God the darkness and the light are both alike. In faith, Jesus descends into hell. We should not be afraid to deepen our faith – even if it is under the cover of darkness. The writer of the Gospel draws this out deliberately. The darkness affects Nicodemus in his mind: who knows what the dawn brought for him? Who knows if the light bathed him, on the other side of the valley of the shadow of death? Did he hear the words of Jesus, that faith means he won't perish but will have eternal life?

Ecce Homo!

Following Jesus blesses us richly with abundant life. But it is a mixed blessing to follow where his footsteps lead. As pilgrims, we learn that the light, the joy and the love of God comes to us through the darkness and death of the crucifixion. As with so many aspects of our lives, we grow in virtue, in wisdom and love when we don't turn away from hard experience, from the valleys of the shadow of death.

Think of friends, Christians, in countries where it's dangerous to follow Jesus. Many face threat and violence for their faith, daily. Christians persecuted, who know the price of the faith that has no price. Many who stand, *Ecce Homo*! Some with none to see them but God alone.

They live by the promise of faith that can face death, having learned not to fear. To have faith enough to suffer, perhaps even to die, for the sake of Jesus Christ, is to know life beyond death. Eternal life: the gift of life that is priceless. A gift which is ours, when we turn to Christ, take up our cross and follow him.

As we journey onwards through Lent, let us know the gift of faith and love. The gift means we dare to stand and be counted. Let it be said of us: *Ecce Homo*! Look! There they are: Christians who know the love of God that brings eternal life.

Frances Ward

Hymn suggestions

Praise to the holiest in the height; Lead us, heavenly Father, lead us; Take up thy cross, the Saviour said; Guide me, O thou great Redeemer.

Second Sunday of Lent 5 March
Second Service **Living Your Best Life in Christ**
Ps. 135 [*or* 135.1–14]; Num. 21.4–9; **Luke 14.27–33**

Millennials' and Gen Zers' imperative

In an age where Millennials and Gen Zers through social media are redefining world views, this generation is poised to change the world. They follow influencers who promote the ideal of 'living one's best life'. Influencers are successful to such an extent that they shape how companies allocate advertising budgets. Apart from shaping fashion, protest and popular culture, Millennials and Gen Zers are also providing fresh perspectives and engagement on important issues such as social and environmental justice. Millennials and Gen Zers are intentional in wanting to solve macro problems, from confronting unjust policies and unfair norms to combating climate change and challenging the lack of gender equality. Social media offers a platform for an imperative to right the wrongs of their predecessors. However, is this 'wokeness' enough, or is there a spiritual dimension to 'living one's best life'?

Living your best life in Christ

In Jesus' ministry, the crowds were constantly gathering around him. He offered healing, teaching, compassion and a new vision. Like Millennials and Gen Zers, the people of Jesus' time longed to see a change in the unjust systems and structures that oppressed many people – slaves, the poor, orphans and widows. Many people value community and want to solve the problems in our society. We all want to live well and better together. But how do we live our best life in Christ? Jesus draws us into a life of discipleship, a life that costs us everything. It is impossible to hate those we love. There can be only one priority. For divine love, we must be prepared to carry the cross and give up our possessions. There is sacrifice to truly knowing and experiencing love.

When we watch the Olympics, we observe athletes who have made incredible sacrifices over many years – training, relationships, other interests – to give themselves a shot at a medal. We may not be elite athletes, but we know how to make costly sacrifices. Why do we make such sacrifices? We do it because these things are important to us. The question is when it comes to living for Christ, what sacrifices are we willing to make and at what cost?

To live our best lives in Christ we are called to love God and love others. It isn't about pursuing the world's definition of wealth and success, because, as we read in Luke 14, 'none of you can become my disciple if you do not give up all your possessions.' God doesn't promise health, wealth or success in this life. Jesus gives us the gift of wholeness in this life and hope in an eternal future.

A spiritual dimension

To be a disciple means that we are called to remain in Christ, committed to living lives that glorify God. We are called to be servants who praise the name of the Lord. Thus, our focus should be on chasing after God with the passion, energy and determination of an elite athlete. As we journey on in our relationship with God, we learn how to be more like Christ in every area of our life. God is concerned about our whole selves, seeking for us to flourish as integrated beings. Our relationship with Jesus shapes who we are, characterizes our relationships with others and determines the authenticity of our lives.

We are called to live our best life, not as the world determines but by kingdom standards. We are called to be like Jesus, trusting him in both wilderness and mountain-top moments. Perhaps we are being asked this week to reframe our priorities through a spiritual lens so that our lives might be transformed by the love of Christ. Perhaps we are being invited to total surrender, offering every aspect of our lives to God. Because in this generation, we have hope and a future as we serve a faithful God who cannot be outdone in generosity.

Catherine Okoronkwo

Hymn suggestions

Faithful one, so unchanging; O Jesus, I have promised; Be thou my vision; King of kings, Majesty.

Third Sunday of Lent   12 March
Principal Service   **Tools of Engagement**
Ex. 17.1–7; Ps. 95; Rom. 5.1–11; **John 4.5–42**

How do relationships grow? How are friendships forged? In countless ways no doubt! We might, however, want to identify different, deepening stages in a mysterious process that starts with two people meeting, grows through talk or activity around a common interest, and finally arrives at a trust that allows for sharing deeper truths about who we are. But these stages don't just describe human relating. They also tell us something about the way we come to know God.

God-given encounter

Today's Gospel explores the way our relationship with Christ can grow. The story begins with a meeting, initiated by Jesus. Jesus encounters a solitary woman at a well. In the ancient world, women were associated with the home, but as it fell to them to fetch water, the well was considered an extension of their home space. Instead of coming to the well with other women in the cool early morning, this woman – an outcast – avoids them by coming alone in the midday heat.

The woman is also a Samaritan, racially deemed by Jews as unclean. Crossing the great divides of Jesus' day, the encounter – humanly speaking – thus draws together male and female, powerful and powerless, Jew and Samaritan. Depicting a man entering the space of an unrelated woman blurs the strict protocols separating public and private spheres. Scandalous! At a more mysterious level, of course, it also brings together the divine nature of Jesus, the Word made flesh, with the humanity of the woman. No matter how invisible or unacceptable we may feel we are to others, Jesus sees and seeks us.

Human request

Christ doesn't just come to meet us: he recognizes and values what we can give. The relationship between Jesus and the woman develops as it moves to the second stage: a request and a shared interest. Jesus asks for a drink and the conversation proceeds around subjects of mutual concern: water and thirst. Jesus draws the conversation from an earthly understanding of water to a heavenly one. Just as God had once provided water for his people as they thirsted in the wilderness, Jesus speaks of the 'living water' he himself offers. The woman, fascinated, doesn't understand this reference to the Holy Spirit, but still senses that this living water will renew her life. She asks Jesus to give her some.

God-given insight

With divine insight, Jesus now takes the relationship to a richer, more truthful level. The woman doesn't need to tell Jesus her circumstances: he already knows them and understands. Traditionally, commentators have taken the woman's five husbands as evidence of repeated unfaithfulness, and have considered her now to be living with a man outside of a marriage contract.

However, perhaps we need not judge the woman so harshly. In the ancient world, a host of reasons could lead to a woman's being rejected, from infertility to her burning food. Meanwhile, as younger women were frequently given in marriage to older men, this woman might also have been widowed several times. If so, the man with whom she currently lives may be her father, son, brother or brother-in-law. Whatever her circumstances, Jesus offers not a hint of judgement.

When we understand that God fully knows us and loves us exactly the way we are, something inside us opens up. We start to blossom. This is the woman's experience. She moves from asking how Jesus can benefit her, to simply thirsting to know the truth about Jesus. Who is this stranger who offers living water? She's still confused, but as she follows Jesus' leading, her trust and belief deepen. Initially surmising that Jesus is a prophet, she eventually becomes the first of many in John's Gospel to hear the words, 'I am'. Jesus reveals his true identity: he is the Messiah!

Human transformation

Although, like the woman, we don't always understand, our relationship with Christ brings us new life. Despite her confusion, the woman is dramatically transformed by her encounter. This is the fourth stage. It's as if the joy and relief of being accepted and loved, plus the wonder of believing who Jesus is, all bubble up inside her. Leaving her earthly water-jar behind, she hurtles off into the village to share with others the mystery and miracle of her heavenly encounter. Before, she was isolated; now, she finds community. First, it was Jesus who crossed boundaries; now, it's she who does. Entering the public arena with all the excitement of a new missionary, she points forward to the future mission of the Church.

The God-given journey

Encounter, request, insight, transformation: while this particular story compresses our relationship with Christ into a few verses, our own spiritual journey will take a lifetime. We may find that sometimes we inhabit more than one stage at a time. At which stage – or stages – are you, at the moment? What is Christ asking of you, and how thirsty are you for the living water? How has your knowledge of Christ grown and how are you being transformed?

Mary Cotes

Hymn suggestions

Jesus calls us here to meet him; Have you heard the raindrops; O God, you search me and you know me; I heard the voice of Jesus say.

Third Sunday of Lent   12 March
Second Service   **Into the Fray**
Ps. 40; Josh. 1.1–9; **Eph. 6.10–20**;
Gospel at Holy Communion: John 2.13–22

Historical re-enactment is an important pastime for many people. I live in Tewkesbury where every year, over the second weekend in July, the town is transported back to 4 May 1471. On this weekend, 25,000 people come from all over Europe to re-enact the Battle of Tewkesbury – the decisive battle of the War of the Roses. It's the largest medieval battle re-enactment in Europe. Tewkesbury Abbey – where I am vicar – is at the heart of this modern-day gathering, just as it was in the original event.

Around the battlefield, on which we celebrate the Eucharist on Sunday morning, has grown a tented village selling all sorts of equipment for re-enactors. A smithy is erected so that armour, after the battle, can be realigned and repaired. Stallholders selling swords, daggers and chain-mail do a roaring trade. For the authentic re-enactor, it is all a very serious business.

A ready-made visual aid

St Paul surely had Roman soldiers in mind when he developed his analogy of the whole armour of God in his letter to the Ephesians. Scholars have suggested that Paul brought together the teachings of the Older Testament with a visual aid that would be standing on guard outside any public building. St Paul spiritualizes the centurion's armour, armour that Emperor Constantine would have been familiar with, and armour you can still pick up in Tewkesbury on the second weekend in July. The whole armour of God may seem a strange or difficult analogy for us today, but for many Christians the armour of God has been a potent metaphor for centuries.

Belt and breastplate

First, we put on the belt of truth. The belt holds all things together, without it you won't get very far. Truth is essential in all our relationships. We need to speak the truth about God and God's love for all in Jesus. We need to tell the truth when speaking to those around us: our spouse, our children, our parents, our grandparents, our neighbours and colleagues. Finally, we need to grasp the truth about ourselves. Living truthfully rather than living a lie is a core value that the world today needs.

Next, we put on the breastplate of righteousness. This is about right relationships and healthy relationships. We are to grow good relationships with all those around us and even with ourselves. We are to be in right relationships, not wrong, abusive and self-seeking relationships.

Shoes and shield

Then we put on the shoes of peace. We should never be looking for a fight with our family, neighbours or workmates. Legitimate conflicts are to be worked through in mature ways that focus on resolution and peace – whether between individuals, groups or nations. We are to be peacemakers, working diligently for and towards peace in all relationships. And we are to be peacekeepers too.

Next, we put on the shield of faith. The shield reminds us to trust God. We trust that God is with us, and in us. We trust that God will strengthen us for every situation we face. We can't prove God. We can't prove God's inner strength. We can't prove eternal life. The gift of faith enables us to trust. We trust our inner spiritual self. We trust God's slow plan for salvation and wholeness for all people. Though we can't see it, we can trust God's plans for our future, on both sides of the grave.

Helmet and sword

Then, we put on the helmet of salvation. This is a gift that enables us to know that we are totally and utterly loved by God, that there is nothing we can do to earn or merit that love: it's a free gift from God. We don't have to worry about being saved, we just have to live it. We don't have to question whether or not we deserve it. Eternal life is a gift.

Lastly, we put on the sword of the Spirit that is the word of God. There is power in the Bible, in the word of God. The words of Jesus in the Gospels, the wisdom of the Older Testament and the advice of the apostles are not merely words printed on pages of a dusty book that we pull out in emergencies. God's words are living words, intended to live in us and through us. We should learn them, perhaps even memorize them so that we can recite them when the going gets tough and the battle is long.

The armoury

Where do we find this suit of armour that St Paul encourages us to wear? At the armoury! It would be lovely to welcome you to the Tewkesbury re-enactment to get you kitted out, but there's an easier place to do that. And that's in the Christian community, the Church, where the people of God gather and the body of Christ is formed. From the Church, the body of Christ, we learn about faith ... and right and good relationships ... and peace ... and trust ... and salvation ... and the Bible. These qualities can be found in the Church, God's armoury. There we can each pick up all these essential Christian elements and learn to wield them well in service to the world under the standard of Jesus.

'Put on the whole armour of God, so that you may be able to stand ...'

Paul Williams

O Jesus, I have promised; Stand up, stand up for Jesus; Put peace into each other's hands; My eyes have seen the glory.

The Fourth Sunday of Lent   19 March

(For Mothering Sunday, see p. 88. For Joseph see p. 300.)

Principal Service   **The Man Born Blind: Healing and Wholeness**

1 Sam. 16.1–13; Ps. 23; Eph. 5.8–14; **John 9**

Today's Gospel relates what appears to be a straightforward healing miracle: a man, blind from birth, receives his sight. But beneath the surface lie several questions:

• Why was he blind in the first place?
• What might 'healing' mean?
• What does it mean to 'see'?
• Is there a link between physical affliction and sin?

In Jesus' day, it was assumed that illness was God's punishment for sin. An illness from birth was believed to be the result of parental sin. Hence, when they encountered a man born blind, the disciples' question to Jesus is quite natural. This might seem primitive to us, but even in the 1662 Book of Common Prayer we find this line in the order for the Visitation of the Sick: 'whatsoever your sickness is, know you certainly that it is God's visitation.'

Jesus' answer, though, is clear: neither the man nor his parents had sinned. Would that the Church through the ages had taken these words to heart!

Seeing and believing

Jesus went on to heal the man, and the passage teases out the contrast between blindness and sight. The man's physical blindness does not prevent him from 'seeing' who Jesus is, yet the Pharisees are so steeped in sin and 'spiritually blind' that they are incapable of recognizing Jesus. Characteristically, the writer here references a major theme of the Fourth Gospel, which later comes to fruition in Jesus' post-resurrection words to Thomas: 'Blessed are those who have not seen and yet have come to believe.'

Healing and wholeness

But what exactly did the man receive from Jesus? His sight, certainly – but more than that. Before the miracle, he would have begged; with sight restored, he could work for a living. Blind, he would have lived on the margins of society; with sight, he would have been fully part of his community. Above all, the man's healing enabled him to become more fully himself – the person God intended him to be. He received wholeness and integration: his life started to come together. His physical cure was a part of the picture, but part of something much bigger.

Healing is a thorny subject, not least the distinction between healing and cure. The man born blind *was* cured. But cures don't always happen. In public ministry, I have seen cures that have been little short of miraculous, but many more cases of serious illness where there has been no cure. We all struggle as Christians – as human beings – with the question 'Why?' and it's foolish to suggest there is a reasonable answer. Nor can we simply duck the issue by claiming that the absence of a cure 'must be God's will'.

Nevertheless, God's offer of wholeness always stands. The Gospel is about becoming, in Christ, the people God created us to be: whole, functional, integrated people. Humans are a complex mixture of body, mind and spirit; God's healing is about the wholeness of all three. If any one of these becomes disordered (or dis-eased) then there's likely to be a knock-on effect elsewhere.

For instance, someone living with uncertain mental health might also suffer physical or spiritual symptoms. Likewise, someone with a debilitating physical illness might easily fall prey to mental distress. A person who gets mixed up in the wrong type of spirituality can end up suffering serious psychological trouble. We can't split the human personality. God's healing is about the integration – the wholeness – of all three.

And although illness isn't caused by sin, spiritual, mental and physical well-being (or lack of it) are linked. On the occasion, described in Mark's Gospel, when friends lowered a paralysed man through the roof to reach Jesus, Jesus said to the man – whom he had healed – 'your sins are forgiven.' Illness is never a punishment for sin, but there might sometimes be a link: complex beings that we are.

Letting in the light

In the New Testament reading, Paul writes of letting in Christ's light to expose areas of darkness in our lives, so that they may be seen more clearly and dealt with, and we may grow in wholeness. Self-examination in Lent is not unlike spring-cleaning: shining light into the hidden corners of our life and removing the cobwebs.

Each of us is inevitably dis-eased, in some way or other: in body, mind or spirit. God's will is that we should be made whole: set free to be the people he made us to be. A crucial step towards that wholeness is for us to face up to the people we are now – by praying for Christ's light: the light of insight, the light of judgement, the light of healing.

> The almighty Lord,
> who is a strong tower for all who put their trust in him,
> whom all things in heaven,
> on earth and under the earth obey,
> be now and evermore our defence.
> May we believe and trust that the only name under heaven
> given for health and salvation
> is the name of our Lord Jesus Christ. Amen.[7]

Peter Moger

Hymn suggestions

Amazing grace; Awake, awake, fling off the night; I heard the voice of Jesus say; We cannot measure how you heal.

Fourth Sunday of Lent   19 March
Second Service   **More than the Sand**
Ps. 31.1–16 [*or* 31.1–8]; Micah 7, *or* **Prayer of Manasseh**;
James 5; *Gospel at Holy Communion*: John 3.14–21

Not a good man

The Prayer of Manasseh is found in the Apocrypha but the story of the man who prayed it is told in the Hebrew Bible. One version, a very damning one, is told in 2 Kings; another with a more redemptive ending is told in 2 Chronicles.

Manasseh was a king of Judah. It could be said that, like A. A. Milne's poem about King John, Manasseh was not a good man, he had his little ways.

Those little ways, according to the accounts in the Hebrew Bible and the annals of the kings of Israel and Judah, included idol worship, desecrating the Temple with altars to foreign gods, deep involvement in the occult, resorting to child sacrifice to appease Moloch, a Canaanite deity, and executing the prophets who spoke out against him. Tradition has it that he put to death the prophet Isaiah by ordering that he be sawn in half with a sword. No, King Manasseh was not a good man!

Son of King Hezekiah, Manasseh came to the throne when he was just 12 years old. Perhaps that went to his head, all that power so young. Lacking guidance and parental care, his reign went awry, leading the people away from their faithfulness to God for over half a century. The writers of Kings and Chronicles account Judah's exile into Babylon as a direct punishment for the deeds of King Manasseh.

A man who repents

But Chronicles includes a part of the story that Kings leaves out: Manasseh's repentance, his turning once more to God and seeking forgiveness.

The prayer reveals that he saw the error of his ways. Perhaps he had thought that he was invincible. Or perhaps when he was captured by his enemies, the destruction of his kingdom made him see that the desperate measures he had taken to appease count- less deities had come to nothing. He turned back to the God he had heard of in his boyhood, the God of Israel. Chronicles records that he prayed to the God of his ancestors, although not the prayer itself. Those words are found in the Apocrypha.

In this prayer, Manasseh contrasts himself to the patriarchs, Abraham, Isaac and Jacob, whom he describes as sinless. Now, anyone who has read the stories of those characters will know that they could not, with any accuracy, be described as sinless. They made grave mistakes along the way, messed up big time more than once. But through those mistakes, they learned more about God and what it meant to be faithful to God. Perhaps Manasseh learned that too, although we don't hear the details of how his life was turned around so starkly. Only that he prayed for forgiveness. But perhaps the message is that if God could forgive and redeem one like King Manasseh, then there is hope for all.

Manasseh confesses that the sins he has committed are more in number than the sand of the sea. This echoes God's promise to Abraham – that God would make Abraham's descendants as many as grains of sand upon the shore and as many as the stars in the sky. It also has echoes of Psalm 139, the song of praise to the inescapable God. In it, the Psalmist says, 'How weighty to me are your thoughts, O God. How vast is the sum of them! I try to count them – they are more than the sand; I come to the end – I am still with you.'

A God who is our home

God's thoughts, God's wisdom, God's goodness, God's promise of blessing far outweigh our sin, even the sin of a king whose reputation for evil was considered by the writers of his history to be responsible for the destruction of the holy Temple in Jerusalem and the exile of God's people. For even from such destruction and exile God redeemed. A remnant returned to the land and rebuilt the holy place. There was a new beginning, new life, forgiveness and transformation. And that is the heart of the gospel.

So, the Prayer of Manasseh matters. It has its place in our liturgy and our lectionary. It is included as one of the canticles in *Common Worship*, a prayer of penitence. Manasseh bends the knee of his heart. In Jewish understanding the heart was the seat of thought, feeling and will. To bend the knee of the heart was to show a free choice, not a forced obedience. At a time when the king was forced to obey a foreign power in exile, the choice of his heart was to worship God. Like the prodigal son, Manasseh's penitence is a longing to return home yet a sense of utter unworthiness to look upon the one who is that home, that sanctuary, that dwelling place. But God's loving-kindness is to welcome us all home. So, the great narrative of the people of Israel in the Hebrew Bible mirrors God's longing for the whole world, the great and loving kindness of God to be revealed in Christ.

Carey Saleh

Hymn suggestions

O Love that will not let me go; Purify my heart; Praise to the holiest in the height; Lord, we turn to you for mercy.

Mothering Sunday   19 March

(All-Age Mothering Sunday, see p. 366.)

Reclaiming Mothers' Day

Ex. **2.1–10**, *or* 1 Sam. 1.20–end; Ps. 34.11–20, *or* Ps. 127.1–4;
2 Cor. 1.3–7, *or* Col. 3.12–17; Luke 2.33–35, *or* John 19.25b–27

The well informed among us might assume I have made an error
in calling my sermon 'Reclaiming Mothers' Day' – after all, don't
preachers usually try to reclaim the Church's Mothering Sunday
from Mothers' Day? Don't preachers usually remind their hearers
that originally this day was for people to worship at their mother
church – the largest in the area, or the one where they were baptized?
And in later times it was a day for domestic servants to take a day
off and go home. Well, maybe. But today, in light of our readings,
I want to reclaim Mothers' Day.

The Mothers' Day story

At the end of the nineteenth century in West Virginia, a woman
called Ann Jarvis said, in her daughter's hearing, 'I hope and pray
that someone, sometime, will found a memorial mothers' day com-
memorating her for the matchless service she renders to humanity
in every field of life. She is entitled to it.' Ann died in 1908. Her
daughter Anna held a memorial service on 10 May. In 1914, Presi-
dent Woodrow Wilson declared the second Sunday in May to be
Mothers' Day in America. The idea spread and in Britain the fourth
Sunday in Lent eventually became our Mothers' Day. Sadly, by the
time Anna Jarvis died, the idea of celebrating women's service to
humanity had become a day on which to turn a profit. Anna named
it Hallmark Sunday. The purpose was completely missed.

Hiding Moses

Today's story from Exodus helps us to refocus on that purpose.

This is a story of three women: Moses' mother, his sister and
Pharoah's daughter. Their brave decisions lead to the salvation of
the Hebrews from slavery in Egypt. Imagine for a moment, or if you
have experienced it, take yourself back. At the time our story takes
place, Moses is three months old. His family have kept him hidden
until this point. They were an oppressed people. Oppressed peoples
live in homes that are squashed close together. If they were slaves,

they would have lived in homes separated from their neighbours by little more than a reed wall. This was like hiding a baby for three months behind a garden fence!

Imagine how much work his mother had to put in to keep him quiet. Ready to feed him every time he cried, to change him every time he stank. This was commitment. But at three months his cries were getting louder and more insistent. Hiding him was next to impossible.

Hatching a plan

Moses' mother and sister hatch a plan. They've heard good things about Pharoah's daughter, perhaps. Maybe she's already done secret acts of kindness for her father's slaves. They hide Moses in a place where the princess will find him. She sees the child and makes a decision. Pharoah's daughter is not fooled. She knows this is a Hebrew baby boy, one that her father had ordered should be killed. And yet she takes him into her home. Moses' sister steps out and offers to find the child a nurse – his own mother. Now, instead of hiding the child as he goes through toddler tantrums, Moses' mother is paid to look after him.

'If it weren't for Hermione'

I don't know whether you've seen the t-shirt slogan that says, 'If it weren't for Hermione, Harry would have died in book one'. For those who don't know, Harry is Harry Potter, the wizard hero of several novels by J. K. Rowling. In book one, Hermione saves him by solving a puzzle. He may be the hero but his existence depended on someone else. It's the same in our Exodus story. Moses becomes a great hero – but if it weren't for three women, he would have died in chapter 2. Whatever else we remember this Mothers' Day, let's remember the hidden heroes, the women on whose shoulders we all stand.

The women in our story are courageous and bold. They refuse to do as they are told and choose to do what is right. There are many such women down through history, largely ignored and unknown. Even if they were not biological mothers, like Pharoah's daughter they play a part in raising children and seeing justice is done.

So, Mothers' Day is important. Not because of the car, flower or chocolate industries, but because it reminds us that women have played and still play a vital, but largely unseen, role in the life of our communities and our wider world.

Liz Shercliff

Hymn suggestions

We gladly celebrate and praise; For Mary, mother of our Lord; God of Eve and God of Mary; Mothering God, you gave me birth.

Fifth Sunday of Lent (Passiontide) 26 March
Principal Service **Lazarus and Passiontide**
Ezek. 37.1–14; Ps. 130; Rom. 8.6–11; **John 11.1–45**

Today, on the Fifth Sunday of Lent, we experience a gear change: we cross the threshold into Passiontide. Jesus has set his face towards Jerusalem, and he now takes us with him into new territory, as the cross looms nearer. So why, if we are moving towards the cross, do we read today about the raising of Lazarus? Surely, the story of Lazarus, with Jesus' great saying at its heart, 'I am the resurrection and the life', would fit better in Eastertide. But this is no mistake: the lectionary choice is spot on for the beginning of Passiontide.

Cross and resurrection

We need to remind ourselves that the first to hear the Fourth Gospel would have known the end of the story: that Jesus' death was followed by his resurrection. For the writer of the Gospel, death and resurrection are all of a piece. The crucifixion is Jesus' glorification as he is 'lifted up' and 'draws all people to himself', and the resurrection is about his vindication. The cross isn't merely a prelude to resurrection, nor is the resurrection a postlude to the cross; the two belong together.

At one of my churches at this time of year (when the sun shines!) the shadow of a memorial cross falls on the wall next to the church door, creating a view of an open door with the outline of a cross next to it. This is a powerful reminder that in Passiontide – as we focus on the whole of God's saving work in Jesus – we see the empty tomb through the shadow of the cross. The cross and the resurrection belong together.

Resurrection is not about a happy ending that sweeps away the pain and anguish that have gone before. Resurrection takes the past and transforms it so that a transformed past can become part of an eternal future. We see this most clearly in Jesus himself. After his resurrection, Jesus' hands and side continue to bear the marks of the nails and spear. These marks were there in Jesus' *resurrection* body. The resurrection didn't obliterate the suffering of the cross but took that suffering into a transformed future.

The God who weeps

For Lazarus to be raised, he had first to die. It's likely that Lazarus wasn't old; his death would have been traumatic for his family and friends. When eventually Jesus came in response to Martha and Mary's pleadings, he didn't arrive with all guns blazing and, victorious, pull a risen Lazarus out of the tomb. Jesus, the incarnate Son of God, wept with his friends. At the heart of the Christian gospel is a God who weeps, a God who suffers with us and alongside us. At the heart of the gospel of resurrection lies the brokenness of the cross.

The God who suffers

There was once a time when theologians maintained the impassivity of God – that God in Jesus had suffered once and for all on the cross, but now death was defeated. God remained compassionate but incapable of being changed or affected by the suffering of the creation. No more so. Christian theology, as the Holy Spirit leads us into all truth, has had to adapt as it has struggled to make sense of the harsh reality of a suffering world. The experience of two world wars fuelled a revolution in Christian thinking. The trenches of the first war and the Holocaust in the second meant that what we had been taught to believe about God would no longer pass muster. 'Where was God in the midst of such suffering?' The American-Jewish writer Elie Wiesel was asked this question as he watched the harrowing execution of a child in a Nazi concentration camp. He answered that God was himself hanging on the gallows.

It was not that 'God had once been there, in Jesus' suffering on the cross' but that God was present in that moment – in the midst of that child's suffering. God continues to suffer with us and for us. Jesus did not simply say to Martha and Mary, 'It's OK, I am the resurrection and the life' – Jesus wept as he shared their pain. The resurrection makes sense only when it is seen with the shadow of the cross in front of it – the suffering and the glory belong together as God's saving work.

Isaiah wrote of the suffering servant – words immortalized in Handel's *Messiah* – 'Surely, he hath borne our griefs and carried our sorrows.' And not only that he has borne them, but bears them *now*, and will *continue* to bear them in the future – until such time as God's saving work is complete. The raising of Lazarus speaks loud and clear: that God, in Jesus – the resurrection and the life – suffers with us and weeps with us, as well as offering everlasting life in all its fullness.

Peter Moger

Hymn suggestions

In the cross of Christ, I glory; Morning glory, starlit sky; Praise to the holiest in the height; We sing the praise of him who died.

Fifth Sunday of Lent (Passiontide)   26 March
Second Service   **Entitlement**
Ps. 30; Lam. 3.19–33; **Matt. 20.17–end**

Images of God

As a priest, you often get asked to do odd things at unexpected times. At least I do. I was on a packed tube once at Hyde Park Corner in London. I was with my father, and we had just been to the Proms at the Royal Albert Hall. The carriage of the tube was jammed packed, to the extent that you wondered if you could get another person into it. I was in my dog collar when the guy next to me said really quite loudly: 'Give me a blessing father,' and so I offered him God's blessing with my father next to me and in earshot of a great crowd of people.

What is your God like? I know that sounds a rather simple question, but I don't think it is. There is the God we can describe and talk about, but then there's the God we really believe in. Often we can discover what the latter is like when we ponder our image of God. In today's Gospel reading we have two sets of people asking very different things of Jesus, and therefore unknowingly of God, and they give us contrasting depictions of their images of God.

Mothers and their sons

I guess most mothers want the best for their children, or at least what they think is the best for them. They want to have pride in them. To be able to boast about them. The mother of the sons of Zebedee (interestingly, we don't know her name) wants a favour from Jesus. She wants them to have the best seats – for ever: to be the top disciples. To share in the glory of heaven. This is beyond first class university degrees and Olympic medals; this is eternal merit. Notice that she kneels before Jesus, she knows he has power; but notice also what he asks: 'What do you want?' I wonder what she really wants? Recognition for her sons? To know that they are of value and ultimate worth? That they are significant?

Healing

Later in the story, we have two blind men (again unnamed by the roadside, and they seem to have a very different attitude from the mother of the sons of Zebedee). Their cry seems not to come from a sense of entitlement (you know my sons and therefore you know me) but from dire need. They call out in desperation: we are given a sense that they know that this is their only chance to engage with this man, and they won't give up, even when asked to do so. It's like those persistent needs within us that keep calling out until they are heard and listened to. Again, Jesus asks them: 'What do you want me to do for you?' He doesn't impose his own projected needs on them, he wants to know what *they* want. He responds to their need with healing.

Suffering

In Passiontide, we are drawn ever deeper into the mystery that is God. A God that can never be adequately described or represented by human beings. A God that Lamentations describes as a God of 'steadfast love' which never ceases, and for Christians is most vividly displayed on the cross. For Jesus' disciples, and maybe for us too, a God who enters into powerless vulnerability, suffering, torture, mockery and death is hard to imagine. All-powerful, mighty gods are so much easier to fantasize about. Yet, in this gospel passage, we are confronted with a God in Jesus who acts so differently from our expectations. He is not doling out the best tickets for the top seats in heaven: far from it. He asks us to go where he goes – to live as servants, and to share in the suffering and pain that being people of love will necessitate. In the blind beggars, we see how he responds to desperate need, and we see echoes of Lamentations: 'The LORD is good to those who wait for him, to the soul that seeks him.'

Worth

At the heart of these passages and of Passiontide, I sense that there is something very important going on about value and worth. Each and every one of us is of equal value to God. There is no entitlement and hierarchy to that, save that all of us are entitled to his love, freely given. Once received, grace flows, and we don't need to find comfort in the best seats at the top table like the sons of Zebedee, but rather we receive the healing that we need like the blind men at the roadside. This is why we as a church are privileged in sharing God's blessing with all, even those packed into a tube train at night, for his love has an abundance and generosity beyond anything that we can imagine, and great is his faithfulness.

Jonathan Lawson

Hymn suggestions

Great is thy faithfulness; There's a wideness in God's mercy; From heaven you came, helpless babe; Jesus is Lord!

Holy Week

Palm Sunday   2 April
Principal Service   **Through Eyes that Have Cried**
Liturgy of the Palms: **Matt. 21.1–11**; Ps. 118.1–2, 19–end
[*or* 118.19–24]; *Liturgy of the Passion*: Isa. 50.4–9a;
Ps. 31.9–16 [*or* 31.9–18]; Phil. 2.5–11; Matt. 26.14—end of 27
[*or* Matt. 27.11–54]

Jerusalem without

All they know of life on the other side of the walls are bits of stories gleaned from travellers passing by. They gather tales of fortunes made and fortunes lost by intrepid merchants from near and far. They treasure rumours of Temple intrigues from priests and Levites on their commute in and out of the city. Now, all they have is the echo of their dreams dashed against the forbidding walls of the city of peace, life stories forged in the crucible of difference.

Locked out of the city, they wait. They watch. They hope. They hold on to the compelling vision of the future that gives them a place and a voice at the table. Like Isaiah's restless watchmen posted on the walls of Jerusalem, awaiting her restoration, they rehearse their faith in God's infallible promise.

Before Oscar Romero, they had learnt that 'there are many things that can only be seen through eyes that have cried'. So, they keep watch, certain that their eyes, accustomed to tears, will recognize the sign when it appears.

Like Samuel and Anna in the Temple, their eyes do not betray them when they are first laid on him. Immediately they know. Not the kind of knowledge that relies on demonstrable facts, but the gut-stirring kind of knowledge forged in the cauldron of faith. It is him!

Those that life had stripped of everything, strip out of their own cloaks and, spontaneously, lay them on the ground as a sign of

95

honour and allegiance to the Son of David. Immediately, a song of praise arises from their hearts. It is an ancient song that, in the same breath, names the anguish of oppression and exclusion, and the hope of salvation. Like Dostoevsky, their 'hosanna is born of a furnace of doubt'.

Jerusalem within

As Jesus enters Jerusalem, riding upon a donkey, a persistent rumour suggests that at another end of the city, through a less conspicuous gate, a wholly different kind of procession is taking place. Pontius Pilate, the Roman Governor, riding upon a warhorse and accompanied by mighty Roman soldiers, is making his own entry into Jerusalem ahead of the Passover.

Jesus, the prince of peace, enters a city under occupation, a troubled place, a place of struggle accustomed to conflict and confrontation. How will Jerusalem, the city that has a history of killing prophets, receive him? How will this provincial prophet from Nazareth fare in the metropolis as he encounters the insiders, the local authorities and the might of Rome?

The contrast is obvious between Jesus' reception from those outside Jerusalem and those inside the walls. His entry into the city, accompanied by an atypical procession, fervent in its expression of faith, seems dissonant with the immediate preoccupations of city dwellers.

The commotion that ensues is a reminder of a similar commotion some 30 years earlier as men of science from afar had entered Jerusalem seeking the new king of the Jews to pay homage, only to find a city, her leaders and men of faith and science unready and unprepared.

As Jesus enters Jerusalem, he encounters a people captive behind the walls they had erected. Their lives had become so fluent in the art of negotiating with power that they had lost the ability to engage with the pain of exclusion and marginalization. Their stories had been surrendered to forces of assimilation and conformism to such an extent that they had settled for survival against flourishing, totally desensitized to hope.

Next year in Jerusalem?

As followers of the donkey-riding king, we are called to become a fellowship of the poor, the weak, the vulnerable through whose witness the powerful and glorious divine kingdom is rendered evident to the rest of creation. We are God's messianic people, a foretaste of a new humanity, one that is defined by God's own rejection of power, resisting bombastic self-expression, but revelling in simplicity.

That is the kind of God we encounter in the poem of creation, calling humanity into partnership, not because she is unable to look after her creation but because her essence is community, partnership. We encounter her pleading with Pharaoh to let her people go, not because she is unable to engineer the longed-for liberation but because she desires to orient human agency towards justice and righteousness. Again, we encounter her negotiating with a teenage couple about an impossible proposal that will for ever alter their destinies and that of the whole of creation. Such a God invites us to dismantle the walls around our lives, around our hearts. She invites us to reacquaint ourselves with life beyond the walls. It is the kind of life that will never be a stranger to cries.

Lusa Nsenga Ngoy

Hymn suggestions

All glory, laud and honour; Your majesty; Hosanna in the highest; Faithful through the ages (Promises).

Palm Sunday 2 April
Second Service **A Tale of Two Vineyards**
Ps. 80; Isa. 5.1–7; **Matt. 21.33–end**

Two vineyards

We have, in our readings, a tale of two vineyards. The first vineyard is at the heart of a love song. The vineyard is well situated, the land well prepared, the plot made ready to process the crops. And yet rather than the fine grapes that such a vineyard should yield, it yields wild grapes. And, the prophet tells us, the vineyard owner is the Lord, the vineyard is the house of Israel, in which is planted the people of Judah; the harvest God expects is justice, and the harvest it produces is bloodshed.

The second vineyard is at the heart of a parable told by Jesus, and it seems that he has this passage from Isaiah in mind. But the tale goes off in a different direction. In Jesus' parable, the owner goes away and leaves tenants in charge of the vineyard. The owner sends slaves to collect the harvest, but the tenants want to keep the harvest for themselves, so assault and murder first one, then a second party of slaves, and finally the owner's own son.

Who are the tenants?

This parable is sometimes interpreted, using Isaiah's vineyard analogy, to tell us that the Jewish people are the tenants, refusing to acknowledge God's prophets – the slaves – or Jesus – the owner's son – but abusing and killing them. This kind of interpretation has been used to justify anti-Semitism with awful consequences over many centuries. But you can't transpose Isaiah's interpretation on to Jesus' parable *quite* like that.

In Isaiah's parable, there are no tenants or slaves. So, if we hold on to Isaiah's interpretation, we can still have God as the owner of the vineyard. We can still have the vineyard as the house of Israel, and the vines as the people of Judah. Who, then, are the tenants? Those who are entrusted with the tending of the vines; the nurturing of God's people. We have the answer in our Gospel reading – 'When the chief priests and the Pharisees heard his parables, they realized that he was speaking about them.'

Putting themselves in the place of God

So, what is going on? The problems with the two vineyards are different. What emerges in the vineyard of Jesus' story isn't that the vineyard isn't productive, it's that the tenants act as if they own it. They begrudge the owner the produce; they want the harvest and the inheritance for themselves. The Jewish leaders are putting themselves in the place of God, and putting their interests above God's. They have disregarded their duty as caretakers of God's people – rather than working for the owner of the vineyard, they have looked out for themselves. When God has sent messengers – the prophets, and God's own son – the religious leaders have silenced them.

It's not the Jewish people who kill the son, but their leaders, whose political machinations compel them to silence Jesus, the one who comes from God to tell them that Israel is God's, not theirs. As we enter Holy Week, we are confronted with the complex web of desires and motives that drive those who hold power in Jerusalem.

This is encapsulated in the words of Caiaphas, the high priest, in John 11: 'It is better for you to have one man die for the people than to have the whole nation destroyed.'

Defending or building?

The stewards of the vineyard are trying to defend it. They do not want to let anyone in or let any of the harvest out. They are so protective of it that they refuse to acknowledge that anything might change. They are trying to keep a kind of stasis, wanting to maintain their own precarious positions of power and influence.

What they are not doing is building the kingdom. Jesus follows this agricultural parable with a building metaphor, but he returns to that image of fruits. What the owner wants is for the vineyard to grow – not to be defended but to be expanded. And with an abundant harvest, there is no need to defend or fight over what grows. Those stewards of the vineyard could be builders, but they have rejected the stone. But those who build rather than defend – who incorporate Jesus into what they do, rather than throw him out and try to silence him – those who build, produce fruits. They grow the kingdom of God, which is big enough for everyone.

How does the story end?

In this version of this parable, rather than telling his listeners how the story ends, Jesus invites them to complete the story. He asks them what the owner would do to the tenants, and they answer: 'He will put those wretches to a miserable death, and lease the vineyard to other tenants who will give them the produce at harvest time.' That is what *they* would do, those are the rules *they* play by – in their world view, the landowner whose son is murdered by his tenants would put the tenants to death. But as Jesus prepares to go to his death, his response to those who will kill him is not about revenge, but building God's kingdom.

Kat Campion-Spall

Hymn suggestions

My God, I love thee; My song is love unknown; Morning glory, starlit sky; Ride on, ride on in majesty.

First Three Days of Holy Week   3–5 April
Wasteful Worship?
(These are the readings for Monday in Holy Week, but the sermon may be used on any day.)
Isa. 42.1–9; Ps. 36.5–11; Heb. 9.11–15; **John 12.1–11**

There is no agreed order of events in Jesus' final days, but this meal in Bethany with his friends was probably one of them.

Imagine it. The city, four miles away, is pervaded by chaos, confusion, acrimony, hostility and mistrust. The people seek a Messiah who will come to reign. The leaders are intent on keeping hold of power. The high priest has already issued a warrant for Jesus' arrest. Caiaphas has already uttered those well-known words, 'It is better for one man to die for the people.' The world is hostile to Jesus.

Yet in the middle of it, he, the hunted man, sits down to dinner with his friends. In the midst of a political storm, Jesus remains calm.

Look who's there

Lazarus is there, the friend Jesus had raised from the tomb. I wonder whether he looks around the room, thankful to be enjoying another meal with his friends; thankful simply to be alive. I can't help wondering about the conversation between Jesus and Lazarus, the man preparing for death and the one who had recently been through it.

Martha and Mary are there too. Martha who had gone out to meet Jesus on the road when he finally arrived to grieve for Lazarus. Now she must be buoyed by her realization in that meeting that Jesus is 'the Messiah, the Son of God, the one who is to come'. Mary didn't go out to meet Jesus when he came. Too upset with him for arriving late, perhaps. But now she knew, because Jesus had sent for her, that, in Jesus, God reaches out over and over.

To Mary, Jesus is worth everything she has and everything she is. She plans an extravagant act of worship. Bringing an expensive pot containing expensive ointment, she pours it all over Jesus' feet. This is planned worship, a testament to the fact that things have changed. Mary probably gives all that she has.

'What a waste!' says Judas, the treasurer.

Wasteful worship?

'That ointment could have been sold to help the poor. What a waste.'

Judas was correct. Had the ointment been sold, in today's terms, it might have raised the equivalent of the current Jobseeker's Allowance for two.

Was Mary's worship wasteful?

Mary's actions were a declaration of love for Jesus. But perhaps there is more here. Jesus, and his friends, knew that he was going to die. The authorities were out to get him. This could be their last meal. Mary's actions were not simply about her expressing her love. They show care for Jesus, understanding of his needs.

Mary could have simply handed over her expensive gift for Jesus to do with as he wished. But she doesn't. She anoints him. In Jesus, there must have been nervous anticipation of what faced him. He must have felt the stress of being a hunted man. What better thing than to sit down with friends, for the perfume of nard to fill the air, and to have aching muscles massaged?

True worship

Was it wasteful?

No more wasteful than giving up careers, or time, or money to advance the kingdom of God in some way. No more wasteful than giving up time to train as a lay minister, or sing in the choir, or any of the other practical things that are part of worship to God.

And what are we to make of Judas in the end? The root problem with Judas isn't greed, or dishonesty, or suspicion, not even the betrayal for which he is so well known.

It is his lack of worship. His comment reduces Jesus' mission to simply doing good. Mary's perfume could indeed have been sold to help the poor. But our Christian calling to see that the Church changes the world, to challenge injustice and show compassion, begins not with the imperative to be good but with the inescapable fact that we are made to worship.

When we start there, then we do things differently. When we recognize Jesus among us, we recognize others as our brothers and sisters. And then we move away from Judas' generalization of helping the poor, to recognizing who needs help and how. We move away from the deadness of giving money to salve our consciences, and into a place where giving and doing are part of our worship.

The heart of the matter

I began by reflecting on the people gathered around the table with Jesus. We have met the grateful, the worshipful, the serving, the cynical. We have been reassured that there is room for all at the table of the Lord. Come, asking which you are: grateful, worshipful, serving, cynical.

Whichever you are, Jesus welcomes you to the table.

Whichever you are, come.

Liz Shercliff

Hymn suggestions

A prophet woman broke a jar; When I needed a neighbour; My God, how wonderful thou art; Just as I am.

Maundy Thursday   6 April
Loving to the End

Ex. 12.1–4 [5–10] 11–14; Ps. 116.1, 10–end [or 116.9–end];
1 Cor. 11.23–26; **John 13.1–17, 31b–35**

Faithful to the end

In October 1940 the authorities in Warsaw announced the establishment of a Jewish Ghetto. Subsequently, the city's Jewish residents, one-third of its people, were forced into a space that took up just 2.4 per cent of the city's surface area. To them were added refugees who had been transported to Warsaw, taking the Ghetto population up to around 450,000 people.

Surrounded by walls and under strict guard, they were cut off from the outside world. The conditions were unbearable. On average, six or seven people lived in one room and the daily rations represented just one-tenth of the minimum required daily calorie intake. Epidemics were hard to prevent. More than 80,000 Jewish people died there. Yet despite these appalling conditions, intellectual, cultural, creative and religious life persisted. In July 1942 the deportations to the Treblinka death camp began. That summer, 300,000 Jews were sent to 'the east', code for the death chambers at Treblinka.

Many left behind began to plot what we know as the Warsaw Ghetto uprising. One courageous revolt took place in January 1943. Another significant moment came towards the end of April. Cruelly the Nazis had chosen the week leading up to Passover for the final destruction of the Ghetto. As their soldiers moved in, the Jewish resistance fighters rose up. This resistance took many forms. Yad Vashem, the Holocaust History Museum, gathered descriptions, including one of Rabbi Maisel on that first night of the Seder. To a terrifying backdrop of explosions and gunfire, his family assembled together with glasses of wine as Rabbi Maisel read the Haggadah and recounted the age-old story of deliverance.

The thought of Rabbi Maisel and his family celebrating Passover amid the danger and devastation all around them is profoundly arresting. It is also humbling and convicting, for they suffered at the hands of Gentiles. In an echo of the events of the original Passover, these courageous people were faithful, to God and to one another – to the end.

As we hold in mind Rabbi Maisel and his family our thoughts might also go to another Jewish rabbi and his companions coming together for a meal in Passover week, sharing cups of wine, singing hymns, praying to the God of Moses even as turmoil gathered around them.

Loving them, and us, to the end

The clock had been ticking since the previous Sunday with Jesus' highly visible entry into Jerusalem. The clock had started ticking long before, of course, but the arrival of Jesus into the city and the enthusiasm of the crowd had caught attention. The military rulers were on edge. Even one of his own had been to the authorities offering to betray Jesus.

Amid this backdrop of impending danger, what did he choose to do? To flee, to fight? John's Gospel tells us that Jesus, 'Having loved his own ... loved them to the end'. He got up, knelt before them and, one by one, he washed their feet. An amazing glimpse into the heart of God.

Betrayal, arrest, false accusation, mockery, beating, all await Jesus that very night. At that moment he would have every right to be self-absorbed, frightened, angry or bitter, but this was not what preoccupied him. What was on his mind was ... love.

Jesus understands the time, that his hour has come, and it brings him to his knees, in love. The God who descended to take on our flesh descends once more and kneels before humanity.

One by one God lifts and bathes dirty feet – even the feet of the one who would soon betray.

This mutual act involves proximity, availability, vulnerability and a choice whether or not to accept and to be accepted.

It is both comforting and challenging, unnerving this loving and being loved to the end. For God in descending, in loving them to the end, overturns our tendency to make distinctions between ourselves and those we deem to be 'other', and especially the distinctions we make between 'us' and those we deem to be 'inferior'. Between those who wield power and the apparently powerless.

May we who seek the Saviour this Passiontide be granted the grace to reject the temptation to reinstate the distinctions and the separations that he, in kneeling before us, has swept away.

Tricia Hillas

Hymn suggestions

From heaven you came; I will offer up my life; Ubi caritas (Taizé); A new commandment.

Good Friday   7 April
Principal Service   **Watching Death**
Isa. 52.13—end of 53; Ps. 22 [*or* 22.1–11, *or* 22.1–21];
Heb. 10.16–25, *or* Heb. 4.14–16; 5.7–9; **John 18.1—end of 19**

The human condition

So, we fix our eyes on a man dying on a cross. Jesus the one in whom we put all our hopes and trust, the one whom we thought would save us. This man is dying.

In his book *Every Third Thought*, Robert McCrum talks of how life and death are woven together, in a mixture of fear that is familiar. Death is our human condition, and Jesus is fully human, sharing a human death, with a body that will fail, breath that will cease, a heart that will stop. And we watch.

Watching death is tough. Many of us will have wept at death in all its different guises. We gasp at a sudden death in a book or film and we weep at the episode of *Call the Midwife* when Barbara slips away peacefully with people at her side and the words of Psalm 23.

It's how we all want to die – peacefully, at home, surrounded by loved ones. But a vigil with the dying is not always like this. Caring for someone in pain is tough, very tough. There is the endless paraphernalia of pain relief, the invasive moments of the body, the need to see and do things you never wished to see or to do, and then there are the long nights, when the pain breaks through and the person whispers, 'I thirst'. It seems to me no coincidence that we talk of labouring for breath, the work of dying, just as we laboured for birth. Yet, even in those relentless moments, far away from the world of TV and radio, there is something more at work.

Labouring for breath

In the best-selling book *When Breath Becomes Air*, Paul Kalinithis' wife describes the end of his life and how the family kept vigil by his bedside. He took fewer and fewer breaths, his eyelids were closed, and his face untroubled. It felt as though the room was 'saturated with love'.

And Jesus – is his death saturated with love?

He is alone. With friends and family at a distance, or simply hiding far away. The rejection of all that Jesus proclaimed and all that he lived out is final. There are no more miracles, no more crowds to hang on his every word, nor even any more enemies to argue with him, only those who feel victorious left to laugh. So where is love now for this man who has spoken love to so many? This is where we watch for meaning and try to find purpose and vision, join dots and make connections, and, as the great football manager Alex Ferguson would say, try to see beyond the situation into the future.

Finding meaning

In John's Gospel, the whole story has been heading towards this moment – a moment of love and victory. On the cross, we see a man who speaks love, and knows love, and has held on to the hope of God to the very end. 'It is finished,' he says, proclaiming the promise of God whose whole purpose has been to love us, draw us home and bring us healing and salvation.

As we watch Jesus on the cross, as we look at his broken body, we see the love of God and we see every step of the journey God's people – us – have made in response to that love.

God creates us and God loves us, but we destroy and we hate. God calls us back to himself, again and again, offering grace and forgiveness, but we isolate ourselves. God gives us visions and dreams, plans and purposes, but we reject his ideas, preferring our own solutions.

God holds out hope and healing for all, but we prefer to struggle on, inflicting more pain through our actions, our exclusions and our anger. But John's Jesus is the Christ on the cross who has triumphed over death, and who will always be drawing us back to life.

The hope of light

In Liverpool Cathedral there is a contemporary painting of the crucifixion by Craigie Aitchison. A huge cross dominates a dark sky. The body of Jesus is still on the cross, but there is light in the picture, which means the stars shine in the blackness, a rainbow arches above the cross, the shadows are pushing backwards and the things we love – in this painting, the artist's dog – are caught in that light. It is not a picture of what happened, but a picture of meaning.

On Good Friday we pause, as silence falls, to hold before Jesus all our disappointments, failures and sin. And we find meaning as we look at the light of his love, there on the cross, for us all.

Sandra Millar

Hymn suggestions

When I survey; My song is love unknown; Man of sorrows (Hillsong); Were you there when they crucified my Lord?

Easter

Easter Vigil 8–9 April
On Not Needing a Hero

(*A minimum of three Old Testament readings should be chosen. The reading from Ex. 14 should always be used.*)
Gen. 1.1—2.4a *and* Ps. 136.1–9, 23–end; Gen. 7.1–5, 11–18; 8.6–18; 9.8–13 *and* Ps. 46; Gen. 22.1–18 *and* Ps. 16; Ex. 14.10–end; 15.20–21 *and Canticle*: Ex. 15.1b–13, 17–18; Isa. 55.1–11 *and Canticle*: Isa. 12.2–end; Bar. 3.9–15, 32—4.4 *and* Ps. 19, *or* Prov. 8.1–8, 19–21; 9.4b–6 *and* Ps. 19; Ezek. 36.24–28 *and* Ps. 42, 43; Ezek. 37.1–14 *and* Ps. 143; Zeph. 3.14–end *and* Ps. 98; Rom. 6.3–11 *and* Ps. 114; **Matt. 28.1–10**

The mystery

Several years ago, I read all the Agatha Christie 'Miss Marple' novels in order. Miss Jane Marple is an elderly woman from a tiny village who watches everything, has an unusually sharp mind, and deploys both to solve murders. Towards the end of many of the stories, Miss Marple gathers all the characters together in a room to explain her thinking and dramatically expose the murderer who is then dragged away by the police. Usually, this means that the other characters can suddenly find a new lease of life and live happily ever after.

I have often wondered if humanity is inclined towards approaching the story of the death and resurrection of Christ as though it were a crime novel or film. The Church, the gatekeeper of the event, more than at any other time in the year, focuses on a plot and a story. We forensically pick over the details of who did what and when. If you have been going to church for a few years you build up layers of potential meaning and meanings, glimpses of possible implications. And yes, there is a cruel death. Perhaps we build ourselves up to need Easter Sunday to be the moment when, gathered in community, we hear someone explain it all.

The hero

One of the things that traditionally has been used to understand the resurrection of Christ has been the human experience of fighting and warfare. So, we talk of Christ defeating, conquering and triumphing over sin and death by the cross and resurrection. And theologians have built up an understanding that when Christ descended into hell he went there to triumph over it and so release all those imprisoned. We call it 'the harrowing of hell', from the old English word, to harrow or to despoil. The resurrection of Jesus then becomes the final moments of his rise from hell and his bursting from the tomb as the all-conquering hero who has even defeated death itself.

The reset from the wings

Yet nowhere in the Bible do you find stories of Jesus after the resurrection acting like a triumphant hero. In Matthew's account of the after-effects of the resurrection there are earthquakes and powerful angels and experienced guards who are so frightened they run away. Jesus isn't in those things. He isn't even in the still small voice that tells the women who have been quietly watching and waiting by the tomb, 'Don't you be afraid.' That part is played by an angel. Jesus appears in stories where all the crowds are gone. The public stage has gone. These are stories of Jesus talking to individuals. Stories of Jesus in private rooms, on a deserted beach and on a road. This is not the story of a warrior hero who has conquered death, hell and sin. These are stories of love – unconditional, uncontrollable, unassuming love. Love which led Christ to die in solidarity with all the marginalized, unfairly treated, victims in history. Love which led Christ to somehow – let's be honest, we know not how – spend time after his death with his friends, comforting them and giving them a sense of hope and of purpose that would sustain them for years to come.

My life has been defined by a violent murder, committed some years ago one Easter Day, just as the sun was rising. I cannot escape that, any more than anyone else who has experienced a violent trauma can. There have been times when I have wished that death had never happened, times when I longed for a hero to rescue me from the multiple bereavements involved. But gradually, over the years, the distressing evil of that event has on the whole slipped into the background and what has taken centre stage is the presence of the unconditional, unassuming and uncontrollable love of God in how I have tried to understand it and live life to the full after it, after death. It is there, just there, and any words beyond that are too thin. Somewhere in there is the true meaning of redemption.

This for me is the story of the resurrection – the revelation of the faithful love of God for the world. Love which takes us all, both individually and corporately, a lifetime on earth and then some more after death to explore and find the multiple meanings of. Love which is simply present, in the face of the most extreme evil, in the company of the most distressed, at the moments when anything beyond death and complete ruin seems impossible. And, so, history is reset, not by a process of tidying up and making sense but by an event that is beyond all our frameworks of understanding, seeing, knowing and feeling. History, corporate and personal, is reset by the resurrection to give us the possibility of being – to borrow a phrase from a prophet – the people who survive the sword and find grace in the wilderness.

Esther Elliott

Hymn suggestions

We sing a love that sets all people free; We cannot measure how you heal; Now is eternal life; Within our darkest night (Taizé).

Easter Day   9 April
Principal Service   **Beyond First Impressions**
Acts 10.34–43, *or* Jer. 31.1–6; Ps. 118.1–2, 14–24 [*or* 118.14–24]; Col. 3.1–4, *or* Acts 10.34–43; **John 20.1–18**, *or* Matt. 28.1–10

A few years ago, a UK television advert for a newspaper unfolded something like this: as a car pulls up, we see a skinhead running towards us down the street. It looks like the skinhead is running away, perhaps from the scene of a crime. Then the camera angle changes and we see that the skinhead is running towards a very respectably dressed man holding a briefcase. The skinhead grabs the man and immediately we think he's about to steal the briefcase. Finally, the camera pans out and we see the whole scene: the skinhead has in fact run towards the man to grab hold of him, push him out of the way of falling masonry, and thereby save him. As the ad finishes, a voice-over says that it is only when you get the full picture that you can fully understand what's going on.

The advert reminds us that first impressions are really powerful. Indeed, there are situations where the capacity to make snap judgements or process information quickly is the difference between life and death. This is the classic 'fight-or-flight' reflex which kicks in in moments of extreme danger. However, first impressions can also lead us into error and foolishness.

At first glance

When we come to reflect on the joy and wonder of Easter Day, I often think about the power of first impressions and the importance of waiting to get the full picture. For the account of the resurrection in St John's Gospel should not only fill us with a simple joy which invites us to shout, 'He is risen, he is risen indeed!'; it also challenges us to live our lives with new insight and understanding of reality. In its mystery, Easter Day takes us into God's fuller picture.

In the realm of first impressions, surely Mary Magdalene's reaction is a reasonable one: she comes to Jesus' tomb and finds the stone rolled away. She runs off to give Peter and John the headline interpretation of what she's seen: the tomb is empty and – horror! – she does not know where the grave-disturbers (robbers? soldiers? Temple guards?) have taken Jesus. Her response is surely sound, for bodies were no more raised from the dead in Mary's time than in ours.

Reacting to the headlines

Upon hearing Mary's report, Peter and John rush back to verify what she has witnessed. Perhaps they don't quite believe her because she is a mere woman; perhaps they would want to check out the scene with their own eyes no matter who had reported the news of the disappearance of Jesus' body. These are all people suffering under the effects of shock: their leader and dearest friend, their teacher, has been cruelly murdered just days before. It is hardly surprising that they react as they do. To discover that on top of the trauma of Jesus' execution his body has been stolen would only add insult to injury.

Peter, ever the bold, enters the tomb and finds irrefutable evidence that Jesus' body is gone. It is as if, for John and Peter, that's that. They've witnessed all they need to know the truth: Jesus' body has been taken.

Through grief or arrogance or shock they cannot perceive a deeper truth: Jesus is risen. And so, without grasping the wider picture, they leave.

Waiting on God

Mary does not leave. She who came to the tomb first, while it was still dark, cannot bring herself to leave just yet. She stands and weeps. She tarries and abides and she looks into the tomb again. There is no hurry now. She is beyond the first reactions of her 'head' or instinct. The adrenaline of fight or flight has departed. Rather, she encounters the situation with her tearful heart and, in doing so, she encounters angels. More than that – though at first, she cannot comprehend it – she encounters Jesus.

Again, her first impression is that Jesus is the gardener: 'Sir, if you have carried him away, tell me where you have hid him, and I will take him away.' It is when Jesus calls her by name that she recognizes him for who he is.

I cannot see how any of us can ever get a full grasp on the wonder and mystery of Easter Day. Resurrection blows our minds. Nonetheless, it is in waiting on God to show himself more clearly to us that we enter his fuller reality. To take the risk of waiting or even of offering our grief and our longing as Mary Magdalene does is a risk worth taking. Certainly, to wait on God to show himself, rather than be sure of what is going on based on first impressions, is the wiser path. Along that path we may know the joy of the truth: 'Jesus is risen. He is risen, indeed!'

Rachel Mann

Hymn suggestions

Led like a lamb; Thine be the glory; Christ the Lord is risen today; The greatest day in history (Hillsong)

Easter Day   9 April
Second Service   **Finding and Being Found, Seeking to Hold and Being Held**
Morning Ps. 114, 117; Evening Ps. 105, *or* 66.1–11;
S. of Sol. 3.2–5; 8.6–7; John 20.11–18 *if not used at the Principal Service, or* Rev. 1.12–18

Footsteps in the quiet of dawn

After a fitful sleepless night, parted from the one for whom her soul longed, I can picture the lover in the Song of Solomon rising ahead of the dawn. Like the women who also got up early on the first Easter Day, her footsteps sound in the deserted streets as the light grows. Those women had seen Jesus die, his body taken from the cross, and from them, laid to rest in the enclosing darkness of the earth. The lover had sought her beloved but could not find him; she called for him but received no answer. The women made their way through the city streets of Jerusalem towards the tomb. The lover makes her way in the streets and squares hunting high and low. Loss and separation echo with each footstep.

But as the Spirit had once hovered over the void and, as at the divine Word, the chaos had fled before the light of creation, so now the divine Word speaks again, even into the deepest most wretched separation of death.

Ecstatic at the reunion with her beloved, the lover of the Song of Solomon takes hold of him and refuses to relinquish him. We may recall that the impulse of Mary Magdalene is also to reach for Jesus. He directs her, though, to take hold of life in him in a different way. The old and the new are being united. Things are not what they were, and what was is not how things will be.

The changes of life and death

Change, whether the death of someone we have loved dearly, the ending of a relationship or a phase of our work career, can profoundly disturb our sense of there being a straightforward road mapped out ahead. Afterwards, life can find a new, even joyous, equilibrium, but it is always different. Even new and welcome life can be disarming. The most well organized of parents-to-be can be surprised by the changes accompanying a new arrival. From waking and listening for the steady sound of breathing, to the number of bags making even the simplest outing an epic undertaking; nothing will ever be the same.

At a human level, birth and death touch the very core of us and can throw us into powerful, joyful, sorrowful disarray. They are messy, capable of interrupting well-made plans and of disrupting our sense of control.

The birth, life and death of Jesus interrupted the flow of human being; God with us, interrupting our ways of being towards self, others and God, and in the process confounding our treatment of our enemies and our understanding of power, meaning and every aspect of life.

The disarming disarray of resurrection

Why then should his resurrection cause any less disarray? Not simply a satisfying resolution, a happy ending to a difficult, emotional week, but a cosmic turning of the tables. Not neat, not tidy, but the death of something and the birth of something new which was messy, powerful and creative.

Ancient icons and the paintings of English artist Stanley Spencer depict well this newness, with their untidy resurrection morning depictions of people being pushed and pulled and scrambling out of tombs, be they Near Eastern or those of Cookham churchyard.

When *we* talk of, say, resurrecting an idea or a project, what we often mean is recapturing what *was* rather than what could be. But the God of resurrection takes the past and makes of it a new creation – life born from love, which pitted against death emerges victorious. Love which neither many waters can quench nor floods drown.

Little wonder that, so I'm told, some Christians in Tanzania dance from the close of the Vigil on Holy Saturday up to dawn on Easter Day. Tiny humanity joining in with the foot-stomping joy of creation.

This day we are invited to share in the disarming disarray of resurrection; recognizing that resurrection in our lives, as well as in the world, is likely to be wild and messy, an overturning of the old order.

Come Tuesday, we *could* assume that it's business as usual, only with our waistlines a little stouter from chocolate indulgence. We *could* try clinging to the old deception of being in control, of having everything planned, being people of our own making, carrying on digging our own graves. Or we can join the dancing band of those who in searching have been found and who in desiring to take hold of God find themselves held, in love. May our footsteps lead us to the empty tomb and to the joy of being found and held in Christ.

Tricia Hillas

Hymn suggestions

Low in the grave he lay; Now the green blade riseth; He is risen; Blessed assurance (Cornerstone).

Second Sunday of Easter 16 April
Principal Service **My Lord and My God**
Ex. 14.10–end; 15.20–21 (*if used, the reading from Acts must be used as the second reading*), or Acts 2.14a, 22–32; Ps. 16; 1 Peter 1.3–9; **John 20.19–end**

A week on from Easter Sunday – but in the Gospel, it's still the same day for the disciples. It's evening and they're huddled together behind locked doors, too frightened to venture out. Too frightened, despite the news from Mary that she has seen the Lord.

The doors are shut. No one can enter. But the risen Christ is suddenly there. And what a gracious entrance. Jesus doesn't say, 'Where were you?', 'Why did you betray me?', 'What are you doing here locked away?' He doesn't say any of the things he could say. Instead, he greets them with, 'Peace be with you.' 'Peace' – the Hebrew word is 'shalom' and means 'well-being' in the fullest sense. Jesus is saying to the disciples – may you be whole, may all the blessings of the kingdom of God be yours.

And then he breathes the Holy Spirit on them, filling them with the power of God to go out – to be Christ's body on earth, the ones who are sent by the Father. God's mission – the proclaiming of Jesus as 'Lord and God' in words, actions and lifestyle – is a godly activity. Our commitment to mission as individuals and as a church is a measure of how Christ-like we have become, and an indication of our growth into the stature and maturity of Jesus.

My Lord and my God: for Thomas

Thomas isn't there. We don't know why. Thomas misses the disciples' first encounter with the risen Jesus. Despite their detailed stories of what happens, Thomas is sceptical, stating that he won't believe until he sees for himself and can touch the reality of wounded flesh. You can't blame him. We're not just talking about new life – this is not a fluffy chick and daffodil event. The resurrection is a completely new happening – a new creation – never heard of or possible before. No wonder he doesn't believe it. No wonder people find it hard to believe today. Dead people don't come back to life. But that's the point. This is a God event. God is a God of new creation, of surprises, of breaking the rules. It is in God's very nature to do new things. God can't help Godself. It's who God is.

Thomas doesn't have to wait long – just a week, the first anniversary of Easter Day. The disciples are together again, and this time Thomas is with them. Jesus returns with peace for the group but gives individual attention to Thomas. Jesus answers Thomas' request to see and touch. Thomas' faith leaps. Not only does he see and believe, he worships and proclaims Jesus as 'My Lord and my God'. He is the first person to do this. His desire to see leads to a place of firm and committed faith. We should never underestimate the place of searching and doubting in our journey to Jesus.

My Lord and my God: with scars and wounds

Thomas draws attention to the scars and wounds of Christ. The resurrected Christ is a new creation, a new being – not a ghost, or a resuscitated man like Lazarus, but a being who can pass through locked doors, come and go at will, eat and drink. But he still bears the marks of the cross. Resurrection doesn't come without crucifixion. As Christians, we hold in tension death and life, suffering and joy.

To be a Christian is to suffer in some shape or form, at some time. We are part of the body of Christ, and that body still bears the marks of trauma and violence, even in resurrection. The traumatized body doesn't recover, it's re-made. Peter in his letter writes to a persecuted Christian community. He reminds them of their need to hold two dimensions of faith together – rejoicing and suffering. Writing to the dispersed Christians, he reminds them to keep hope alive – as they suffer – because they are assured of eternal life through the resurrection of Jesus. There are 250 million persecuted Christians in our world today. It is the message of Easter that gives the Church courage to continue, even in adversity, to proclaim Jesus as Lord and God.

My Lord and my God: for us

The risen Christ comes to us today in word and sacrament. He comes not to scold but with peace. He comes to quash our doubting. He comes bearing scars in solidarity with our hurts and struggles: he has been there too. He comes to breathe the Holy Spirit into our lives – to turn us from frightened lukewarm followers into committed disciples, fired up with the good news of God's love. He comes to reveal the new creation made possible through the resurrection, which is promised to us both now and for ever. He comes to surprise us, to make us think again, to breathe new life into places where our lives have become stale or predictable. To remind us that nothing is set in stone.

The message of Easter is exciting and disturbing, surprising, comforting and challenging. May the risen Christ take each of us by surprise again, and call us to declare afresh, 'My Lord and my God'.

Catherine Williams

Hymn suggestions

Love's redeeming work is done; Breathe on me, breath of God; Jesus, stand among us; Put peace into each other's hands.

Second Sunday of Easter   16 April
Second Service   Show Must Go On
Ps. 30.1–5; Dan. 6.[1–5] 6–23; **Mark 15.46—16.8**

Donatello and a number of Renaissance artists developed a sculpting technique that consisted of only sculpting part of a block of material, leaving the figure to appear as caught within the block. This technique, called *non-finito* (unfinished in Italian), was a homage to the Platonic philosophical idea that no work of art could ever perfectly mirror its heavenly counterpart.

While we celebrate and marvel at the ingenuity of artists, the truth is that we live in a world where closure is what we seek. We long for refinement, completeness; not merely suspensive punctuations to the events and circumstances of our lives. However, closure is not always an available option. Instead, many of us often find ourselves suspended in a place of unfulfilled anticipation.

Non-finito?

'The beginning of the good news of Jesus Christ, the Son of God.' As Mark the evangelist opens his volume on the life of Jesus, he seems to set the tone in such unambiguous terms that the reader and hearer would be right to assume that this story might indeed end on a positive note. Instead, we are left a little perplexed as Mark concludes his account with *amazement*, *terror* and *silence*.

This apparent anti-climax had prompted earlier readers to have a go at improving the ending. First, supplementing it with a succinct description of what happened next, then offering a longer precis of some of the choice cuts of Easter tradition and narratives.

And yet, the unresolved tension of the cliff-hanger of the Gospel of Mark's original ending has the merit of holding the reader and hearer to attention. Though it leaves us puzzled, it has also the quality of inviting us deeper with the central claim of this story. If Jesus is indeed the Son of God, how might his resurrection inform the responses of his followers to the unpredictability of the life and journey of faith? How might we respond to the unexpected challenges of life as those claiming to walk in the footsteps of the risen one?

In Joseph, who meticulously wraps Jesus' body and rolls the stone on the tomb hewn out of the rock, we encounter an embodiment of our longing, and often compulsive need for completion and closure. Jesus' body cannot be left hanging on the cross. His story, however tragic, needs to be brought to a close in a way that tends to cultural, religious and social imperatives. All this happens in the presence of three women, Mary Magdalene, Mary, mother of James, and Salome, inadvertent witnesses of this desperately sad epilogue to 'the beginning of the good news'.

Every end is a new beginning

It seems, however, that there is a twist or two left in this tale. Seeking their own closure, these three women arrive early at the tomb, carrying with them spices to conclude funeral rites. They arrive laden with unbearable sadness and ponderings, only to encounter an unexpected situation. They meet a young man who informs them that the story they were coming to lay to rest once and for all is being appended as Jesus has been raised, and has set a rendezvous for a reunion with them and the other disciples in Galilee.

Alarm, amazement, terror and silence are all they can offer in response. In many ways, this is in keeping with Mark's narrative. Throughout the Gospel, the evidence suggests that those closest to him persistently fail to fully comprehend the true nature of who Jesus is, and how this beginning of the good news is manifested amid all the turpitudes of their lives.

Conversely, demons have no difficulty in understanding who Jesus is. And it is from the mouth of a Roman soldier, one of those directly involved in his execution, that we finally hear the most limpid confession of Mark's central message: 'Truely, this man was God's Son.'

Words without end

As we join the story, we participate in the composition of not merely an appendix or an afterword but the redaction of a new volume. 'The beginning of the good news' is a call to be attentive and to actively engage with a story that is likely to leave us confounded and constricted.

In contrast to the silence of the women on which Mark ends his account, there is a hint that silence is not the most suitable location for the story of the one John refers to as the Word. Instead, as seen in subsequent attempts to give an appropriate end to the story, it only makes sense in the commitment to gossip the gospel in words and deeds.

Mark leaves us suspended, not as the last word on the story but as an invitation to enter more deeply into that story, just like the women entered the tomb. There is no prerequisite to understanding and comprehending the whole story, but a willingness to stand as witnesses to the fact that this story continues. Indeed, this story is not primarily preoccupied with conclusion and closure. Instead, it is a story of beginnings, of retelling, literally of reliving.

Lusa Nsenga Ngoy

Hymn suggestions

Were you there; O, happy day; Give thanks to the Lord, our God and King (Forever); Blessed assurance.

Third Sunday of Easter 23 April
Principal Service **The Breaking of the Bread**

Zeph. 3.14–end (*if used, the reading from Acts must be used as the second reading*), or Acts 2.14a, 36–41; Ps. 116.1–3, 10–end [*or* 116.1–7]; 1 Peter 1.17–23; **Luke 24.13–35**

The feast at the end of the road

> Come, my Light, my Feast, my Strength:
> Such a light as shows a feast,
> Such a feast as mends in length,
> Such a strength as makes his guest.[8]

There is a painting by Caravaggio in the National Gallery of the supper that is described in the Gospel. Caravaggio was a close contemporary of George Herbert, who wrote these words, though I wonder how they would have got on.

Imagine the disciples, walking the seven or so miles to Emmaus. A stranger has joined them: the only stranger in Jerusalem who hasn't heard the news. They walk, he talks, filling their minds and hearts with the Scriptures, all about the Christ. They arrive at their destination, and he makes to continue, but they press him to stay and eat with them.

Caravaggio, painting in the early seventeenth century, captures the moment when their eyes were opened and they recognized him as he takes and breaks the bread – then disappears from their sight. On the left, a disciple, with his green jacket, torn elbow thrusting out into our faces; on the right, St James, with a scallop on his lapel, the symbol of pilgrimage, arms extended deep into the picture behind the Christ, hand reaching out towards us. Another disciple, in the space behind, face obscured, looking down on the central figure, who sits, calm, focused on the bread before him. A beautiful Christ, in rough contemporary clothes, red and white, long dark hair. Again, an arm stretched out, inviting us to join the party.

Caravaggio depicts the moment with characteristic clarity. And obscurity. For the shadows are there. Faces obscured; hinting at more from the darkness. And a bowl of fruit, toppling on the foremost edge of the table. About to fall out of the picture. All that fruit, scattered across the floor at our feet. Or falling into our lap. Depending on how far we are, or how close we have drawn towards the table.

Easter in ordinary

Their despondency on the road was transformed as their hearts burnt with the word he speaks. And now, sacrament too. They would have recognized the action. Taking, blessing, breaking, sharing the bread, just as at the Last Supper, before his body was broken on the cross.

This post-resurrection story lends itself to Caravaggio's vernacular style. The ordinary words and actions, the journey and meal, companionship and conversation fold about the Easter Christ. The ordinary, the material, speaks across the centuries into our preoccupations, our hopes and fears, as the picture spills out, into our time and space. An ordinary late afternoon walk becomes a pilgrimage, a journey of significance to a meal to which we also are invited. All that is despondent, bitter even, within us, our emptiness, futility, dashed hopes; and we are offered a bowl of grapes, pomegranates, pears and figs.

A sense of Easter call

A sense of calling is often like this. You start off on the road, in control of your destination. Then the encounter, by something, someone, who addresses you. The narrative of the road to Emmaus is the journey towards the invitation to come to thanksgiving, to Eucharist. Come, my way, my truth, my life, we sing. To respond – wholeheartedly – is to breathe on the road, fresh air, new ideas, to see the truth differently.

What Caravaggio does, remarkably, is allow the dark shadows to say as much as the explicit subject matter. Our imaginations are stirred into the sudden realization that God-in-Christ is present, where the darkness and the light are both alike.

Imagine their return journey, back to Jerusalem. The disciples now altogether different. No longer are they in darkness, but now they bear the light for others. They now know 'a life as killeth death'. To encounter God in Christ is to be addressed by a loving truth that calls forth the best in each of us, making us human, in the light and in all our dark despair. What was so original about Caravaggio was the abiding mystery that the finished painting does not wholly resolve. It is to be continued in our minds.

The fruit, fallen into our lap

> Come, my Light, my Feast, my Strength:
> Such a light as shows a feast.

The bread and wine which we receive as the body and blood of Christ are real, this sacrament of the Eucharist, in a way that gives reality to all our eating and drinking. We are guests at a feast that gives meaning to our lives, ultimate meaning, fulfilling all desires. Christ's resurrected body is present now, to us today, as the body and blood we receive, a gift of grace. Where there is always more to receive, to know and understand, to give in turn. It is to receive the fruit that falls into our lap.

Frances Ward

Hymn suggestions

Come, my Way, my Truth, my Life; Alleluia, sing to Jesus; Will you come and follow me; Just as I am.

Third Sunday of Easter 23 April
Second Service **The House in the Centre**
Ps. 48; **Hag. 1.13—2.9**; 1 Cor. 3.10–17;
Gospel at Holy Communion: John 2.13–22

God's house

Why build a house for God? Because God wants to be at the centre of life. That doesn't mean that God needs to be the centre of attention. But God's desire is *for* us, and thus God has a propensity for being *with* us. How do we know? We see it in Eden, with the tabernacle, in the incarnation of the Word, through the Spirit of Pentecost. And here, with these remnant people, in the Temple.

God doesn't need a penthouse apartment or country estate. Yes, there are particular regulations for building this house, but it isn't about the house itself. The Temple points to God's heart to have a space among us human beings. God's heart is to live in the village, in the town, in the city – to be in the midst of our lives and therefore known by us. How? By the Holy Spirit – the one who has been hovering over the earth since creation. The Spirit is present in this passage, living in Zerubbabel and in Joshua, primed to be manifestly present in the Temple, and thus with the people.

'I am with you,' God says to Zerubbabel and Joshua. This is the gospel, the good news of the whole of Scripture: Immanuel, God with us. God has come to fill the house, the neighbourhood, the nations – more than that, God has come to be with us all.

It is interesting that God 'stirs up' the spirits of Zerubbabel and Joshua. We probably need stirring up to remember where God is. I certainly do. We sometimes cry out 'Help!' to God when we are desperate. But there is more for us than that. God is ready to be at the centre of every area of our lives. We see this in this great building spoken about in the passage. That is why this meticulous and exhausting work is so vital. It speaks of the importance of God's life in the midst of everyone and everything involved: in the lives of all the various craft workers building the Temple, in the lives of the farmers who provide the sacrifices, in the lives of the priests performing their duties. In other words, in the lives, occupations and priorities of the entire community.

Our house

Of course, in some countries, the UK being an obvious example, people love to own a house. But if we feel we've made it when we get on the property ladder – that this is the true point of life – then something is amiss. Is our security in ownership of bricks and mortar? We can live for the sake of other things besides owning a house: getting our dream job, achieving a certain level of fitness, even things in the Christian life. These things are well and good. But what do we really need and who do we really want to become? We need God, and for the sake of the earth we need to seek the presence of the Holy Spirit. We have seen that this is what God wants too. God wants to be tabernacled, templed, incarnated and poured out among us.

The real bold move is to let God build a temple in our lives. After all, our bodies, says St Paul, are temples of the Holy Spirit. Joshua and Zerubbabel needed courage to build the Temple. It took everything they had to give. We need courage to say yes to God being at the centre of our lives. But just as we need courage, we know too that this can only be a good thing. When Christ comes, when the Spirit of Pentecost comes, we know that we are in safe hands. Is there a cost for us? Sure, daily. But we do not walk this way alone, and the one we walk with is good.

Everyone's house

Does God want a house? Yes: in us, in our neighbourhoods, across the nations, everywhere. And as we allow the Spirit entrance, we find that our hearts are turned to the things of God, to the cares of God, to the priorities of God. We find that we can have courage for the demands of life. We find too that we can share God's big heart for being present with everyone else. We live in an age, of course, where God is not given so much space. But God is well able to meet that challenge and is in no way absent because of it. God does not want a fancy temple but is instead knocking at our door. Will we answer?

Mark Amos

Hymn suggestions

Be thou my vision; Love divine, all loves excelling; Jesus, be the centre; My hope is built on nothing less.

Fourth Sunday of Easter   30 April
Principal Service   **The Gate of Grace**
Gen. 7 (*if used, the reading from Acts must be used as the second reading), or* Acts 2.42–end; Ps. 23; 1 Peter 2.19–end;
John 10.1–10

For those of us who live in urban or suburban settings – which is most of us – the language of shepherds and sheep can feel a little alien. Indeed, Jesus' agrarian context can seem very distant from modern life's extended supply chains and pre-packaged food. We are not peasants or, for the most part, farmers or fisherfolk.

Nonetheless, for those of us who are regulars in church the language of sheep and shepherds is familiar. We are used to the fact that the Bible has a lot to say about shepherds. We are used to Jesus' use of shepherd language, which draws on images from the Scriptures he would have known and loved.

God of surprises

Jesus, of course, has a genius for surprising us. His use of shepherding metaphors and images does not stop with familiar images for

God and Israel. He takes metaphor to the next level. Thus, his state-ment, 'I am the gate for the sheep.' It creates all sorts of resonances. Indeed, while I know that many people in our world do not see Jesus as their lord and saviour, surely even for the most cynical it is hard to deny that Jesus had a genius with words. For me, the state-ment, 'I am the gate for the sheep', is an example of his brilliance, full of possibility and strangeness. Jesus says, 'I am the gate.' What on earth can he mean?

If concepts of shepherds and sheepfolds do feel distant, the idea of a gate is surely immediate and contemporary for everyone. It is something both everyday and comforting yet at the same time has complex and troubling resonances for our divided world. For if gates can make us think of something as mundane as a garden gate, 'gates' also have implications of boundaries; they can mark the line between what counts as 'inside' and 'outside' or 'public' and 'private'. There are gates set up at the end of Downing Street to signal that this is special, protected ground. Sometimes we need a security code to get through a gate. If we lack the code, we cannot expect access. Increasingly, folks live in 'gated' communities.

Who's in? Who's out?

It would seem that we live in a time when barriers, gates, walls – all of those things that act as boundary markers – seem to have become huge cultural and political issues. Some politicians seem keen to erect physical walls along borders or feel the need to police, ever more ruthlessly, the attempts of some to cross seas and land barriers in search of a different or better life. The boundaries of inside/outside and public/private are policed. Gates have social and political significance.

So, when Jesus says, 'I am the gate for the sheep', we might, in the light of modern political obsessions, see him as a gatekeeper who polices the boundary between those who are in God's king-dom or God's Church and those who are beyond the pale and do not belong to the saved. This is a picture of Jesus which, for many, would be unduly authoritarian. This is Jesus as a kind of security guard; this is Jesus as the (armed) police officer who stands at the door of 10 Downing Street.

A gate of grace

That surely will not do. In saying that he is the gate it is not that Jesus is a security guard for God. Rather he wants to emphasize that it is in relationship with him that abundant life is to be found. He is not a gate that requires a security pass or special access. He does not represent an elite club. Rather he is the Son of God who wants everyone to have abundant life. To have it, one simply needs to meet and trust him.

I suspect we could all come up with a list of the threats to our flourishing. Our society holds within the capacity to be as exploitative as any other in history, including Jesus'. In our society, as much as in Jesus' time, some wish to take advantage of us and lead us away from what makes for a good and full life.

When we come into relationship with Jesus, we enter a place of safety where those who would exploit and abuse us cannot come. He offers not only a safe place to rest – the sheepfold – but total freedom to come and go into abundant pasture. This is Jesus not as gatekeeper but as the one who genuinely brings the fullness of life: 'Whoever enters by me will be saved, and will come in and go out and find pasture. The thief comes only to steal and kill and destroy. I came that they may have life, and have it abundantly.'

Rachel Mann

Hymn suggestions

The king of love my shepherd is; Abundant life; For the healing of the nations; How sweet the name of Jesus sounds.

Fourth Sunday of Easter 30 April
Second Service **The Temple Made of Prayer**
Ps. 29.1–10; **Ezra 3.1–13; Eph. 2.11–end**; *Gospel at Holy Communion*: Luke 19.37–end

Mind games

Mindfulness: the latest answer to stress and anxiety, bringing peace of mind when life is tough. It's a Buddhist practice, one of the seven elements of the path to enlightenment, to enable us to become calm and wise, to alleviate a variety of mental and physical conditions.

Its very simplicity commends it. And the more you practise it, the easier it becomes to find the zone inside where you can let worries fade away and live in the present moment. For, yes, we do live in anxious times. We can become ever more self-reflexive, excessively self-conscious, existing in a hall of mirrors, a cage of intense absorption with the latest image, where reality becomes ever more virtual. We fail to attend to what is outside the hall; we can no longer see the sky, the Otherworld that exists beyond our narrow horizons.

In C. S. Lewis's *The Last Battle*, Aslan – the real Aslan – exposes the fraud Shift and the donkey Puzzle, dressed up in a lion skin. A recurrent theme in the book is how easily we are deceived by what seems real, but is not. The Dwarves play a key role, caught as they are in their own world view, dominated by their own desires and selfish goals. Towards the end of the book, they are huddled around, absorbed in their own concerns. Lucy pleads with Aslan to do something for these poor Dwarves, so Aslan shakes his mane. A great feast appears for the Dwarves: but even though they eat, they can't appreciate the delicious food. Instead, they believe they're eating hay, turnips, raw cabbage leaves. C. S. Lewis illustrates what happens when our minds are trapped in solipsistic frames of reference that interpret our experience with closed minds.

The Other who transcends

The attractive thing about Buddhism, at least to many people in today's world, is that it doesn't require God. There is much good in mindfulness – it helps us get through the stresses and strains of life. For me, though, it's the lack of the Other that I miss. A personal God who encounters us, meeting us in prayer and sacrament as wholly Other. We are stirred in our imagination, out of the all-too-human, self-referential thought traps and mind games.

The foundations of life and self

It comes down to the question of what we base our lives upon. Foundations. In Ezra, we hear about the builders who laid the foundation of the Temple of the Lord. Singing and dancing accompanied the completion, praising God in worship: 'For he is good, for his steadfast love endures for ever towards Israel.' The people responded with a great shout because the foundation of the house of the Lord was laid. Weeping and joyful shouts could not be told apart as all the people came together to celebrate.

To build ourselves on the foundations of something Other than ourselves enables us to engage with a reality that is beyond ourselves, a real temple to a real God.

The cornerstone

St Paul uses the metaphor of foundations and buildings. He reminds us that we are founded upon Jesus Christ; he is the cornerstone. The new temple, in whom 'the whole structure is joined together and grows into a holy temple in the Lord; in whom you also are built together spiritually into a dwelling-place for God'. To see ourselves in a lifelong – indeed beyond this life – relationship with God-in-Christ is to base our lives on prayer. Prayer of different sorts. Contemplation is remarkably like the techniques of mindfulness. Meditation takes a phrase or a word to repeat in our minds, chewing it over to digest inwardly (called *lectio Divina* within Benedictine traditions of prayer). Or we lay ourselves and our own concerns aside, and pray for others, holding them in intercession. Or we ask God for something we want, and learn through prayer that we are most healthy when we desire what God desires, rather than our own wants.

Christ is our peace

Paul claims that in Christ is our peace. The peace of mind that comes through prayer is a gift of God-in-Christ; we receive it as a grace, not as a result of our own endeavours to be mindful. Certainly, we will use many of the same techniques – centring ourselves, quietening our busy minds, breathing slowly and steadily, recalling the eternal now of the present moment. But we will do all this in order to make ourselves ready to receive a peace that is beyond us, that comes to us as the gift of a personal God who loves and cares for us as infinitely precious in his sight, no longer a stranger and an alien, but a member of the household of God, a dwelling place for God.

Frances Ward

Hymn suggestions

Christ is made the sure foundation; Breathe on me, breath of God; Be still, for the presence of the Lord; Let all the world in every corner sing.

Fifth Sunday of Easter 7 May
Principal Service **The Way, the Truth and the Life**
Gen. 8.1–19 (*if used, the reading from Acts must be used as the second reading*), or Acts 7.55–end; Ps. 31.1–5, 15–16 [*or* 31.1–5], 1 Peter 2.2–10; **John 14.1–14**

Eastertide encourages us to ask what it means to live in the light of the resurrection. Today's Gospel is read twice this year during this season: today and on 1 May, the feast of the apostles Philip and James. They were among those who encountered the risen Christ in person. But what might this passage mean for us?

The context

It contains one of Jesus' great 'I am' sayings as part of an extended conversation between Jesus and the disciples spanning four chapters. The writer places it between the washing of feet at the Last Supper and Jesus' agony in the Garden. By squeezing such a large body of teaching into this supposed time frame, the writer can emphasize its relationship to what is about to happen in real time. Over a relatively short space of time, Jesus will be betrayed, denied and tried, then crucified, buried and raised, after which he will return and give the Holy Spirit. These events form the entire basis of Christian worship between Holy Week and Pentecost; they sit at the heart of the gospel of redemption. It's as though the writer is suggesting that here, in Jesus' great discourse, is the teaching the disciples need to see them through the events that lie ahead.

Asking questions

Most of these four chapters are taken up with Jesus speaking. But now and then, one of the disciples says something; in today's passage, we have a question from Thomas. Thomas' *great* moment is after the resurrection where he declares his faith, recognizing his Lord and his God. Today's Gospel reveals another great moment. He asks an honest question, and this leads to Jesus' 'I am' saying. Thomas is prepared to ask without, it seems, worrying about looking stupid. He's quite possibly asking the question that all the disciples were thinking but didn't dare to ask: 'Where are you going; how can we know the way?'

Through Thomas' question, we are permitted to ask questions.

Questioning is crucial if we're to grow in faith – and we need to be prepared that there won't always be a straightforward answer. Christian faith is not about a series of prescribed questions to which there are correct answers. Tools such as a catechism and courses in Christian basics help set a framework for faith. But there will never be a direct answer to every question. The world is complex and at times confusing; living as a human being – as a faithful Christian – must involve living with unanswered questions.

Jesus the way

But we don't live alone. In reply to Thomas' question, Jesus gives not a direct answer but an open answer, an answer that requires him (and us) to keep thinking. Jesus doesn't tell Thomas the way: he has to work it out for himself. To discover what Jesus means, Thomas – and we – must commit to *following* the way of Jesus, *believing* in Jesus as the embodiment of truth, and *living* in and with him. Only then will we discover what he means.

Jesus does not say 'I'll show you the way' but 'I *am* the way'. Some years ago, on holiday in Japan, my wife and I found ourselves utterly lost at a Tokyo metro station. It was morning rush hour, and the station was packed with people hurrying to work. A Japanese man, on his way to work, stopped in the middle of the rush and asked where we were going. We thought he might give us directions. But instead, he beckoned, 'Come with me', and took us through the labyrinthine network of tunnels and escalators to a platform in the depths of the station and said, 'It's the next train from here.' He didn't tell us the way, or even show us the way, but took us in person – he *was* the way.

We don't learn Jesus' way fully through absorbing his teaching (important though that is), but by travelling *with* him: he *is* the way. After the resurrection, the disciples discovered a relationship with the risen Christ. As Christians, our faith – our life – is rooted in that relationship too. We have guides for the way, foremost among them the words of Scripture. This points us in the right direction – 'a lantern to our feet and a light upon our path', as it says in Psalm 119 – it helps show us the way. But it is not itself the way. The Bible points beyond itself to reveal the Word of God: the incarnate, crucified and risen Jesus, the one with whom and the way *in whom* we travel.

Peter Moger

Hymn suggestions

Christ the way of life, possess me; I am the light whose brightness shines; O changeless Christ, for ever new; Thou art the way, by thee alone.

Fifth Sunday of Easter 7 May
Second Service **What If the Candle Blows Out?**
Ps. 147.1–12; **Zech. 4.1–10**; Rev. 21.1–14;
Gospel at Holy Communion: Luke 2.25–32 [33–38]

If asked to name a prophet, I doubt that many of us would think first of Zechariah, one of the minor prophets about whom little is known. That near anonymity may be important, in that it makes the prophet's message (rather than his person) of primary importance.

Zechariah is associated with Haggai (in the book of Ezra), and their ministries coincide, occurring when the exiled Jews returned from Babylon with a mission to restore the people to the Promised Land and rebuild the Temple. The traditional date for the return of the first exiles is 538 BC.

Zechariah is a seer, a visionary. The book bearing his name mixes visions and oracles. (Stylistically his book of visions is reminiscent of that of Ezekiel.) The vision that our passage recounts, his fifth vision (there are eight in the book), may have come to Zechariah around 520 BC.

Visions require interpretation, either by the messenger or by the recipient of the message (the prophet) or, perchance, by ourselves as we seek their meaning for today.

Vision or dream?

The vision begins in a familiar way: the angel (a divine messenger) returns. (He acts as both speaker and interpreter.) Zechariah is 'wakened' as if from sleep ('stirred up' may be a better translation). He must not cease from his seeing, assuming that Israel is now secure. The angel prods Zechariah, asking him what he 'sees'. The prophet then describes his vision of an unusual gold lampstand and two olive trees.

It is difficult to visualize the lampstand that Zechariah sees, largely because later Jewish tradition would assume that a lampstand with seven lights would take the form of a menorah, but this is an anachronistic assumption since such lamps (ritual objects) are first depicted in the Roman era. Zechariah's lamp has a bowl at the top allowing oil to flow continually via seven channels to seven lights. Perhaps those seven lights form a circle? I read a commentary that suggested that it might have been similar to a ceramic lampstand of the era from Syria-Palestine that had pinches in the clay rim of the bowls allowing multiple wicks to burn in each bowl. Despite the helpful illustrations, I can't visualize it. Suffice it to say that it is a stunning gold lampstand with many lights.

The two olive trees are close by ('on either side' or 'above', depending on the translation of the wording) and keep the lamps supplied with olive oil so that they can burn constantly. Can the light represent the presence of God? Presumably not, because it relies on an outside source of power/fuel. Maybe it signifies the life of the community, that life which God is promising to maintain.

'What are these?' asks Zechariah. (Is he asking about the lights or the trees?) The angel answers that, 'This is the word of the LORD ...' Suddenly the nature of the vision and the discourse between angel and seer changes and there is a message for Zerubbabel (in the only reference to him in Zechariah, though he is central to the book of Haggai). Do the trees represent Zerubbabel and Joshua (the high priest), the two community leaders who are 'sons of oil'? If they do, then those two here become sources of oil. We know that, in worship, olive oil was used to light the Temple and oil had a special place and significance in rituals of anointing (signifying appointment and empowerment).

So, is the vision intended *for* Zerubbabel? Or is it *about* him, the governor, the Temple-builder? He is to bring out the capstone, the last stone in the rebuilding of the Temple, with due ceremony. This is to be done 'not by might, nor by power, but by my spirit', says the Lord. Zechariah and Zerubbabel are God's instruments, so it seems that the words of verse 6 are to warn them not to get above themselves. Zerubbabel has an important, God-given, task to fulfil, the completion of which will verify Zechariah's prophecy.

What if the candle blows out?

That curiously designed lampstand may be vision, dream or nightmare, for what if the light were to be dimmed or extinguished? Surely if it represents the promise of God to his people, he will keep the lamp burning. God will maintain the life of the community while it completes the work it has been assigned. We are accustomed to light signifying hope.

I can remember being involved in a selection process wherein candidates for ministry were asked what they would do 'when the candle blows out', when hope was extinguished. Many spoke of periods when they had felt distant from God, when they were uncertain of his will for them. All spoke of their personal devotions, of prayer and Bible study, some told of consulting with a spiritual guide or trusted Christian friends. A few mentioned the reassurance found as they continued to be faithful to attendance at public worship ('praying through' their experience).

Are we, therefore, as contemporary members of the faith community, those who must tend the lamp, maintain the life of the community and be constant in worship, until God's messenger comes to us?

Zechariah's vision assures him that the lamp cannot go out (the source of oil is unending) and that the task of Temple-building will be completed. This is not just a dream (lost upon awakening) nor is it a nightmare. It is God's spectacular promise.

Wendy Kilworth-Mason

Hymn suggestions

Give me the faith which can remove; Great is the darkness that covers the earth; Light of the world, you stepped down into darkness; Shine, Jesus, shine.

Sixth Sunday of Easter   14 May
(For Matthias, see p. 309.)
Principal Service   **Never Alone**
Gen. 8.20—9.17 (*if used, the reading from Acts must be used as the second reading*), or Acts 17.22–31; Ps. 66.7–end;
1 Peter 3.13–end; **John 14.15–21**

Being rescued

Most of us, I suspect, can relate to the feeling of relief and thanksgiving when someone comes to help us. Whether we have broken down in our car, or the gas won't work, or we've hurt ourselves and called an ambulance. Knowing that someone is coming to save us is profound.

Jesus said, 'I will not leave you orphaned; I am coming to you.' Remember where we are in the story. This is the night of Jesus' betrayal. And what does Jesus say to the disciples, who were by the end of this night going to be scattered across Jerusalem and the surrounding area? On this night of confusion, fear, betrayal and mystery, he says, 'I will not leave you orphaned; I am coming to you.'

Being Easter people

We live in the extraordinary period between the resurrection and the culmination of the kingdom of God, the moment where potential becomes reality, where promise becomes, in John Donne's word, 'possession'. This means we have to try to be people who can live in the space in between the promise and the possession. To be Easter people is to be people who can exist, who can do our living and working and breathing, our praying and hoping and loving, with something that is less than certainty but is much more than a vague dream of something better to come.

Built into us is a desire to seek God. That's partly what St Paul is trying to say to the people at the altar to an unknown God. Longing for relationship with God is natural. What Jesus says on the night before he dies is that it is not we who need to travel to *God* but God who, through the events that are about to unfold in Jerusalem, will come to *us*. 'I will not leave you orphaned; I am coming to you.'

Sure and certain hope

That promise, that 'sure and certain hope', as the funeral service puts it, helps us to make sense of this in-between place in which we live. This place where, though we profess that we 'look for the resurrection of the dead and the life of the world to come', nonetheless is a patchwork of glory and pain, of despair and hope, of deep troughs of depression as well as the occasional mountain-top experience. We all know how brittle life can feel. We all know how brittle life can be. We live our personal tragedies, alongside those of our communities, our nation and our world. How is this the life of the resurrection? How are we an Easter people with alleluia as our song?

Well, as in almost everything to do with the Christian life, it comes back to the font. It comes back to the water of baptism. Jesus is not an impervious, waterproof Superman zooming in from somewhere else and whisking away everything awful and replacing it with a set of lovely things. The resurrection is about the person of Jesus Christ, fully human and fully divine, passing into the very depths, and rising, gathering up and transforming and transfiguring and hallowing all of that experience.

Jesus disappears into the waters of death and rises again, and we go with him. Breaking the surface of the font and emerging into the life of the resurrection where we still carry the marks of our sufferings, just as he does, the risen body of Christ bearing the marks of the nails and the spear, but now we know that those marks are hallowed, and so are ours.

Our suffering is shared

None of this of course fully addresses the fairly arbitrary nature of suffering in this world. Why does one person get an incurable disease or get murdered on the streets of the city, and some other person doesn't? But the reason that we can live in this in-between world, this place where the tomb is empty, where Christ is coming to us, where the world is pregnant with the potential of the kingdom, is because the sort of God who dies and rises again for us is the sort of God who knows what it is like to be us because Christ also suffered. And he is with us in our suffering too.

You are not alone. To be Easter people is not to be people who escape the realities of the world, is not to be people who, by being part of God's 'crew' get a free pass from the suffering and awfulness that life entails. But it is to be people who know that although we go down into the waters of death, we come back out again, and as our heads break the surface and our eyes see the glory of the kingdom of God, we do so accompanied by the Christ who is no longer an unknown God but is the parent of children – children who find that they are no longer orphaned because God has come to us.

Tom Clammer

Hymn suggestions

Now is eternal life; The head that once was crowned with thorns; See, what a morning; Thou, whose almighty word.

Sixth Sunday of Easter 14 May
Second Service **Girls and Boys Come Out to Play**
Ps. 87, 36.5–10; **Zech. 8.1–13; Rev. 21.22—22.5**;
Gospel at Holy Communion: John 21.1–14

Safety

The global pandemic of Covid-19 has made us think about safety in completely different ways. In order to keep our children safe, we had to close playgrounds and schools. But then we found that many of these children had no safety at home – from deprivation, ignorance or violence. We thought our vulnerable elderly people were safe in care homes, but then many of them ended their lives without either home or care. We even learned to be good Samaritans by crossing over the road to keep other people safe – from ourselves!

And at the same time the Church, along with other institutions, has been rocked by scandals of abuse. We have had to think all over again what it means to keep one another safe, to protect the vulnerable – the very young, and the very old. We are learning, all over again, what we should have known long ago – what it means to safeguard one another.

Zechariah's vision

Into these issues and memories, the prophet Zechariah whispers – from the unread margins of the Bible and culture, from long ago and far away: this gentle and reassuring picture of the city of God. Zechariah could imagine the city of God to be a place where girls and boys are playing on the streets, and where the old, living out the full term of their lives, are there with them. This might not look like much! Compared with the golden city of Revelation, this may seem an unambitious, even secular, vision of paradise!

But in a time of violence and exile, in a time when ordinary life was more and more precarious, this portrait of an ordinary street must have seemed like a Utopian dream.

Imagine if little boys could be safe from raiding parties that might co-opt them to be slaves or boy soldiers.

Imagine if girls could play in the open, safe from violence, abduction and rape.

And, of course, these are abuses that are still happening all too frequently in our world today.

Zechariah's vision is a story of *once upon a time*, that is, a dream of possible futures. He imagines a deep homecoming – exiles stream from the east and the west, a people coming home. He imagines a sowing of peace, a harvest of fruit, a gentle rain.

Indicators of peace

After years of coal smoke, all around the city of Manchester, even up in the hills, all the drystone walls used to be covered with a deposit of grime and soot. But after smokeless zones were introduced, living things started to grow again – mosses and lichens that live on the surface of the stone walls. These lichens will grow and flourish only when there is no pollution. They are indicators. And in the streets of the city, the presence of these children, and their ability to play freely, is an indicator of a special kind of peace.

This vision of the city of God constantly extends to include those who are very young. It makes room for the laughter of the child. It offers the child freedom. This city constantly opens its arms to provide shelter and a resting place for the very old.

Safety and freedom

It is a city where safety is not just seen as a kind of refuge, a kind of safe bomb shelter, but rather a place in which there are spaces for people to be free. In this city, there is both safety and freedom. Sometimes it happens that our concern for safety, our own and others', can end up binding us in fear. But this city of God is a place of freedom from fear.

God's love, God's grace, flow into us. And our churches at their best become places where that grace flows out to others. We build together a fellowship of peace and love, a place where no one is turned away. A place where there is 'neither Jew nor Greek, slave nor free, male nor female'. A truly inclusive Church where all are safe, where all are free.

An inner welcome

And it may be that these movements also occur within us. Within each one of us, there is a history, a life of experience – often a story of pain, loss and exile. And the city of God can welcome even the inner child of our hearts – who also may have been obscured or suppressed – to come out and to play in the streets without fear.

And in this city, the parts of us that are weary and old begin to hear the invitation to come and rest, in safety.

'I will save you and you shall be a blessing,' Zechariah says in the voice of God. May we find safety and refuge in God. May we dream of a place of safety and joy, for the youngest and the oldest, and may we bring that dream to life by our welcome.

Andrew Rudd

Hymn suggestions

Christ is the world (A touching place); Here in this place (Gather us in); For the healing of the nations; Let us build a house.

Ascension Day 18 May
Principal Service **Can I Get a Witness?**
Acts 1.1–11 (*must be used as either the first or second reading*), *or* Dan. 7.9–14; Ps. 47, *or* Ps. 93; Eph. 1.15–end, *or* Acts 1.1–11; **Luke 24.44–end**

The experience of corporate worship in the African American tradition is, at its core, a participative moment and movement. This is particularly evident in the rich repertoire of songs that draws the congregation and leaders in a call-and-response dialogue. Classics such as 'A Train's A-coming, Jonah', or the relatively recent 'O, Happy Day' are only two examples of the cultural and spiritual staple for countless generations of enslaved Africans and their descendants singing to the liberator God their anguish and hope from a strange land.

The tradition of call-and-response is pervasive to black homiletic experience, making every sermon not a monologue but a conversation. In these conversations, the preacher seeks the support and affirmation of the community, recognizing that the truth of a statement is not in the compelling nature of the argument, but in its capacity to mobilize and elicit the assent of the congregation, the community.

'Are you with me?' 'Can I get an Amen?' 'Can I get a witness?' These are not betraying the preacher's anxiety, neither are they performative devices. Like punctuation, they give rhythm to the sermon, inviting some kind of improvization on the theme. It is a collective composition that always leads to a shared commitment to transformed and redeeming living that extends the experience of faith from the sanctuary to the streets, reducing the gap, the distance, between sacred and profane.

This is the tradition upon which many of the civil rights movement leaders in the USA built their action, leaving us a legacy of compelling sermons, discourses and writings that continue to shape the efforts of many contemporary activists for justice around the globe.

Active listening

If call-and-response is a conversation, its first movement is rooted in a commitment to attentive listening, a posture that assumes decentring from self and reorientation towards God, an interconnected and interdependent leaning on the other. It is a commitment to weave our particular stories into the universal story of God's love and grace as heralded by prophets of yesteryear and recorded in holy Scripture.

It is a call to testify of the death-defying encounter with the risen One. An encounter that challenges estrangement and isolation, oppression and marginalization, and gives us the courage to hope where hope is unbearable. In this encounter, we are offered the opportunity of reframing knowledge and understanding, releasing our imaginative capacity to conceive of a future that will be transformed and redeemed.

The call to a life of witness is a call not framed around doing but being. It is not about a collection of activities and strategic plans. In the words of the risen Christ, it is an intimation to stay, to dwell in a place of equipping, of forming and reforming, of impartation of divine essence. Being a witness is about a commitment to embody a quality of being that best reflects the nature and character of Jesus. Our very lives become the unveiling, the unlocking of the mystery of Christ. They become the primary witness of and to the resurrection.

Enter the Theo-drama

Being a witness is a call to a life that both espouses the experience of yesterday while lifting our horizon on to a future that is to be the fulfilment of God's promise of salvation. Furthermore, being a witness is about opening self to a fellowship of the hopeful and the faithful. Such a fellowship is not a static one, but one that obediently follows the guiding of the risen Christ with the Spirit. It is a fellowship that, while mindful of the urgency of change, is never in a rush to run ahead.

It is a fellowship that opens itself to the scrutiny of interrogation, choosing to wrestle with the fracture of the past in repentance that leads to reconciliation. In our era, it would be a community committed to creating safe spaces for the marginalized and minoritized, the exploited and persecuted. Equally, it would be a community unapologetic in creating brave spaces to address and redress all root causes of injustice.

This fellowship is both a receptacle and a channel of the beatific life received in the outstretched and lifted hands of Christ who proclaims blessing over it. Witness, therefore, emerges out of what we now know of God, of ourselves and the world. The intersection of these, when held in healthy balance, might just be what the kingdom of God is about.

Luke opened his account of Jesus' ministry with the story of his temptation in the desert. In that story, Jesus rejects the lure of expediency, the appeal of performance, and the burden of existential anxiety. Matthew suggests that after the devil had departed, heaven opened and angels attended to his needs. As he concludes his account, Luke paints the picture of an open heaven. Only this time, it is Jesus himself who is carried up to heaven. Instead of angels attending to him, his disciples seem to take over the task to worship him, perhaps as a way of testifying to the fact that their lives have been touched by that heavenly quality that only elicits one response.

Lusa Nsenga Ngoy

Hymn suggestions

Bless the Lord, O my soul (10,000 reasons); Jesus, my passion in life (Above all else); All hail the power of Jesus' name; Soon and very soon.

Ascension Day 18 May
Second Service **Absence, Presence and More Than a Brief Encounter**
Morning Ps. 110, 150; Evening Ps. 8; Song of the Three 29–37, *or* 2 Kings 2.1–15; **Rev. 5;** *Gospel at Holy Communion*: Mark 16.14–end

Absence

Forty days ago, we began to celebrate: he is risen!

That cry echoed around this building and in our hearts – and still it continues. Yet now, we gather to recall his ascension, his departure in the presence of his gathered disciples, after those remarkable days among them.

Now, often when I think about the ascension I'm taken to the film *Brief Encounter*. That venerable black and white 1945 film by David Lean, starring Celia Johnson and Trevor Howard, based on Noel Coward's earlier play, revolves around hard choices and heart-rending partings. There are hints of the turmoil and the actual partings of the recent war years, made all the more striking because of the film's restrained pathos.

Many of us will know the wide sea of emotions that ebb and flow around separation, absence and endings. So, I wonder about those disciples of Jesus. What a time they'd had: crowds cheering on Palm Sunday followed quickly by the betrayal, arrest and brutal crucifixion, the silence of the Saturday, the triumph of the empty tomb and then the exhilarating way in which the risen Jesus had been present to them over the past few weeks.

Now it seems that they must get used to living in a world without him. Disorientating, even frightening – what happens next? Is it back to tax collecting, to fishing? His coming had been celebrated by angels, the name given to him – 'Emmanuel' – meant 'God with us'. And now he is leaving? Had it all just been a brief encounter that was now over?

Maybe not ... *maybe* there is more to absence and presence than we might think at first glance.

Presence

I wonder if you have come across the work of a contemporary Chinese artist called Lui Bolin. You can of course search for his work online. One of his exhibitions, held in London, drew together a number of his pieces under the title 'The Heroic Apparition'.

Bolin uses his own body as a canvas, painting himself, with the help of an assistant, to merge with his background. These pieces of performance art, captured in photographs, have earned him the title 'the invisible man'. Each piece takes around ten hours to complete and when photographed it can be near-impossible to spot him at first glance. This phase of his work began after his Beijing art studio, along with the studios of other artists, was shut down by the authorities in 2005. The government had stipulated that it didn't want artists gathering and working together. Bolin decided to use his art as a means of silent protest. It's continued from there and he has painted himself into ordinary settings like a supermarket display stand, a market stall, and socially loaded backgrounds like Tiananmen Square, Wall Street and the Tiles for America 9/11 memorial. In all this work the artist might seem to be absent, banished, but is actually profoundly present.

On Ascension Day we do well to note that sometimes in apparent absence there is a deeper presence. Jesus' promise, 'I will be with you, always', still holds true, truer than anything else. Our risen, ascended, Spirit-sending Lord has not absented himself, but he invites us to see with renewed eyes, to listen for his voice with renewed attention. For, as our reading from the Revelation to John conveys, Jesus has risen not only from the dead but to glory!

The living, reigning God before whom the throne room of all heaven quakes in awe and worship. This God invites us to be present as God is present to us; it is to this God that the prayers and worship of all the saints rises.

More than a brief encounter

This was no brief encounter – God is not absent but deeply present to his world, through his Spirit and in his people.

God is still present to you and me – even if sometimes we have to look hard and it seems like the artist has disguised himself most cunningly. It's as if he loves to invite us to find him through our pressing into the world with our eyes and ears open to discern him – perhaps where we might expect to find him least.

God also longs to be present to his world *through* you and me. As he prepared to ascend, Jesus asked his disciples to wait for the coming of the Holy Spirit. They had a task to do, a calling; they were to be those whose lives revealed the presence of God.

An interesting question then, one with which to close: the extent to which my life implies the presence, or the absence of God, to the world? Our risen, ascended and glorified Saviour.

Tricia Hillas

Hymn suggestions

Alleluia! Sing to Jesus; All hail the power of Jesus' name; Open my eyes, Lord, I want to see Jesus; The head that once was crowned with thorns.

Seventh Sunday of Easter
(Sunday after Ascension Day)   21 May
Principal Service   **In-between People**
Ezek. 36.24–28 (*if used, the reading from Acts must be used as the second reading*), *or* **Acts 1.6–14;** Ps. 68.1–10, 32–end [*or* 68.1–10]; 1 Peter 4.12–14; 5.6–11; **John 17.1–11**

A storyline

Some people like stories to reflect their orderly view of life: with a beginning, a middle and an end, having a pattern and purpose that can be seen and understood; having a conclusion that ties up the loose ends, leaving people with a sense of completion and satisfaction. When the book is closed there are no more questions to be asked: it is complete.

Other people prefer their stories to be open-ended, because they believe that life is like that: with a variety of loose connections and accidental happenings; having a development that can never be fully grasped; not having a tidy ending, because tidiness can never contain either the muddle or the mystery of life. When the book is closed the questions keep coming.

Depending on your own point of view and preference, you can read the story of Jesus' ascension, which we celebrated last Thursday with its echoes still present in our Gospel reading this morning, as a story that completes everything or a story that leaves everything open-ended.

The ascension does complete the mission of Jesus: it is the last act of the cycle of his life, death and resurrection which celebrates the return of Jesus to his Father.

The ascension is also open-ended, for it marks the beginning of a new time in which the apostles learn to live with a different kind of presence of Jesus from the one they knew. They have to come to terms with the fact that Jesus will never again walk with them on the roads of Palestine. They won't see him in person healing the sick, nor hear his teaching first-hand. That time is over. That age is gone. Something new is beginning.

The birth pangs

The birth pangs of a new age are very painful indeed – 'the fiery ordeal that is taking place among you to test you'. Life is indeed messy and muddled, and here is a tension between how things are and how things ought to be, between the 'now' and the 'not yet'.

Not only is this process of the in-breaking of the kingdom of God continuing, but we don't know if we are at the beginning of the Christian movement, in the middle of it, or near the end. It could all end tomorrow. It could continue for another thousand years. We don't know. All we know is that we are somewhere between the beginning and the end and that we are confronted by the same challenge to keep the story of Jesus alive as were those first disciples looking up into heaven.

In-between people

We are an 'in-between people', we find ourselves in the middle of a complex variety of stories that compete for our attention. None of us can begin at the beginning of those stories because we are 'middle people'. None of us started from zero: we are all born into a world that is already in motion; we found ourselves amid a history we did not initiate; we were ushered into a family and a tradition we did not form. We inherited the times we live in. We could make a start for ourselves only because we were given a start by others. Before we owned anything we owe everything.

The story of Jesus is a powerful gift that has been given to us, a gift of life that helps shape the world around us. The story does not simply reflect how things are but calls us beyond ourselves to a kingdom that is larger than the boundaries of geography and nationality, culture and even time itself.

His-story

The story of Jesus' ascension reminds us that Jesus is beyond us and can never be contained. But the same story also reminds us that the Lord is working with us as he did with those early disciples by confirming our word with signs of the kingdom. A truth that is beyond us, and yet of ourselves.

So, this Sunday, we rest in that space between ascension and Pentecost. It is a puzzling space, a place of unknowing. But the space of unknowing is where we often live most of our Christian life: 'to be in the world but not of it'. The gospel beckons, calls us on and challenges us to move beyond the boundaries that are set by our fear, weakness and short-sightedness.

Our stories are not finished, the last word has not been written, the final scenes are still open-ended. Where the future is a mystery, there is still hope working in the hopelessness of the world. That is the good news: the truth that is beyond us, and yet of ourselves. Our stories are his-story.

Paul Williams

Hymn suggestions

Lord, enthroned in heavenly splendour; In Christ alone; Blessed assurance; Crown him with many crowns.

Seventh Sunday of Easter
(Sunday after Ascension Day) 21 May
Second Service **All in All**
Ps. 47; 2 Sam. 23.1–5; **Eph. 1.15–end**;
Gospel at Holy Communion: Mark 16.14–end

Fell walking

I am a keen fell walker, and my favourite place to walk is in the Cheviot hills: but please don't tell anyone else about them, because nobody seems to know that they are there! In the wonderful solitude and silence of those hills is to be found a different perspective. The first is historical. Some of the ancient drovers' roads passed through the Cheviots as did Dere Street, a Roman road, and there was a large Roman hillfort at Chew Green. There are remains too of Bronze Age burial grounds and archaeological sites that mark former medieval settlements, as well as wild goats to be seen wandering around today, which are thought to be descended from those who have been there for many centuries. I find myself deeply connected to a history bigger than my own there: it provides a larger framework for my life. But, second, like any set of mountains and hills, there are also incredible vistas. From some peaks, you can see for miles into Scotland, northern England and to the coast and the North Sea. There is vast space, for almost as far as the eye can see. If you are fortunate enough to stay there on a clear night in winter or autumn, the stars are quite indescribable, and you can see the Milky Way and what appears to be literally thousands of stars. Another staggering part of God's creation laid out overhead. Another perspective.

Funerals

For those who have the privilege of officiating at funerals, I guess that I may not be the only one who is conscious that the words that I write on a couple of pieces of A4 are a meagre summary of a person's life. How do you sum up a life in words, stories and images in so short a space of time? How can you do that person justice? For all the richness or emptiness of a person's life, what is the sum of it? How can we describe it?

Maps

I have always rather loved maps, although they are somewhat out of vogue now, what with mobile phones and GPS. I love the detail, the sense of plotting what is on the ground so that you can visualize the whole that cannot be seen when you are standing in one spot. How hard it is, and how odd, that we rarely get to see the map of our own lives, with all its contours and significant markers, places of interest and less significant landscapes. Only, maybe at the end of our lives, as with David in the reading from 2 Samuel, do we get to see the bigger picture: the journey of our earthly lives and how it starts and concludes. Maybe at a funeral that is what we try to do: to set out the map of a person's life, and to highlight its particular features, oddities and joys.

The divine perspective

As someone involved in the ministry of spiritual direction, a not uncommon invitation is to invite an individual to ask for the grace to see things through God's eyes. This time of the liturgical year as the Church celebrates Christ's ascension into heaven, this is a time when we focus on his reign in heaven and his authority over all. After walking the earth as a human being, particularity gives way to generality, and Christ reigns over everything. Instead of standing in one place on the map, he sees (and reigns over) the whole thing. The reading from Ephesians we are given today is in the form of a thanksgiving prayer, which stretches our imagination with the most glorious images. Words are hurled about, such as 'immeasurable' and 'far above', but the ones my attention was drawn to are, 'who fills all in all'.

The whole

We live in a world where modern communication makes the news very immediate. We hear of things very quickly. There is often little time to process what we are being told. It can be really hard to put things into context, to know the whole story about something. We have perhaps lost some of the wisdom of waiting on God and listening. Today's readings remind us of the bigger picture, of the whole sweep of time and eternity. That there is a bigger map than just the journey of our lives and the lives of those around us. Every so often, if we are given the precious grace, God gives us the bigger picture, the larger perspective, his view on the world and the universe. It seems that special grace is here today in holy Scripture, as the writer of the letter to the Ephesians shares with us a vision of the heavenly realms, and of a God whom one day we shall come to know as 'all in all'.

Jonathan Lawson

Hymn suggestions

How shall I sing that majesty; God is working his purpose out; Immortal, invisible, God only wise; Majesty, worship his majesty.

Day of Pentecost (Whit Sunday)   28 May
Principal Service   **Come Out of Hiding!**

Acts 2.1–21 (*must be used as either the first or second reading*), *or* Num. 11.24–30; Ps. 104.26–36, 37b [*or* 104.26–end]; 1 Cor. 12.3b–13; **John 20.19–23**, *or* John 7.37–39

On this day of Pentecost, we have two accounts of the outpouring of God's Holy Spirit upon the disciples. Two different accounts indicating that God works in many ways, and the Spirit can be experienced differently at different times. On both occasions the disciples are scared, hidden away, fearful behind locked doors, watching and waiting.

Called from behind closed doors

In Acts, despite witnessing the resurrection and ascension of Jesus, the disciples were not confident about what to do next. God's Spirit comes upon them very dramatically. Luke struggles to describe the scene. It's like a violent wind. It's like tongues of fire. All receive the ability to speak in other languages. These disciples – whose local accents were laughed at – are now able to communicate with people from every part of the Roman Empire. God's Spirit empowers and liberates ordinary people.

In John's Gospel, it's the day of resurrection. Again, the disciples are in hiding – deeply bereaved, confused and frightened. Again, the outpouring of the Spirit is dramatic but in a very different way. The risen Christ appears in the room bringing peace, hope, comfort and support – the things that grieving people need. Jesus breathes the Holy Spirit into the disciples. The breath of God is a very important image in the Jewish tradition. God breathes life into Adam, God breathes life into the valley of dry bones in Ezekiel – so that the house of Israel is restored and renewed. Here is God in Jesus breathing the Holy Spirit who empowers and liberates. Freed from the power of death, the disciples are raised to new and confident ways of living.

In both cases, those filled with God's presence and power are called out of hiding – out of cosiness and introspection – out into the world, to be witnesses to the love and goodness of God.

The example of Peter

Peter is a great example of this. Peter was always getting it wrong, getting confused. Peter denied Jesus and ran away. Here he is on the Day of Pentecost addressing thousands of people, making clever theological connections with the Hebrew Scriptures, witnessing in such a way that 3,000 people are converted. It was a very courageous act – it's not that long since Jesus was crucified and there were plenty of people in Jerusalem out to get Jesus' followers.

Peter, by the power of the Spirit, is entering into who he is truly called to be. Jesus saw the potential in Peter and that potential is enhanced and realized through the Holy Spirit. Peter is on his way to being a true witness to Christ. The power of God helps him lead people into the truth of Jesus.

And us?

What's the good news for us on this Day of Pentecost? First, God the Holy Spirit comes to us in different ways. We may have dramatic experiences of God. The Holy Spirit can be like a mighty wind and flames of fire. But God the Holy Spirit is also the Comforter, the Counsellor, the Advocate – who brings peace and reconciliation. So, our experience of the Holy Spirit may be quiet, a deep-down affirmation and consolation.

The gift of the Holy Spirit was given at our baptism and we grow more and more into that gift as we grow deeper into God throughout our lives. The Holy Spirit enhances our God-given potential both as individuals and as community. The Spirit helps us to be all that we can be and often takes us to new places within ourselves, our church and our community. We may need to learn to accept our worth, we may need to take on new tasks that stretch us, we may need to give more time to a relationship.

Where the Spirit is at work, we would expect to see boundaries being broken down, prejudices challenged, fears and anxieties overcome. Those fully committed to the journey of 'becoming' never give up on the process of growing deeper into God. People who are passionate about unity, about building bridges and working for reconciliation. Where the Spirit of God is at work the Church doesn't stand still, isn't content with being cosy – is willing to take risks and is outward-looking.

Being sent

The gift of the Holy Spirit for each of us is given ultimately so that we can be sent out as the Father sent Jesus. Sent out to witness to Christ at work in the world wherever we find ourselves. We don't always do that best with words. Often our day-to-day living among others makes people wonder about God. But we do have to be ready when the time is right to give an account of the hope that is in us.

Respond to the Holy Spirit at work in you. Do something risky for God. Do something to bring reconciliation or healing. Be God's person in God's world. Let God empower and liberate you. Let God work in you so others may be empowered and liberated too.

This Pentecost, come out of hiding to share the amazing love of God – far and wide.

Catherine Williams

Hymn suggestions

Holy Spirit, gift bestower; Spirit of God, unseen as the wind; Come, Holy Ghost, our souls inspire; Come down, O love divine.

Day of Pentecost (Whit Sunday)   28 May
Second Service   **All Change**
Morning Ps. 87; Evening Ps. 67, 133; Joel 2.21–end;
Acts 2.14–21 [22–38]; *Gospel at Holy Communion*:
Luke 24.44–end

It is now some 60 years since Martin Luther King delivered his famous speech in which he dreamed a dream: one day, little black girls and boys would join hands with little white girls and boys, and former slaves and former slave-owners would sit down together. Inspired by the visions of the Hebrew prophets, King's daring words denounced injustices and pointed to a world lived more in tune with God's purposes.

All together

Knowing the impact that King's speech had on his audience perhaps helps us understand something of the power that Peter's words must have had on his listeners in Jerusalem. The gift of the Spirit has fired Peter's vision and turned him into a powerful speaker. Something new is happening, he declares. This is God's new day. God has acted in Jesus the Messiah and established the end times promised by the Hebrew prophets.

Peter is addressing a huge number of fellow Jews gathered together in Jerusalem. Coming from as far away as Rome and North Africa, they represent different cultures and customs. While the vast Roman Empire sought to draw nations together by using military force and political strategy to subdue them, Peter announces that ultimate power to unite comes from on high, from the God of love made known in Christ.

All prophets

God's Spirit is dramatically and devastatingly inclusive. Quoting words from the prophet Joel, Peter affirms that God's Spirit has been gifted not just to the elite, but to each and every one. Joel's apocalyptic vision of the Day of the Lord had described the shatteringly extraordinary way in which, in the last days, God's Spirit would be poured out upon all humankind regardless of gender, age or social position. Joel's prophecy has now been fulfilled, declares Peter. The proof is that the Holy Spirit has been poured out upon the likes of the followers of Jesus – a motley crew if ever there was one!

It is often thought that in writing the Acts of the Apostles, Luke was attempting to tell the Church's story in a manner that was acceptable to Roman power. Yet there are undeniable ways in which Joel's words, spoken by Peter, necessarily have fresh resonance for those who live as subjects of the Roman Empire. This was a patriarchal world in which wealthy and powerful men held sway. Against this background, Peter declares that God's Spirit has been lavished upon both men and women, rich and poor alike. In God's purposes, the way of the world is not to be decided by the richest people with the loudest voices, nor is the power to speak God's words to be reserved to priests alone. How might our world be different if richer nations were to listen to the voices of poorer nations as much as the other way round? Or if we were to pay more attention to the inspired dreams of artists, actors and musicians? Peter's words challenge us to change our mindset and listen for inspiration in the voices of others, regardless of their gender, ethnicity, background or social status.

All servants

Such inclusivity implies not the power of some over others but the servanthood of all. Joel's vision foretold the way God's Spirit would be poured out even upon slaves: the most powerless of all. Peter, however, now understands the slaves or servants of Joel's prophecy to refer to all those, male and female, who serve God and follow Jesus. In the new community brought into being by the gift of the Holy Spirit, the duty of serving will not, as in a patriarchal household, be expected solely of women and slaves: all will be called to be servants of God, living in obedience to God and mutual submission one to another.

All invited

This new community established by the gift of the Holy Spirit is open to all, just as God's salvation is offered to all. Continuing to cite Joel, Peter declares that everyone who calls on the name of the Lord will be saved. This again has powerful resonance for his listeners. The Roman Empire required the nations it subjugated to acknowledge Caesar as Lord. Peter, however, unambiguously refers here to the divine Lord. Those who call on *this* name will not be oppressed but saved. God offers blessing and belonging, forgiveness and reconciliation. Although at this stage Peter is addressing his fellow Jews, his open invitation to 'everyone' already points to the moment when Gentiles – those who are not Jews – will be welcomed into the Church.

All of us

This scripture offers no invitation to apathetic acceptance of the way things are. If God's Spirit has indeed been poured out on young and old alike, that includes each of us. Yes – you and me! How does Joel's inclusive prophecy challenge you? What dream would you share if you found yourself in front of a crowd? What's your vision for our church or our town? For your workplace or home? Pentecost makes each of us a dreamer for God. Let's not leave the dreaming to others.

Mary Cotes

Hymn suggestions

Let us build a house; Breathe on me, breath of God; We are called to be God's people; Enemy of apathy.

Ordinary Time

Trinity Sunday 4 June
Principal Service **The Mind of the Maker**
Isa. 40.12–17, 27–end; Ps. 8; 2 Cor. 13.11–end;
Matt. 28.16–end

What captures the imagination?

It's an interesting expression, isn't it – to think of your imagination being captured, or caught. The experience when some idea, or passion, or image sparks a response in our minds, engaging our heart, mind and soul. Good art – music, painting, literature, poetry – does this: we are absorbed and taken out of ourselves.

Our imaginations can be captured in unhealthy ways, by stuff that stirs fear and despair, depression and mental health problems. Think of advertising that tells us that we're worth it – that our lives will be transformed by shampoo. Or some computer games that lock us into obsession, dark places of cruelty and barbarity. Of relationships that control through emotional manipulation, such that we imagine ourselves much less than we are, unable to resist the bullying of someone who dominates us. Or cult religion, where ideological forces hold us trapped. There are any number of ways, today, where our imagination can be captured, with destructive and devastating impact. The 'Selfie' becomes a nightmare of narcissistic addiction. Or the false ecstasy of drugs takes over our minds.

Instead, we can turn to poetry, the landscape and seascape, music – by a combination of many things – classical and contemporary compositions or art that offer resonances, a conversation, down the centuries, as a modern composer captures the spirit of Bach or Handel and reinterprets it to another time, another place. Taking the canon of the best that has been thought and said, and re-presenting it, so the imagination expands with something new. To help us grow in moral and emotional knowledge, to recognize and articulate a more sophisticated range of emotions and make judgements that mean we live life more abundantly. 'They shall mount up with wings like eagles, they shall run and not be weary, they shall walk and not faint,' says Isaiah. With our imaginations captured, we soar like eagles, we run, we are energized, we live life to the full.

'Elitist'?

This is not elitist, but it is to recognize that today's society is expanded by a wholehearted engagement with the musical and artistic heritage of the very many different cultures that come together to make a modern nation, so that those talented enough to become the composers, the artists, of the future, are better for having their imaginations captured, inspired, shaped by the rich feast of the past. The more richly and diversely we are formed, the more imaginative will be our contemporary offering. Alongside other religious and cultural traditions, the Christian heritage continues to have a profound impact, over centuries, on how we imagine, how we shape our experience, how we frame our morality and emotions. Without those varied repertoires, we are impoverished as a culture. It needs refreshing in every generation, a living tradition that continues to enrich human reality, in dialogue across the ages and across the difference of culture.

Creating, redeeming, sanctifying

Today is Trinity Sunday. God, who is experienced most richly as the Trinity, creating, redeeming, sanctifying. God the Creator who authors, who composes, who brings into being, *ex nihilo*, from nothing. Out of chaos comes order and pattern. Out of darkness, there is light. Out of non-being, being. Dorothy L. Sayers said we create as we share in the mind of the maker. Our imaginations then stretch into new realms when we contemplate God the Creator, for, says Isaiah, 'The LORD is the everlasting God, the Creator of the ends of the earth. He does not faint or grow weary; his understanding is unsearchable.'

God the Creator loves matter – created material that is hallowed by God's only begotten Son who becomes human like us. The incarnation is the greatest affirmation of material imaginable. With all its hard resistances, its pain and suffering, its greed and cruelty, God redeems this world through a love stronger than death. And it doesn't stop there. God sends his Holy Spirit to be with us: 'remember, I am with you always, to the end of the age.' The comforter, the advocate, the inspirer, the enthuser. The paraclete – the Holy Spirit who captures our imagination with a love that passes our understanding.

Imaginations captured by faith, love and hope

Today we affirm our belief in God: Creator, Redeemer, Sanctifier – Father, Son and Holy Spirit. God seeks to capture our imaginations by inspiring us with the stories of Jesus Christ, interpreted through the ages by musicians, artists, poets. Let us rejoice today in that glorious, profound, intriguing, challenging heritage that is ours, and give thanks to God for all the opportunities to create with imaginations captured, shaped and inspired by faith, love and hope.

Frances Ward

Hymn suggestions

Holy, Holy, Holy; I, the Lord of sea and sky; I bind unto myself today; Immortal, invisible, God only wise.

Trinity Sunday 4 June
Second Service   **A Change is Gonna Come**
Morning Ps. 86.8–13; Evening Ps. 93, 150; **Isa. 6.1–8**;
John 16.5–15

Awakening

In August 2018, a 15-year-old girl concerned by the lack of urgent action concerning environmental emergency decided to mobilize and organize her community and nation to take action in addressing what presented to her as the most urgent issue of our era. Greta Thunberg, the diminutive Swedish teenager, has since become a global force in the struggle to revert the effects of climate change, drawing and inspiring millions in her struggle.

Her commitment was birthed out of the realization that she lived in a society marred by inaction and a sense of apathy that was driving it to inevitable destruction. Her voice holds a prophetic quality that calls most of us to awaken to the need for urgent action in attending to our own practices and habits. Hers is a challenging prophetic message warning of impending doom if nothing is done.

In Isaiah, we encounter a kindred spirit to Greta. He too is called to a prophetic ministry birthed out of a similar realization of his own failings and that of his society. Long before Greta, Isaiah's eyes were open to the reality that the future was only guaranteed through a commitment to an introspective posture towards life, and humble openness to God. This awareness of inhabiting a broken world becomes the catalytic experience towards prophetic awakening and the opportunity of a life-altering encounter with God.

Dwelling

The mystics describe an awakened person as one who has nothing, desires nothing, worries about nothing and plans nothing. Such a person is closely attuned to the heart of God and agile in their ability to respond to God's call because they are grounded in worship, meditation, reflection and contemplation. That, in many ways, could be a series of qualities that define Isaiah.

Isaiah is found in the Temple, possibly trying to make sense of the demise of his King Uzziah whose act of rebellion had disqualified him from access to the place of God's presence. And in that place, perhaps lost in his wonderings, he is suddenly transported into an alternative reality that offers him a fresh understanding of himself, his people and of God. Usual Temple imagery takes on new significance and vividly conveys the sense of God's presence. The smoke from the incense burning on altars and running through the Temple, the flickering flames on lampstands, the singing of the Temple choir all convey a sense of divine immediacy.

From that place of contemplation, we are invited to discover that holiness is not a moral notion, neither is it a divine attribute. Instead, it is God's own nature. From that nature, we discover that the purpose of God is redemption. This is not of our doing but is the work of God's Spirit, healing and transforming. Divine pedagogy aims at leading to a place of understanding. Understanding, not as an aggregation of knowledge, but an invitation to relate, to connect from the deepest places of our persons.

Holy imagination

Hineni. Here I am. This is not merely about geolocation. Rather, it is a bold statement of intent, an indication of the location of Isaiah's heart and its orientation towards God's future. It's the response of Abraham to God when asked to offer Isaac in sacrifice; it's the response Eli instructs the child Samuel to give when God calls him in the middle of the night. By saying *Hineni,* Isaiah writes himself into a lineage of people of faith willing to yield totally to God's call and become the herald of a new world.

This world becomes possible and viable through imagination. Indeed, imagination has powered in no small way radical changes throughout history, fostering a collective narrative of a world none of us has lived in, but long for. In the words of Howard Thurman, the African American spiritual activist and mystic, imagination leads to the quality of relationship that enables each person to be 'alive to life'. Thurman invites us to experience and acknowledge the truth that God consents to meet us in the only sphere we can know, the sphere of bodies and birdsong, the laughter of children, the wondrous dance of quarks and infinite expansion, and the deep longings of the human heart. It is this world through which God manifests the generosity and presence of the Trinity, and it is in this world the Spirit waits to receive a total yielding, a throwing wide the gates of our total being.

This yielding is not performative utilitarianism. It is a letting go of our attachment to the world system and surrendering to the light: giving ourselves over to the light. It is a commitment to resist, better still denounce, the limits of the fractured world in which we are inducted. Therein we receive the freedom of who we are called to be, liberated from the tensions of our false selves.

Grounded and strengthened by the mysterious presence of our three-in-one God, as we learn to tune out the demands of this world, we can respond to God's call: 'Whom shall I send?' and heed it by saying, 'Hineni' – 'Here am I; send me!'

Lusa Nsenga Ngoy

Hymn suggestions

Come down, O love divine; Holy, Holy, Holy, Lord God Almighty; Worthy is the Lamb; I, the Lord of sea and sky.

First Sunday after Trinity (Proper 5)   11 June
(For Barnabas, see p. 316.)
Principal Service   **Everyone Laughed at Jesus**
(*Continuous*): Gen. 12.1–9; Ps. 33.1–12, *or* (*Related*):
Hos. 5.15—6.6; Ps. 50.7–15; Rom. 4.13–end;
Matt. 9.9–13, 18–26

Inappropriate laughter

There is a very odd phrase in the middle of this Gospel reading. We have heard the story of a woman whose life was so limited by her disease that she could barely move in a crowd, and of a father willing to risk everything because his daughter was near death, and indeed dies. Then we find these words: 'and everyone laughed at Jesus'.

This isn't the kind of laughter that so often patterns times of grief and loss, when we share memories and stories, and tears dry as we begin to smile and laugh. Relationships are founded on memories of good times and shared moments, so this kind of laughter amid loss is normal and expected. But not the kind that interrupts here. This is strange and awkward. These are professional people, hired to mourn. These are family and friends devastated by loss, and this is Jesus, a teacher and rabbi, a man who should at least be respected. Yet into the midst comes laughter. Awkward laughter happens for all kinds of reasons. Sometimes it's out of embarrassment, out of anxiety or fear, or mockery, born out of incredulity and disbelief.

The unclean woman

What is it about Jesus that makes them laugh? Maybe his behaviour has made him a figure of fun, maybe they have lost all respect for him as the stories and rumours circulated. Already people knew that Jesus was not always proper. We know, they knew, that he broke the Sabbath, touched lepers, had meals with tax-collectors, talked to prostitutes, and now he has been touched by an unclean woman. The gynaecological condition suffered by the woman has meant that she was permanently unclean and that everything and everyone she touches will also become unclean and need to be cleansed. Twelve years and no explanations. Even with all the wonders of twenty-first-century medicine, this can happen. Perhaps this woman had heard that Jesus moved among the unclean; perhaps she thought he already was unclean, and therefore touching him would be acceptable. So, she does. Not only does he notice, he publicly acknowledges what has happened. Jesus is not ashamed, not angry. He just knows someone needs help and healing.

The laughter of disbelief

Imagine the stories and rumours that have flown back to Jairus' home, this respected leader who has also risked everything. No wonder they are laughing as Jesus approaches and then says something outrageous, denying their purpose and their grief: she is not dead, but sleeping. Imagine the women swelling with indignation at this unclean man from the country, claiming to know something different from them. Imagine the men of the household, anger rising in them, as a stranger interferes, adding to the shame they already feel at the way their master, Jairus, is behaving. So, everyone laughed at Jesus. Maybe they laughed out of uncertainty and fear as to just what else this man might do. In the Narnia books, Lucy famously says of Aslan: 'You see, he's not a tame lion.' Jesus has shown himself to be unpredictable, and unpredictable people are dangerous. Just how far will this man go? For Jesus is more radical than anyone knows.

How far will Jesus go?

For, those who laughed did not understand that Jesus is prepared to go as far as he needs so that he can walk with those who suffer, stay with them through death, hold their hurt and pain, and transform it with his healing love. He will spend more time with the outcast and the unclean. He will spend time with women and children, with the mentally unstable and the unloved. He will go further than anyone wanted, as he takes on all the pain of the world and infuses it with hope, through his death and his resurrection to new life.

Jairus' daughter lives! A woman is healed – and two families begin a new life, because of Jesus' willingness to go further and keep on reaching into human lives, getting dirty, getting laughed at, getting hated. It doesn't make any difference how much people laugh at him, he is still at work healing, walking with us in our pain and griefs, strengthening us with his hope, inspiring us with unexpected joy. People will still laugh at the audacity of hope in the face of despair, in incredulity and in mockery. In our world today, Christ has no hands but ours, and just maybe we will need to be the ones who are willing to have crowds laughing at us as we move alongside the outcasts of our world, going further than we thought possible, as Jesus leads us on.

Sandra Millar

Hymn suggestions

Jesus, stand among us; Open our eyes, Lord; Blessed be your name; We cannot measure how you heal.

First Sunday after Trinity (Proper 5)   11 June
Second Service   **Jesus at the Margins**
Ps. [39] 41; 1 Sam. 18.1–16; **Luke 8.41–56**

Where Jesus stands

Jesus, it seems, stands with the powerful.

He stands with those who define sin, determine worship and dictate doctrine. He stands, it seems, with those who asked Christians newly arrived from the Caribbean as part of the Windrush generation not to come back to church because they frightened the parishioners.[9] He stands, it seems, with the privileged who speak on behalf of the working classes, rather than allowing them to speak for themselves. He stands, it seems, with those who reject women's ministry. He stands, it seems, with those who would exclude children from being full members of the Church. In today's reading, he stands, it seems, with those who use verses from Leviticus as a means of excluding others.

In today's gospel story, Jesus stands with Jairus, the synagogue ruler who has the authority to determine who is allowed into the synagogue for worship and who is not; who has the authority to banish from community anyone who does not fit in with its demands and prescriptions.

The law in Leviticus is clear: 'If a woman has a discharge of blood for many days ... she shall be unclean.' There can be no doubt, this woman is unclean and must bear the consequences. Jesus, it seems, stands with the powerful, and the law appears to be on their side.

Change starts among the ankles

It's sometimes said that real change starts at the grass roots. Greta Thunberg sat alone outside the Swedish parliament for many Friday afternoons before others began to join and a movement to raise climate consciousness globally was born. It took 11 years for Tarana Burke's #MeToo movement to gain influence. Real change starts at the grass roots – or, in this story, among the ankles of the crowd. For as Jesus stands alongside Jairus, an insignificant woman, shrinking from public view, definitely not 'one of us', reaches out to touch his cloak. In her desperation, she resists the status quo and seeks out Jesus.

He notices his power diminish in some way. Jesus does not hold on to power as so many do; he not only gives it freely, he allows it to be taken. Because he knows what has happened, Jesus searches for the one who has taken power from him. All eyes are surely on the powerful. What will Jairus do when he realizes who has stopped Jesus en route to healing his daughter? As the crowd watches, Jesus moves. No longer alongside the powerful, he stops and stoops for the powerless woman to tell her story.

The full story

This woman's story is important. It's told in three of four Gospels. In Luke, she tells Jesus, and the crowd, what had brought her to this point and why she reached out to touch him, her full story. I wonder whether Jesus prompted her narrative with questions like, 'How did you feel about that? How did you manage?' It's clear that he fully understood because his first recorded word to her is 'daughter'. In one word, he gives her an identity and a place in a family, the things she has been deprived of for so long.

As a ruler of the synagogue, perhaps Jairus had helped to determine that this woman was unclean. She was excluded from her community, maybe even to the extent of having to shout out that she was unclean in case others got too close. The law supported Jairus' decision. Yet Jesus ignored it. He stopped and listened, restored and raised up the least and the lone.

From the time the Roman Empire adopted Christianity as its religion, through our own history of Crusades and overseas missions, to today's efforts to impose our own views on others within our churches, Christians have too often assumed that when we are in power, Jesus stands with us. I wonder, however, as we see the numbers of assaults on gay couples, global majority people and women increase year on year, whether Jesus has moved. No longer alongside us, I wonder whether Jesus is among the persecuted, betrayed and broken. And whether that is where he wants his Church to be too.

There is a corollary to the story, of course. Jesus spending time with the woman did not mean he had no time for the powerful. He did go with Jairus. He had power enough to restore his dead daughter. I wonder whether the Church too might be restored if we were to pay attention first to the marginalized.

Liz Shercliff

Hymn suggestions

Beauty for brokenness; The kingdom of God is justice and joy; Longing for light, we wait in darkness; Make me a channel of your peace.

Second Sunday after Trinity (Proper 6)   18 June
Principal Service   **God's Treasured Possession**
(*Continuous*): Gen. 18.1–15 [21.1–7]; Ps. 116.1, 10–17
[*or* 116.9–17]; *or* (*Related*): Ex. 19.2–8a; Ps. 100; Rom. 5.1–8;
Matt. 9.35—10.8 [9–23]

What's your most treasured possession? If you were burgled or your house caught fire, what would you try to save? When it comes to the crunch, for many of us the most treasured possession wouldn't be a possession at all – but more likely a person, or group of people. For the majority of us, our relationships are more valuable than the things we own. On this Father's Day, I hope there are dads throughout the country who know they are treasured by their children and partners. We are much more likely to run into a burning building risking life and limb to rescue a loved one than an item, however valuable.

Loved by God

In the reading from Exodus, the Israelites have reached Mount Sinai. God has rescued them from Egyptian oppression in dramatic fashion beautifully expressed: 'I bore you on eagles' wings and brought you to myself.' God and the people are linked by the covenant, a promise founded on mutual love. The people of Israel are God's treasured possession.

That love is experienced as growing and developing down the centuries and we see it most clearly in Jesus Christ, God for us – prepared to die for all. The power of that love breaks down every barrier – even death. St Paul can write to the Romans that through the resurrection all peoples, both Jew and Gentile, are now God's treasured possession – those whom God chooses to rescue for eternity.

Loved by Jesus

In the Gospel, Jesus looks at the people and is filled with compassion. They are like lost sheep, going round in circles, lacking guidance and direction. He remarks that the harvest is plentiful but the labourers are few. There are far more people needing rescue than rescuers. Jesus appoints 12 apostles to help him in leadership. He appoints them by name. They are individuals, unique, from different places and trades. Their task is to bring to God those who are harassed and helpless.

Their first task is to go to the Israelites who've got lost along the way. They are to proclaim the good news – to tell the story of God's love. The kingdom is near. The apostles demonstrate that by curing the sick, raising the dead, cleansing lepers and casting out demons – all biblical signs that God is at work. They go to the Israelites first but with the coming of the Holy Spirit at Pentecost the mission field opens up and all peoples are included in God's rescue plan.

Called to be disciples

We too are God's treasured possession. But not just us – all people everywhere are loved and treasured by God. Sadly, many in our communities are going round in circles and need to be rescued – to hear God's love for them. Jesus calls and appoints each of us – just as he called the first disciples. He calls us by name through our baptism. Calls us to go and tell people the good news of God, to demonstrate to them by godly acts that the kingdom is near. We probably won't be raising the dead – at least not physically, but many are spiritually dead and we can bring them to a new understanding of living life in all its fullness. God still shows himself to our generation in startling ways – in acts of grace, generosity of giving, unexpected forgiveness, fresh starts, acceptance, welcome and hospitality.

Making a difference

You may think there's little you can do to make a difference but you'd be wrong. Helping people see that they are loved and treasured makes a whole world of difference. I heard a story recently of a handyman working for a company. Each job he does has a set time – so long to change a washer, so long to unblock a loo, so long to mend a window. When he'd been working there for a few weeks he went to his boss and asked why no time was allocated for interacting with the person whose house or flat he was in. He said he was often doing jobs for elderly or vulnerable people and he needed time to introduce himself, set their minds at ease and have a chat. He might be the only person they'd see that week. The boss listened and eventually agreed that he could have 20 minutes extra in each property to talk to the clients. It worked so well that the system was changed – and became more human. That's a really good example of being an agent of hope, a disciple of good news – someone who can bring in the kingdom of God by an ordinary, sensitive, thoughtful act, which makes a real difference to everyone. Carrying hope that does not disappoint.

We are disciples – each called by name. And it's our calling and joy to work with Jesus to gather in God's harvest of souls. We each carry the message of hope – that all are God's treasured possessions, loved beyond measure. Who will you tell today?

Catherine Williams

Hymn suggestions

You shall go out with joy; Build your kingdom here; I, the Lord of sea and sky; Go forth and tell.

Second Sunday after Trinity (Proper 6)   18 June
Second Service   **With Me or Against Me?**
Ps. [42] 43; 1 Sam. 21.1–15; **Luke 11.14–28**

Similar, but different

If you read through the Gospel of Luke and reach the words of
Jesus in this passage, 'Whoever is not with me is against me', they
might seem familiar. Just two chapters before our reading from
Luke, Jesus says something very similar – similar, but actually
very different. In Luke 9, Jesus says to his disciples, 'Whoever is
not against you is for you.' But in this reading, what Jesus says is
reversed: 'Whoever is not with me is against me.'

Let's reflect on those two statements for a moment. The first,
'Whoever is not against you is for you', feels the more open of the
two. If we're not in opposition to each other, then we can bump
along together fine, without getting in each other's way. 'Whoever
is not against you is for you' leaves room for sitting on the fence
– Jesus is suggesting that anyone not opposed to the disciples, and
therefore his teaching that they share, is implicitly an ally – they will
not resist the spreading of the gospel, so they are not an opponent
of the gospel.

That is not the case in this reading. 'Whoever is not with me is
against me' leaves no room for apathy. If you are not actively on
the side of Christ, you're on the other side. So, what has changed in
the space of two chapters to turn those fence-sitters from friends to
enemies? Immediately after Jesus says 'Whoever is not against you
is for you', in the very next verse, we read, 'When the days drew
near for him to be taken up, he set his face to go to Jerusalem.' Jesus
embarks on his final journey to Jerusalem where he will die.

No room for apathy

This brings a change of focus, a change of tone. Jesus is no longer
someone who is tolerated by the authorities, but a wanted man.
And in that context, 'Whoever is not with me is against me' makes
more sense. The cross is the locus of a cosmic battle between good
and evil, between love and hate. What we see there on a human
level resounds at a spiritual level throughout and beyond the world,
and the ripples of that play out still. There are times when we feel
those ripples – when evil and despair and horror feel like they
might overwhelm us. Those are the times when there is no room

for apathy when those who choose no side are not somehow by default on the side of good, not on the side of hope, not on the side of peace or love.

Are we complicit?

It's easy to be appalled and horrified by atrocities, disasters and injustices in the world. But if we do nothing about the systemic injustices that make them happen, we're actually complicit with that injustice. That could be the kind of corporate cost-saving corner-cutting that leads to something like the Grenfell Tower disaster, the global inequity between those who emit the most CO_2 and those whose lives are most impacted by the effects of climate change, or government policies that allow the rich to get richer and the poor to become more deeply entrenched in poverty. If we are appalled by the consequences but do nothing to address the causes, we are complicit – 'Whoever is not with me is against me.'

Uniting on the side of Christ

But there are always signs of hope where people come together to bring about change, where differences are laid aside and people are united in compassion to work for justice. This is what Jesus is talking about when he says, 'every kingdom divided against itself becomes a desert, and house falls on house' – if we can't work together, we will achieve very little. As Christians, we have a distinctive calling and voice in the world. But that doesn't mean we can't be united with others on the side of Christ. Evil is real. And if no one stands up to evil, it gains power. Every stand taken against evil, however small, whoever makes it, is a step towards the coming of God's kingdom. Very often, even if we do not believe exactly the same thing, even if we do not share a culture or a language or a faith, we can choose the path of hope and goodness and life, honouring every human being, and walking together with others who choose to act against evil. If we choose that path and walk on it, then we are united and we are on the side of Christ.

Kat Campion-Spall

Hymn suggestions

Enemy of apathy; Be thou my vision; There's a spirit in the air; Take my life and let it be.

Third Sunday after Trinity (Proper 7)   25 June

Principal Service   **Disturbing the Comfortable and Comforting the Disturbed**

(*Continuous*): Gen. 21.8–21; Ps. 86.1–10, 16–end [*or* 86.1–10];
or (*Related*): Jer. 20.7–13; Ps. 69.8–11 [12–17] 18–20
[*or* 69.14–20]; Rom. 6.1b–11; **Matt. 10.24–39**

Comfort and disturbance: essential for growth

For those of us who know our fickle failings in discipleship and long for deeper relationship with God, the Gospel passage both disturbs and comforts – and the Church needs to experience both movements of God.

Where we have become lazy, disengaged, playing at religion like Sunday golf club members, the words of Jesus come with disturbing force. Where we have become fearful and felt small and helpless before powers that ridicule faith, mock belief and actively persecute, Jesus' words come with comfort, encouragement and strength. We need to experience the full force of both aspects of Jesus' teaching. We need to be disturbed and we need to know comfort.

The spiritual life is a journey. Sometimes we might especially need to experience the divine soothing of being reminded that God knows the numbers of hairs on our heads and cares for us deeply. God is the One who holds life and death in his hands and is more powerful than every human agency that might do us harm – bigger than bullies, abusers, terrorists – who are all subject to death, whereas God is the God of life, who brings life to his faithful people. Nothing can ultimately overcome this, not even death. When we feel defeated and afraid, bruised and broken, we need to be reminded of this bigger picture. We need to be comforted by the God who loves us tenderly.

A divine kick up the backside is a heavenly gift

But there is more to the passage; these are disturbing words and, as much as we might want to resist, we need disturbing. A divine kick up the backside is a heavenly gift. We can become too at ease, making faith into a get-out-of-jail-free card, cheapening grace, softening the radical call of God. We do it out of fear. We do it out of that very human desire for an easy life. But if we desire God then this life of ease will never be enough. It is dissatisfying. Like gulping down salt water when you are dying of thirst. The deep desire for God, given by God, calls for a reordering of priorities – it opens us to discomfort because we realize that anything less than God is just not enough. We need to be disturbed. It's a divine gift.

There *will* be trouble ahead

Jesus warns that if we identify with him then we can expect trouble. 'They called me Beelzebub – what do you think they will call you?' Jesus expects his disciples to speak aloud what we know of him. Are we willing to speak openly about what we have learned through prayer and worship, study and experience about the nature of God? Or are we ducking down into a privatized, cosy little faith? Jesus warns of persecution – and while we know that thousands of believers the world over are persecuted for their faith, do we consider persecution part of our discipleship? That's a disturbing thought for many of us.

Jesus' words about family division are especially disturbing, reminding us that all our relationships and commitments need to be ranked behind commitment to God – such that when conflicts occur, which they will, there is no doubt where our loyalty lies. Jesus' teaching cuts across our spiritual laziness and ease and calls us deeper into the life of faith, trust, risk and hope.

Now what?

I read this passage and feel convicted that my life of faith is too little, too fearful, too hesitant, a shrunken version of what it could be. The spiritual danger here is the fall into despair, which is paralysing. Too much discomfort and many of us freeze, gripped by the monster of our own inadequacy. We need to know God's reassurance. Yet, too much comfort and we rest at ease and grow spiritually flabby and undernourished.

We need to run to the God who knows the number of hairs on our heads as well as she knows our multiple failings. Come running to God in search of the strength to speak up, the courage to bear up, the willingness to grow up into the stature and maturity God desires for us.

In this way, disturbance leads us back to God and opens us to new possibilities. Comfort keeps us from despair and opens up the doorway to deeper trust, firmer faith and a renewed willingness to walk with Jesus on his way.

Today's reading weaves together warning and encouragement, and we need both elements. It calls us to re-evaluate our priorities, and reset the compass course of our lives. What will I live for? What matters most to me? Jesus disturbs our self-satisfaction and comforts our despair. This way is the path to life in all its fulness.

Kate Bruce

Hymn suggestions

I surrender all; Forth in thy name, O Lord, I go; Take my life and let it be; Jesus be the centre.

Third Sunday after Trinity (Proper 7)   25 June
Second Service   **Have You Been Invited?**
Ps. 46 [48]; 1 Sam. 24.1–17; **Luke 14.12–24**

Who is allowed in?

In a former parish where I served, I was asked by a lovely guy who had become a friend: 'Am I allowed to come to your church?' Anyone who knows me well understands that I very much dislike any idea that a church is mine, as it is of course God's church; but the whole tenor of the question deeply upset me. How does someone get the idea that a church is not for them, or that they might not be welcome? What kind of message have they received and where did it come from?

Exclusivity

Another friend of mine when he was a vicar in London showed me around the church that he served at the time. The church building itself had had a chequered history and could easily have closed at some point. It now had a new roof, which had somewhat saved the day, but the inside was pretty tatty, with bare and decaying plaster, and the lighting was fairly ropey and makeshift. We talked about it, and he said that he rather liked it, because he felt that no one would feel that they couldn't come in and feel welcome there. That story has stayed with me. There are lots of subtle barriers that prevent people from coming to church, and one of those can be that the church gives an air of being so grand and ornate that only people of a certain background and status feel that they can enter. Having said that, even grand palaces can be welcoming! How a church makes itself welcoming and gives a genuine sense of that is, I would suggest, worth pondering.

Party people

Jesus seems to like a party. I hope that is not a shock to anyone. His first miracle in John's Gospel is at a wedding celebration, and he helps the festivities along by providing vast quantities of wine. A lot of the stories he tells, like the one in today's Gospel reading are about celebrations. Today's parable is pretty radical, in line with most of Jesus' teaching. In today's story, Jesus makes explicit that the invitation goes to the uninvited – precisely those people who are never included on the guest list. The story of the martyrdom of St Lawrence tells us that when he was told to bring forth the treasures of the church which were in his care, instead of bringing out gold and silver as his persecutors had expected, he brought to them the poor: the true treasures of God's Church. Christ is quite clear: that his kingdom and his invitation is to the uninvited, the excluded, the marginalized.

All are welcome

The idea that churches are a place where all are welcome seems a lovely idea, but how is it worked out in practice? Do we really mean it? What has to be in place to help people feel welcome? To be welcomed takes more than just a greeting of 'Welcome', although that helps. I guess it also takes a disposition and a sensitivity to what might exclude people. A very simple thing can be our use of words. Early on in my ministry in Heaton in Newcastle, a parishioner very thoughtfully and kindly challenged what the notice sheet said at church: 'You are very welcome to join *us* for tea and coffee after the service.' As she pointed out, this created a sense of 'us' and 'them', rather than all being equal and welcome. Ever since then I have become very aware of avoiding the 'us' word whenever possible in church life and public notices.

Strangers

As children, we are taught not to talk to 'strangers', and thus potentially starts a lifelong distrust of those we don't know. But Jesus' kingdom is full of those that no one wants to know, except him. His radical sense of love and acceptance of the unacceptable clearly upsets many, particularly the religious people of his day. It is outrageous behaviour. However, there is a deeply spiritual side to this too. For if God is the mystery we believe him to be, then he will often be surprising, both in his reality and in his actions. People of faith are called to be open to a God who regularly astonishes and challenges us, and pulls us away from our expected tasks into unexpected places. As such, we are called by Jesus to welcome the stranger as if they are Jesus himself, and to love our enemies. This may also involve us loving the enemy within – the strange parts of ourselves that we hide so effectively from others, but beg by the roadside of our lives to be invited in, accepted and loved. What then? Perhaps it's only then that the party can really begin.

Jonathan Lawson

Hymn suggestions

Let us build a house; O Lord, all the world belongs to you; Beauty for brokenness; When I needed a neighbour.

Fourth Sunday after Trinity (Proper 8)   2 July
Principal Service   **Passing the Test**
(*Continuous*): **Gen. 22.1–14**; Ps. 13; *or* (*Related*):
Jer. 28.5–9; Ps. 89.1–4, 15–18 [*or* 89.8–18]; Rom. 6.12–end;
Matt. 10.40–end

It's a part of life, surely everyone has had an experience of being tested. Perhaps you recall sitting examinations at school or college; maybe on hearing the word 'test', you immediately remembered your driving test. Some among us may be awaiting the outcome of medical tests. Hence, the word 'test' can conjure up all manner of recollections and emotions. I think most of us would agree that being tested can be a stressful experience.

Today's narrative tells how Abraham was tested by God. It's a compact, succinct story, the last major episode in the Abraham cycle, whose meanings have been interpreted in a variety of different ways. Perhaps it gives glimpses of the era of the patriarchs (around 1800 BC). Though it tells of Abraham, maybe it reveals the faith understandings of those who put the story in its current form (from traditions that were collated in the time of King David and revised during the exile).

Within the story words about *testing*, *obedience* and the *fear of God* recur: are those its themes?

Does the story explain why the Israelites didn't practise child sacrifice (though their neighbours probably did)? Was it crafted to say why a place had been named Jehovah Jireh (the Lord will provide)? In the tradition, the place of near-sacrifice came to be identified with the Temple Mount in Jerusalem, so this story became that of the founding of that holiest of places.

Picture this ...

One way of trying to understand a story is to decide how to depict it in a single picture. To the Cloth Guild of Florence, one scene stood out. They chose it in 1401 as the competition panel piece for those who sought their commission to cast new bronze doors for the baptistery of the cathedral.

Two panels (of the seven original entries) survive to this day. Following the competition rules, both depictions are the same size as each other. Both competitors focus on a point fraught with drama. When Abraham lifts his knife to slay Isaac, suddenly the angel intervenes. Brunelleschi's angel actually reaches out and grasps Abraham's arm to push his hand away. By contrast, Ghiberti's entry, though depicting the same scene, seems restrained. His foreshortened, understated angel presumably commands by word, not gesture. Drawing the eye is the classically beautiful form of the kneeling Isaac, the calm figure amid the storm.

This dramatic pivotal point is crucial to our understanding of the story. Abraham is being horribly tested: how can he sacrifice his son, the son on whom the promise depends, his only son says the text (for the illegitimate one has been cast out in the previous episode). Is Abraham to give up his hopes for all that God promised, all that he has committed his life to since he answered God's call and left Haran?

Our modern culture cannot comprehend a society that would regard children as expendable. Let's accept that child exposure and child sacrifice (to appease the gods) were not unknown in

Abraham's age. We need to set aside our modern sensibilities to find the meaning of the text for us, while our theology struggles to accept that God would demand such a price.

Abraham knew that all things came from God: he did not question God's right to ask for anything to be returned to him. One who fears God will keep his commandments.

Testing, obedience and the God-fearing

Abraham passes his test with flying colours. He proves his total obedience to God's will; irrespective of what the personal cost of obedience might be. The angel proclaims that now he knows that Abraham is God-fearing. 'Fear of God' is not the same as being afraid (though we might say that God frightens us in this story). Abraham so reveres God that he must demonstrate his faith in extravagant action.

Because of Abraham's obedience, the sacrificial ram is provided by God. Abraham names the place 'God provides', or it may be translated, 'The Lord will see to it'. Certainly, Abraham 'sees' an assurance of God's future intentions, as the angel calls for a second time from heaven and reiterates God's covenant promises.

Abraham learns the cost of obedience. Isaac, though not slaughtered, was given up to God. Perhaps the father–son relationship was irrevocably altered by the events of this story. They separate: Abraham returns to Beersheba but Isaac is next heard of in Beer-lahai-roi.

Abraham was asked by God to undertake something extraordinary, something we struggle to understand or make sense of. How do we react when God asks challenging or demanding things of us? Will we take risks for our God? What does obedience mean for us? Do we have the faith of Abraham? Would we pass the test?

Wendy Kilworth-Mason

Hymn suggestions

The God of Abraham, praise; Deep in the shadows of the past; O for a heart to praise my God; How great thou art.

Fourth Sunday after Trinity (Proper 8) 2 July
Second Service **Saul's Dark Night**
Ps. 50 [*or* 50.1–15]; **1 Sam. 28.3–19**; Luke 17.20–end

Saul and his shadow

Meet King Saul, selected by Samuel to be the first king of Israel. He is head and shoulders above everybody else. But it doesn't go well. Jung, the psychologist, said that 'The taller the person, the longer the shadow'. From the outset, Saul is plagued with depression and anger. The rise of David, the one who will succeed him, only intensifies the fault lines of Saul's character.

Most lectionary passages have some sense of hope or redemption. The whole Bible is, after all, grounded in the mercy and love of God. But this story seems without hope. Saul here encounters the darkness of his own shadow.

It may be good, occasionally, to stay with such darkness. It's all too easy to slip into an easy belief that there are always happy endings, that everything can be fixed.

Every one of us has a shadow side: things about ourselves that we are ashamed of, that we deny even to ourselves. And sometimes when we reach the end of our tether, and everything gets 'out of hand', aspects of ourselves come into the daylight that we did not want to be revealed.

It is telling that Saul has 'cut off the mediums and the wizards from the land'. Now, in his extremity, he turns to the very people he has denied. In our own times we look on with disbelief as televangelists, preachers of homophobic hatred, come to be discovered with rent boys. Even closer to home, it's so easy to preach the love of God and yet be found wanting in our own relationships. To talk about acceptance, even as we despise and belittle others.

Unanswered prayers

Saul turns to God but gets no answer. This is such a familiar feeling, isn't it? To pray, to plead with God – but have no sense whatsoever of an answer. Sometimes we pray and pray for someone to be healed, and then they die. What Saul doesn't realize and, I think, what we ourselves often forget, is that God is not there to give answers. God is not an oracle, a promise box or a slot machine to meet our needs. The God of love desires to relate to us in love, in a real relationship that does not depend on what happens around us. God is the source of questions – questions rather than answers.

If we bring ourselves before God with our whole selves – including our shadow side – we become open to the possibility of change. It has to be said that this is never easy. Even if we have a deep understanding of the love of God, we still have a natural tendency to draw back, to go our own way. We turn, too easily, to other sources of meaning, other places where we might find guidance, even if those places are destructive.

Saul gets no answer from God, but from the medium he gets more answers than he expected. Maybe she too gets more than she bargained for! In place of her usual smoke and mirrors, mysterious knockings or ectoplasm, it seems that Samuel shows up, grumpily disturbed from the sleep of death.

It's almost as if God says, 'You asked me for an answer – well, here's your answer!' Maybe we need to learn to live in that place where there are no answers, in uncertainty, in a kind of darkness – but to live in trust.

The question

Saul's only hope would be to live with the intolerable question. It's natural to look for answers, to see God as a kind of parental figure, an almighty fixer – and sometimes that seems to be true, particularly in the childhood of faith. But God is also the one whose love seeks out our presence – earnestly, relentlessly. God comes to us as ultimate question: 'Do you love me?'

Saul falls back, as we do, on things that have worked for him in the past. Samuel is someone who gave his life some meaning and mediated God for him. But even if Samuel appears from the other side of death, Samuel is not the answer. There is no answer to be found unless Saul begins to live with the questions, and these may be our questions too.

Living with uncertainty

Do I settle for the things that have worked for me in the past? How can I live with the experience of loss, the experience of extreme challenges to my own identity?

May God give us grace to live in uncertainty, in tension, in darkness and failure. May we hold on to hope in what is not seen, finding a place of ultimate trust in the goodness of God.

At the heart of our faith stands the one who hung on a cross, the darkest place of all, and said, 'My God, my God, why have you forsaken me?'

But by remaining there, and 'because of the joy that was set before him', he saved us all.

Andrew Rudd

Hymn suggestions

Dear Lord and Father of mankind; Lord Jesus, think on me; Who can sound the depths of sorrow; Within our darkest night (Taizé).

Fifth Sunday after Trinity (Proper 9)   9 July
Principal Service   **The Blame Game**
(*Continuous*): Gen. 24.34–38, 42–49, 58–end; Ps. 45.10–end, *or Canticle*: Song of Sol. 2.8–13; *or* (*Related*): Zech. 9.9–12; Ps. 145.8–15; Rom. 7.15–25a; **Matt. 11.16–19, 25–end**

She started it – no, he started it!

The blame game is so easy to get caught up in – it seems to be one of humanity's favourite pastimes. Those of you with children in your lives may well be regularly called in to referee between them and find each child insisting that it's all the other's fault. But even if you don't have children around, it's fairly common to spot this behaviour in adults too – we only need to look on social media threads or political life to see people blaming each other in a way that just seems to keep escalating.

This is what Jesus is picking up on at the start of our Gospel passage. In a game that moves back and forth between the boys leading a wedding dance and the girls a funeral march, something has gone awry, and now both groups are hurling blame across the marketplace: 'We played the flute for you, and you didn't dance!' 'Yeah, but we wailed, and you didn't mourn.' And so rather than playing happily together, the children are caught up in the back and forth of an argument, trying to blame each other for things falling apart.

It's not my fault!

The people Jesus is talking about didn't listen to John because his asceticism didn't please them; but when Jesus came celebrating life in all its fullness – well, that's not where they wanted to find God either. They're clearly not engaging with the teaching from God about the coming of the kingdom but, as far as they're concerned, that's not their fault. They're happier squabbling like children over the deficiencies of those around them than taking responsibility for their own behaviour.

This even, at first glance, seems to be what Paul is doing in this passage from Romans: 'For if I do what I do not want, it is no longer I that do it, but sin that dwells within me.' This might look like he's passing the buck, and refusing to take responsibility for his actions.

But there is more subtlety to what Paul is saying than may first be apparent. What seems so often to be at the root of human evil is misplaced desire. Desire for power, wealth, status, however that expresses itself, is usually really a desire to be loved, valued, to be wanted by the people around us. But that misplaced desire can lead us all too often in the wrong direction, to do the evil we do not really want. Jesus knows the burden of that inner struggle we all face. It's a burden we often try and relieve ourselves of by trying to convince ourselves that we're not at fault, someone else is to blame. We try and avoid confronting our failures by magnifying the failures of those around us. When things go really awry, we end up like the children in the marketplace, squabbling about how it's everyone else's fault and refusing to take responsibility – or, worse, uniting around a scapegoat and piling all the blame on them.

Lay down your burden

But Jesus says:

Come to me, all you that are weary and are carrying heavy burdens, and I will give you rest. Take my yoke upon you, and learn from me; for I am gentle and humble in heart, and you will find rest for your souls. For my yoke is easy, and my burden is light.

And this image of a yoke is extraordinary. A young ox would be yoked to a mature one who knew how to obey the driver's instruction; the young ox would be guided by its partner until it learnt to follow the will of its master or mistress. If we translate this image into following Jesus, it's not really following at all – it's going together, side by side, and being guided by him as we learn to discern and obey the will of the Father.

If we submit to this yoke, we will exchange our heavy burden for a light one. So, our burden of failure, of anxiety, of loneliness, of dissatisfaction; of feeling like we haven't achieved the power or wealth or belonging we desire, this is surrendered when we surrender our desire to choose our own path and follow our own way. On the path that Christ walks with us, we are taught that we are loved, that we do matter, that we are wanted and liked and precious. And as we take on the yoke of Christ, we pick up a different burden, one that is shared with Christ and all his people – the burden of the victim. By stepping out of the self-interested blame game, we have to be prepared to be the ones who are blamed, who are scapegoated, as Jesus was. We walk alongside the poor in spirit, the meek, the mourning, the peacemakers, the persecuted. The burden is not trivial. But it is not crushing, because it is carried by the blessed ones, and it is shared by the one who brings life out of death.

Kat Campion-Spall

Hymn suggestions

I heard the voice of Jesus say; Jesu, lover of my soul; Dear Lord and Father of mankind; When I needed a neighbour.

Fifth Sunday after Trinity   9 July
Second Service   **What We Don't See**
Ps. 56 [57]; 2 Sam. 2.1–11; 3.1; **Luke 18.31—19.10**

Short-sighted

Being short-sighted runs in our family, and I have needed the use of glasses from the age of seven. My great uncle Henry was similarly short-sighted, but like many of his generation, he was determined to serve king and country in the First World War. Such was his determination (and fear of failing the medical on the grounds of his diminished sight) that when he was being examined for the army medical, he learnt the eyesight chart off by heart, hoping and praying that it would be kept that way around for his sight test. It was, and he was recruited to serve in His Majesty's Armed Forces, and he went to fight for his country at the latter end of the First World War, writing about his experiences of the trenches later in life, which is why I know this story. I can see next to nothing without my glasses, a peculiarly vulnerable feeling when on the rare occasion I don't have my glasses to hand. It takes some courage, I would suggest, to go to war, particularly knowing that you might not be able to see if your glasses are broken or lost.

What we cannot see

I wonder if you have had that rather embarrassing experience in a shop where you have asked a member of staff for something that you cannot find, only to discover that it was right in front of you? There are things in life that in hindsight can seem so obvious, but at the time, for some reason or another, we could not see them. Today's Gospel reading seems to be about three types of not seeing – the first of which was something the disciples did not want to see.

'Group think'

We have been introduced in recent times to the idea that groups of people sometimes cannot see something because of 'group think': a form of knowing that precludes other world views. It seems very likely that the disciples understandably went with the messianic belief system of their day, which expected a new Davidic king who would rule Israel with mighty power and overthrow the Romans (the then occupying power). As a consequence, it seems the disciples cannot get their head around a man they have followed so faithfully these last three years talking about suffering, being mocked and finally being killed: and then being raised from the dead. They cannot see that happening. It is beyond their imaginations, and therefore beyond their sight and expectations. They can only see what they want to see.

Physical blindness

The story of the disciples is juxtaposed by Luke in the next part of the Gospel story by a man who cannot physically see anything. But he knows a great deal, as many that are blind do: he knows that this man can heal him. There is something that this blind man can see that others cannot, despite his visual impairment. His seeing that Jesus has this power, helps him to see again. His faith, that which sees within (the eyes of faith), brings him sight.

Climbing to get a better a view

Lastly, we come to Zacchaeus, that most hated of people of Jesus' day: a tax-collector – who did the occupying force's work of collecting money through taxation. He wants to see Jesus. He desires to see Jesus, and because of his short stature, he finds a good vantage point to get a better view. By doing so, he becomes far more conspicuous than he would have been in the crowd, and as a consequence he is seen by Jesus. Jesus, throughout Luke's Gospel, sees and calls those who traditionally were neglected by organized religion: the poor, women, sinners, outcasts. He sees them, engages with them, gives them a sense of value. When they are seen, acknowledged, drawn in, their lives change, as Zacchaeus demonstrates today. Seeing is not only believing but life-changing. Life-transforming.

Questions to ponder

Today's Gospel reading leaves us with some interesting questions to ponder. What can we not see because of our world view or group think? How do we broaden what we see? How do we get to see what we cannot see? The blind man reminds us that there are things that we can know and see, without always having seen them physically or having been taught them. I wonder what those things are? Zacchaeus reminds us that sometimes we need a different perspective to see the bigger picture and that meeting and knowing Jesus – being seen by him – creates the possibility of changing our lives for good. How has Jesus done that for you in your own life?

Jonathan Lawson

Hymn suggestions

Amazing grace; God's Spirit is in my heart; God is love, let heaven adore him; Thou, whose almighty word.

Sixth Sunday after Trinity (Proper 10)   16 July
Principal Service   **Turning the Soil**
(*Continuous*): Gen. 25.19–end; Ps. 119.105–112;
or (*Related*): Isa. 55.10–13; Ps. 65 [or 65.8–end]; Rom. 8.1–11;
Matt. 13.1–9, 18–23

The parable of the sower is such a well-known story that it's quite easy to glance over it without a second thought. But is it clear? Why would the sower purposely throw seeds on to the soil where they had little chance of thriving? Today's farmers use all sorts of technology from GPS to computer-controlled crop spraying to ensure they achieve the best results. Or, to put it another way, if the sower was a person in business their resource mismanagement would soon result in them getting the sack! So, what was Christ saying with this parable?

A simple farmer

Some in his audience were hoping for a Messiah who would not only rescue them from their exile and oppression but restore the fortunes of Israel to greatness beyond imagining. Yet here Jesus is talking about seedtime and harvest, about failure and success. These are not the words of a great and powerful leader but a simple farmer.

Christ was trying to turn assumptions upside down as well as challenging faith. He uses the ordinary to guide us into learning about his extraordinary plan about the kingdom of God and our place within it. The soil Christ is referring to is us. The second half of the reading from Matthew tells us that. But have you ever wondered how soil changes over time? The same crop planted in the same soil year by year will eventually become diseased and the yield will drop. The goodness of the soil will be used up if it's not refreshed. Or if rocks are not cleared away the soil may become stony, preventing roots from growing deep into the ground.

Different types of soil

Yet, how are we like the soil Christ talks about? Surely once we become followers of Christ, that's it, isn't it? We go to church regularly, join in all the activities and perhaps even volunteer to help out. Surely, we are the good soil?

Well, yes and maybe no! For, like soil, we change over time because life happens. Choices are made for good or for ill. Such decisions were the best we could do at the time but the impact upon our hearts is perhaps not so good, perhaps making them a little stonier or completely paved over. Maybe there was a time when finding out about Jesus and his ways was new and exhilarating. Yet now that thrill, that sense of first love, has diminished. The surety of faith has waned. The demands of the world, from work and family, the lure of 'have it now culture' darken and choke our imaginations. We all have barren times, and sometimes it's hard to remember the good. But it is during these difficult times that we must just keep going.

Turning the soil

Sometimes our spiritual lives need a change, a kick-start if you like, back into a refreshed, positive routine that deepens and nourishes our faith. So, Jesus reminds us that growth in faith requires good soil. And good soil doesn't just happen – it needs to be cultivated, fertilized and ploughed, crops need to be rotated and sometimes the soil needs to be left fallow to recover its goodness. How are we ensuring that the good soil of this parish laid down over hundreds of years is being attended to so that we can all flourish and produce good fruit – even up to a hundredfold?

Good soil will be produced when we turn or re-turn to Christ and put him first in our lives. When we allow the Holy Spirit dwelling in us to guide our minds, hearts and behaviours. Good soil will be laid down when we are faithful in prayer, and study of the Scriptures, when worship is the most important event of every week and every day. When justice and hospitality are high on our agenda, and when the most vulnerable in our communities are given worth and a place at the table. Every time that the Eucharist is celebrated in your church it is celebrated for everyone who lives in your parish – whether they come to church or not. What a privilege and responsibility and deep joy to do that for our people.

Success

The prophet Isaiah writes during the exile. God's people are battered, downtrodden and far from home. God says that his word sent to them will not return empty and his purposes will succeed. The prophet tells the people that they will leave Babylon in joy and return home to Jerusalem in peace – and the whole of creation will join in celebration together. He doesn't say it *might* happen; he says it *will* happen.

So, we all need to work together on that good soil – so that we may all flourish and grow in the love of God, filled to overflowing with the Holy Spirit and following and serving Christ faithfully, trusting that the rich harvest promised by God will come to fruition – here and beyond.

Paul Williams

Hymn suggestions

Lord, for the years; O for a thousand tongues; To God be the glory; Seed, scattered and sown.

Sixth Sunday after Trinity (Proper 10) 16 July
Second Service **Ending in Peace**
Ps. 60 [63]; 2 Sam. 7.18–end; Luke 19.41—20.8

Victory and defeat

Defeat and victory are big psalm themes. But why does God enable Israel's victory one day and their defeat the next?

With Israel, God calls out a people. They know God's presence or absence like none other on the face of the earth. God is their advocate, even in their approach to war. However, in this psalm, we see that God has allowed Israel's defeat. Has Israel been rejected, asks our Psalmist?

God's commitment to Israel is defined by covenant. Israel is God's and God is Israel's. Because of this, God is for them as companion, redeemer and Lord. Israel is loved by the God whose purposes for creation will come to fruition. However, God will not wholly shield Israel from the forces that press in. That wouldn't be a covenant, it would be protectionism. It would be stifling to the point of suffocation, and would ultimately stop Israel from growing.

Although hard pushed here, Israel was not called to rejection, but to be a beacon of God's love. It is our end too. Israel, and ultimately the human race, have an advocate. We, like Israel, have gone astray, but God has not given up on us and is always acting for us. Yes, calamities will come, and yes, God might have something to do with them, but the covenant, the will of God for us created beings, is one to which God is eternally committed.

This psalm is attributed to David, that most famous king of Israel and Judah. Although it narrates a defeat, it is likely set within a larger period of kingdom expansion and success. Through this time, David has learned much about God. For all his failings, he knows the God of the covenant. It is to this same God that he must now turn in defeat. Although seeming to show anger here, God is not vindictive or tyrannical. As much as David is in pain, his former experience tells him that God is in the business of growing people, not keeping them pushed down.

But we are still left in a hard place with this psalm. The threat of defeat still lurks at the door. Death and destruction still ravage our world. However, the fulfilment of the covenant has arrived. Christ has come! God's growing plan for humanity has a new dawn. In Christ, the covenant promise given to David and his forbears has a centre. And from this centre, God blesses the world. God's story is growing again, and we are included.

Covenant of love

Actually, the covenant always had a universal end: Israel was to be a light to the nations, a signpost to the God of love. Christ is that light and love. And he brings this ruptured world, where violence still holds sway, towards his own heart of love. Yes, there is violence in this story, but God's end with human beings is peace.

We might not win at everything – God forbid that we do – but we can know an advocate: one who allows us to act, to pray, to make mistakes and, yes, sometimes succeed. But we have to know that Jesus is no more on our side than on anyone else's. Those who follow Christ cannot claim success if success means final defeat for others. Our successes are not the heart of the story. The heart is the God who draws all people together in love. That is the fulfilment of the covenant, and where the travel of the Christian life is finally heading.

Kingdom of peace

War will cease; defeat and triumph will be no more; God will be all in all and all will see. In the meantime, God has set aside a people who are called out to recognize the presence of Christ and Spirit; a people who signpost a future kingdom of peace. The kingdom

184

will not be war, so let us live for peace now. We live for a future in which there will be no winners and losers, so let us not press down or exclude anyone now, whether in our neighbourhoods, work-places, churches or lives together. Whatever we turn our hands to, we do so not to win but to point towards a kingdom of love. In this kingdom, we choose to do what will bring growth, not what will bring glory to ourselves.

Through the Spirit, the shoots of the kingdom are already arriving even while calamities come. And as a people, we can point to this kingdom coming now as it is in heaven.

Mark Amos

Hymn suggestions

The splendour of the King; Shine, Jesus, shine; Make me a channel of your peace; The kingdom of God is justice and joy.

Seventh Sunday after Trinity (Proper 11)   23 July
Principal Service   **Let God Be the Judge**
(*Continuous*): Gen. 28.10–19a; Ps. 139.1–11, 23–24
[or 139.1–11]; or (*Related*): Wisd. 12.13, 16–19, or Isa. 44.6–8;
Ps. 86.11–end; Rom. 8.12–25; **Matt. 13.24–30, 36–43**

Wheat and weeds

During this season of Ordinary Time when we explore what it means to be a Christian, we're revisiting the parables. Last Sunday we had the parable of the sower. This Sunday it's the turn of the wheat and weeds.

Jesus speaks about the good seed being sown in the good soil. However, during the night an act of bio-terrorism occurs. An enemy sows weeds among the wheat so that both wheat and weeds spring up together.

The farm workers want to uproot the weeds. The wise farmer, concerned for the crop, suggests waiting: letting both grow together so that it will be easier to separate them during harvesting. Jesus helpfully explains his analogy of the kingdom ending with a fierce and scary picture of judgement – the wheat makes it into the barn, the weeds end up in the furnace. 'Let anyone with ears listen!'

So there's wheat and there are weeds. How can we tell which is which? How do we know the difference? Does it matter?

Growing together

The farmhands are very keen to keep the wheat 'pure' by rooting out the weeds. But that isn't their job. The wheat and the weeds can co-exist, can grow together. We're being warned here not to give a premature judgement about what is 'good' and what is 'bad'. We can be very quick to decide who we think is 'in' and who is 'out'. But Jesus suggests that everyone is 'in', at least for the time being. So whoever you are and wherever you come from you are welcome in God's kingdom, even if you think you're not. Stay, explore, grow, bring diversity, enable all to learn more of the kingdom. Who's to say which is wheat and which are weeds?

Recently I went for a walk on the Mendips with a friend, and there we walked on a path through the middle of an enormous field of wheat – it stretched as far as we could see and it appeared to be all wheat until we slowed down and looked more carefully. In among the wheat, there were lots of 'weeds' – wildflowers: campion, cornflowers, thistles, scabious – a rich diversity. On the weeds, there were insects galore, especially bees and butterflies. I saw ringlets, skippers, gatekeepers and fritillaries. The 'weeds' in this field were enabling rich biodiversity alongside the wheat, and all of it flourishing. Could it be that the weeds are a 'gift'?

Judgement

So far, so good. There's room for all to live and grow together in God's kingdom. But what do we make of the end of the parable – that scary picture of judgement that makes us squirm. It's really important to remember that judgement belongs to God. Judgement is in God's hands, not ours. And what we know of God can ease our fear about judgement.

The book of Wisdom gives us a picture of God who is sovereign and just. God is Lord over everything, and chooses to 'spare all'. God judges with mildness and great forbearance. God has the power to act and fills his children with hope. God gives repentance. Second, third, fourth, endless chances and opportunities are offered for a fresh start for each of us. God's mercy is wide.

God in Jesus

This is the God who in Jesus was and is and will be alongside us. Jesus models for us what humanity can be like at its most whole – made in the image of God. God was sacrificed for us in Jesus so that we could be reunited with God for ever. This is the God who filled us with the Holy Spirit at our baptism so that we could be adopted into God's family as heirs. We are not slaves to God but children, loved unconditionally – without beginning or end.

St Paul says the whole creation – wheat and weeds – waits with eager longing to be liberated into the glorious freedom of God's kingdom. We are saved – not through anything that we have done, but through what God has done for us in Jesus. And we wait in patient hope for the fulfilment of God's eternal plan. Meanwhile, life can be tough. Difficult things happen and we suffer. Some of that doesn't sit easily with a loving God. It can make us question, struggle and sometimes lose hope.

Important then to hold on to the eternal dimension, to press forward and allow hope to colour our daily living. Practise tiny acts of righteousness, kindness, goodness and love to extend God's kingdom step by step. Make a stand, saying, 'I choose the way of hope. I choose the way of God. I will carry and witness to hope for those around me.' Be great-spirited and overflowing with generosity. Concentrate on growing into the wheat that God longs to harvest, and encourage others to do the same. God's loving-kindness and mercy will address the weeds.

Catherine Williams

Hymn suggestions

Build your kingdom here; Christ will come again; God is working his purpose out; The kingdom of God is justice and joy.

Seventh Sunday after Trinity (Proper 11) 23 July
Second Service **The Discernment of Solomon**
Ps. 67 [70]; **1 Kings 2.10–12; 3.16–end**; Acts 4.1–22;
Gospel at Holy Communion: Mark 6.30–34, 53–end

What an upheaval! After a reign of 40 years, David, the great king of Israel, has died and has been buried in his city, Jerusalem. Can you imagine how the people must have felt as a reign that had lasted for a long time, for more than a generation, came to an end? How many of them would have genuinely mourned the king's passing? Who would not have feared for the uncertain future? As Solomon ascended his father's throne, surely they would have asked of each other, 'What kind of king will he be?' Could he ensure the safety of the state, govern and judge (as had the Judges)?

As we have heard, the Deuteronomist, the author and/or editor of the traditions in 1 Kings, tells a story in the third chapter of the book which gives an insight into the character of the new king and sets the tone for his reign. This story has sometimes been given the title 'The Wisdom of Solomon' or 'The Judgement of Solomon' but since, in the Old Testament context, 'wisdom' and 'judgement' are susceptible to a variety of meanings, perhaps a slightly different title should be used: the discernment of Solomon.

The discernment of Solomon

You may have noticed that, in the (NRSV) narrative, the king is not referred to by name. Is the king in this story of two prostitutes really Solomon? One possibility is that what is essentially a well-known folk tale may have been borrowed from, or modelled after, a story from another ancient Near Eastern culture. (It has similarities to stories from Egyptian and Indian sources.) Perhaps the point is to note that the Deuteronomist is attesting to Solomon's God-given ability to exercise practical wisdom in the meting out of justice (whether or not it's 'history').

Here is a king who listens carefully, even to women of little account. We're told that they are prostitutes, which explains why two pregnant women are living together, with no 'man of the house'. The women were alone in the house (with their infant sons) when the incident occurred, so they alone can bear witness to what happened.

The drama is played out in the style and format of a legal case brought before a judge and the narrative takes a combative, dialogical form. First, each of the two women tells (her version of) the story, appealing to the king for justice. (The background to their story is tragic: the child of one of the two has died and each woman now claims that the surviving child is hers.) Second, having listened, the king speaks, calling for a sword in order to divide the contested child into two halves.

(What is this? Insane justice or the casual brutality of a king/judge who is wearied of this dispute?) Traditionally this intervention is seen as an act of brilliance, as the turning point in the story.

Third, each woman speaks again. The reactions of the two women to the king's suggestion enable him to make a judgement. While one woman was content that the child be divided between them, the other cried out: better that a living child be raised by the other than that it be put to the sword. The king decrees that the child should be given to this more compassionate woman; 'She is the mother,' he declares. Has the true (birth) mother been identified? The passage does not say, but it surely suffices that the child is given into the care of the better parent.

As the conclusion to the passage, the Deuteronomist says that all Israel heard of the judgement, they saw that the king could carry out justice because of the wisdom of God that was in him, they were awestruck.

Wisdom, justice and discernment

How reassured the people must have been as to the character and competence of their new king! Were such a story to be told about a contemporary new ruler, would we be reassured? In modern societies, I doubt that we would want kingly (or presidential) intervention in a domestic matter! Where were the specialists who could determine such matters: social services or the family courts? The story reminds us that we live in very different times. Israel was a small nation, where power and authority (under God) was vested in the monarch.

Solomon, assuming the role of ruler and judge, is depicted as wily and guileful. He's precocious: he displays practical wisdom beyond his years or experience. His is a discerning mind that is not found wanting. However, is there a modicum of underlying criticism in the Deuteronomist's concluding statement, an implication that kingly judgements can be corrupted? It is fortunate that God's wisdom has prevailed and it has saved the living child.

189

Perhaps we are too prone to put our trust in the sophisticated mechanisms, the inbuilt checks and balances, of our social systems. Is there justice for women of little account? Are our social supports adequate for the vulnerable? Is God-given wisdom, justice and discernment evident within the social structures of our secularized states? Should we look again at this story about godly wisdom exercised by a ruler, praying that we, and those whom we select as our rulers, maybe as discerning as Solomon?

Wendy Kilworth-Mason

Hymn suggestions

Give to me, Lord, a thankful heart; Heaven shall not wait; It is God who holds the nations; The kingdom of God is justice and joy.

Eighth Sunday after Trinity (Proper 12) 30 July
Principal Service Did You Hear the One About the Kingdom of God?
(*Continuous*): Gen. 29.15–28; Ps. 105.1–11, 45b [*or* 105.1–11], *or* Ps. 128; *or* (*Related*): 1 Kings 3.5–12; Ps. 119.129–136; Rom. 8.26–end; **Matt. 13.31–33, 44–52**

Who makes you laugh? There are all sorts of comedians. The ones I like can tell a story about ordinary events, family life and so on, and make them so funny. Timing is everything, but a one-liner, well placed, can't but help make you smile.

Jesus comes out in front of the crowds and starts his teaching. In rapid fire, he serves up parable after parable. His timing is masterful, and word pictures hit their mark with precision so that you can't help but see. The comedian makes you laugh, but Jesus makes you see.

A gospel routine

The routine Jesus offers in today's Gospel is amazing: five short parables all in a row about the kingdom of God. All of them are gems: mustard seed, treasure buried in a field, a precious pearl and a fishing net. Then there's the one about yeast in the flour. It's a one-liner. You may have missed it, but it goes like this: 'The kingdom of heaven is like yeast that a woman took and mixed in with three measures of flour until all of it was leavened.'

Three measures of flour. Do you know how much that is? It's about 80 pounds! This woman is no pastry chef whipping up a couple of delicate, exquisite little biscuits. This woman is a baker! She's emptying 16 five-pound bags of flour into the big mixing bowl. She's pouring in 42 cups of water. She's got a mass of dough in her hands that weighs over 100 pounds. She is kneading this lump of dough, shaping it, pounding it. It looks like some scene at the end of a professional wrestling match. Here we have a no-nonsense operation. A woman, with her apron dusted with flour, her fingers deep into the dough.

Patience and discernment

Yeast takes time to work. We must be patient as the dough rises and comes to life. Equally, this dough is not a dead lump, a hopeless, shapeless pile, but instead it's a universe where opportunities become real.

We must exercise this same patience and discernment about the world around us. Life is something other than a bag of flour and a dab of yeast. Life is a lumpen, promising mass of dough, on its way to becoming rich bread. Just as yeast permeates the entire lump, so the kingdom is present everywhere, and everywhere it becomes real for those with eyes to see.

If we look around us and within us, we can recognize the presence of the kingdom. That kingdom is at work, just as yeast is active in the dough. As yeast is invisible and known by its effects, so the kingdom is hidden, concealed, buried deep in ordinary circumstances, yet known by its results.

Look at your life in the light of God's love. Something is there for you to find – whether your life seems successful or disastrous, whether you call yourself a winner or a loser. That something is the activity of the kingdom, yeast bubbling away in your corner of the lump.

And when you find the kingdom among the realities of your own life, then it's only a short step from finding that same kingdom in events around you, in the lives of other people, and everywhere you choose to look.

Hidden but potent

A word of caution. The kingdom does not come with fanfare trumpets; it's not the subject of headline news and public announcements. We are talking here about yeast working invisibly in the dough, a hidden yet potent activity.

As it takes hope to believe that bread will rise, so too faith is necessary to see the signs of the kingdom in the everyday and the ordinary. We must exercise patience and discernment wherever God places us. Then we will see that what seems like a dead lump is in fact bubbling with divine life.

May each of us, as we encounter places, people and circumstances, look for the kingdom: not as distant, but near at hand; not as obvious, but hidden; not as static, but alive and real. When we look for the kingdom, we shall find it present, abundantly present. So present that whenever and wherever bread is broken Jesus is revealed and becomes known to us. Thus we discover Jesus' one-liner to be true: all the world is a lump of dough, flour with yeast mixed in, and SURPRISE! God is a baker-woman making bread.

Paul Williams

Hymn suggestions

Lord Jesus Christ, you have come to us; I am the Bread of Life; Seek ye first the kingdom of God; Jesus, remember me (Taizé).

Eighth Sunday after Trinity (Proper 12) 30 July
Second Service **The Paradox of Buildings**
Ps. 75 [76]; **1 Kings 6.11–14, 23–end**; **Acts 12.1–17**;
Gospel at Holy Communion: John 6.1–21

Buildings and the Bible

The Bible has an ambivalent relationship with buildings. In some parts of Scripture the image, the metaphor, of a building is used very positively. St Paul, for example, refers to the early Church as 'God's farm, God's building'. And of course, in one of the favourite parables from our Sunday school days, we remember that Jesus uses the image of a sturdy house built on a firm foundation in the parable of the wise and the foolish man. Buildings, in both of these instances, seem to stand for something enduring, something stable, that might offer us protection and security, and be a place of community.

In other places, Scripture is a little more reticent. Our first reading today is part of the story of the building of the Temple in Jerusalem. It's actually a section from towards the end of that story. We are hearing about Solomon finishing the Temple. But do you remember that when David, Solomon's father, first suggests that it might be a good thing to build a temple, God is not keen? Throw your mind a few years earlier in the story. King David is newly victorious, settled in Jerusalem with his own lovely palace, and he wants to build a house, a temple, for the Ark of the Covenant. Fundamentally he is planning to build a church. And Nathan the prophet comes to him and says, 'No, don't do that. The whole point about the Ark is that it is mobile. It moves.' 'I have not lived in a house since the day I brought up the people of Israel from Egypt to this day, but I have been moving about in a tent and a tabernacle.'

Solomon's vision

Isn't that interesting? At times the Bible is quite nervous about buildings. There is a slight nervousness when King David first has the idea of building a temple, that building a permanent place might make us forget about how mobile God is.

And yet, in our reading from the first book of the Kings today, we jump ahead. Solomon has succeeded David as king, and he has built the Temple that his father first had a vision of. And we're right at the end of that project now. It's taken seven years, and in our first reading we hear of the care, the concern and detail that went into the building of the Temple. The building of what seems to be, for Solomon, an offering of a prayer in stone to the God of Israel.

Holy places, holy spaces

So, there is that ambiguity again. Buildings. Good or bad? Well of course it's a bit of both, isn't it? And all of us who worship in church buildings, whether ancient or modern, whether stone or brick, wood, metal or glass, know that buildings are a funny mixture. Buildings matter. Of course, they do. They always have done, they always will. For all the reasons that motivate Solomon. These are the holy spaces where we sink into prayer most easily. These are the spaces that bear the marks of our ancestors, the alterations of our liturgical, community and civic journey. These stones are pregnant with the prayers of those who have gone before us, to which we join our prayers for those who will follow after. On many church walls, there are tablets and memorials to the people who prayed here before us. Many churches are surrounded by the graves of those who taught us to pray. So of course these places matter. They help to form us, they remind us where we have come from and, at their best, they can be a stony sacrament of praise.

Locked doors imprison us

But, of course, buildings have doors, and those can be tricky too. They can exclude as well as include. They can deter people, as well as be flung open in welcome. In our reading from Acts today we hear of how God, by his angels, can open the sorts of doors that can trap or imprison us. That can make us less free than we ought to be. Less free than God wants us to be. In Peter, we can find ourselves: when we are imprisoned by whatever it is that hems us in and traps us – the past or the present, circumstance or our own choices, or something visited upon us from outside – we too can find that the chains fall off our wrists and even gates of iron open on their own accord.

Doors are essential

God is at least as interested in opening doors as he is in building houses. And I suppose if we can take one thing from the two readings today, it is that if we are to have a building, it is absolutely essential that it has doors in the walls. And we should expect God to open those doors unexpectedly, and often. And that might unsettle us a bit.

So, we open our hearts to the God who can swing wide the gates of even the darkest prison, who dwells on his throne in heaven as well as in this building, and most particularly in our receptive and waiting hearts and minds.

Tom Clammer

Hymn suggestions

And can it be; We love the place, O God; Let us build a house; God is here, as we his people.

Ninth Sunday after Trinity (Proper 13)   6 August

(For Transfiguration, see p. 330.)

Principal Service   **A Little Goes a Long Way**

(*Continuous*): Gen. 32.22–31; Ps. 17.1–7, 16 [*or* 17.1–7];
or (*Related*): Isa. 55.1–5; Ps. 145.8–9, 15–end [*or* 145.15–end];
Rom. 9.1–5; **Matt. 14.13–21**

The ability to make a little go a long way is a true art form, and
one that my generation brought up in the affluent 1960s and 1970s
is not very skilled at. Those of you who have lived through leaner
times will be much better than me at making a little go a long way.
Perhaps you can emulate the Bootstrap Chef – Jack Monroe. I find
myself envying Jesus' miracle with the loaves and fishes. How useful it would be if we could multiply food.

A tale of wonder

I first heard the loaves and fishes miracle when I was about six. I
can remember sitting on the story carpet at school and having it
read to me. I didn't come from a Christian family so Bible stories
were new for me, and this one was a tale of wonder. I remember
wishing that I could give my packed lunch to Jesus so he could do
something special with it, and feed many people. Perhaps you have
childhood memories of this story too: it's such a popular one.

The story of the feeding of the 5,000 was very important to the
early Church. We know this because it's in all four Gospels, and in
two of them feeding miracles come more than once. The story has
been honed and refined as it's been written down. The theology
has been worked through and crafted so that the first Christians
and now us can make important links with the Eucharist. So, we
have the fourfold eucharistic actions – taking, blessing, breaking
and sharing – which you see at every Eucharist. Matthew too makes
the point that the Christian community, the body of Christ, is to be
inclusive. The people are not sent away to find their own food but
are encouraged to stay with Jesus and with each other. Matthew
mentions women and children as well as men, showing that they
were included.

Ordinary/extraordinary

Bread and fish were ordinary everyday food – staples in the diet. Jesus takes the ordinary and does extraordinary things with it – makes it holy – just as we ordinary people are made holy by the presence of the Spirit within our lives. Bread and fish are both symbols for Jesus – the people are fed with Jesus by Jesus. And we believe that in Holy Communion we receive the body and blood of Jesus at the meal where Jesus is the host. The feeding is placed in the context of healing people. Jesus heals the sick before he feeds them. The Eucharist is a supreme healing moment in the life of the Church. All things come together to make a whole when the Eucharist is celebrated, and the ordinary becomes extraordinary.

Brokenness

How interesting too that all this was happening at a very low moment in Jesus' life. He had withdrawn to grieve the murder of his cousin John. They met for the first time before they were even born – at the meeting of Mary and Elizabeth. Jesus has known John all his life. So, he goes away by himself to grieve. He's in a difficult place emotionally. And yet from that place of brokenness, Jesus can trust God sufficiently for a miracle to be worked through him. From the breaking of bread and fish comes abundance – sufficient to maintain life in thousands.

An abundance of food and drink in the Bible is a symbol of joy and fulfilment. Isaiah the prophet calls people to drink and eat even when they have no money because he is referring to the goodness of God that is on offer. As with Jesus, the invitation is open – much wider than usual, beyond the boundaries of Israel.

Fulfilment

The feeding of the 5,000 has links to the Isaiah passage, but it also links with the feeding of the Israelites in the wilderness with manna in Exodus, and with the feeding of the army by Elisha in the book of Kings. Matthew points to Jesus fulfilling the Law and the Prophets. So, Matthew is looking both back and forward. The feeding of the 5,000 is a glimpse of the heavenly banquet and a foretaste of what is to come for those who love God. Fulfilment of God's promise, which we remember at every Eucharist.

In the presence of God, we may feel very little, worthless even, and we come with empty hands to worship. God takes the little, the 'nearly nothing' we have, and does incredible things with it. God can and does work miracles, and the ordinary becomes extraordinary. The food we receive for the journey might seem very little too – a wafer, a sip, a few verses – but with God a little goes a long way.

Catherine Williams

Hymn suggestions

Guide me, O thou great Redeemer; I am the bread of life; Bread of heaven, on thee we feed; Eat this bread; drink this cup (Taizé).

Ninth Sunday after Trinity (Proper 13)   6 August
Second Service   **Where is Wisdom to be Found?**
Ps. 80 [*or* 80.1–8]; **1 Kings 10.1–13**; Acts 13.1–13;
Gospel at Holy Communion: John 6.24–35

Journeying

I wonder where you would travel to and why. To visit someone perhaps? To discover something new? To flee to safety? In search of treasure? The Bible is full of stories about people embarking on journeys: in fact, the Bible as a whole could be described as the story of humanity's journey with God. For people of faith, a journey might be described as a 'pilgrimage' to a particular shrine, city or holy place. The experience of pilgrims is often that the journey itself reveals things that were never expected when the person originally set off, and that the journey is as significant (if not more so) as the destination.

The magi

One of the most well-known journeys in the New Testament is told in the Gospel of St Matthew and recounts the story of the magi who set out to find the new king, born to be King of the Jews. They naturally seek out the current ruler in Jerusalem to see if he knows where this child is to be born, thus setting off a destructive chain of events that they could never have imagined when they asked their innocent question. Expecting to find a newly born king in a palace is not an unreasonable expectation, but the New Testament story speaks of a God rarely found in the places where we expect. They go home a different way, and the holy family themselves set off on another unexpected journey, fleeing for their lives, this time to safety in Egypt.

The search for Wisdom

The book of Job raises the question: 'But where shall wisdom be found?' In the story of the visit of the Queen of Sheba to King Solomon, the answer is plain and clear. It is this king whom she has come to visit who has the wisdom, although of course it is ascribed (along with his fame) to God. But there is an important truth that all wise people know, that all have the potential to be wise, and we would do well to trust the wisdom within ourselves, above all else. The Queen of Sheba might have 'spun' the story that King Solomon was a great purveyor of wisdom, but it seems likely that the historical context is that she was there to sell her wares, whatever they may be, to create better diplomatic relationships with the King of Israel, and also to develop some trade deals with him to boot. 'There is nothing new under the sun!', as Ecclesiastes says. Perhaps the Queen of Sheba has a bit more wisdom to her than the text suggests. It seems unlikely that she came away empty-handed herself.

The wisdom of Jesus

In his first letter to the Corinthians, St Paul speaks of Jesus as the one who 'became for us wisdom from God'; the one we anticipate in the first of the Advent antiphons:

O Wisdom, coming forth from the mouth of the Most High,
reaching from one end to the other mightily,
and sweetly ordering all things:
Come and teach us the way of prudence.

For Christians, it is God who always initiates the journey and, in Jesus, God journeys into the world in substance of our flesh, so that human beings can see him, touch him, converse with him, know him, believe in him.

The Jesus within

A favourite question of mine when people share something of their inner life with me is: 'Where do you find God?' Many of us search for God in places that we are told we *should* find him, only to discover that he was already there in the places we already knew, waiting to be found, it is just that we had never realized it was him. Many, through his grace, come to realize that God often works through subtle (and less subtle) nudges and prompts: through intuition and desire. Eventually, on our journey of faith, we can come to realize that the wisdom and the knowledge were within all the time, waiting to be discovered, listened to, embraced. The message of the incarnation, of God become human, is that God can dwell in us, and live in us, if we invite him to do so: that the divine can be found in human existence, in our very being. He is as close to us as our breath, if we would only recognize that. Whatever was achieved by the visit of the Queen of Sheba to King Solomon, I wonder what she really learnt from her journey, and what she took home. Might she have found something that she had already had but had never known? What might that be called? Where is wisdom to be found?

Jonathan Lawson

Hymn suggestions

Be thou my vision; Immortal, invisible, God only wise; Praise to the holiest; The perfect wisdom of our God.

Tenth Sunday after Trinity (Proper 14) 13 August
Principal Service **The Stories We Tell Ourselves Really Matter**
(*Continuous*): Gen. 37.1–4, 12–28; Ps. 105.1–6, 16–22, 45b [or 105.1–10]; *or (Related)*: **1 Kings 19.9–18;** Ps. 85.8–13; Rom. 10.5–15; Matt. 14.22–33

The stories we tell ourselves really matter

The Old Testament reading for today parachutes us into the story of Elijah. Just before our passage starts, Elijah is hunkered down under a solitary broom tree, wishing his life were over. What a change! Not long before, he had triumphed over the prophets of Baal – winning a huge spiritual battle – a prophet at the top of his game. Now, the glory days have evaporated like the early morning mist. Queen Jezebel has promised to snuff out his life at the earliest opportunity. How the mighty have fallen. Understandably, Elijah sees his story in shadows. He has lost sight of the light. He is hunkered down in his cave.

Like Elijah, our lives can be so full of contrast – profound seasons of spiritual richness can be followed by deep and terrible desolation. In the bleak times, notice how easy it is to lose perspective, to frame our story in utterly negative terms. Spiritual forgetfulness has rugby-tackled our man. He has forgotten the God of the mountain-top victory. We see him informing God that he is the *only one* left. *All* the Israelites have broken faith with God. *All* the prophets have been murdered. There's just him. He might as well be dead. Elijah narrates to himself a story of utter hopelessness. Alone, he sits in his cave, in darkness. He tells himself a story of fear and abandonment. 'I alone am left.'

What story do you tell yourself?

The story we tell ourselves shapes our perception and experience of reality. What story do you tell yourself today about the world and your place in it?

Fast forward to the end of the Old Testament reading and we see a different picture. Elijah, you are not alone! God tells of seven thousand who have remained faithful. It is so easy when the chips are down and fear stalks the internal landscape, to focus on the negatives, to magnify our sense of pain and powerlessness, to lose perspective. When that happens the spectres of hopelessness, fear and futility take on tangible form and we can fall into despair. It's a horrible, painful place to be.

God tells a different story

Notice how God deals with Elijah. God doesn't rebuke him, tell him to pull himself together and stop being a misery guts. 'Come on, Elijah, put on your happy face.' There is no patronizing, simpering pep talk here. God takes Elijah's distress seriously, compassionately and powerfully. This is very good news if you happen to find yourself alone and wretched. The God of love is powerfully present to Elijah, drawing him out, into a different story.

At this point, what does Elijah, broken, bowed and despairing, need? A violent wind occurs, but God is not in the storm. Elijah has enough storm as it is. A great earthquake happens, but God is not in the earthquake. Elijah is already shaken to his core. Then fire roars forth, but God is not in the fire. Elijah already tastes ashes; he doesn't need to be further burned. Elijah does not need a God of fire and fury who shakes the earth. He needs to be met in stillness, presence and closeness. He is. It is this which draws our broken man out to the entrance of his cave, to the threshold of a new story.

A new chapter

It is easy to forget the love and compassion of God when the storm hammers around us, the foundations of our world shake, and the fire of fear and fury burns. But God is always near, in silence, in the still points, in the reassuring whisper that reaches into the hidden places. God will not leave Elijah entombed in his cave of fear. This is not where the story ends. There is more to life than the reduced horizons of Elijah's misery; there is work to do, a future to create, Elisha to anoint, train and equip. There is new life beyond the black shroud of Elijah's depression. There is hope and a future beyond his bleak despair. God takes Elijah there, into a new chapter of his story.

The Gospel reading resonates with a similar theme. Peter steps out on to the water and sinks, confidence lost – but he is met in the outstretched hand of Jesus who knows his lack of faith, yet loves him still. Failure is simply a bend in the story – not the final full stop. There is always more. With God even death is a semicolon; the resurrection clause has no full stop …

The stories we tell ourselves really matter.

Kate Bruce

Hymn suggestions

Empty, broken, here I stand; Take, O take me as I am; Dear Lord and Father of mankind; What a friend we have in Jesus.

Tenth Sunday after Trinity (Proper 14)   13 August
Second Service   **A Leader Who Listens?**
Ps. 86; **1 Kings 11.41—12.20**; Acts 14.8–20;
Gospel at Holy Communion: John 6.35, 41–51

Peaceful transition of power

King Solomon has died, the king presented in the Jewish Bible as the wisest of kings. Solomon has presided over a golden age, but now he's gone. So now that most fragile of moments has arrived: the peaceful transition of power. Power has come to an end – how is it to be resumed? There will be a new king – how is he going to handle his new role? What is the will of the people?

Rehoboam is the son of Solomon, and so he has a claim to power. But then, in this fascinating story, he explores, with his advisers, how this power will be expressed. What kind of leadership will Rehoboam offer? His father was in every way a hard act to follow.

A delegation of the people come to the new king with a request. They want a kind of Magna Carta – if he will be a benign leader, then they will serve him gladly. Rehoboam hesitates – perhaps he already likes the idea of being king too much. Perhaps he has already got the taste for power, and what he *can* do is more enticing than what he *should* do?

Good and bad advice

Rehoboam consults his advisers, just as our presidents and prime ministers consult their staff. The older advisers, who worked with his father, suggest that he be gentle: 'If you are a servant to these people, they will serve you for ever.' But the young advisers, his peers, talk up his strength, his force of character. They advise him to be ruthless, to exert his power to the full.

Rehoboam chooses what he sees as 'strong leadership'. It turns out to be the wrong choice: the people rebel, the kingdom splits. The legacy of David, and Solomon, is destroyed.

In our time, strong leadership obviously has a great appeal. Populist dictatorships have sprung up around the world, The slogans of leaders, the promises they make, seem to have an enormous effect.

And it seems as if strong leadership is often seen primarily as a matter of speaking. Strong leaders are those with strong, even aggressive, words. This idea is prevalent in society, and even in the Church. There are often those who want, or even demand, that the Church should exercise leadership by offering strong, clear opinions in the public arena.

Is this a helpful idea? Does it really fit with the mission of the Church? What words do we really need in times of change? How do we respond when leadership comes into question?

A leader who listens

This story of Rehoboam is a direct challenge to these ideas of leadership. A good king, it suggests, will be a leader who listens. Listening is more important than speaking.

This is a theme that develops all through the narrative of Scripture, and finds its fulfilment in the gospel, in the understanding of incarnation, of Jesus, the servant king.

God who listens

Because, ultimately, this all hinges on the nature of God. Hearing God, listening to God, is fundamental, but we listen to God first of all because God listens to us. That is the deepest foundation of our relationship with God – God first loves us. First of all, before anything else, God searches and knows us. Any love we have for God is a response to God's eternal love.

God is the one who listens for the footsteps of the returning Prodigal. And so, a follower of God must also be, first of all, a listener. Listening is at the very root of our being. Bonhoeffer says, quite rightly, that if we stop listening to one another, we stop listening to God.

However small or great our role, or ministry, we each have a choice to make about our power, and how we exercise it. It can be so easy for any of us, if we are given power, to mistake ourselves for God. We may imagine that because we may be doing God's work, that in some way we represent God. That can be really dangerous. To listen is to exercise love for others. To listen shifts the balance of power away from myself. To listen is to open myself more fully to the possibilities of life in God.

And the message of the gospel points us to the idea that God is most present, most visible, in the powerless. If I don't, as a leader, listen to the powerless, I may not be able to hear what God is trying to communicate to me. May we learn to lead as servants of God, leaders who listen.

Andrew Rudd

Hymn suggestions

From heaven you came; Brother, sister, let me serve you; Meekness and majesty; The King of love my shepherd is.

Eleventh Sunday after Trinity (Proper 15)
20 August
Principal Service   **Challenging Jesus**
(*Continuous*): Gen. 45.1–15; Ps. 133; or (*Related*): Isa. 56.1, 6–8; Ps. 67; Rom. 11.1–2a, 29–32; **Matt. 15.[10–20] 21–28**

A challenging voice

In our Gospel today Jesus is challenged: challenged publicly by a Canaanite woman. She comes to ask for healing for her daughter. She is vocal and persistent. The disciples try to get Jesus to send her away. They perceive her as difficult and demanding. But she won't go until she's received what her child needs. I'm reminded of Jacob who wrestled all night with God saying, 'I will not let you go, until you bless me.'

Jesus declares that his mission is only to the lost sheep of the house of Israel. He says it's unfair to take the children's food and throw it to the dogs. These are harsh words from Jesus – though 'dogs' can be read as 'puppies' in the original, so maybe a little softer. The woman comes straight back with a great riposte: 'even the dogs eat the crumbs that fall from their master's table.' She knows what's on offer. She's prepared to fight for it. And what's on offer is healing, transformation, salvation for *all* – and it isn't a new idea, we can trace it right back to the prophets and beyond.

Going to the lost

Our Old Testament passage from Isaiah was compiled after the Israelites had returned from exile in Babylon. It was a difficult time. Everything had changed. The Temple was no more, the king was no more, many foreigners had married Israelites both in exile and in Jerusalem, and the Israelite faith was challenged and in danger of being compromised.

Isaiah calls the people to do the right thing. To keep the Sabbath and not do evil. For if they hold to God's promise of love, and serve him, then whoever they are they will be welcome. Foreigners who serve God will have a place in his house. God's house will be a house of prayer for *all* peoples and the promise is that many others will be gathered to God in the future. The vision is that those outside the Jewish faith will be welcome in God's house, in God's kingdom. That promise stretches way back to Noah in the early chapters of Genesis, and in Isaiah we hear, 'Thus says the Lord GOD ... I will gather.'

Jesus is indeed sent to the lost sheep of Israel – so that they may turn again and be renewed in their faith, so that the kingdom is opened up to all. Some of that will come about by the example of those who are considered to be outsiders – like the Canaanite woman. Paul's mission to the Gentiles after the death and resurrection of Jesus leads to a new and renewed faith as all are beginning to be gathered into the kingdom. And the fervour and challenge of those who were previously 'outside' renews and opens up the original core so that all may be gathered in.

Gathering everyone in

What I find exciting in our Gospel today is that the presence of Jesus enables an outsider to have confidence and courage to stand up and challenge the current thinking. As a woman and a Canaanite, this person crosses significant boundaries as she challenges Jesus. There is something about him that liberates her to bring into the light the truth: that all will be gathered into the kingdom. She speaks the good news the disciples have failed to grasp – that her daughter has as much right to receive God's grace as anyone else. And she does: Jesus heals her instantly as he recognizes and proclaims the woman's faith.

So, if the vision is that God wants to gather everyone into the kingdom, whoever they are, then we may have to think again about how the Church enables that to happen, and what our priorities need to be. We gather week by week to be fed by God in word and sacrament and then we're sent out, scattered to order to take the good news of Christ and live it so that those around us may encounter Jesus and in that encounter be liberated to challenge the status quo in their lives and in the Church, claiming the truth for everyone.

Look around you this morning. Who is not here who should be here? Who in our community is not represented? Who is missing from the table? Who is challenging the status quo?

Are we listening? What are we going to do about it?

Catherine Williams

Hymn suggestions

When I needed a neighbour; Jesus Christ is waiting; Go forth and tell; There's a wideness in God's mercy.

Eleventh Sunday after Trinity (Proper 15)
20 August
Second Service   **God's Open House**
Ps. 90 [*or* 90.1–12]; 2 Kings 4.1–37; **Acts 16.1–15;**
Gospel at Holy Communion: John 6.51–58

Can you remember a time that you were made to feel truly welcome? Or that you were excluded? You probably can, because the way we are greeted and treated by others often makes a lasting impression. It can have a long-term impact on our self-confidence and sense of self-worth. Today's reading tells the story of a welcome that took place in Philippi and invites us to explore more deeply the nature of the hospitality the Church is called to extend.

Welcoming the gospel

First, we're to welcome the gospel itself. Luke, the author of Acts, has been describing the gospel's whirlwind journey across the known world. After Pentecost, the good news has spread increasingly widely from Jerusalem until, guided by a dream, Paul and Silas arrive in Philippi. There they encounter Lydia at a place of prayer. She's a God-fearer, a Gentile with a measure of allegiance to the Jewish faith. When Paul starts talking, something important happens to her. She listens intently, and the Lord opens the door of her heart. She welcomes the gospel message and is immediately baptized.

In many ways, Lydia's story is our story. God entrusts to human beings, like you and me, the unspeakable treasure of the gospel of Christ. Our calling is not to treat it as a distant acquaintance, easily brushed off, but as a loved, honoured guest, to be received with joy and open arms: attended to and engaged with. Our own response to the good news may not be as immediate as Lydia's: we may take months, years or even decades to come to a point of deep and authentic welcome. But the process is the same. We never know quite what will happen when we dare to take that step of truly listening and finding room for the gospel in our lives.

Welcoming others

Then, we're to welcome others. Lydia is not content simply to welcome the gospel into her life. Here she is, inviting the missionaries as guests into her home. She's really insistent! She seems instinctively to know that the two welcomes go hand in hand. In the ancient world, strong dualistic ideas divided people along the lines of race, gender and social status. Yet when the newly baptized Lydia invites Paul to her home, we're given a picture of the Greek welcoming the Jew, and the woman welcoming the man.

We may also have a picture of the former slave welcoming the free man. Luke introduces Lydia as a businesswoman, a dealer in purple fabric. As the dirty and heavy work of dying fabrics was carried out by slaves, it's suggested that Lydia may have been an emancipated slave from Thyatira who had set up a co-operative in Philippi. As Luke never tells us that she was married or widowed, it might well be that her origins were very modest, not to say poor. With Paul, she becomes the co-founder of the first church in Europe, based in her home: a prophetic place of cross-cultural welcome for all, no matter their background, gender or ethnicity. In depicting the creation of this church, Luke reminds us of what every church is called to be.

All welcome?

For some years I worked with a minister from another tradition who had been born in Jamaica. On arrival in Britain in the 1960s, he had been warmly welcomed into a local Nonconformist church and married a white woman he met there. But that was as far as the welcome went. When he asked for acceptance on the ordained list, the powers that be told him that the denomination wasn't ready to accept a black minister. Thank God, a different tradition finally welcomed him with open arms.

We might well be shocked to hear such a story. But being shocked isn't enough. If we're to be communities that offer gospel hospitality, stories and experiences like these – even from the past – must propel us further towards a whole change of heart and mindset for today. We need to ask ourselves the tough questions. How welcoming are we – really? We may well say we're an open community and write 'All welcome' on the noticeboard outside, but how does that get translated into the different areas of our church life?

Lydia's story reminds us that our welcome of God's good news is measured by the depth of hospitality we offer to others and to all, and by the level of our openness across all the structures of the Church. We urgently need all who have experienced exclusion to share their stories, not so that we can just hold our hands up in horror, but so that together we can build a church that discovers the meaning of true community in Christ.

God entrusts to the Church as to each of us as individuals the good news of the gospel and the extraordinary welcome it contains. How well do we know one another's stories of being welcomed or sidelined? How can our welcome become, like Lydia's, more open?

Mary Cotes

Hymn suggestions

Let us build a house; Jesus calls us here to meet him; One is the body and one is the head; In Christ, there is no east or west.

Twelfth Sunday after Trinity (Proper 16)   27 August
Principal Service   **Practical Paul**
(*Continuous*): Ex. 1.8—2.10; Ps. 124; or (*Related*): Isa. 51.1–6; Ps. 138; **Rom. 12.1–8**; Matt. 16.13–20

'Ever so 'umble'

Perhaps I had recently read Charles Dickens' novel *David Copperfield* the first time I consciously heard a sermon on this passage from Paul. However it happened, his words about not thinking of yourself more highly than you ought became synonymous in my mind with that most unattractive of characteristics – being 'ever so 'umble'. Later, as I heard preachers extolling the virtues of humility, I would look around the congregation. There was really no need to tell many of them not to think highly of themselves. Their lack of a good education, secure employment or simply respect from others told them daily that they were of little value. 'What would happen', I wondered, 'if these people thought even less of themselves?'

How might we read this passage then? Paul gives us a clue right at the start – 'therefore'. What he is about to say is based on what has gone before, in other words. Let's briefly look at how Paul has led us here.

Summarizing Paul's message so far

The first 11 chapters of Romans are rooted in one notion – the righteousness of God. God *is* righteous and God *ascribes* righteousness – that is, God declares that God's people are also righteous. We don't earn it, we haven't been found not guilty, but God has declared we are righteous – all of us. Three central ideas flow from that: God is impartial, God's grace is radical, humanity is made to be in solidarity with the whole of creation.

So what?

Therefore all of you, all genders, black and white, young and old, able-bodied and disabled present your whole self to God – body, mind and spirit. Therefore, let your thinking be transformed. If God is not impartial, how can the Church be? If God's grace is radical, how can we treat others harshly? If we are to be in solidarity with the whole of creation, how can we abuse it?

Here's my problem again: 'For by the grace given to me I say to everyone among you not to think of yourself more highly than you ought to think, but to think with sober judgement.' As I said, I felt that the world could have been a better place had several members of the congregation thought more of themselves. So, what does Paul mean? In his argument so far, Paul has emphasized the righteousness of God – God's superiority to us, and unity among human beings, our equality with others. That changes everything.

As we wrestle in society and in the Church with some big issues, seeing others through the lens of God's impartiality, God's radical grace and our solidarity with them will change things. In some areas of the Church, debates about women's ordination or human sexuality still rage. How would it be if we all looked at those with whom we disagree not as wrong but as declared righteous by God? How would it be if we regarded those who are different from us because of skin colour or gender or ability as those with whom we are in solidarity?

Thinking less of ourselves because we think little of others simply denies God's radical grace. Thinking of others through the lens of God's righteousness gives right esteem to all.

Being body – practical Paul

That might seem hopelessly idealistic. If we're all equal, can't we all do the same things? No need for theological training for clergy or lay preachers, then. No need for safeguarding training for those who work with the vulnerable, perhaps. 'Nonsense!' I hear Paul say.

Having said that because of God's righteousness we should each present ourselves as a living sacrifice, and each think rightly of ourselves, Paul becomes intensely practical. We're a body, each part has different attributes and is designed for different things, 'so do them', he says.

If you are naturally a helper – help; if you are a teacher – teach. An encourager? Encourage. A giver? Give. A leader? Lead. You get the idea. It isn't just freeing, it's revolutionary. Paul establishes a foundational principle for churches and church leaders in these few verses. Don't look at what needs to be done, look at what gifts the body of Christ in this place has, then think about how to use them. For God's people it means not trying our hands at everything, or doing what we do least well as a matter of discipline. It means identifying what gifts God has given us and seeking ways to develop and use them.

I want to finish with some words from a hymn written by John Bell of the Iona Community:

Take, O take me as I am;
I present my body as a living sacrifice,
and my mind to be transformed.
summon out what I shall be;
I want to use my gifts for God and God's creation.
set your seal upon my heart;

So that I play my full part as a member of the body of Christ,
and encourage others to do so too.
and live in me.
Bring to life the gifts I have been given.[10]

Liz Shercliff

Hymn suggestions

Take, O take me as I am; We have come, God's living temple; God's
Christ who is my righteousness; Just as I am.

Twelfth Sunday after Trinity (Proper 16) 27 August
Second Service **What is Faith?**
Ps. 95; 2 Kings 6.8–23; **Acts 17.15–end**;
Gospel at Holy Communion: John 6.56–69

What is faith?

Faith is a tricky concept. What does it mean to have faith? It is
something to do with belief, isn't it? It's something to do with
believing that something is true, but at the same time not having
absolute solid proof about it. There is a certain rather lovely Christmas film in which a young girl is trying to convince a courtroom
that it is reasonable to believe in Father Christmas. As part of her
argument, she presents the judge with a dollar bill. On American
money are printed the words, 'In God we trust'. And this piece of
evidence is sufficient for the judge to proclaim that if Americans
are content to use trust in God, whom they have never seen, to give
value to their currency, faith in other things that we cannot see
might be reasonable too.

Now the purpose of this sermon is not to argue for belief in
Father Christmas, but to illustrate that even in popular culture
this conversation about what it might mean to have *faith* in, or to
believe in, something that we cannot see is a live topic.

The paradox of faith

If you are anything like me, faith is experienced a bit differently
from time to time. There are moments where faith seems to come

really easily. Perhaps during a very uplifting act of worship. Perhaps, as many people describe, when we are struck with wonder by the extraordinary beauty of natural creation. Perhaps at those moments where it seems that our prayers are answered.

Then there are times when faith seems really very difficult to keep hold of. Those moments where we do not seem to be able to hear God. Those moments where life is very dark, very difficult, and our prayers seem to disappear into a great void. Where we worry that all of this might be complete nonsense.

And then of course there is the in-between experience, where probably most of us operate most of the time.

What can we see? What can we believe?

Interestingly, both our readings today are all about what we can see, what we might believe, and the distance between those two things. Chariots of fire are a great theme in the books of the Kings, and they usually symbolize a moment where the reality of heaven, the reality of God's economy, breaks for a moment into human existence. Do you remember that when Elijah is assumed into heaven he departs from earth on a chariot of fire? And here again, when his successor Elisha wants to avoid an awful slaughter in battle he prays to God and the vision of horses and chariots of fire appear, symbolizing God's presence among the people of Israel. The reality of the wonder of God leaks into the mundane human experience, just for a moment.

Another example is the transfiguration of Jesus, which the Church celebrated only a couple of weeks ago. Do you remember that story? Jesus takes Peter, James and John up the mountain, and just for a moment he appears to them in his true glory. They see him dazzling, shining, blazing, talking with Moses and Elijah, heaven and earth meeting in a snapshot of the true reality before that fades again and they have to go on with the memory of that experience to remind them of the truth.

The reality beyond our hope

And then in our second reading today we have a slightly different angle on this same conversation. Paul sees an altar to 'an unknown God'. In his preaching to the people in Athens, rather than scolding them for worshipping blindly, he gives this really interesting sermon about what we can see, and what we cannot see. What he is saying to them is that there is a reality behind all of the natural instinct to want to worship. Humanity has always tended to worship, tended to look up into the sky and look for answers, look for reasons why the world is the way it is. What Paul is saying here is: I can give you a name. I can give you a person who is at the heart of all that wondering. And that person's name is Jesus. And we hear that, 'When they heard of the resurrection of the dead, some scoffed; but others said: "We will hear you again about this."'

Sometimes the reality of our faith is really easy to see. At some other times, it is almost impossible. And that's OK. We are unlikely to see chariots of fire daily. And sometimes it's going to feel as if we are groping in the darkness towards God. But we can take heart that this challenge has been faced by people of faith from the beginning and that our little faltering steps are all that God asks of us. He simply opens the door, so that we would 'search for God and perhaps grope for him and find him – though indeed he is not far from each one of us'.

Tom Clammer

Hymn suggestions

And did those feet in ancient time; The duteous day now closeth; Immortal, invisible, God only wise; Christ, whose glory fills the skies.

Thirteenth Sunday after Trinity (Proper 17)
3 September
Principal Service   **Bearing the Unbearable**
(*Continuous*): Ex. 3.1–15; Ps. 105.1–6, 23–26, 45b, *or* Ps. 115; *or* (*Related*): **Jer. 15.15–21**; Ps. 26.1–8; Rom. 12.9–end; **Matt. 16.21–end**

Sooner or later, all of us must bear something unbearable. In bearing the unbearable, we realize how little control we have over much that damages our society and ourselves. As grief, rage, anger and fear surface in our thoughts, what sort of conversation can we have with God?

Lament

Biblical scholars call it 'lament', but we would be far better off calling it 'a song of rage'. In a tradition that can be traced back to Moses, and forward to the book of Job, the prophet Jeremiah gives voice to unbearable pain, anger and misery at unspeakable horrors and uncontrollable events that surround him in his life as God's prophet. His relationship with God has ceased to be a joy and delight and has become an unceasing pain and incurable wound. He is full of rage at his fellow human beings who torment him and asks God to 'bring down retribution for me on my persecutors'. He is equally hostile towards God: 'you are like a deceitful brook, like waters that fail.'

Jeremiah is bearing something unbearable, and all he wants is for the misery to stop. But even when God comes to him, in response to his outburst of rage, it is troubling: the misery is not going to go away – there'll be no rest from his torments and horrors. God simply assures Jeremiah of his presence, to strengthen him to withstand more misery. Throughout his ministry, Jeremiah appears the most plaintive and broken-hearted of all the prophets: his name has become a byword for complaining.

Hurt and bewildered

Jeremiah is commissioned to tell his people that their sins have earned them defeat and exile. He warns them that God's help is not automatic, that they might as well surrender to their enemies because God will not help them. Jeremiah's message is heard as treason; he is attacked by the crowds, imprisoned and tortured. His painful vocation isolates him from his family and friends; he becomes a laughing stock around the streets and the city.

Jeremiah is no robot; he is hurt and bewildered by how people respond to him. Many people just ignore him. And during all his anguish and pain normal life goes on in the city. People continue their daily routines. Business is as usual. Reflecting on how suffering happens amid the ordinary, the poet W. H. Auden noted how the Old Masters always depicted in their painting someone eating or opening a window, dogs doing doggy things.

Approaching Jerusalem

Suffering happens while the sun shines, while others carry on as usual, while traffic continues to flow. Those who have lost loved ones know that clocks are not stopped, the telephone is not cut off, the dog is not prevented from barking. As Jeremiah spoke of his approaching suffering in Jerusalem and his troubled relationship with God, so Jesus in today's Gospel prepares his disciples for his approaching ordeal in Jerusalem. He speaks of it as necessary – not a necessity that lies in the nature of things, not a tragic fate, but the will of God made known through the prophecies. Like Jeremiah, Jesus has to face the stark truth that his relationship with God involves personal anguish, suffering and rejection. More than that, it will lead to a violent death.

Peter is frankly appalled at the prospect and tries to deflect Jesus from the path that lies ahead. After having declared Jesus to be the Messiah, as we heard last week, a title associated with victory and glory, Peter now denies: he denies that Jesus must suffer. Peter wants to banish suffering from the agenda; Jesus brings the subject to the forefront of the conversation. Let's be blunt – to understand Jesus means to understand suffering and the way of the cross. That is the essence of his teaching to Peter at this time, and that is why Peter is denounced so strongly. Peter wants Jesus to be immune from frustration, suffering and contempt. The Christ of his dreams is all glory and prestige, untouched by vulnerable humanity, unscathed by our suffering. It is a world away from the Messiah that Jesus has to grow into, a future of suffering which he is about to enter.

Via Dolorosa

The Via Dolorosa, the way of the cross, which Jesus followed passed through streets and markets, by houses and shops, by windows and doors. While it happened, people went about their business. Suffering must run the course of the familiar. As we go through suffering, as we walk our own Via Dolorosa – as we all must – know that our way of the cross does not go unnoticed. Jesus is our suffering companion; he proves to be our strength; his power is mighty in our weakness. If the cross is the price to be paid for love, then carrying it is love's proof in action. For Jesus, that was enough, for Easter was just a step away.

Paul Williams

Hymn suggestions

Be still, my soul, the Lord is on thy side; My song is love unknown;
Great is thy faithfulness; Through the night of doubt and sorrow.

Thirteenth Sunday after Trinity (Proper 17)
3 September
Second Service   **Unlikely Saviours**
Ps. 105.1–15; **2 Kings 6.24–25; 7.3–end**; Acts 18.1–16;
Gospel at Holy Communion: Mark 7.1–8, 14–15, 21–23

Desperate times

This passage from 2 Kings begins at a very bleak moment for the
people of Samaria. They are under siege by the Aramean army;
their food supplies have all but disappeared, and they are resorting
to desperate measures to survive. The people are eating what would
usually have been considered rubbish – we hear that a donkey's
head is worth eight months' wages, even dove's dung is being sold
for food. What we are spared in the portion missed out from our
reading is a story of women cannibalizing their own children –
desperate times indeed.

And what we so often find in times of desperation is that those
on the margins are pushed even further out. Such is the case here
in Samaria. After we are introduced to what's happening inside the
city, we are taken to the no man's land between the city wall and
the besieging army. There we find four men with leprosy – outcasts
who would have been dependent on the charity of others – and in
these circumstances there is nothing to spare. No one would have
wanted lepers draining extremely limited resources. And so they are
starving to death.

Desperate measures

They are realistic about their prospects and see three options. Try
and go into the city, and die of starvation; stay where they are,
and die of starvation, or desert to the enemy camp. This is a pretty
desperate option in itself, as lepers were unlikely to be welcome in
the camp, let alone lepers from the enemy side, but it was the only
place where food was available, and the only chance of survival –

and if they died, they were no worse off than they would have been if they'd chosen either of the other options.

So, these four desperate outcasts take a chance – and it pays off. Unknown to anyone in Samaria, the Aramean army have abandoned their camp and left everything behind, fearful that allies of the Israelites are on their way to liberate the city. The four feast and secure their futures by hoarding gold, silver and clothing. But instead of helping themselves and leaving quietly, they have an attack of conscience – 'What we are doing is wrong. This is a day of good news.'

Liberated by outcasts

And so, the liberation of the city is led by the outcasts, the four men with leprosy, as they pass the message of the army's desertion to the king via the gatekeepers, and all the starving people of Samaria feast on the food left in the camp. How long would it have taken the watchers of the city to realize that the siege had ended? The noise of a fleeing army didn't seem to have reached their ears. The good news shared by the four must have saved lives. But how many of those inside the city cared about the lives of their four saviours?

Who is left behind?

In our society, too, in times of difficulty, our worlds seem to contract – our attention is drawn to those closest to home. We only need to look at the news headlines to see that disasters and atrocities far away are often eclipsed by events nearer to home. Like the reduction in overseas aid during the Covid-19 crisis, resources are pulled in and those on the edges are left behind.

In our story of the four men with leprosy, what is striking is that those who are rejected are the bearers of good news for everyone. Despite being abandoned to starvation, they have compassion for those who rejected them. They feared the consequences of keeping the news to themselves till morning, and with the resources of the whole camp behind them, they could quite easily have cut and run if they wanted. But they chose to bring life and hope to those who had abandoned them.

Messages of hope from unlikely places

The story invites us – encourages us even – to be always open to the possibility of good news coming from the most unlikely sources. That's great, but the responsibility that gives us is to listen to the people we don't want to listen to, the people who disgust or frighten us, the people we don't really want to be with, the objects of our pity. And that's a challenging thing to do.

The king was probably not pleased to be woken in the middle of the night because of a message from some lepers – until he heard what they were saying. There will always be important words spoken at inconvenient times by people we don't want to hear from – to us as individuals, communities and society as a whole.

There are people whose survival and well-being our society may often seem less interested in promoting, especially when times are hard. But those are the very people that just may have a message of salvation for all of us if only we would listen.

Kat Campion-Spall

Hymn suggestions

There's a spirit in the air; Tell out, my soul; Put peace into each other's hands; Just as I am.

Fourteenth Sunday after Trinity (Proper 18)
10 September
Principal Service   **Together in Community**
(*Continuous*): Ex. 12.1–14; Ps. 149; *or* (*Related*): Ezek. 33.7–11; Ps. 119.33–40; Rom. 13.8–end; **Matt. 18.15–20**

Reconciliation is at the very heart of Christianity. However, we can keep this truth at a distance by theologizing on a cosmic scale around the cross: God being reconciled to humanity, and humanity to God in Christ. This is absolutely true, but how does that cosmic truth play out in our relationships with each other? What do you do when someone hurts or offends you? Do you keep the hurt to yourself and brood over your wounds? Or do you face up to the person and give voice to your annoyance, anger and hurt? To tell or not to tell: that is the question. There is a poem by William Blake, 'A Poison Tree', which imaginatively explores this problem:

I was angry with my friend:
I told my wrath, my wrath did end.
I was angry with my foe:
I told it not, my wrath did grow.

The poem continues with the anger towards the foe being fed and watered by the poet's emotions so that it grows into a beautiful tree with poisoned apples which eventually kill the enemy. The moral is that unvoiced anger and hurt can do deep, lasting and permanent damage.

Issues in the Christian community

In today's Gospel reading, Matthew advises addressing issues and problems that arise in the life of the organized community of the local church. He is writing at a time when Jesus is present, not in the flesh but in Spirit, whenever two or three are gathered in his name. The theme is the relationship of the members of the church, to one another, in an offence that violates the bond of fellowship. Matthew writes this instruction in a setting of an address given by Jesus to his disciples.

The advice is straightforward: 'If another member of the church sins against you, go and point out the fault when the two of you are alone.' The Gospel says that the offended party, not the offending one, should first seek reconciliation. That makes perfect sense, for how do I know if I have offended someone if I'm not told? It counsels personal intervention and honest talking. It encourages members of the church – and this is one of the few places in the Gospels where *ekklesia* (church) is used – to straighten things out with each other privately if at all possible. Christians are to deal with each other with truth and grace and with each other personally – no anonymous complaints to the authorities, no whisper campaigns and no running away from the fellowship. The purpose of confronting another who has wronged you is not to humiliate them, but to be reconciled with them. It is an honest attempt to avoid the poison tree springing up between Christians.

If private reconciliation fails, another attempt must be made by invoking the help of one or two others, who are to try to settle the matter before it goes public. Exclusion from the local community is the very last option, and even then we are asked to treat the offender like a Gentile or tax-collector whom we know Jesus associated with and never stopped loving.

Taking responsibility

All the practical advice in the Gospel centres on Christians taking responsibility for each other. Belonging to a community implies being involved in the life of its members. Of course, this is not a charter for the snooper and the busybody, but a procedure for a caring community to follow. It is a way of handling hurt and anger. Just as conflict is sure to happen in a community of sinners, so gracefully confronting someone can be the language of love. Like the story of the poison tree, the refusal to face up to your anger and hurt ends up as the refusal to love.

St Paul tells us in today's New Testament reading, 'Love does no wrong to a neighbour; therefore, love is the fulfilling of the law.' If love is real, it cannot avoid facing conflict. If a relationship is broken, then it is important to recognize that brokenness, for it is in brokenness that we find Jesus: his broken body on the cross, and in the Eucharist. Doing nothing in the face of perceived wrongdoing and hurt is precisely what the Gospel opposes.

Today's Gospel is tough and not easy to follow. But with grace and truth, we approach each other with care, trusting that our halting efforts at giving voice to our hurt will be accepted in the best spirit. It may not work, but it is better than planting a fatal orchard with our anger.

So, I encourage you to think of one person with whom you are at variance, perhaps someone who has hurt you. Pluck up courage and speak to them with grace and truth. Begin the process of healing, trusting that where two or three are gathered Jesus is there too and that in God all things are possible. Let's take time to grow together in fruitful love and trust.

Paul Williams

Hymn suggestions

Bind us together; As we are gathered; For I'm building a people of power; The Church's one foundation.

Fourteenth Sunday after Trinity (Proper 18)

10 September

Second Service   **Meeting the Holy Spirit**

Ps. 108 [115]; Ezek. 12.21—13.16; **Acts 19.1–20**;

Gospel at Holy Communion: Mark 7.24–end

Those who hadn't heard and those who had

'We haven't even heard that there is a Holy Spirit,' they said.

How sad that was! And how wonderful that Paul was able to introduce those disciples in Ephesus to the Comforter, the Advocate, the Wind of God. *Ruach* in Hebrew: the Spirit who was present at creation, present in the incarnation, present at the baptism of Christ, present at every baptism since, present with us today.

But sadder still, perhaps, for those who have heard of the Holy Spirit and yet forget her. Those who work so hard in the service of the church, in the one who came to give us life, and yet do so in our own strength rather than the strength of that wonderful Spirit.

Do we in the church get so lost in process, policy, faculties, endless meetings in which we record the minutes that run into years, sorting out the service rotas and filling in our mission statistics, that we don't experience the presence of God in our souls and bodies, the joy of knowing what it is to love and be loved? Do we forget in our constant organized busyness to pay attention to what God is calling us to be? Have we forgotten the longing of our souls; or that God longs for us to know abundant life and freedom?

I wonder if we are so caught up in anxiety about the survival of an institution or even simply the survival of our own part of it that we have forgotten why we *are* the Church and what it means to *be* the Church: people living as a witness to the transformative love and grace that is the gospel.

Repentance – open to change

Paul explained to the Ephesians that John the Baptist had brought a message of repentance. We've given repentance a rather complicated status. We tend to see it as a means of punishing ourselves and others, beating ourselves up so much as to suggest we are beyond redemption. Whereas repentance means to turn in a new direction. It is about being open to being different. Repentance is the first step to transformation. It is about facing the possibility of change. That can sound a dangerous and alien concept to many in the Church. Change is something we like to avoid at all costs.

Perhaps that's why our relationship with the Holy Spirit tends to be on nodding acquaintance only, as though we've never been properly introduced. We prefer to keep our distance. For 'change', in the best sense of the word, is one of the Holy Spirit's middle names.

Do we hold on to what we have always done, resisting change and defending our role and our position and our argument to the hilt but missing the transforming breath of the Holy Spirit?

To be open to what God longs to do in us and through us is what John taught as a first step in the process; his baptism of repentance. Jesus showed that openness in coming to the Jordan. It's where his ministry began so that he could reveal the next step in the process. For when he came up out of the water the Spirit descended upon him. 'You are mine. With you, I am so delighted.'

This was the baptism of the Holy Spirit, the baptism of affirmation, confirmation and new life. God's natural response to our openness, the anointing of the Holy Spirit, is to enable us to be what God has called us to be. It is an invitation to life. We become a part of something bigger.

Holy Spirit, we welcome you

The writer of Acts points out that there were 12 of them who received that new anointing that day. Twelve is a significant number in Scripture. The 12 sons of Jacob founded the 12 tribes of Israel. The 12 disciples of Jesus were the first to know and understand his mission to the world and so help to found, with others, the early Church. And we who have heard of that healing, transforming, life-giving Spirit could be part of all God longs for the Church and for the world in the next 12 months and beyond. It is a metaphorical number for new possibilities.

I dare to wonder what might happen if we burned the books that contain the many minutes of many meetings that have filled the years of the many congregations and church councils that make up the Church – and instead spent more time being open to what God's Spirit longs for us. Remember to make time for Jesus who came that we might find rest for our souls. Remember the wind that brought life out of the chaos and light in the darkness and who embraced humanity with the presence of divine Love. If we remember the wonder of that truth then God might do extraordinary things among us, things that speak of healing and life and transformational grace. Do we dare to welcome such holiness, such renewal in such a Spirit?

Carey Saleh

Hymn suggestions

Holy Spirit, we welcome you; Come down, O love divine; Spirit of God, unseen as the wind; Holy Spirit, gift bestower.

Fifteenth Sunday after Trinity (Proper 19)
17 September
Principal Service   **Forgive**
(*Continuous*): Ex. 14.19–end; Ps. 114, *or Canticle*: Ex. 15.1b–11, 20–21; *or* (*Related*): Gen. 50.15–21; Ps. 103.1–13 [*or* 103.8–13]; Rom. 14.1–12; **Matt. 18.21–35**

Forgiveness is the gospel

Forgiveness, it seems, is not as popular as it was. We still want people to say sorry when they have done something wrong: individually, collectively, presently, historically. But forgiveness is more difficult than sorry. In fact, the term 'unforgivable' is more in keeping with the spirit of the age. Unforgiveness means that we get to define the terms, to keep hold of our power over the situation.

Forgiveness and unforgiveness have something in common: they judge the other person guilty. However, forgiveness gives up the right to hold the moral high ground; it cedes the need for retribution; it lets the past go. That makes it very difficult to do. But forgiveness is powerful. It is the gospel.

At first glance, Jesus' teaching in our parable seems severe. It has a context, of course. The key players – a king and some servants – evoke various people from first-century Palestine: Rome, Herod, the Temple authorities, the poor, the despised, even slaves. Jesus is clearly saying something about those who judge and those who are judged; about the powerful and the weak. The word that he speaks into this court of judgement is 'forgiveness'.

Jesus seems to be addressing the religious teachers and other authorities who had tasked themselves with looking after God's people. It seems they were judging various folk as guilty according to the law, while not recognizing that they, too, had fallen short. In fact, because they had judged others, Jesus implies, they will be more liable to judgement themselves.

The gospel, of course, is that we all, like sheep without a shepherd, have gone astray. We all need God's forgiveness; we are all unable to give what we owe to each other, to God and even to ourselves. But the same gospel says that one has come – this very Jesus – to forgive us our debts, even as we forgive our debtors.

The heart of forgiveness

Why so much anger from the king towards the first servant – the one who was forgiven? Because he has missed the heart of forgiveness and imposed in its place a version of morality not possible to keep on the other servants, a version of morality that he has failed to live up to himself. How often do we expect from others what we cannot manage ourselves? But more than that, how often do we place loads on the shoulders of those who already have the greatest burdens?

We are not those who have the final judgement on our neighbours. God is, and God's judgement, manifest in his son, is 'forgiveness'. Jesus *is* forgiveness. He speaks God's word of forgiveness in his welcome of sinners, and through his death as a common criminal. If Jesus has forgiven, like it or not, all are forgiven, regardless of our attitude towards them.

It is easy to condemn, but have we known what life is like at the margins with those who are condemned? Jesus knew life at the margins. He knew condemnation: he was judged, way before he faced Pilate, as a liar, as in league with the devil, as a mere son of a carpenter. And yet in him, we have God in our midst, we have the rightful judge of all human action. We have the one who has the authority to forgive sins.

Maybe we don't think we need forgiveness or even that we have nothing to forgive. But there is more to the heart of this parable. Yes, the authorities of Jesus' day knew forgiveness was important, but what they had missed was the heavy burden they were placing on others – those who didn't fit the system: the sick, the poor, the destitute – when they should have been modelling the grace shown by the vineyard owner.

We all need the forgiveness that has arrived in Christ. So, let us also remember to forgive each other, however minor or grievous the crime. And let us have open eyes and hearts to those who are most judged by society today – those with the biggest debts, the biggest burdens, the biggest hurts.

We need to forgive ourselves in the light of Christ's forgiveness. We need to forgive others in the light of Christ's forgiveness. We need to receive the forgiveness of others in the light of Christ's forgiveness. None of this is easy or popular. It means acknowledging wrongdoing, injustice and pain. It means saying that these things will not have the last word. But this is the gospel and the freedom to which we are called.

Mark Amos

Hymn suggestions

Amazing grace; Dear Lord and Father of mankind; You alone can rescue; Praise my soul the king of heaven

Fifteenth Sunday after Trinity (Proper 19)
17 September
Second Service   **A Life in Christ**
Ps. 119.41–48 [49–64]; Ezek. 20.1–8, 33–44; **Acts 20.17–end;**
Gospel at Holy Communion: Mark 8.27–end

Life, a series of goodbyes

Due to my parents serving with the United Nations in the Middle East, I attended boarding schools in England for my secondary education. From a young age, I understood that saying goodbye is a natural part of life. As a family, we often said goodbye to my father who was posted to numerous duty stations during his 30 years of service. As we shuffled back and forth to our boarding schools over short and long vacations, my siblings and I were often waving tearful goodbyes to my parents at the airport. Goodbyes are difficult, but particularly painful when they are final in the case of the death of a loved one. Although I've been saying goodbyes all my life, it has never got easier. In my opinion, no one ever gets used to saying goodbye.

Paul, as a missionary, would have said many goodbyes in his time and throughout his ministry. And he too would have felt the pain of parting and being separated from those he had a deep concern for and loved. Yet, in this farewell talk, we encounter Paul not dwelling on the awfulness of the inevitable goodbye, but rather encouraging the elders to follow his example and live a life of sacrifice.

A work of love

In this Acts passage, after spending three years with this community of believers, Paul says his final goodbye to the elders. As he prepared to travel to Jerusalem, he exhorted them one last time, commencing his speech by explaining what being a minister is all about.

He recounts his missional life, one that had encountered all manner of trials and hardships. He shares his story, not to gain sympathy but rather to testify to what a sacrificial life in the service of God calls for. He gives a glimpse of how God uses people to build a worshipping community. Thus, in his goodbye message, he seeks to counsel and encourage the elders who will be carrying on the work of God. And, like the Psalmist, he invites them – and us – to keep God's law continually, for ever and ever, to walk at liberty and seek God's precepts. Paul reminds us that his has been a holistic ministry where he not only preached the gospel but also lived out its message. Put another way, he embodied the gospel message he preached so fervently, by casting away the detestable things which defile our lives.

Humility in service

We need to be consistent in our messaging of who God is and what our faith is all about. Though not always easy, what we preach, how we preach and live out the gospel, really matters. Because the gospel message has the authority and power to create gospel-centred mission and ministries. And it is the body of Christ, the community of believers, redeemed by the blood of Jesus, that is set apart to establish the kingdom of God on earth as it is in heaven. There's an imperative on us who truly believe the promises found in the Bible to pay attention to how God might be wanting to use us to draw people to the divine. In the midst of all that is going on in our frail and fragile world, there is an urgency for us to communicate the gospel message of God's far-reaching love and compassion with humility. We serve a God who wants the very best for all humanity, so let's not waste a single day of our earthly lives as we endeavour to share the gospel with others.

Catherine Okoronkwo

Hymn suggestions

Let everything that has breath; Give thanks with a grateful heart;
Only by grace can we enter; I will offer up my life.

Sixteenth Sunday after Trinity (Proper 20)
24 September
Principal Service   **It's Not Fair!**
(*Continuous*): Ex. 16.2–15; Ps. 105.1–6, 37–end [*or* 105.37–end];
or (*Related*): Jonah 3.10—end of 4; Ps. 145.1–8; Phil. 1.21–end;
Matt. 20.1–16

It's not fair! How often have you heard that said? It's the sort of
thing small children say – especially siblings. 'It's not fair: he sat in
the front last time.' 'It's not fair: she's got more ice cream than me.'
It's not fair! We carry some of those messages with us into adult-
hood. 'It's not fair! She does nothing and she gets all the attention.'
'Why is he famous, or rich or healthy when I'm not? It's not fair!'

Hiring labourers

The parable of the labourers in the vineyard doesn't seem very fair
either, does it? Workers are hired at several points in the day. Some
work all day in the burning heat, and some just an hour, but at
the end of the day they are all paid the same. It's not fair! What to
make of it?

We believe God is a God of justice, who both upholds fairness
and overturns injustice to enable those at the bottom of life's heap
to stand tall and flourish. The last will be first and the first will be
last, says Jesus. The ways of the world are not God's ways. God's
ways sometimes seem topsy-turvy. Equity not equality is the order
of the day.

The owner of the vineyard paid what he promised to those who
worked all day. He was faithful and just. But then he was even
more generous to those who struggled to be employed, whom no
one wanted to hire, who were rejected over and over again. 'Are
you envious because I am generous?' Asks the manager. Did those
who worked all day expect to be paid even more for their diligence
than was agreed? Did they need perhaps to check their privilege?

God's love

In the world, we are generally rewarded for our efforts. Non-achievers are often looked down on. But with God things are different. The kingdom of heaven, suggests Jesus, is different from our worldly expectations We do not earn the right to enter the kingdom. God does not love us in proportion to how much we do to please him. We might serve God in all that we do. We might have served God for years, struggling on in good times and bad, working through the scorching heat of our days. This does not buy God's love and approval. God loves us completely and utterly whether we know it or not, whether we think we are serving God or not. And from time to time this extraordinary generosity and outpouring of love takes people who are on the edges by surprise. If you never, ever did anything ever again God couldn't love you any less than God loves you right now.

... and mercy

Jonah got very angry with God when God changed his mind and chose not to destroy the Ninevites. 'It's not fair!' thinks Jonah. I've done all these things for God and the evil Ninevites deserve to be destroyed. And yet, as soon as they turn towards God and away from their wickedness, God relents. Jonah gets himself wound up looking at the way others are behaving. God indicates that anger is not the way forward. In his self-centredness, Jonah has missed the amazing news that more than 120,000 people who do not know right from wrong have turned back to God for a fresh start.

... and grace

When we expect to be rewarded for our faith, we don't always recognize God's unconditional love and acceptance. We sometimes think we have earned it – that we are entitled and have a claim on God because of our behaviour. But in the upside-down world of grace, those who struggle, who are late-comers to God, who feel unworthy, can be astonished and surprised by the generosity and love that God offers equally to all. No one is worthy of God's love, but wonderfully it is offered to all.

To experience God's grace is to recognize that we are all late-comers to the kingdom. The differences between us are inconsequential to the one who calls, gathers and loves us all completely.

We are not loved more because we work hard, we are not loved less when we struggle, want to give up or break down. We are loved completely and utterly, and always – for eternity. Even death cannot separate us from God's love. The sacrifice of Jesus on the cross was for everyone, everywhere, in all circumstances, for all time. Paul writing to the Christians at Philippi urges them to live their lives in a manner worthy of the good news of Jesus Christ. What does that mean for you this week? What might that look like in your life? When others look at you, what do they see of Jesus within you?

May the Holy Spirit of God lead you to a new level of generosity towards God and others. May all that you do each day be a reflection of God's love for you shining out towards our broken and weary world. And may you experience the expansive and capacious love of God for you and all those around you – love beyond measure.

Catherine Williams

Hymn suggestions

There's a wideness in God's mercy; O love that will not let me go; Faithful One, so unchanging; Amazing grace.

Sixteenth Sunday after Trinity (Proper 20)
24 September
Second Service   **Are You Listening?**
Ps. 119.113–136 [*or* 119.121–128]; **Ezek. 33.23, 30—34.10**; Acts 26.1, 9–25; *Gospel at Holy Communion*: Mark 9.30–37

They hear but do not obey

For any preacher, the opening words of this passage from Ezekiel are somewhat discouraging: 'They come to you as people come, and they sit before you as my people, and they hear your words, but they will not obey them.' This isn't to suggest that preachers require obedience. However, sermons should be worth listening to – offering encouragement in the way of faith, provoking thought, reflection and prayer, and even prompting changes in behaviour, as preacher and listeners walk together on our journey of Christian discipleship.

This passage offers us insight into what can go wrong between prophets, pastors and people, and there may be a lesson there for each of us to heed. Because the people aren't the only ones that cop it in this reading. The religious leaders – referred to here as 'the shepherds of Israel' – are roundly condemned for neglecting their duties and abandoning their sheep, the people entrusted to their care.

Hearts set on gain

The root issue is the same for both groups – those who hear but do not act, and those who neglect the sheep. Of the people – 'their heart is set on their gain'. Of the shepherds – 'the shepherds have fed themselves, and have not fed my sheep'. The problem is that everyone is thinking first about themselves, about their own gain and their own needs, before thinking about God or anyone else.

The people ignore Ezekiel because what he is telling them is costly to hear. He is telling them that they cannot expect to receive God's favour if they persist in ignoring the path God has set out for them to follow – a path of honouring and worshipping God alone, a path of living well together with others. The people have been lured off the path by self-interest and refuse to heed the warnings God has sent them.

Leading away from God

The shepherds are, if anything, worse – they take from the flock but put nothing in. 'You eat the fat, you clothe yourselves with the wool, you slaughter the fatlings; but you do not feed the sheep.' They expect the rights but take none of the responsibilities of leadership. And they clearly set no kind of example to the flock:

> You have not strengthened the weak, you have not healed the sick, you have not bound up the injured, you have not brought back the strayed, you have not sought the lost, but with force and harshness you have ruled them.

Where the leaders should have been leading the people in God's way, they have instead been in turn exploiting and ignoring them, leaving them uncared for and vulnerable – so no wonder they have strayed so far from God's path.

How do we listen?

So what lesson is there for us as we hear the words of Ezekiel? If we don't want to fall into the traps as the people of Israel did, we must really listen to God. That can be easier said than done – whether you're a shepherd or one of the flock. How do we listen? Our reading from Acts gives us an example of someone who *really* wasn't listening to God, so God had to resort to extreme measures – with blinding light and a voice from heaven. This is unlikely to happen quite as dramatically to us, but there are aspects of his experience that we can relate to.

We may not have been blinded by God's light, or fallen down in a faint because we were so overwhelmed by God's presence, but we probably have felt our hearts lift, our spines tingle or our heads reel. We may have sensed that we were in a holy place, seen or heard something that came to us as a blessing. That could be God speaking. Listen.

We may not have heard God's voice in our heads, but we may have had a sense of God's will – a word of the Bible that seems as if it was written just for us, a phrase from the service or a hymn that suddenly makes perfect sense, a persistent sense of something, a nudge from several different places in one direction. That could be God speaking. Listen.

God's loving voice

As Saul discovered, what God says isn't always easy to hear – but it is always said in love. God says to Saul, 'Why are you persecuting me? It hurts you to kick against the goads.' God isn't hurt by Saul's attacks, but Saul is. It is for Saul's benefit that God wants him to stop his behaviour. And we all get caught up in patterns of behaviour that are as destructive to ourselves as to others around us – I don't need to list them because I suspect we all know deep down what they are. And we probably have all heard that little voice inside that says, 'Stop'. That could be God speaking. Listen.

God speaks to us all. We just need to learn how to listen.

Kat Campion-Spall

Hymn suggestions

O Jesus, I have promised; Lord, speak to me that I may speak; Loving shepherd of thy sheep; Dear Lord and Father of mankind.

Seventeenth Sunday after Trinity (Proper 21)
1 October
Principal Service   Challenged by the Word
(*Continuous*): Ex. 17.1–7; Ps. 78.1–4, 12–16 [*or* 78.1–7];
or (*Related*): **Ezek. 18.1–4, 25–end**; Ps. 25.1–8; Phil. 2.1–13;
Matt. 21.23–32

It's not fair!

'It's not fair,' say the Israelites to God in the passage from Ezekiel: 'The way of the Lord is unfair.' We thought we understood the rules, we thought we knew where we were – but it's all changed!

'O house of Israel,' says God: 'Is my way unfair? Is it not your ways that are unfair?' It's simple, really. Turn away from being righteous, from doing good, and you will lose your life. Turn away from transgressions, from sin, and you will save your life. What could be simpler than that? How is that being 'unfair'?

'It's not fair,' say the chief priests and the elders to Jesus. 'We want to know by whose authority you are doing these things.' 'Answer this question,' responds Jesus. 'Did John's baptism come from heavenly or earthly authority?' This is a tricky question with implications whichever way it's answered: 'We do not know,' they hazard. 'Then I'm not going to tell you about my authority either,' says Jesus. And he goes on to tell a parable guaranteed to make the earthly religious authorities squirm.

Challenged by the Word

In these passages, the protagonists are being challenged by the word: the word of the Lord through the prophet Ezekiel; the word made flesh in Jesus. And an encounter with the word of God makes them think again, changes their outlook, moves them from complacency to new ways of thinking about God.

In both these passages, God's people – first the Israelites, the Chosen Race, then, second, the religious authorities, the chief priests and elders of the Temple – are challenged to keep growing in their faith. It's not enough to rely on the past, on a position held, on a family tie, on historic happenings. God is a God of the present and the future who expects people to journey to new places, geographically, mentally and spiritually.

It's not just what our ancestors did that matters to God, but what we do now and in the future. 'All lives are mine,' says God – the parent as well as the child – and though we may be related to one another it is still what we do ourselves in our relationship with the living God that counts.

Continuing to challenge

Jesus continues to challenge. It is not enough to say the right religious words. It is not about having a particular position in the religious hierarchy, but about being open to the new things that God is doing and being prepared to do the will of God, whatever that might mean. The religious hierarchy didn't recognize God's messenger, John the Baptist, and challenged the authority of God in Jesus. However, tax-collectors, sinners and prostitutes flocked to John the Baptist. They knew their need of grace, took the opportunity to turn around and live. And so, warns Jesus, they are well ahead when it comes to the kingdom of God.

Jesus challenges us to consider which is better: to make fine promises, speak fine words about all we will do and then not do it, or be rebellious, refuse to do what's required, but then have a change of heart, turn around and walk the path of obedience.

Obedience and humility

What does the Lord require? That, made in God's image, we follow Christ and grow more into the likeness of Christ. To be Christ-like is to be humble: to exercise humility by regarding others as better than ourselves. To be looking to build up the best in others. To know that we don't have all the answers and that God is much bigger and much more surprising than we realize.

Following Christ in the way of obedience and humility may lead to humiliation – none of us wants to go there, but Jesus did. It may lead to sacrifice – not as dramatic as Christ's unique sacrifice on the cross, but we may be called to make other sacrifices so that God and God's ways come first in our lives.

Responding to the challenge

We're called to respond to God's ongoing challenge. We cannot rely on some glorious past. It's not sufficient to come to church week by week and say the same words – important though that is.

It's not enough to rely on the faith of other people; we have to be developing and deepening our own relationship with God – being obedient to his will, which may challenge and call us into new ways of thinking, believing, worshipping and being.

So, a challenge today from the living word – a challenge for all of us – warning us not to sit still and stagnate in our faith. Calling us to explore and be open to God in new ways. Reminding us not to be complacent in our relationship with the living God – but to be continually bowing the knee at the name of Jesus Christ and walking humbly and obediently into his future.

Catherine Williams

Hymn suggestions

All my hope on God is founded; Majesty, worship his majesty; Trust and obey; Rejoice, the Lord is King.

Seventeenth Sunday after Trinity (Proper 21)
1 October
Second Service   **God's Dwelling Place**
Ps. [120, 123] 124; **Ezek. 37.15–end**; 1 John 2.22–end;
Gospel at Holy Communion: Mark 9.38–end

Where is God?

Or, to put it another way, where is God's dwelling place?

Before the Babylonian exile, the Israelites would probably have answered with confidence: God's dwelling place is the Temple in Jerusalem. That is God's house, God's dwelling place. But once the city of Jerusalem had been taken, the Temple destroyed, and the leaders and people of Jerusalem exiled to Babylon, what then? If there is no Temple, no house for God, where does God dwell?

Ezekiel's vision

Ezekiel had his own understanding of that. In chapters 10 and 11, he is given, by God, a vision in which the glory of God departs from the Temple, departs from Jerusalem, departs from the people. Ezekiel believed that God was no longer with the Israelite people due to their behaviour. The terrible events that had befallen them were their own fault, because again and again they rebelled against God, turning away from the one who was so faithful to them. Where is God's dwelling place?

But the book of Ezekiel is not all doom and gloom. Immediately before this passage, Ezekiel has a vision that I'm sure you are familiar with, in which dead dry bones in a desolate desiccated valley are filled with God's breath and become living people again. It's a beautiful, powerful image of hope, of God's faithfulness even to the most lost of causes. And what we hear in today's reading is a less dramatic vision, but one that has its own power.

Reconciliation

Ezekiel has a word from God about reconciliation. Reconciliation between two groups who have been divided for over 300 years – the northern and southern kingdoms. These were, until the end of the reign of Solomon, the kingdom of Israel. After Solomon, the people of Judah, the southern kingdom, accepted the rule of his son Rehoboam; but the people of Israel, the northern kingdom, rejected him, and the kingdom was divided. It was a deep and entrenched division. So much so that God knows the people won't understand the message: 'Take a stick and write on it, "For Judah, and the Israelites associated with it"; then take another stick and write on it, "For Joseph (the stick of Ephraim) and all the house of Israel associated with it"; and join them together into one stick, so that they may become one in your hand.'

That might not sound like a very sophisticated metaphor, but for the Israelite people of Judah in exile in Babylon, reunion with Israel was simply not on the agenda. Returning to Jerusalem, yes, the rebuilding of the Temple, yes, but the northern kingdom? So far off the agenda that God's word to Ezekiel continues: 'When your people say to you, "Will you not show us what you mean by these?"' *When* they say it. How else would they respond? What is clear is that while God's people are divided from each other, they are divided from God.

Reunion

Ezekiel gives us a beautiful vision of the future, with the people united, under one shepherd, the new David, secure in the land God gave them for generations. Where is God's dwelling place? 'My dwelling-place shall be with them,' says the Lord, 'and I will be their God, and they shall be my people.'

This is a radical change from Ezekiel's vision of the Lord departing from the people. But it is significant that here it is linked with the reunion of Israel. Ezekiel is suggesting that being reconciled to each other is an important part of the process of being reconciled to God. They need to dwell together if God is going to make God's dwelling place with them.

In our New Testament reading from the First Letter of John, we hear several times the idea of the believer abiding in God. The word in Greek which is translated as 'abide' can also be translated as 'dwell'. 'If what you heard from the beginning abides [dwells] in you, then you will abide [dwell] in the Son and in the Father.' If we allow the gospel to dwell in us, to inhabit us, to remain with us, then we will dwell in the Son and the Father. So John is saying that God will dwell in us.

In our society, as in the time of Ezekiel, as in the time of John, deep divisions exist between people on all levels. Culture, ethnicity, religion, class, gender, age. Some play out on the international stage, some within communities or institutions, some within families. Some are so deep that reconciliation is simply not on the agenda – that holding two sticks together as Ezekiel did would leave people bemused. Where is God's dwelling place?

Something happens when people begin to look at the barriers that separate them from others and start to work for reconciliation. When people who are divided start to imagine dwelling together. When, like Jesus, people begin to transgress boundaries. Because that is where God is at work, where God's dwelling place is made.

Kat Campion-Spall

Hymn suggestions

Let us build a house; Brother, sister, let me serve you; In Christ, there is no east or west; When I needed a neighbour.

Eighteenth Sunday after Trinity (Proper 22)

8 October

Principal Service   **Provoking Jesus, Disruptive and Wild**

(Continuous): Ex. 20.1–4, 7–9, 12–20; Ps. 19 [*or* 19.7–end];
or *(Related)*: Isa. 5.1–7; Ps. 80.9–17; Phil. 3.4b–14;
Matt. 21.33–end

There was a prayer I remember from being very young: 'Gentle
Jesus, meek and mild …', it began. Heresy for the very young!
Focusing in on events in Matthew 21 we don't see a Jesus who is
meek or mild. We see him throwing over the tables of the money-
changers – bringing clatter and disruption. We do witness his welcome of the blind and lame in his acts of healing. There is kindness
here, but not mildness. We see him cursing a fig tree for its lack
of fruit. He is engaged in ongoing conflict with the Pharisees who
question his authority. They are clearly riled by him; he keeps on
provoking, needling them with parables to expose their hypocrisy.
My childhood prayer would have been more theologically accurate
had it read: 'Provoking Jesus, disruptive and wild.' Less soothing,
but much more interesting.

In the crosshairs of this parable

The parable we read today is obviously told with the Pharisees as
clear targets (but don't imagine that lets the contemporary reader
off the hook). The Pharisees know they are in the crosshairs of
this parable, and it fuels the growing tension that will lead to their
brutal actions against Jesus.

What's going on here? Fundamentally, the Pharisees are being
criticized for corruption; they don't deal honestly and fairly with
the landowner. They look after their own interests and seek ultimate control of the vineyard, withholding 'rent' through increasing
acts of violence. The tenants' brutal murder of the landowner's son
reminds the reader of the growing tension between Jesus and the
Pharisees, which will lead to him being thrown out of the city and
killed at Golgotha. Another murdered son.

It's interesting that when Jesus asks the Pharisees what the landowner will do with the wicked tenants their response is merciless:
'He will put those wretches to a miserable death.' Jesus does not
respond directly to their judgement. They offer no mercy, which
speaks volumes about where they position themselves in the parable.

237

They imagine themselves as the wronged landowner, rather than the duplicitous tenants. They seem to have gravitated to the best seat in the house!

Shifting metaphors

Jesus moves the metaphor on. Now the Pharisees are builders – choosing to reject the stone that will hold together a marvellous new edifice. This stone is dangerous. You don't want it to fall on you, or to land on it. Jesus is the stone that breaks and crushes. He breaks our pride and shatters opposition to the love of God. Ultimately, he shatters death itself. That's some disruption!

Jesus speaks of the kingdom being taken away from those who don't produce fruit from its resources. The Pharisees are not impressed by this disruptive threat to their power, prestige and position, and choose an adversarial response. What about us?

Mirror, mirror on the wall

If we read this passage as though it's all about those Pharisees, with nothing to say to us, then we will have failed to comprehend it, failed to hear its call, and missed the grace within Jesus' disruptive stance. Jesus pursues the Pharisees relentlessly. Why? Is the end goal simply to expose and humiliate them? What would be the point of that? Had any one of his hearers sought him out and looked for a different way to live, would he have turned them away? I don't think so. This disruptive, wild Jesus looks for change, for a humbling of the human heart in order to provoke a return to God. He holds up a mirror to the Pharisees. They look but fail to see their true reflection.

When we gaze into the mirror of this parable, do we see something of ourselves reflected back? Perhaps we squirm. I do. The violence of the actions of the tenants is not how I behave! I want to put some distance between myself and this disturbing parable. But, listen to the questions the parable provokes. They are disruptive gifts.

Disruptive gifts

- How do I use power?
- How am I using resources?
- In my corner of the kingdom, am I producing fruit?

- Where is my focus, my chief concern?
- Am I working with and for the vine-owner, or am I more focused on my own perceived interest?

Unless we actively direct it, the human heart will always bend to its own will. Unless I challenge myself with the disruptive gifts of this parable, I will take the best seat in the house and look to what I perceive are my own interests. When we are shown our shortcomings, we have a choice. Will we deny, avoid or blink the truth away? Or will we come in repentance, seeking reformation? No – it isn't comfortable. But perhaps wisdom lies in seeking disruptive, life-giving discomfort over the narcotic ease of self-righteousness.

My childhood prayer went like this:

Gentle Jesus, meek and mild
Look upon a little child.
Pity my simplicity,
Suffer me to come to thee.

Perhaps a more theologically accurate and honest adult prayer might be:

Provoking Jesus, disruptive and wild,
look upon your wayward child.
Pity my duplicity,
enable me to come to thee.

Kate Bruce

Hymn suggestions

Come, thou fount of every blessing; Just as I am; Empty, broken, here I stand; My lips shall praise you.

Eighteenth Sunday after Trinity (Proper 22)
8 October
Second Service   **For Everyone Born, a Place at the Table**
Ps. 136 [*or* 136.1–9]; Prov. 2.1–11; 1 John 2.1–17;
Gospel at Holy Communion: **Mark 10.2–16**

For better or worse?

From antiquity, diptychs have been a creative way of bringing two art panels together to help tell a coherent and cohesive pictorial story. Gospel writers have also carefully crafted their narratives in juxtaposing literary tableaux that help them convey a particular insight into the life and ministry of Jesus. Today's Gospel seems to offer us some sort of literary diptych. However, the attempt of weaving these two stories together seems a little clumsy at first glance. What cohesive narrative might the association between inquisitive Pharisees concerned with legal issues, and carefree children in need of a hug offer?

Seemingly, there is little to no obvious relation between these two tableaux of Jesus' life. And yet, I wonder whether Mark, in coupling these two stories together, is wanting to draw the hearer's attention to a subtle and nuanced insight about Jesus' heart regarding family matters in particular, and regarding what it means to be human in general.

The contrast between these two expressions of Jesus may be somewhat unsettling when read as a single pericope. On the one hand, we encounter a Jesus who seems radical and quasi-inflexible in his assessment of Mosaic law concerning divorce and adultery. On the other hand, we discover an extravagantly generous Jesus who speaks with such tenderness about children and God's kingdom.

How do we hold apparent rigidity with abundant generosity? What might this diptych be telling us? What cohesive narrative might emerge out of these two panels painted for us by Mark the evangelist?

The first cut is the deepest

In his attempt to thwart the Pharisees' renewed efforts to test and discredit him, Jesus invites them to re-engage with the statement of God's purpose in creation highlighted in the divine arithmetic that speaks of plural humanity bonded into singular existence: 'and the two will become one flesh'.

His disciples, it seems, are perplexed by this exchange and want to interrogate Jesus further. In the intimacy of exchange with his disciples, Jesus seems to push the argument one step further as he redefines parameters for adultery.

While we cannot detract from the matrimonial element in this exchange, I wonder whether Jesus' argument here is making a point that transcends matrimony, and underscores the interconnected and interdependent nature of human existence. Humanity is fully realized when allowed to flourish in a rapport of mutuality and intimacy. That, Jesus argues, is the heart of God's purpose in creation. To conspire against it is to contravene with this divine mandate for unity that God has given humanity. In that perspective, divorce becomes not simply the separation of two individuals but the intentional fragmentation of a unit. It is not just the parting of two, but the cutting off of what is one, of what is complete.

Despite their mastery of Mosaic law, the Pharisees fail once more to understand the simple yet compelling insight of God's character and how it manifests in creation. Instead, they have espoused a utilitarian approach to human relations, setting them as essentially transactional exchanges.

Such an approach tends to foster fragmentation, competition, and does not particularly favour collaboration, mutual support and care. It could be argued that an approach that justifies the fragmentation and separation of humanity will have little regard concerning the integrity of the rest of creation, only considering it as disposable resources whose value is assessed according to the measure in which it served individuals or collective interests in their quest for domination and subjugation.

Family matters

The contrasting picture of Jesus gathering children to him and blessing them only adds strength to the point he seems to be making to his disciples and the Pharisees. Where they seek arguments to justify separation, Jesus offers acts that promote the intersection of human stories. Where they lean on to the force of law and their right, Jesus centres his attention, energy and posture towards those with little to no legal or social power.

Divine ecology tends to offer a wholly topsy-turvy vision of the world in which full self-realization assumes a shared commitment to ensure that the least privileged, the least powerful are afforded equality of opportunity and outcome in their quest towards self-realization. Furthermore, it is a world where there is an intentional levelling down of social norms, a radical reorientation towards kingdom values and ideals.

Significantly, Jesus' spontaneous response towards children and their families hints towards what an actualized vision of the kingdom might look like. It hints towards a world where it becomes possible to tell afresh the story of God's purpose in creation, not as an academic exercise drawn from legislative literature, but as an embodied, corporeal reality. Interdependence and interconnection are essential in such a world. Interdependence and interconnection that are not exclusively preoccupied with nuclear relationships, but that recognize the universality of the bonds that bind us to one another, to the whole of creation and, most significantly, to the Creator.

For Jesus, our creation family matters because it speaks of God's love. Family matters because it offers an avenue to express God's love.

Lusa Nsenga Ngoy

Hymn suggestions

Jesus loves me, this I know; Lord of all hopefulness; Hope of the world; For everyone born.

Nineteenth Sunday after Trinity (Proper 23)
15 October
Principal Service   **Dressing for the Occasion**
(*Continuous*): Ex. 32.1–14; Ps. 106.1–6, 19–23 [*or* 106.1–6]; or (*Related*): Isa. 25.1–9; Ps. 23; Phil. 4.1–9; **Matt. 22.1–14**

Since 'Waterloo' and the Eurovision Song Contest, there is little doubt that Abba can write a good tune: a tune you can whistle. To bring together many of the top Abba hits in a stage show and two films, *Mamma Mia*, guaranteed sure-fire success. Although a little contrived, the storylines are filled with exuberant joy in and for the human condition. There are weddings and feasts and celebrations with steaming plates of food, much to drink and enthusiastic dancing. Marvellous!

Frequently in literature and drama, weddings are the setting for a joyful resolution, when young lovers surmount numerous hurdles on the road to the altar, or the finale of an unfolding tragedy. So too in the Bible. The prophet Isaiah chooses the image of a feast of rich food and fine wine where God will destroy death and wipe away every tear as God invites all nations to the table. And Jesus, when he envisions how God's reign will culminate at the end of history, tells of a king hosting a great wedding feast for his son.

All dressed up and nowhere to go

The banquet is prepared, everything is ready and the king, perhaps somewhat satisfied, summons the guests. Shockingly, some simply ignore the invitation while others head out of town. 'The rest' beat up and kill the king's messengers. The generous host becomes the spurned 'Godfather' and sends his armies to wipe out the invited guests. Instead of sulking, though, he orders other servants to go to the highways and byways and invite everyone they see, both the good and the bad.

Matthew, Luke and the second-century non-canonical *Gospel of Thomas* recount this same parable but with very different applications. In Luke, the substitute guests are 'the poor, the crippled, the blind and the lame', an epitome of the Lucan Jesus who preached good news for the poor and welcomed the outcasts into the kingdom of God. In the apocryphal *Gospel of Thomas*, there is nothing elaborate but a simple dinner. The guests refuse because the invitation conflicts with their business interests – money locked up in offshore investments.

Wearing the wrong clothes

Matthew's story is so complicated that it is easy to forget that the central image of God is as a gracious host who hopes that everyone will come to the banquet. This central image, at the heart of Matthew's parable, is easily lost amid the contrary symbols, where roast oxen get cold while a military expedition torches the city. And after that, when the king sees that among the bad and good picked up from the streets there is a party-pooper not properly dressed, he has him bound and thrown into the outer darkness. All this makes it difficult to hold on to the original image of a generous host who knows how to throw a party.

There was another storyteller around at the same time as Matthew, Rabban Johanan Zakkai. In his story, a king invited his servants to a feast, without saying what time it would take place.

The wise among the guests prepared themselves at once and waited for the palace gates to open. They believed that a palace could prepare a feast very quickly. The foolish guests went off to their work. They believed that preparations would take a long time and leave them plenty of scope to roll up when the party was in full swing. Suddenly the king announced that everything was ready. The wise ones came immediately into the royal presence as they were ready to go and dressed in clean clothes. The foolish arrived as they were, in their dirty work clothes. The king welcomed those who were properly dressed and commanded the others to stand and look on at the joy they had lost.

Clothe yourselves

For ourselves, we hold a precious image of a God who calls everyone to his banquet, both good and bad. The expectation is that we will prepare ourselves now by being dressed appropriately for the occasion. So, what are we to wear? Well, St Paul gives a hint in his letter to the Philippians: 'whatever is true, whatever is honourable, whatever is just, whatever is pure ...'. This is developed in the letter to the Colossians: 'As God's chosen ones, holy and beloved, clothe yourselves with compassion, kindness, humility, meekness and patience ... Above all, clothe yourselves with love, which binds everything together in perfect harmony.'

What an outfit! With clothes like these, we will never be thrown out of any banquet.

Paul Williams

Hymn suggestions

O thou who camest from above; Amazing grace; At the Lamb's high feast we sing; Come to the feast.

Nineteenth Sunday after Trinity (Proper 23)
15 October
Second Service   **Don't Airbrush Out the Difficult Stuff**
Ps. 139.1–18 [*or* 139.1–11]; Prov. 3.1–18; 1 John 3.1–15;
Gospel at Holy Communion: Mark 10.17–31

Removing jigsaw pieces

Imagine doing a jigsaw and discovering pieces have been removed. How frustrating! What if the pieces were removed as an act of censorship? That would be plain patronizing.

The people who compile the Sunday readings have been guilty of jigsaw-piece removal when it comes to today's psalm. The ending has been airbrushed out, removing some challenging statements and lopping off the final verses which give a sense of completeness. This seems offside!

Let's hear those difficult verses:

> O that you would kill the wicked, O God,
>   and that the bloodthirsty would depart from me –
> those who speak of you maliciously,
>   and lift themselves up against you for evil!
> Do I not hate those who hate you, O Lord?
>   And do I not loathe those who rise up against you?
> I hate them with perfect hatred;
>   I count them my enemies.

I imagine editing was done to spare us the uncomfortable themes. The problem is we need these verses if we are to fully mine the riches of this psalm.

Truth in a tight spot

Without the ending, the psalm is simply a beautiful meditation on the omnipresent and intimate nature of God. Seen thus, the raging verses are an embarrassment, but if we see them as part of the whole, we will grasp that this moving meditation on the nature of God's presence and knowing takes place in a context of hostility. This matters.

I imagine the Psalmist in a tight spot, back against the wall, scribbling words on the ancient world's equivalent of a fag packet.

Invoking God to kill the wicked, calling for the bloodthirsty to be gone, and speaking of hating with a perfect hatred suggests the writer is in significant difficulty. The tricky verses speak of malice and evil. Perhaps the Psalmist stands unjustly accused, facing uncompromising opponents, without mercy.

I picture this person chained to a radiator, tortured, dragged before a camera to read a statement they do not believe, while someone points a gun at them. Seeing the psalm written against the ancient world's equivalent of this backdrop, we begin to sense the depth of the writer's trauma. The harsh verses, rather than being an embarrassment, are essential to our understanding. Truth can sustain us in trauma of whatever magnitude.

Deep words in dark places

This profound meditation on God's creative seeing and knowing is wrung out of a person walking in shadow, not meandering in a dappled glade.

The Psalmist emphasizes that God knows everything about them, all their movements, thoughts, ways and words. Perhaps some of them are deeply bitter. Whatever the accusation, only God has the full picture. This reality of being known utterly is overwhelming. It is like asking an atom of salt to comprehend the sea. God lays his hand upon the writer in an image of comfort, protection, causing profound awe.

All of life is stretched out before God's awareness. This truth relativizes all our concerns. We think that this issue or that is the be all and end all and become wrapped up in our 'all-important' concerns. Have you pondered the enormity of the reality of God? Pull back the camera. There is nowhere God is not: the places of peace and happiness, the arenas of discomfort and death. In all situations, God will lead those who trust and the right hand of God will hold on tight.

In deep distress, the Psalmist wonders if the darkness will swallow them utterly – before realizing that darkness is like light to God. Nothing can separate them from God. Not even the extremis of their present distress. God knows. This matters.

From womb to tomb and beyond

The writer reframes their troubles in the light of the God who knitted them together in utero. Here is mystery, intimacy, creativity and love. There is nothing that God does not know about the poet. The God beyond time sees and knows all. Before this Creator the Psalmist has no need to pretend or hide; such things are futile. They can simply be and know that they are known – warts, rage and all, even to the very end. There is such blessed relief here.

It is on the back of this theological meditation that the Psalmist launches into their tirade against the wicked, the bloodthirsty, and those of malicious and evil intent. The person is speaking their truth to the God who sees and knows. Faced with the reality of evil, the poet affirms their desire to be found with God and for God. On the basis of this, they invoke the searchlight of God's loving presence to scan everything about them:

> Search me, O God, and know my heart;
>   test me and know my thoughts.
> See if there is any wicked way in me.

This is a statement of profound trust, uttered in difficult circumstances.

The psalm affirms that whatever we face, however dark or unjust, God is present as God always has been and always will be. Here is awe, mystery, comfort and relief wrought from the dark places.

So, don't airbrush out the difficult stuff!

Kate Bruce

Hymn suggestions

O God, you search me and you know me; O God, our help in ages past; Great is thy faithfulness; Abide with me.

Twentieth Sunday after Trinity (Proper 24)
22 October
Principal Service   **Tough Questions**
(*Continuous*): Ex. 33.12–end; Ps. 99; *or* (*Related*): Isa. 45.1–7; Ps. 96.1–9 [10–13]; 1 Thess. 1.1–10; **Matt. 22.15–22**

A few years ago, there was an advert for McCain oven chips on TV which depicted a child on the way home from school asking herself the very difficult question: 'Who do I love most: Daddy or chips?'

She ponders this all the way home until her meal – with chips – is put in front of her. As she settles down to eat, Daddy comes in the door, ruffles her hair and steals her chips. The question is settled: chips, she nods sagely. And we all laugh.

It's a tough question – the question of what we love most, or what we care about most. And tough questions are at the heart of our Gospel today, as Jesus moves closer to the scene of his death, and both questions and answers take us beyond the expected into new directions. That's probably why we don't really like tough questions. We prefer to be entertained by easy questions, questions that will make us and them look good, except when the tide turns and we want to see a public figure exposed. Then we want to hear the audience on *Question Time* asking tricky, ambiguous questions, designed to make the person feel hunted and haunted and to trip themselves up in their answer.

The question trap

The Pharisees and the Herodians were asking Jesus these kinds of questions. They wanted to trap him, to ask a double-edged question that would land him in difficulties whatever he answered. So, they come with the first of their questions: 'Is it lawful to pay taxes to the emperor, or not?' They preface their question with lots of grovelling about how they respect Jesus and know he is teaching the way of God with integrity.

The trap is this: many of Jesus' followers want him to overthrow secular Roman rule, so if Jesus says no, he is aligned with the zealots and is a marked man. But if he says yes, then he has disappointed his followers, shown himself to be no different from other politicians.

Jesus, always an excellent teacher, asks for a coin, a visual aid, and gets them to tell him whose head is on the coin: it's quite probable that this coin is a denarius, equivalent to one day's wage, and that the tax being referred to is the head tax, paid by each person to the Roman government and, like all such taxes, deeply unpopular.

The tough answer

Tough questions need tough answers, and Jesus gives a very tough answer. It is not the wily answer of the politician who avoids the question altogether, nor yet the answer of the diplomat, soothing troubled waters. Jesus gives an answer that conceals another question: who are the questioners really serving? For Jesus brings them face to face with God and God's demands on their lives. He deals directly with the issue of taxes, giving them a rightful place within the economy of God, and faces them with the real issue: acknowledging God in their lives and recognizing Jesus as God among them.

'Give to Caesar that which is Caesar's and to God that which is God's' has become a byword in our world, making us feel that we can know the answer to the tough question of priorities in our lives and balancing sacred and secular, church and state.

We so easily gloss over Jesus' answer to the tough question, missing the breathtaking idea offered in his answer. For when we start to think about giving to God the things that are God's, we find ourselves facing the impossible, for what does not belong to God?

God created heaven and earth; God provides for our daily needs, fills our lives with family and friends, and reveals his love to us in myriad ways. In response, we are asked to love him with all of our heart, mind, strength, soul – everything. So, giving to God what is God's is a huge challenge.

The priority of love

The answer is not really about taxation at all but is rather about love and best love. Which brings me back to the advert. Who do you love most: Daddy or chips? We laugh because the answer is wrong. We know that the child should love her daddy most – chips are just one of the passing delights of life, but not comparable to family love.

But perhaps we also feel discomfited, because we know how easily love becomes measured in the visible, tangible goods we can see and own, and we know how easily material things take our energies and our priorities. Jesus' answer poses us with a tough question: who do we love the most, what do we love most – is it the trappings of our lives or is it God, the author and finisher of our faith, the one who deserves all that we can offer?

Sandra Millar

Hymn suggestions

Christ's is the world; O for a closer walk with God; Take my life and let it be; All my hope on God is founded.

Twentieth Sunday after Trinity (Proper 24)

22 October

Second Service   **By This We Know**

Ps. 142 [143.1–11]; Prov. 4.1–18; **1 John 3.16—4.6**;
Gospel at Holy Communion: Mark 10.35–45

By this, we know

How can we know about God? How do we know how to live in this world? This First Letter of John addresses these enormous questions. The author digs into the language of the Gospel of John and comes out with startling statements that provoke us into thinking about life and spirituality.

Yes, it's a difficult text. It's not difficult to read in that it is complicated, or technical – the words John uses are simple enough – but it has a particular kind of difficulty. It seems designed to stop us in our tracks. The words suddenly arrest us. They turn from the text and look us in the eye.

This is a favourite word of John's. What's happening now, in your life? *This* place, *this* moment – to John, *this* is where the life of God is to be found. It is *by this you know*.

So, this text is not information, but invitation. If I'm fully present to this text, I believe I will be changed – not just by learning new things, although that might be the case – but subtly becoming different from the way I was when I began.

To put it another way, nobody meeting Christ goes away empty. And if I can start to recognize and encounter Christ in this text, then Christ will change me. *By this, we know.*

In this passage, the writer calls us to look at three moments of knowing. Each one has a different tense – past, future and present. He starts by inviting us to look back over our lives

By this, we have come to know

By contemplation of Jesus, the one who laid down his life for us, we have *come to know what love is*. Until we looked this way, into this mirror, we didn't even know or understand love. Of course, that's how a child learns what love is – by what is mirrored from a parent. Unless they see love, how will they learn to love? We too began to understand, says John, as we *saw*, right before us, this self-giving, outpouring love of Christ, shown to us in events and people.

We experienced these small revelations – and by this, we started to know love for ourselves.

And that leads us to what we will know in the future.

By this, we will know

We will know by this (by our integrity, our loving actions) that we belong to the truth.

According to John, we are *of the truth*. I think he means that the truth is where we live. The truth is our home, our dwelling place, our belonging.

For myself, I usually think of truth as something I have or don't have; something I search for, my understanding of reality that belongs to me – *my truth*.

John turns that idea upside down. The truth is not *our* property, *our* object – we are *its* object. By this, we will know that we belong to the truth. In our loving actions, we will begin to recognize that we are part of truth itself, a greater reality than we knew before.

Not *out of* but *into* the truth. We don't live *out of* the truth – putting into practice what we know. But rather, says John, we live *into* the truth – we learn to live in love and faith, and then discover the truth we inhabit, the truth we belong to. Truth possesses us.

This turns us towards our future: *we will know*.

By this, we know

And finally, John looks at this present moment. By this, we know that he lives in us.

In our present, there is this presence, this life. Might it be that this whole passage is actually an unfolding of Jesus' words in the Gospel of John: 'I am the way, the truth, and the life'?

A way seen in love.
A truth known in action.
A life known from the Spirit in faith and love.
By this, we know he lives or abides in us.

Knowing to John is always a present reality, a dynamic relationship. *We* are not the people who are marked out by some special understanding, some difference from others. *We* are only *we* because we participate in this life of God. So even the word *we* itself calls us into reflection and self-awareness. As I hear it, I ask: does this word include me? Exclude me? Invite me?

And as I participate I become part of the *we* – that in the end is God.

May *we* be those who *know*, moment by moment, the mirroring of love, the belonging to truth, the presence of God within us.

Andrew Rudd

Hymn suggestions

All I once held dear (Knowing you, Jesus); Love is his word; Be still, for the presence of the Lord; Spirit of God, unseen as the wind.

Last Sunday after Trinity (Proper 25)   29 October
(For Bible Sunday, see p. 257.)
Principal Service   **A New Song, Shaped by Grief and Loss**
(*Continuous*): Deut. 34.1–12; Ps. 90.1–6, 13–17 [*or* 90.1–6];
or (*Related*): Lev. 19.1–2, 15–18; Ps. 1; 1 Thess. 2.1–8;
Matt. 22.34–end

Season of unexpected disruption

In September 2021 my father passed away. Though he was a week shy of his eighty-second birthday, his brief illness and death was an unexpected shock to the family. We were devastated, this loss indescribable and unimaginable.

Since the beginning of the coronavirus pandemic, many lives have been disrupted by devastation and suffering. Plans and dreams have been interrupted and upturned. Some of us hoped to spend more time with family and friends following months of lockdowns. I had been looking forward to visiting my family in Ghana, but this plan was inevitably shelved. Sadly, the last memory of my father was over a WhatsApp video call after two years of not being able to travel to visit. Without warning, I found myself in a landscape of grief, one that will take months and years to navigate.

In the midst of suffering, who is our neighbour?

Amid our personal griefs and losses, we are called to be people of comfort to our neighbours. We are invited to be Christ-like to those who have endured heartache and wounds of all kinds. I am reminded of George Floyd, who was killed because of systemic and structural racism, and the suffering his family and friends live with because of his death.

In a suffering world, we need to re-evaluate who we consider 'other', 'stranger' and 'neighbour'. Defining the parameters of 'who is neighbour' and 'who is not' is incredibly challenging. We are quick to draw up a shortlist of who we define as neighbour or not, who is in and who is out, as a means of determining who we can serve. The danger in this is that we don't just exclude the undesirable neighbour but we also exclude the presence of God.

We are called to see Christ in all humanity. Within all of creation, God's desire is for us to work together using our unique gifts and talents in God's kingdom work. But when we define 'neighbour' as those who look like us, think like us, or act by our expectations we work against the gospel message of offering love, justice and mercy to all made in the image of God.

A new song

The good news is that as Christians, even in a life of struggle and suffering, we have hope and a future. This good news of Jesus offers us a new song, an alternative way to frame the many griefs and losses we will experience in our lifetime. As followers of Christ, we can be intentional in creating a different world where love for our neighbour exists and prevails over pettiness, power and hate. We can be intentional in creating a world where love – the radical and transformative love Jesus talks about – can make room for 'the stranger', a world where all humanity is respected, valued and affirmed. Yes, we can create a world where we see Christ in 'the other'.

In my mind, what makes this commandment so hard to live out in our lives is it requires that we more fully, and above everything else, put God and love of neighbour at the centre of who we are. This isn't always an easy thing for us to do because it requires us to love the people around us even when it is most challenging for us to do. In my personal season of grief, I am still called to offer Christ's love to those that I minister among. Even when life pulls the proverbial rug from under our feet, we are invited to cling to God.

As we grapple with the interruptions and disruptions of life, we don't have to remain as we are. Jesus' mission and ministry are about transforming us, not just personally, but he also came to transform our communities to be oases of freedom and justice. In a generation groaning under the weight of immense suffering, what part are we going to play in transforming God's world and offering a new song in this age?

Catherine Okoronkwo

Hymn suggestions

When I needed a neighbour; I, the Lord of sea and sky; I will offer up my life; I want to serve the purpose of God in my generation.

Last Sunday after Trinity (Proper 25)   29 October
Second Service   **Eyes on the Prize**
Ps. 119.89–104; Eccles. 11, 12; **2 Tim. 2.1–7**;
Gospel at Holy Communion: Mark 12.28–34

Lean into the harness

Spiritual malaise is caused by the human tendency to take our eyes off the prize of pleasing God. We can drift, prone to wander, becoming tepid in faith and unfocused, like the church in Laodicea – 'neither hot nor cold'. Today's snippet from the Second Letter to Timothy offers a remedy. It reads like a coach calling out tips to their protégé.

The coach is urging Timothy to be 'strong in the grace that is in Christ Jesus'. The image that springs to mind is of a person abseiling, relaxing into the harness and trusting the ropes and the person belaying to get them down to the ground. It's a picture of trust. Being 'strong in the grace that is in Christ Jesus' is the spiritual equivalent of leaning into the harness. It is about the faithful willingness to trust Jesus' presence, strength and goodness, even if that's a hesitant and wobbly willingness.

The coach urges Timothy to pass on what he has heard, and presumably what he has learned for himself, to others: the coached becomes a coach.

Soldiers, athletes and farmers

We are offered three metaphors. First the soldier. Anyone who has been through basic military training will grasp this one. The pressure is often on. You want to get it right. The recruit who graduates on the parade square has suffered. Late nights spent working on kit – bulling shoes, knife-edge creases in uniform, kit laid out with precision. Early morning inspections. Physical pain and mental strain on exercise. The ability to handle pressure and stay focused on the mission takes intention and no little determination. What would it mean to be as spiritually focused on seeking to please God – the enlisting officer? 'Switch on!' says the soldier in this picture. 'Focus.'

The metaphor now shifts to the athlete. Emma Raducanu won the US Open at the age of 18. She didn't get up the morning just before the competition began and think, 'I'll have a go at that.' For years she learned the game, mastered the rules and the moves. She didn't land on court, lob a shot out of play and tell the umpire, 'I've changed the rules, it's still in if the ball goes out.' Like all successful athletes, she is dedicated and focused – learning how to compete at the highest level. The passage suggests the disciple should be more Raducanu.

The metaphor shifts again to the farmer. The farmer who does the work should have the first share of the crops. What is the metaphor driving at? If we take the time to focus on God, wrestle and ponder Scripture, remain with God, we will have the first share of the crops in the sense of the spiritual sustenance and learning that comes from these practices. If you aren't being fed by God, you don't have any resources to offer others. As with the soldier metaphor, there is something here about pleasing God and hearing the words from Matthew's Gospel, 'Well done, good and faithful servant'.

God our coach

All the metaphors are pictures of people who have focused their efforts on a particular enterprise. Timothy is instructed to think over these pictures, to focus on them, 'for the Lord will give you understanding in all things'. We are not left alone to work out what things mean and how to apply them. God is our coach, guiding and instructing alongside us. There's such encouragement here.

From quilting to car restoration

Perhaps the metaphors of soldiers, athletes and farmers feel a bit alien to you. No matter. Think of your life, of the things you do that require effort, focus and determination. Perhaps you are a quilter. No quilt was ever made without vision, planning and careful execution. Maybe you've written a thesis or passed an exam. Such things take focus and determination. No one raises a family well without considerable focused effort! Perhaps you've restored a car to its former glory, manual in one hand, spanner in the other. That doesn't just happen.

Find a picture that speaks to you of intentional focus and remind yourself that this is what God wants from you and will work for, in and with you.

Focus. Focus. Focus

Maybe you find you have wandered off, lost your passion, fallen into some tedious besetting sin. What now? Set your eyes on the prize. Make God your first thought as you open your eyes in the morning, and your final thought as you close them at night. Carve out stopping-off points in the day – to pray, reflect on Scripture, and simply notice God's presence. Take time in nature to allow God to speak to you through creation. Like a helm steering a compass point, keep pointing the bow of your life towards God.

All this demands that we focus, focus and focus again, conscious that God is always lovingly focused on us.

Kate Bruce

Hymn suggestions

Come, thou fount of every blessing; I will follow; Be thou my vision; And can it be.

Bible Sunday   29 October
The Revolutionary Work of Seeing Life

Neh. 8.1–4a [5–6] 8–12; Ps. 119.9–16; Col. 3.12–17;
Matt. 24.30–35

Seeing differently

One of the things living through traumatic events does to a person
is to change their perception and how they see things. Thanks to
Covid-19, for a time all the packaging, the tins, the boxes and
wrappings for my groceries became potential carriers of a deadly
virus and the arms of my glasses became the only safe way to
scratch my nose. Hands became either safe or infected, eyebrows
became the new way to smile and screens the primary way to meet
people. Traumatic events, such as pandemics, remind us that how
we understand what we see and what we hear is dynamic and sometimes surprising.

To see well is an art form with many components, as any blind
or partially sighted person will tell you. It takes focus and attention, discipline and self-knowledge, intuition and learnt skills and
courage and patience. We could all probably name people who we
would say can't see what's in front of their face or see the world a
bit differently. And we could also probably name those people who
are so intense in how they stare at you and the expressions they
use in response that they make you feel uncomfortable and want to
squirm. We know what it is to feel seen and to be ignored.

Seeing layers

The Gospel reading for today is overloaded with complicated stuff
in layers about understanding what you are seeing and what you
are listening to. There are two layers of obvious and literal, 'if this
then that' thinking. If the leaves appear on the tree, then you know
summer is near. More fragile is the statement, if the physical sun
and moon go dark then something is about to happen. And then
there are layers about less obvious things. Seeing stars falling from
heaven and the Son of Man coming on the clouds of heaven, seeing
and hearing all the tribes on earth mourn, hearing angels playing
a trumpet call, knowing that he is near, at the gates. Are these
literal things – shooting stars, comets, clouds, trumpets, gates – or
metaphorical things? How do I distinguish between the sound of

an angel playing the trumpet and the sound of an angel dancing on the head of a pin?

Seeing whole

Perhaps one way into this text is to see the whole rather than the detail. Seeing well, like listening well, I would suggest, is not just a great people skill to have, it is an attitude and a way of life that forms and builds depth and breadth, colour and shade in everyday life. To put it in another way, and a way that directly relates to the text before us, it is an act that brings the sacred, the divine, into the ordinary. Seeing and listening well is revolutionary work that puts at the centre of the stage that presence that is constantly leading us into wholeness, that love which will not let us go. It is work that is about art, awareness and intuition, and which holds fast to the belief that our perceptions can change, sometimes beyond what we can imagine.

Seeing life

Today is Bible Sunday. I wonder how and why you practise the art of seeing or looking at, or even into, the Bible. It is, I think, a complicated and layered activity. Sometimes the Bible is simply a physical object; an ancient book passed down through generations, a book given in celebration of a life event, a copy that is well used and acts as a transitional object through changes in life. Sometimes the Bible is seen as a sign or a symbol; being a Bible-believing Christian can mean something very specific. Sometimes we look at the Bible as a book of history, culture, interpreted text. Sometimes we look at it for comfort or hope or inspiration. Sometimes we look at or for a specific bit to soothe or comfort or back up an argument. Sometimes we read the stories of very human humans within it and see ourselves. We call it The Bible, or My Bible, or Scripture, or God's Word, or A Sacred Text.

Many of us have had an experience of a part of the Bible that has been useful, taught us something, corrected us, something has expanded our minds and our thinking, so our understanding and perception have changed. Perhaps that has been traumatic, perhaps led to a whole change in lifestyle and behaviour and the things around us will never seem the same again. Many of us live with a sense of seeing the Bible as a more general thing; how we understand it and it understands us is harder to put into words, but we are glad of its presence in our lives, and we feel and know that we are seen. We look at the Bible over and over again and see the world, ourselves and God being reformed, renewed, renamed and, ultimately, realized.

Esther Elliott

Hymn suggestions

O Love that will not let me go; How firm a foundation; I will sing the wondrous story; Lord, for the years.

Fourth Sunday before Advent   5 November
(For All Saints' Day, see p. 350.)
Principal Service   **Not One Stone Will Be Left**
Mic. 3.5–end; Ps. 43 [*or* 107.1–8]; 1 Thess. 2.9–13;
Matt. 24.1–14

A golden temple

Places of worship are some of the richest treasures of the Church. They are full of history and tell a complex story of faith. For many, as they worship, there is a great privilege – to look around at beauty. Norman pillars, medieval walls, the drama of the roof, the complexity of the woodwork and the organ, the richness of stained-glass windows. Now imagine, if you can, all of that beauty vandalized, demolished, and the site cleared so completely that nobody will be able to tell that there was once a church.

That scenario might give us a little glimpse of the impact of Jesus' words in this passage. The Temple he looked at, rebuilt by Herod the Great, had so much gold on it you had to shade your eyes to look at it. Built of huge gleaming limestone blocks, it was designed to impress, to hold thousands of people. It was the centre of the worship of the Jews. At special moments in their lives, everybody would go to the Temple. When you prayed you would close your eyes and think of the Temple, the place where people could meet God.

And Jesus said: 'Not one stone will be left here upon another; all will be thrown down.'

A temple demolished

And then, less than 40 years later, it happened. Jewish rebels were holed up in Jerusalem. The Roman armies of Emperor Titus surrounded it. Thousands died, and the city and Temple were engulfed in flames. The site was cleared completely – Temple, city, buildings, trees. Can you imagine the effect on Jewish worshippers?

Matthew is probably writing this Gospel after the destruction of the Temple, so it is not primarily about predicting the future. It's about how the individual finds *endurance* in times like these. It's about how we react to catastrophic events, and how we interpret them. It's about how we expect things to stay the same, how we rely on them, and how they never do stay the same. All things must pass – places, people, relationships, even the expressions of our faith.

There are times in all of our lives where we suddenly find we have lost our centre. What we had relied upon is suddenly removed. What we thought was for ever turns out to be passing and transitory.

World events in our time bring this very close to all of us, whether it is the catastrophic effects of global heating that make our lives more precarious or a pandemic that changes everything. This is tragic daily life for many people in our world.

But none of us, I think, escapes the experience of being transitory, the kind of moment when the world ends – but for me alone. What is there to say about this ending? This loss?

Words for the devastated

It can be so easy to be glib, to try to provide answers where there are no answers.

But clearly, there are passages in the Bible – such as this Gospel reading – that only make sense to people who are under extreme threat. They are people who no longer make assumptions about what is secure, what is safe, what will last. They are under no illusions.

Suffering and tragedy always seem to leave us disillusioned and unsupported, but paradoxically that can leave us open to God. When everything falls away, we may find a new way to live – where we don't depend on ourselves.

We find ourselves in *liminal space* – between one thing and another. In uncertainty and disorientation, in the place that feels like death but turns out to be the place where new life can begin.

New life

Once the Temple was destroyed, it was no longer possible for the Jewish communities that used to look to the Temple as their centre to do so. Deprived of their centre, they started to keep Temple liturgy alive in their synagogues. And in time the book, the scrolls, the Torah, became more important than the Temple that had gone. Without the Temple, they became closer to God.

And instead of being a national faith centred on a temple, a people of buildings became a people of the book. And eventually, the Jewish groups that followed Jesus created and cherished their own books about Jesus – the scrolls that became our Gospels. Christianity began to spread and transform the whole world.

We never know, when suffering begins, what is going to happen. We can't tell, as we feel our lives going into winter, what the spring will be like, or even if there will be a spring. 'Anyone who endures to the end', says Jesus, 'will be saved.'

But that is the source of hope, the deep affirmation of Jesus: the mystery of faith. Christ has died, Christ has risen, Christ will come again. The downward movement leads to the upward movement. That's the way the world is.

Andrew Rudd

Hymn suggestions

All my hope on God is founded; Lord of all hopefulness; Do not be afraid; Great is thy faithfulness.

Fourth Sunday before Advent   5 November
Second Service   **Admitting Vulnerability**
Ps. 111, 117; Dan. 7.1–18; **Luke 6.17–31**

Two versions

Have you ever noticed that there are two accounts of Jesus' most famous sermon? One is in Matthew's Gospel and the other in Luke's Gospel. Today we have Luke's version, and there are some important and challenging differences between the two. That which we usually call the 'Sermon on the Mount' isn't delivered from a mountain in Luke's Gospel. That's what happens in Matthew's story, not Luke's account. Jesus does go up a mountain in Luke's Gospel, but to pray not to preach. After a night in prayer, Jesus chooses his 12 apostles. Then Jesus comes down the mountain to the people following him, and talks with them. Many have come to hear him and are hoping to be healed.

What strikes me here, on the one hand, are Jesus' words and, on the other hand, the listening crowd and the profound respect they have for each other. The crowds come to listen; they also come to have their illnesses cured and their needs met. These people are vulnerable, and Jesus knows that. So, rather than inviting them to take a trek up a mountain to hear him preach, or invite his disciples up the mountain to talk *about* the people, Jesus instead comes down among the people to speak *with* them and to meet *with* them in their vulnerability and need.

Sainthood

We're currently in the season of All Saints and I want to suggest that being a saint means recognizing our vulnerability. Sainthood is not about being perfect, or different, or especially pious, or zealous for the faith. Sainthood is perhaps more about being vulnerable, and out of that vulnerability turning to God in need. It seems to me that there are two types of people prevalent in our society at the moment: sinners who think they are saints, and saints who know they are sinners. No one is more aware of their sinfulness and brokenness than a saint. The healthier we get, the more we realize how sick we are.

Blessings and woes

This also helps us understand Luke's juxtaposition of 'blessings' and 'woes'. We are more familiar with Matthew's account, where, after Jesus proclaims many to be 'blessed', he continues his sermon by telling the disciples that they are the salt of the earth and light of the world. But not so in Luke. Immediately after pronouncing his 'blessing' on the vulnerable poor, Jesus then follows with words of woe to those who are powerfully rich. Matthew, in his story, seems to soften the language by spiritualizing it: not 'poor', but, for Matthew, 'poor in spirit'; not 'hungry and thirsty,' but, for Matthew, 'hungry and thirsty for righteousness'.

Luke's language is starker. Those who are rich, full, at ease and well thought of should watch out. The tables are about to be turned. There is an echo here of the song that Luke has Mary sing earlier in his Gospel:

He has brought down the powerful from their thrones,
　　and lifted up the lowly;
he has filled the hungry with good things,
　　and sent the rich away empty.

The issue is not simply about wealth but about the way we use money and possessions to shield ourselves from our vulnerability: by creating an illusion that we are self-sufficient and not dependent on God. By doing so we blunt our sense of solidarity with and responsibility for the poor, and isolate ourselves from the needs of others. Rather, suggests Jesus, we are to be people of blessing who give away our riches to those who need them. We are to pray for those who lash out at us, and to treat all as we would wish to be treated. This too can lead us to that place of vulnerability.

Vulnerability

However, vulnerability is a nice-sounding word that names a condition most of us would wish to avoid. Vulnerability names a state of need and dependence that is often not comfortable. Our culture regularly discourages us from going there and teaches us that vulnerability is something to avoid at all costs. But while vulnerability is uncomfortable, it is also what makes us human. And when we try to numb those things that are uncomfortable – feelings of sadness, grief and vulnerability – we also numb our capacity to feel joy, satisfaction and happiness.

Church, at its best, can be a place that reminds us that vulnerability is not something to shun or deny. God has promised to meet us precisely at our points of vulnerability, our points of need and our points of brokenness. In the incarnation, God comes to be with and part of humanity in all its vulnerability. God comes down from on high, comes to our level and talks *with* us, not *to* us.

In our vulnerability let's reach out to make contact with Jesus, stretching to receive his healing touch. Let's remember that blessing lies along the path of vulnerability, where knowing our need of God we will practise attitudes and acts of love to all those around us.

Paul Williams

Hymn suggestions

Blessed be your name; When I needed a neighbour; There's a wideness in God's mercy; Bless the Lord my soul (Taizé).

Third Sunday before Advent   12 November
(For Remembrance Sunday, see p. 268.)
Principal Service   **Topping Up the Lamps**
Wisd. 6.12–16, *or* Amos 5.18–24; *Canticle*: Wisd. 6.17–20, *or* Ps. 70; 1 Thess. 4.13–end; **Matt. 25.1–13**

Pivotal times

It's a time in the church calendar of remembering, of looking back into the past and recalling the heroes of our faith, and also of reflecting on our own history and memories. But it's also the kingdom season, a time of thinking about the purpose of our faith, and it's a time to look forward, as on this Third Sunday before Advent we begin to think of the Christ who will come again one day.

The parable we heard is a timely one, which brings past, present and future together as we stand at this pivotal point in the year. Those who were listening to Matthew's Gospel, some 50, 60, 100 years after Jesus' resurrection, were living with a great expectation that he would return, and as year succeeded year their hope became dim. The descriptions of lamps lit, of oil running out and of wedding attendants waiting have all become a part of the images of our faith and our story as we think about how we hold on to hope in our lives.

Weary at weddings

Weddings in Jesus' day took place over many days. They involved feasts at the bride's home and feasts at the groom's home, and processions in between, just as many weddings across the world do today. We only have faint echoes of this now in the changing tradition of hen parties and stag nights, where friends and family of bride and groom gather separately to support and to celebrate. For the bride, female friends, often bridesmaids, played a special part in helping her be ready and in announcing the arrival of the groom. So, the bridesmaids need to be on the ball, keeping watch, alert and poised for action, whatever happened. In Jesus' story, the groom is late.

Waiting isn't easy. Imagine the attendants in that long night, imagine the shadows darkening around, imagine the winds and the rain as the flames flicker, and the fear sets in that the light is growing dim. You might imagine the conversations as time ticked by: shall we go, shall we stay? Slowly they all become tired, worn out with the events of the day, and they all fall asleep, waiting for the groom to come. There is a strange echo here of a time when the disciples listening to this story would also fall asleep, waiting for Jesus, unable even to watch with him in prayer.

It's not easy waiting. We wait for things to change in our lives. We wait for new life to run through our churches. We wait for the hungry to be fed and the homeless to be housed in our communities. And sometimes it seems as if nothing is going to happen. Sometimes, as we wait, we may look at the lamp we hold, and the supplies seem to have run out. A weariness descends. Are we ready for the work of God in our midst after all?

The oil of love and the oil of purpose

At this time of year, we remember the past, we give thanks for all the gifts that God has given – for his faithfulness and presence. We look back at our journey, the relationships that have surrounded us, the unexpected twists and turns that have kept us, above all the love that has never let go. As we remember, our hearts are stirred and our courage is renewed. Our lamps are filled with the oil of love and with the oil of hope. The parable reminds us to keep topping up that love – not tomorrow, but today.

We are also in the kingdom season when we think about God's will here on earth. When we remind ourselves of his purpose and our own role in proclaiming and building his kingdom. Topping up the oil in our lamps is also remembering the purpose to which we are all called – the kingdom of God – and the things we do that, seen and unseen, bear light to a world that is waiting, waiting for the coming of Christ. Being a bridesmaid is about being part of what is happening, being faithful as we stand in our place serving God, and, today, topping up the oil in our lamps with the knowledge of God's love in our lives, and God's purpose at work in our world.

Sandra Millar

Hymn suggestions

Give me joy in my heart; Heaven is in my heart; Christ, whose glory fills the skies; God is working his purpose out.

Third Sunday before Advent 12 November
Second Service **A Special Sort of Justice**
Ps. [20] 82; Judg. 7.2–22; John 15.9–17

God's justice

The God of Scripture both sits on high and dwells in the lowly place. This same God is the judge of human actions and the one who comes alongside the 'weak', the 'orphan' and the 'lowly'. God says 'no' and 'stop' to the wicked and unjust, and 'yes' to the victims of injustice.

This psalm appeals to God's justice. Yes, there are other things that God is: kind, compassionate, powerful, wise; but only God's justice will see things put right. Without justice, there is no hope for the world.

The setting of the psalm is unusual – a divine council, of all places. It sounds like a heavenly place – very otherworldly, with 'gods' and the like. But heavenly places in the Bible relate in no small part to what happens here on earth. We can be sure, then, that justice in the divine realm will find its way here.

Justice is more than fairness. Yes, lady justice holds a set of scales, but God goes further than rolling out a political 'levelling up' agenda. God not only judges from on high, making executive decisions about tax and improving education, but comes to us close and personal. Justice with God is justice that takes skin and bone.

Justice in person

The God who judges from on high steps down from the throne of judgement to pursue both those who have been unjust and those who have faced injustice. In Jesus, we see God the judge, acting in total responsibility for us created beings. He takes our infirmities; he touches the untouchables; he befriends the prostitute. Jesus the judge shares his existence with those most harshly judged by society. Justice for him will be forged through solidarity with the victim.

Jesus is not the remote judge on high, then, but he does deliver a word of judgement. If he didn't, there would be no hope for the victims of injustice. In his life, his death and his resurrection, he shouts 'no' to injustice and to those who judge the vulnerable. And he speaks an all-embracing 'yes' to the victim, the prisoner, the orphan.

Some of us are more inclined towards compassion and mercy than justice. We want to empathize with those who suffer and tenderly come alongside them. These are excellent qualities to have. However, the risk of *only* being empathetic is that we become inactive in seeking justice. Those who have faced injustice often need more than compassion. They need things to be put right. Conversely, the risk of only seeking justice is that we are always on the lookout for fairness, rather than seeking to join with the vulnerable to share their view of the world. To only seek justice can be to prioritize what is 'right' over what is kind.

Justice *and* compassion are needed. Our Psalmist appeals to God, knowing that God's justice includes compassion for the vulnerable. Such justice and mercy are exactly what we see in Jesus Christ. Christ is both just and merciful. This means that the endgame for the world will be justice for all, just as much as it will be mercy, forgiveness and reconciliation.

Living justice

There are days when we are neither merciful nor just. But God can well cope with us in such times. Jesus, the merciful judge, knows us in our weakness and forgives us. We cannot fix the world by ourselves. We will let people down. But we find ourselves in the hands of a loving God, whose future of justice can cope with our imperfections. That doesn't mean that we have an excuse; rather, it means we do not have to see ourselves as the ultimate solution to all problems. We cannot, in fact, be saviours. And that is a liberating thought.

We do have a role to play, however, in rooting out injustice, in living out Christ's compassion, in sharing life with those who have found themselves excluded, misjudged and disenfranchized. We will spot instances of injustice in our day-to-day life with those we meet. When we do, we can first act in solidarity and then venture to establish fairness and justice, always recognizing the grace we have received.

As we seek justice, and likewise mercy and kindness, we know

267

we do so in view of this heavenly council, where ultimate justice is being enacted, where mercy goes alongside, where wrongs will be put right, and where people from all nations will be granted welcome, liberation and a future where injustice, pain and sorrow will cease.

Mark Amos

Hymn suggestions

Tell out, my soul; Give thanks with a grateful heart; Beauty for brokenness; Living hope.

Remembrance Sunday 12 November
Holding On to Loveliness
(*The readings for the day, or for 'In Time of Trouble', or those for 'The Peace of the World' can be used. Readings for the Peace of the World are used here.*)
Mic. 4.1–5; **Phil. 4.6–9**

Hard thinking, hopeful thinking

Remembrance Sunday is one of those times that brings a whole host of stories and scenes flooding back. We might recall all the times we have laid a wreath at a memorial or been part of a parade, or just watched those moving moments from the Cenotaph as the great words of the Act of Remembrance are spoken. Our minds may be full of the pain and horror of war, of individuals whom we no longer see, of families torn apart, refugees pushed across the world, bodies changed for ever, and relationships that have been damaged beyond repair.

In the midst of all this come the words of St Paul in his letter to the church at Philippi encouraging us to think of things that are true, honourable, just, lovely and good. These words make us change our perspective, and listen for the different stories that emerge from war: words and actions that hold out hope. There are stories like that of the group of women who helped create 'home tents' in Kent during World War One, so that young men would have a place full of kindness and comfort before they left for the front. The tents were places where they could gather, games would be played, warm food served, and the women helped them write letters, chatted and talked of the hope of Jesus Christ, the light that would be with them in the darkness. These men were given something pure and lovely and true to hold on to in their most difficult times, as many letters testify.

Contemporary courage

Fast forward 100 years or so to recent TV programmes, where hundreds of people were moved to offer skills, time and resources to build a future for veterans of recent conflicts. Men, women and children whose lives were devasted in Afghanistan and Iraq found hope and loveliness once again, in contrast to darkness and despair. Stories of things that are pure and true can be heard in many different ways, told by many different voices.

We may not have war on our doorsteps any more, but the experiences of those who are pushed out of their homes, who travel long and dangerous journeys, and who simply want to bring up their children and grandchildren in peace and security are in our midst. I remember once talking to a young boy who had come here as a refugee from Angola. I asked him what he liked best about living here, expecting him to say something like McDonalds or football. Instead, he simply replied, 'They don't come to bomb your house.' Thankfully all over the world, people are working to build and maintain peace, through their work or as volunteers or just out of love. It is through the ordinary acts of kindness, the daily choices that people make to help others that the seeds of peace are sown. These are the things that help us all to work for the world that the prophet Micah speaks of, where swords become ploughshares and spears become pruning hooks, and people can sit at peace.

Remembering well

I often walk into the entrance hall of a local farmers' club – not because I am a farmer but because it's used for meetings and events – and in the entrance are large boards with the names of those members who died in active service. The idea of such memorials grew up after the horror of World War One when millions lost their lives. There were moments for a nation to remember together, like the two minutes' silence, but there were also countless memorials built in villages, towns, workplaces, schools across the land. It meant that each relative, colleague and friend could be remembered in lots of ways – in the home, in the community and nationally. As lives from long ago and from years just gone are remembered, we also remember the actions that brought loveliness to lives at home and bring hope in the most difficult of circumstances.

The light of Christ

Think on these things, writes St Paul, as his letter from 2,000 years ago draws to a close, adding that the God of peace will be with those who hold fast, who turn from darkness to light, grounding their lives in Jesus Christ. Today we remember the loss and the pain, but we also remember the courage and the kindnesses, things that are true and pure and worthwhile. As we remember all these things together, we find the courage to build the future, to pray and work for peace and to hold on to light and hope.

Sandra Millar

Hymn suggestions

For the healing of the nations; Peace is flowing like a river; O God, our help in ages past; Brother, sister, let me serve you.

Second Sunday before Advent 19 November
Principal Service **The God of Gift**
Zeph. 1.7, 12–end; Ps. 90.1–8 [9–11] 12 [*or* 90.1–8]; 1 Thess. 5.1–11; **Matt. 25.14–30**

The late poet U. A. Fanthorpe wrote a very funny and poignant poem called 'Getting It Across'. It's told in the voice of Jesus and it is a reflection on how God does not always choose the most gifted or most promising to share the message of grace and love with a disbelieving world. It paints a very funny picture of disciples bored with Jesus' stories, having heard them over and over again. At the same time, it reminds the reader that it is through ordinary people that the good news has reached us.

I think of that poem when I preach on a passage as familiar as the parable of the talents. The standard readings of it are so familiar from Sunday school that it can feel as if there's nothing more to say. When we hear a preacher say of this parable that it is about how God wants us to use our gifts and talents for the sake of the kingdom rather than bury them out of sight, we can be tempted to yawn like those first disciples in Fanthorpe's poem. We've heard it all before.

A living parable

There are ways we can bring a familiar parable, like that of the talents, alive again. Some scholars have gone so far as to deconstruct the parable, suggesting that it is a mistake to identify God with the demanding Master; indeed, some thinkers, drawing on the wisdom of African American liberation theologies, have gone so far as to suggest that the real hero of the parable is the slave who buries the talent in the ground. He is the one who resists the tyranny of the Slave Master. He is the one who refuses to placate the Master.

I suspect such an interpretation, while striking and powerful, might be a bit much for some of us and require a little too much theological theory to justify. Perhaps a better way for us to explore this parable without falling back on cliché is to ask how it relates to our images of God and ourselves.

Speaking for myself, I can say that before I came to faith in my twenties, I was inclined to see God through the eyes of fear, rather like the scared slave. I saw God as 'a harsh man, reaping where you did not sow, and gathering where you did not scatter seed'. In short, I saw God as a stern and tyrannical father figure of my worst patriarchal imaginings. This was a father figure without mercy or love. I was determined to have nothing to do with him, even if he were the creator of the universe and I owed my life and breath to him. I would rather have nothing to do with his harsh and cruel schemes.

A false God

While I think we now live in an age where most people don't even think about God at all, let alone as a stern parent figure, I think the cruel image of God as tyrant persists. I think that many people in the Church are raised to think that they have to walk on eggshells around God for fear of condemnation. We can become risk-averse, thinking that what we have to do is appease this God. Even if we don't feel we have to behave like the 'talent-burying' slave in the parable, perhaps we feel that the only way we can prove our value to God is – like the slaves who are given five and two talents respectively – to double the 'investment' God has made in us. We have to prove that what he has given us is well used.

The living God

I'm not so sure. Since coming to faith, I've encountered a different God. This is not a God who is asking us to add to the investment he has made in us or even one who proves his harshness when we hide our gifts or our life from him. This God is much more challenging, for he is the one who is invitational and loving and forgiving. He is a parent who delights in his children. This is the God whom I want all of us to meet and about whom I love to tell.

The parable of the talents holds depths it is easy to miss. We should wrestle with it rather than treat it as offering simple answers and advice. If we are determined to read it as about our talents and gifts and about using them to their fullest, then I think we are called to share them out of a joyous response to the God who loves and likes us. The living God is not a tyrant or a monster waiting to punish us. He is the God who invites rather than threatens or drives. He is the God who draws us into the fullness of life.

Rachel Mann

Hymn suggestions

And can it be; At the name of Jesus; Bless thou the gifts; Take my life and let it be.

Second Sunday before Advent   19 November
Second Service   **Alpha and Omega**
Ps. 89.19–37 [*or* 89.19–29]; 1 Kings 1.[1–14] 15–40;
Rev. 1.4–18; *Gospel at Holy Communion*: Luke 9.1–6

Who do you think you are?

We are used to identifying ourselves either by our past – our ancestors, place of birth or school we attended – or our present – where we live, who we know, where we shop, what we read. Maybe we live now in the light of what we have experienced. Perhaps our early faith seems naive, our present circumstances unfair. For as long as there have been human beings, we have told each other stories about why things are the way they are.

Alpha stories

These are 'alpha stories', stories of beginnings. Christians often use the birth of Jesus as an alpha story, God came into the world in human flesh and lived among us. For some, it's where we began, and this Christmas we might come to a crib and adore Christ the Lord. Or perhaps Easter is more like our alpha story, life bursting from the tomb, death defeated. Either of these stories could have been an alpha story for the seven churches John is writing to. Whichever it was, the stories identified them as Christian. The church in Ephesus had abandoned its alpha story; the one in Smyrna was to be persecuted for it. The church in Pergamum had abandoned it, the one in Thyatira had adapted it. In Sardis, the story had been forgotten; in Laodicea, it was no longer read with enthusiasm. Only Philadelphia remained faithful. The problem with an alpha story is keeping it alive as we move on.

Omega stories – the arc of God bends down

'Omega stories' begin at the other end from alpha stories. They are John's way of seeing things in his Revelation. 'Look!' John says. 'He is coming.' There is some detail about how Jesus is coming, in the clouds, in a way everyone will see, but I suspect the most important aspect of this passage is its beginning: 'Look! He is coming.' It contrasts with every other way of looking at endings. Whether we are talking about death or the end of our planet, we use words of going – we speak of the 'departed' or of the world 'passing away'. Hollywood blows the world to smithereens in its apocalyptic films. Yet the omega story of the Bible is this: 'Look! He is coming.' As Christians, we have a story with a purposeful ending. If the arc of history bends towards justice, the arc of God bends down, towards the earth.

Omega stories – there is no paradise

I remember being really surprised by a religious tract handed out on the street that depicted a heaven very similar to the Garden of Eden, as though the whole of human history was to be wiped out and everything reset to the beginning; as though the Garden of Eden had been closed for renovations when Adam and Even were kicked out. John's message to the churches is not, 'We're going back', but, 'We're going forward.' There is no promise of an idealized garden; instead, the future is a city. In fact, it's going to be a very disappointing city for some who think only they and those who agree with them will be included in God's future. God's city is huge and open and inclusive – later John will write that the gates of the city will never be shut. People will be able to wander in and out.

Omega stories – there is no church

Finally, and you might be relieved to hear this, the new Jerusalem will have no churches, no temple. The time for beautiful places like this will be gone. There will be no need for holy places, sacred books or sacramental ritual. There will be no ministers – lay or ordained. No need to go anywhere, read anything, do anything to meet with God, for God will simply be there among us and with us. Our natural reaction might be fear, but just as the Son of Man says to John, 'Do not be afraid', so he will say to each of us.

So who are we? We are people with an alpha and omega story, and at the centre of that story is the one who is the Alpha and the Omega. There may be trials ahead, as there were for at least one of the churches that John wrote to, but the arc of God bends towards the earth. Therein lies our identity and our hope.

Liz Shercliff

Hymn suggestions

Lo, he comes with clouds descending; O come, O come, Emmanuel; Hark a thrilling voice is sounding; Alpha, Omega, beginning and end.

Christ the King (Sunday next before Advent)
26 November
Principal Service   **Jesus: Lord of Our Lives**
Ezek. 34.11–16, 20–24; Ps. 95.1–7; Eph. 1.15–end;
Matt. 25.31–end

De-cluttering

Have you seen those programmes on the television where a team is sent to help those who have become overwhelmed by their possessions? People become hoarders for all sorts of reasons and often need sustained help and compassion to overcome the problem. When our living spaces are overtaken by clutter it can seriously affect the quality of our lives.

In the process of helping to clear out clutter, people are encouraged to go through their possessions. What happens is they uncover or rediscover things that are very precious to them and those things are kept and displayed properly when they move back into their house. Treasured memories in photographs are framed and hung on the wall – special objects are placed where they can be seen and appreciated. Things that are never used go to charity to be used by those who need them, and other things are sold so that there's enough cash for a holiday or a treat. People get their lives back into order as they order the living space around them, and they can move on from things that hold them back – events in the past – so that they are focused more on the present and future.

Letting go

Letting go is a very important process and at times a difficult one. But if we cling tightly to things then our hands and hearts won't be open to receive the gifts that God has for us in the future – it's important to let go and let God.

Letting go is a good topic to consider on the feast of Christ the King. Today is the very end of the Christian year. Next week we start a new year with Advent Sunday, which leads us through into Christmas – the birth of Christ – through Epiphany, Christ as a light to the nations, down to Candlemas and then towards Easter.

So, this is a good week to begin to let go and let God. It's a good time to let go as we enter a time of preparation, of watching and waiting, of looking forward in hope to the future, to the celebration of God with us at Christmas.

Today we celebrate Christ as King over our lives. Jesus is the name above every name, servant of all, our hope, who fills all in all. Jesus let go of life itself on the cross and was raised from the dead that we might be one with God. Jesus, seated at the right hand of God in glory. Jesus, who let go and let God.

Christ the King in us

Today's Gospel of the sheep and the goats is not about us rushing around doing good works to earn a place in God's kingdom. The Holy Spirit living within us leads us to recognize and proclaim Jesus Christ as Lord or King in our lives – the one who is of real importance, the centre of all things. And when we let go and see Christ as of central importance, then we are led naturally to feed the hungry and thirsty, to give hospitality to strangers, to clothe the naked, to be alongside people in all kinds of imprisonment.

Christ in us reaches out in love and compassion to Christ in others. It is not what we do ourselves but Christ dwelling in us who does it. We are the body of Christ here in this place and together as a body, a church with Christ as the head, we help to feed the hungry, we put roofs over people's heads, we are alongside people who are in distress. We may not feel that we do it as individuals but we do it as a church, and we're all part of that. And of course, it's not just what happens here either, but outside these walls every day of our lives in all the places that we go, Christ is mightily at work.

But sometimes in the mess and chaos and busyness of our daily living, we forget that Christ within us is King over us – and that through his sacrifice for us our present and our future with God is secure. We are kept in eternal life – we are reminded of that every time we receive Holy Communion. But the clutter that we carry around with us gets in the way and stops us from seeing what is precious and special and holy.

Maybe this is a good time for you to give your soul a de-cluttering – to discover again that which is precious and special and needs looking after carefully, needs nurturing and needs to be enjoyed. Give away what you don't need, sort out that which holds you back in your faith – fears, problems from the past, prejudices, misunderstandings – some of it really needs to go.

If through Advent we can let go of that which holds us back, then at Christmas our hands will be empty and open to give to others and to receive the greatest gift ever – God with us.

Catherine Williams

Christ triumphant, ever reigning; Crown him with many crowns; Meekness and majesty; Our God reigns.

Christ the King (Sunday next before Advent)
26 November
Second Service　**Princesses in the Revolution**
Morning Ps. 29, 110; Evening Ps. 93 [97]; **2 Sam. 23.1–7**, *or* 1 Macc. 2.15–29; Matt. 28.16–end

Monsters

Today is a feast day with a monster feel about it. The theme of Christ the King feels gigantic and like something of myths and legendary tales: a faith version of *Game of Thrones*. Moreover, it's got a sort of two-headed animal vibe going on. It's celebrated on the last day of Ordinary Time, which is also the Sunday before the start of a new liturgical year. In other words, it's a way of looking backwards and forwards at the same time. You can use it as a construct for gathering up and reviewing all the odd bits of theology and festivals, the long haul since Pentecost, and as a way of frontloading for Christmas.

Heroes

Reading the 'last words of David' seems therefore to fit perfectly today. David, the colossal hero right at the heart of the major war-game myths and legends of the biblical text, looks both backwards over his life and forwards to what his ongoing impact might be. David is the sort of giant hero whose legend increases as time passes and stories are embellished. His status meant so much to the people of Israel that he got ten goes at having his last words recorded, of which this passage is just one. Legend in his own lifetime, his status grew and grew until the statements that he was the favourite of God, the person through whom God's spirit speaks and the ruler who rules justly, are completely believable. No one would ever know from these last words that this was a man who had an affair with a married woman; had her husband killed; ignored the rape of his daughter, and caused a war with one of his sons.

Princesses

A few years ago, I discovered a version of the Bible for young children called the *Princess Bible*. The particular one I saw came as a book in a pink cardboard cover in the shape of a handbag, with pink feathers all over it, designed apparently to appeal to every girl's inner princess and assure her that she is, in fact, God's little princess. I have yet to see a direct equivalent *Prince Bible*, but the Bible in combat colours designed to appeal to boys seems pretty close. My first reaction was to be furious that gender stereotypes were being used to sell our sacred text. On reflection, I think there is something more deeply disturbing going on.

Princesses abound in the culture we are steeped in. They are an image, a notion, that provides a ready-made identity for people, usually girls. Princesses, in our culture, are pretty, savvy, loved, secure, confident, valued and treated very well. Increasingly they are throwing off their lifeless passivity of sleepy waiting and becoming agents of positive change. Parts of that are an identity worth trying out, trying on and inhabiting. But princesses and princes have no trouble being all these things because they are part of the elite and the privileged. They are special and superior from the start and thus able to work to a finish, like David's, where they can genuinely believe they were cherry-picked by divine forces.

The revolution

In the government of Christ the King, however, there are no princesses, no princes, no elites, no privileged, special people, no lords and ladies of the court. Everyone is equally loved, valued and honoured. And just as David was loved for all his life story, not just his highlights, so are we and everyone else. We often talk of the kingdom of God as the upside-down or inside-out kingdom where the norms of the world are turned on their head and the last will be first and the first last. We want our leaders and our future to be unmistakably good, so good they are almost divine. We want to be governed by a system of clear justice and unmistakably know what is the right thing to do. But the logic of the government of Christ the King is not existing logic reversed. It is logic beyond what we can currently map, understand and imagine. We are all equally, uniformly – the words begin to run out – and completely, entirely, fully valued and loved by God. That is profoundly revolutionary. It is a half-hidden truth that is world-shattering. We are all loved beyond measure, boundless and free. This is the truth in every soul, the light in every face, the spark in every relationship, the beginning, the middle and the end of every story.

Esther Elliott

Hymn suggestions

Thy kingdom come! On bended knee; Praise with joy the world's Creator; Christ triumphant, ever reigning; Crown him with many crowns.

Sermons for Saints' Days
and Special Occasions

St Stephen, Deacon, First Martyr   26 December
On the Feast of Stephen

2 Chron. 24.20–22, *or* **Acts 7.51–end**; Ps. 119.161–168;
Acts 7.51–end (*if the Acts reading is used instead of the
Old Testament reading, the New Testament reading is*
Gal. 2.16b–20); Matt. 10.17–22

Stephen – a good man

On Boxing Day, between turkey and leftovers, with carols still
resounding in our ears, comes this feast of Stephen. No sooner have
we celebrated the birth of Jesus than we remember Stephen – the
first martyr of the Church!

Something of a shock to the system – but might it be the heart of
the matter? This incarnation is a serious business. Stephen's story
reminds us that the shadow of the cross is never far away. It's a
matter of life and death. That God is for life, not just for Christmas.

Luke presents Stephen as a remarkable person. When there's a
pastoral need in the new Christian community, tensions appear.
'Hebrew' followers of Jesus are at odds with the Greek converts.
These Greeks feel neglected, and so the apostles appoint 'deacons'
to look after practical needs – and maybe mediate as well – while
the apostles 'keep to prayer and the ministry of the word'. Stephen
heads the list. Luke lists his spiritual credentials: 'a man full of faith
and of the Holy Spirit'. A man who goes on to perform marvels
and signs, as if he too were an apostle. This arouses a great deal of
animosity. He's accused of blasphemy, and the people are agitated.

Stephen's defence

Stephen is brought before the council. His defence is a long history of Israel's relationship with God. How again and again the people of God ignore what God says to them. How the people of God rebel against God, and persecute – sometimes to the death – the messengers of God. This doesn't go down very well with the council.

Why does Stephen, the spirit-filled servant of the poor, attack the authorities in this way? He incites the crowd against himself. It leads inexorably to his lynching, to his martyrdom.

Martyrdom

How do we feel about this? Martyrdom has been celebrated and remembered throughout the history of the Church, but do we still see it as a good and glorious thing? This happens so soon after Jesus has been put to death. Death after death – the killing goes on. Does the work of the Spirit, giver of life, always lead to casualties? That certainly is the witness of Scripture. Very few of the apostles and witnesses to the resurrection died peacefully in their beds. Is it so today? Across the world, there are still places where Christians die for their beliefs. This raises uncomfortable questions for those of us who live in more secular, comfortable worlds.

And although we may not be lynched, like Stephen, or crucified like Jesus, could it be that in our culture there are different kinds of stoning? Are some still attacked or even destroyed purely because of their goodness?

Whose authority?

This story is also about religious authority. Stephen's historical analysis still rings true for us. It is all too easy for us, who bear the name of God, to find ourselves opposing God. In the name of God, God is hurt and punished. In the name of defending truth, the God of truth is rejected. Those who see themselves as defenders of the faith try to destroy God. If we allow ourselves to fall into patterns of exclusion, or violence, we always re-enact crucifixion.

Stephen finally talks about Jesus. You have become *his* betrayers and murderers, he says. And, with dreadful irony, they then become Stephen's murderers. And in the end, it is not his speech that enrages them or even his personal attack on their complicity in the death of Christ. It is his *beholding* that enrages them to the point of murder.

'Look, I see the heavens opened and the Son of Man standing at the right hand of God.'

There is nothing so enraging as the dawning realization that we are wrong. That what our opponent sees may be closer to the truth than what we see. The gospel invites us to *come and see*, to contemplate until we begin to know. And this contemplation confronts all the illusions that keep us from love, that keep us from compassion.

A vulnerable God

We behold the child in the manger. We recognize a God without defences, God in vulnerability and weakness. We see God as the one who draws out compassion, who is interested in justice and equity, the care of widows and orphans.

But this vision of the gospel will always enrage the Herods of the world, the religious power elites. It will even enrage *us* – if we are committed to our own self-interest. When this love challenges us, the devices and desires of our hearts will always lead us to reach for a stone to throw.

The lectionary reminds us of the death of Zechariah. Just like Stephen, Zechariah is stoned to death, but his last words are, 'May the Lord see and avenge.' Whereas Stephen echoes the dying words of Jesus: 'Lord, do not hold this sin against them.'

Stephen, in his dying, recapitulates the death of Jesus. He spells out the gospel difference, manifests the God of love. And the feast of Stephen reminds us of something we need to hear again and again. That even as we crucify Christ afresh, by our lives and actions, so Christ reaches out to forgive us. The love that breaks the cycle of violence and invites us home.

Andrew Rudd

Hymn suggestions

Good King Wenceslas; From heaven you came; Love came down at Christmas; Stephen, first of Christian martyrs.

St John, Apostle and Evangelist   27 December
Being at Home with God
Ex. 33.7–11a; Ps. 117; 1 John 1; **John 21.19b–end**

Favourite Gospel

I have done a fair amount of interviewing in my time, and I really enjoy asking questions that seem disarmingly simple (maybe even playful and fun), but the answers to which reveal a great deal. 'If you could change one thing about the Church of England, what would it be?' is one that I am particularly fond of. When I went forward for ordination training, my sponsoring bishop asked me which was my favourite Gospel. A very simple, almost trivial-sounding question, and yet the answer reveals so much. I replied, 'Luke'. He told me, with a twinkle in his eye, that I was almost right: 'Mark would be right and John would be wrong,' he said. John's Gospel is a little bit marmite, as we say in Britain: some love it and some don't!

Theology

I guess why some people might not be so drawn to John's Gospel is that, instead of stories, it has more of a theological focus. Of all the Gospels, it is to some readers the most abstract: it begins not with a story about Jesus' birth, as with Matthew and Luke, but an understanding of what that birth means for us, and it sets the scene for one of the great themes of John's Gospel (of which there are many), that God chooses to abide with us – literally translated, 'pitched his tent among us'. The connection with today's reading from Exodus is I hope obvious. Jesus is the new tent of meeting: the new place to meet and experience God.

What makes home, home?

As I am writing this, my home is upside down, with people working here to replace the kitchen and the utility room. I am incredibly grateful that the work is going on, and with all that is going on in the world it seems such a minor thing, but it is also strangely stressful, with many of my possessions all over the place and much of my living space displaced. There is in my experience a great deal of difference between a house and a home, and there is quite an art to homemaking, to creating a place of comfort and peace.

Where does God reside?

In the theme that runs through John's Gospel of 'abiding', it becomes very clear that God has not only come to abide on earth in Jesus, but that he seeks to abide *with us* and also *in us*. John 15 makes explicit that this can happen through the keeping of his commandment to love one another, and that when we abide in Jesus and he in us, this will lead to much joy as well as fruitfulness. God is now not some distant deity, hard to comprehend and utterly separate from us: he is now close at hand, able to dwell with us and in us. God can be found bodily.

Friendship

John's Gospel refers to the 'beloved disciple', the one whom 'Jesus loved', as is mentioned in today's Gospel. Widely thought to refer to John himself, he is part of the intimate circle that are with Jesus at critical moments in his ministry: the transfiguration and Gethsemane, and John himself is at the foot of the cross with Jesus' mother Mary and reclining on Jesus' breast at the Last Supper. Not only does John's Gospel reveal to us that we can be friends with Jesus, it reveals that we can be intimate with him too. Very close. Have you, have we, asked Jesus to be our friend? Can we hold his hand and cuddle up close to him? Can we let him redefine what it is to be a family?

Always more to learn

As we celebrate St John today, the writer of the Gospel, whose words bring such depth of knowledge about Jesus and the incarnation, there seems to me a particularly important sentence at the end of today's Gospel reading in verse 25: 'But there are also many other things that Jesus did; if every one of them were written down, I suppose that the world itself could not contain the books that would be written.' It seems a significant statement to make at the end of the Gospel: to acknowledge that although we have now met (and hopefully experienced) this more homely God – a God who is so very present to us through Jesus and the Spirit – he still cannot be fully contained in any description of him. A book, or whole library of books, cannot contain all the stories about Jesus, just as no image or set of words can fully contain God. Despite the familiarity, there is still mystery. Maybe this is one of John's great gifts to us: intimacy as well as the unknown. Like any relationship, there is always more to learn, experience and discover about God.

Jonathan Lawson

Hymn suggestions

Thou didst leave thy throne; How shall I sing that majesty; What a friend we have in Jesus; Word supreme, before creation.

The Holy Innocents 28 December
Why Do We Snuff Out Life?

Jer. 31.15–17; Ps. 124; 1 Cor. 1.26–29; **Matt. 2.13–18**

How many children?

Not a scene to include in the infant nativity play. We allow the wise men to go home by another road without wanting to dwell too much on what will happen when Herod – brooding in his palace – realizes that the wise men are not returning to him, and he is consumed with murderous rage. This was not a one-off for Herod: complex, brutal, cruel, unstable. He had secured his crown over Palestine with Roman approval but his political and personal relationships were fraught with suspicion. Seeing his wives and sons as rivals, he had many of them murdered. He gave orders that popular people be executed at the moment of his own death to ensure national mourning even if not for him. While it wasn't carried out, it shows that an order to slaughter a few babies in a scrubby little Judaean town wasn't out of character. Bethlehem, the least of the cities of Judah, would have had very few baby boys at the time. Fewer than the 16 killed in the Dunblane school shooting, considerably less than the 116 children killed in the Aberfan disaster, far less than the 1 million Jewish children of the Holocaust.

Every human life is sacred to God from the youngest to the oldest. By contrast, Herod wanted to eliminate one baby boy so he ordered that every baby in Bethlehem should be killed – just to make sure. Killing was his first defence, his default position.

Rachel is weeping

Joseph is instructed to take his family and flee to Egypt. Egypt of all places! Part of the nation's history and synonymous with slavery and death, yet deliverance. Matthew includes this narrative to show Jesus as the new Moses, whose mother had to hide him. Pharaoh, threatened by the sheer numbers of Hebrews living in his land, put them under slavery. When the Hebrews multiply despite this oppression, Pharaoh decides to cut them off at the source – kill the baby boys. The midwives, as an act of civil disobedience against the oppressor, refuse to do so. These were the wise women of the Exodus narrative. They disobey Pharaoh's orders. In his anger at being duped he orders that every baby Hebrew boy is to be thrown into the Nile. Herod gave the wise men orders. They disobey. He responds with murderous rage.

Not the first or the last. Rachels worldwide and through time weep for their children. Many powerful leaders filled with suspicion and hate have stamped out something that threatened them: a life, many lives, a new idea, a new movement, a new hope. Not just leaders. Ordinary people across the years have acted on the impulse of their insecurities; trampling on the threat of new life, new beginnings, change, light, hope.

We do it often to ourselves.

We stamp out some new thing in us.

Those voices, those odd thoughts at the corner of our consciousness, those longings, those little green shoots – why do we treat them with such suspicion, why the instinct to stamp them out, to throw them into the Nile? Because they are new or different; because they threaten some power, control or status we hold too important? The little living thing within that tells us this is not the way. We stamp it out.

What might have been?

I wonder how different the story would have been if Herod had gone with the wise men with an open mind. If he had allowed his own words – 'for I too long to pay him homage' – to become real? If he had seen the child, the new life, remembered the Scriptures and the stories of his adopted people. If he had understood what real kingship meant. What a difference it might have made to Herod – and Herod's world.

If the Pharaoh who did not know the story of Joseph or his brothers had listened to those Hebrew midwives tell their tales around the fire; had seen the skill with which they brought life into the world; had seen the Hebrew children flourishing because they were loved, and had not hardened his heart. If Hitler had said let our people grow as one community, sharing skills and stories of our past and our heritage, and let us build something new together.

How different might many stories and many lives have been if we had understood truly what the priest of Dunblane had meant when he said, 'When the bullets began to fly in that gymnasium, God was the very first to weep.'

So it is in the many Bethlehems, Egypts, Dunblanes, Aberfans and Auschwitz and the many mistakes of the Church before and since.

Jesus came to that which was his own, and they did not know him. But we – who have seen his glory, full of grace and truth – are called to make that grace known, enable that word of life to be spoken. Called to be the brave midwives of the Word. And see what God is birthing among us.

Carey Saleh

Hymn suggestions

Sing lullaby; Christ is the world's true light; We cannot measure how you heal; Come, wounded healer.

Naming and Circumcision of Jesus   2 January (transferred)
What's Your Name?
Num. 6.22–end; Ps. 8; Gal 4.4–7; **Luke 2.15–21**

Coming out

When I was a tempestuous young curate, back in the last millennium, I preached a sermon in an ancient country church in County Durham at Choral Evensong. My theme was that God had 'come out' in Jesus. I remember it having little or no effect that I was aware of, save for a slightly whispered conversation with me from one member of the church out of concern for another member of the congregation who was not open about being an alcoholic. As we continue to celebrate Christmas, there is still much to ponder about the God who makes himself visible, touchable and knowable in Jesus. Just as a thought remains a thought until spoken or written down, so God manifests himself to us in tangible form in the Word made flesh. It *is* a sort of coming out, in modern parlance.

What's in a name?

What is your name and what does it mean? My name is Jonathan and I am named after my mother's cousin of the same name, and in Hebrew Jonathan means 'Gift from God'; something which I often remind my mother! Throughout history, if fellow human beings have wished to degrade other people or peoples, they have attempted to remove their names, reducing each person to a number: attempting to change them from the unique individual that they are into some form of commodity or item. The concentration camps of the Third Reich speak eloquently of this, but modern computer-based systems and algorithms have the potential to have a similar disposition. For people of faith, and particularly of the Jewish faith, the name given to an individual is very significant. It is not only what they are called by, it is also their reality. Hence, when important times of call come from God, the name is often changed by him, as with Abraham and Sarah in Genesis. Similarly, in the Hebrew Bible, God is never called by name, for to do so is to know God, who can never be fully known.

Identity

Who are you? How would you describe yourself? There are many ways we can tell people who we are, using descriptions of our family relationships, our employment, our culture or our faith. In Galatians, Paul, who at this point in his epistle is writing about baptism, makes clear that our identity is in Christ. We are his children, and through baptism we are siblings in him. We have a new identity. Similarly, in Jesus, we gain a new understanding of God. Now God can be named in Jesus ('The Lord saves'), and his name is a powerful name. His name has been used ever since to call into light those things that are hidden in darkness. It is his name, and his being named, that we specifically celebrate today.

Naming things

An important path on the road to healing hurtful things in our lives can be to name them. To call them out. Any therapist or counsellor knows something of the power that can come with giving an experience or a feeling a name. Jesus himself in his ministry names demons and other forces of malevolence, and as a result gains power over them. But he also does far more than that. He calls out behaviour, particularly that of religious people, which stops others from meeting with God; most dramatically with the cleansing of the Temple. Any institution has to be aware of the things that people feel cannot be named, and over the last years, the Church itself has been forced to listen to those who have been sexually abused by ministers in the Church: experiences that have been hard to name as well as hard to hear. The Church in its turn is called to name in society that which cannot be named: to speak about the marginalized, the oppressed, the ignored. Those who have become a statistic and are not remembered by name.

Vocation

We all have a vocation and that is to be what God made us to be. The book of Revelation speaks about our white stone name, the name that God has given us and the true reality of who we are. The exemplar of a human being who was (and is) truly himself is Jesus: he shows us what it is to be truly us, and in doing so he reveals that we can carry the divine within us too. The journey of our life and faith is to be true to our reality, just as Jesus is true to his, so that when we come to the end of days, God may recognize us as the one he created, and others see that the Lord has blessed us and kept us and that the light of his countenance has shone upon us, now and always.

Jonathan Lawson

Hymn suggestions

At the name of Jesus; Name of all majesty; All hail the power; O for a thousand tongues.

Epiphany   6 January
Journeying On
Isa. 60.1–6; Ps. 72 [1–9] 10–15; Eph 3.1–12; **Matt. 2.1–12**

Happy New Year!
I wonder what this year will hold for you ... What resolutions
have you made? What are your hopes and dreams?
What journeys will you go on – physically, emotionally, spiritually? Who will be with you as you travel? How will you know when
you've arrived? What will you find when you get there?

Marking and measuring time

We like to mark and measure time, don't we? To divide it into
chunks that we can hold and control. I've just bought a new wall
planner for my study – where I can see the whole year and plan my
time and tasks accordingly. It makes me feel secure and productive,
as I place my little stickers on the squares.

My secular year planner would have me believe that Christmas
is over. Fortunately, I also have a liturgical calendar to remind me
that, though the world has finished festivities, the Christmas season
isn't over yet. There's still plenty of time to celebrate the birth of
Jesus – plenty of time to enjoy the Christmas season which runs
through Epiphany to Candlemas at the beginning of February.
Still plenty of time to visit the manger and whisper our hopes and
dreams and longings for ourselves, for humanity, for our planet, for
the cosmos, into the ears of the Christ-child – to give him the gift
of our heart. Still plenty of time to see, to be thrilled and to rejoice.
We're reminded of that as we celebrate the arrival of the wise ones
who come to pay homage to the Christ-child.

The magi

Imagine the magi. They had almost nothing to go on, they travelled
a vast distance, probably close to 1,000 miles. On an adventure
guided by God through the stars, the Scriptures and a dream. These
ancient astronomers believed that what they saw in the heavens
reflected earthly activity. They saw a new star rising – a unique star
– and they believed it pointed to the birth of the new King of the
Jews. So exciting and extraordinary was this that they set off into
the unknown to find this new king, to pay him homage – to worship

him. They were inquisitive, brave, wholehearted and naive in their dealings with Herod who was deeply threatened by their news.

The travellers learnt that the Messiah was prophesied to be born in Bethlehem and that is where the star stopped. They had reached their destination. They were overwhelmed with joy, just as John the Baptist jumped for joy when he came close to Jesus for the first time. They travelled a long way and they were not disappointed with what they found – a poor family with an infant, in humble surroundings.

The magi offered gifts: rich, rare and highly symbolic. Gold – for a king. Frankincense – for a high priest. Myrrh – for sacrifice. The baby's future heralded a new heaven and a new earth. The glory of the Lord promised by the prophet Isaiah was there. The journey, hard and risky, was worth it.

Prophecy fulfilled

Hundreds of years before the birth of Jesus, Isaiah spoke of a time when the light of God would draw all people together. Those who were scattered and exiled would come home. Nations and kings would come from far away. All would pay tribute and vast riches would be brought as all came to worship and submit to God. Matthew surely had that passage in mind as he set about writing his account of the visit of the magi. Here are the representatives of the nations coming to worship the light of the world – the infant Jesus. For Matthew, Isaiah's prophecy is fulfilled.

The divine plan offers salvation for all. No one is outside God's love. With the coming of Christ, outsiders are welcomed into the very heart of God's story. The magi tread the path to Jesus that paves the way for the Great Commission in the closing chapter of Matthew's Gospel when the resurrected Jesus sends his followers out to the ends of the earth to make disciples of all nations. Coming to worship, going to witness – the heartbeat of God's love for the world.

A different way home

Encountering the Christ-child changes the magi – they are warned in a dream not to report to Herod but take a different path home. When we meet with Christ – whether at the manger, in our prayers, in the Scriptures, through the Eucharist, in the people we encounter every day – we must expect to be changed, to find that our path, our way home, is different. We may want to plan, mark out, pin down and control the future, but so often God has other plans. God's dream for humanity is beyond our wildest imagining – it may take us on different roads, chasing stars, far beyond the safety of our little lives into the immensity of love: deeper, richer, broader, higher, purer than we can begin to fathom.

I wonder what this year will hold for you. What resolutions have you made?

What are your hopes and dreams? What journeys will you go on – physically, emotionally, spiritually? Who will be with you as you travel? How will you know when you've arrived? What will you find when you get there?

Catherine Williams

Hymn suggestions

As with gladness; Brightest and best; We three kings of Orient are; O worship the king in the beauty of holiness.

The Week of Prayer for Christian Unity
18–25 January
Body Matters
Readings for the Unity of the Church:
Jer. 33.6–9a; Ezek. 36.23–28; Zeph. 3.16–end; Ps. 100, 122, 133; **Eph. 4.1–6;** Col. 3.9–17; 1 John 4.9–15; Matt. 18.19–22; John 11.45–52; John 17.11b–23

Where and how is Christian unity lived out? Of course, important theological discussions at national and international level go on between churches of different traditions, and vital ecumenical structures enable mission and collaboration on different issues. But in his Letter to the Ephesians, Paul is interested in how Christian unity is practised and experienced at a local level. His words of wisdom speak as much to churches as they relate together as to Christians within the same local church.

Humility ...

If Christians are to live together, true to God's calling, their first priority, suggests Paul, must be humility. This doesn't mean that some should grow expert in being humble while others lord it over them. The Christ-like humility of all lies at the heart of mutual submission: a two-way traffic of giving and receiving. Paul is well aware of the challenge this represents! Christians will need patience and gentleness to bear with each other, he says. Spare no effort! He implies that it's only through struggle, attention and perseverance that we learn the ways of peace.

... and one-ness

Paul keeps repeating the word 'one': one body, one Spirit, one hope, one Lord, one faith, one baptism, one God and Father. This is more than just rhetoric! Paul is intensely aware of the cultural divides threatening the Ephesian church which brings together Jews and Gentiles. There are two principal cultures, two ways of doing things, two ways of understanding what it means to belong, two ways of negotiating the world. This is why Paul is at pains to emphasize that despite these differences, they are called to live in *one* body. Through the cross, God has made the two one! United in Christ, they will need to practise humility to make this unity real. One side can't say to the other, 'It's all got to be done our way.' There needs to be sensitive selflessness on all sides, particularly among those accustomed to holding sway.

At one time, I served as minister of a Nonconformist church that had taken the courageous step to unite with a local church of another tradition. We had already started worshipping together, and different working groups were discussing questions of ecclesiology, theology and ministry. These meetings faded into relative insignificance, however, next to the ongoing debate over that most essential of issues: in the new church, which church's cups and saucers would we serve the coffee in? Yes, it is sometimes culture and not theology that gets in the way of unity!

... and humanity

But we discovered that disputes over crockery could be resolved and healed by growing in love for one another. One day a woman in the other church complained of a sore throat. Three days later she died tragically of meningitis, the first case in an outbreak that ripped through the town. The following Sunday, members of our church welcomed the newly bereaved husband to worship, throwing arms around him and weeping with him. That was a key moment in our journey towards unity. It started not with deciding which liturgy we should use for which service but with our shared humanity and our responding humbly and spontaneously to each other's needs. Christian unity is not lived out at an esoteric level of disembodied spirituality, but in flesh and blood, between everyday people with all their hurts, pride and fears. No wonder Paul uses the human image of the body to describe it.

... and partnership

The more humility we learn, the more our humanity grows and the more honest we become, seeing ourselves through others' eyes. We sense our emptiness and our need for others to teach, enrich and forgive us. This is a whole way of being Christian, which draws us both towards and beyond the unity of the Church. Paul affirms that the one God is the Father *of* all, *through* all and *in* all. God's purposes are to draw *all things* into unity in Christ. As churches whose life is in Christ, we need to seek this God in whom the unity of the Church and the unity of all things hold together.

Today the world faces desperate emergencies: the crisis of climate change; the welcome of unprecedented numbers of refugees. The churches have a calling to respond to these issues, but we can't face them alone. They're bigger than us all. We need partners: experts to teach us, friends to stand with us, and Christ-like humility to enable us to join others of all faiths and none in confronting the challenges.

Our prayer during this special week is one small, prophetic step towards the unity the whole earth cries out for. When we pray for Christian unity, we are also praying for a Christian, Christ-like way of being truly human. Seizing with joy and thankfulness those God-given tools of humility, gentleness and love, we ask that together we might offer – in everyday human form – a reflection of the unity and community of the Holy Trinity: one Spirit, one Lord, one God and Father, of, in and through all.

Mary Cotes

294

Hymn suggestions

Your hand, O God, has guided; Brother, sister, let me serve you; One is the body and one is the head; Christ is the King, O friends rejoice.

Conversion of St Paul 25 January
Conversion: Event and Process

Jer. 1.4–10, *or* Acts 9.1–22; Ps. 67; **Acts 9.1–22** (*if the Acts reading is used instead of the Old Testament reading, the New Testament reading is* Gal. 1.11–16a); Matt. 19.27–end

A friend of mine doesn't much like St Paul's theology. On this St Paul's feast day, he wholeheartedly agrees to pray for his conversion! So, this is an excellent day to ask what we mean by 'conversion'?

Jerusalem

When we come to consider St Paul in our New Testament reading today, two places come to the fore: the road to Damascus and the house of Ananias. But there's another place which needs to be mentioned – Jerusalem. A seeming insignificant figure is picked out in the crowd to hold the coats of the mob that stoned Stephen. The Acts of the Apostles is careful to report that 'a young man named Saul' was the one at whose feet the killers of Stephen threw their clothes. This young Pharisee was neither disgusted by nor neutral to the stoning of Stephen; he was actually 'giving approval of his death'. After all, this violent death was aimed at preserving the truth of the Torah. And yet, Saul's dogmatic assurance was being shaken by how Stephen died. Saul could not escape the memory of Stephen's eyes and one whose 'face shone like an angel'. This incident prepared the young man named Saul for the dramatic encounter with the risen Jesus on the road to Damascus.

We live life forwards and understand it backwards. When we look back, we often find God's fingerprints in the twists and turns of our lives that, at the time, we had missed. When you look back on your own life, do you see God at work?

Damascus

Damascus was the place where Paul had to admit that he had got it wrong. In this moment of realization that he is wrong, Paul is converted. He is converted from his pride, his assuming God's will. He is converted to the possibility of self-doubt: there is no longer certainty about God or Jesus. Rather, God in Jesus is his certainty. Now Paul is confronted with the true mystery of God, and Paul now knows nothing. Paul is released from the chains of being correct and released into new freedom, the loving gift of God's grace. Here is the true conversion: the realization that we do not possess the whole truth. This understanding is the Damascus road experience.

Our conversion to doubt means that we are required to live with an ongoing awareness that we could be wrong, that we might need to change, to develop and to learn. We can no longer maintain that we know everything. We must learn from each other as individuals, from our cultures and the variety of church traditions, new truths about humanity, and God in Christ. This conversion is the beginning of our new journey as Christians together; we have not arrived, but we travel this Damascus road together. Picking up others as we travel, not believing that they must conform to us, but only asking them to consider that they too may be converted as, together, we engage with the mystery that is God.

This is 'the Way', as the Church first called it. A road into mystery: a journey of exploration and learning together, a journey for all peoples and all creation, a journey into the mystery of God.

Ananias' house

The turning point for St Paul was the change of direction: from the pessimism of a persecutor to the optimism of a propagator. The conclusion of this phase of Paul's conversion is made by an unknown believer named Ananias. God used Ananias to complete the work that he started in the death of Stephen and continued on the road to Damascus. The healing touch of Ananias and his reconciling words 'Brother Saul' turns the trauma of blindness into the tranquillity of a new vocation within the community of the Church. God used Ananias to define Paul's ministry as 'my chosen instrument to carry my name before the Gentiles and their kings and before the people of Israel'. Ananias reminds us that a part of our conversion is not just to God alone but also to one another. We cannot be Christian on our own – we need each other. When we acknowledge that, we acknowledge the Church, the body of Christ, and our role within that body for the world's salvation. True conversion must lead to the service of each other and of the world that God loved so much that he gave his only begotten Son.

On this feast of the conversion of St Paul, let's give thanks to God who is intimately involved with our story, a God who acts in the now to shape our future and a God who gives us one another and the grace to serve one another and the world. Conversion is all this. It is never completed and stretches into eternity because it is all this.

Paul Williams

Hymn suggestions

Dear Lord and Father of mankind; He who would valiant be; Amazing grace; All for Jesus.

Presentation of Christ in the Temple (Candlemas)
2 February
Ten Thousand Hours and More
Mal. 3.1–5; Ps. 24.[1–6] 7–end; Heb. 2.14–end; **Luke 2.22–40**

They say that to become a good pianist or a winning golf player, you need to start by getting in 10,000 hours of practice. It takes time to develop your gifting, learn from your mistakes and allow music-making or golf to permeate your way of life. And we might suggest something similar about the way we develop our relationship with God.

A lifetime preparing

Our Gospel for Candlemas presents us with that momentous scene in the Temple in which Simeon and Anna both recognize the specialness of the infant Jesus. They have seen the promised Messiah and they rejoice! Yet what has prepared them for this moment? What has enabled them to recognize that this child is the One they've been waiting for, the One who will bring God's salvation?

Luke invites us to understand that this profound spiritual discernment doesn't just fall on them out of the blue. Both Simeon and

Anna have given not 10,000 hours, but a lifetime in preparation for this moment. The widowed Anna is 84. Meanwhile, as Simeon has been promised that he will not see death until he has seen the Lord's Christ, we assume that he too is elderly. They have spent long prayerful years growing in faith and awareness. They have learnt such deep attentiveness to God that when the significant moment comes they have the sensitivity to be open to the Spirit's prompting.

The outward dimension

First, each is attentive to God through the outward, active practices. Simeon is upright. This suggests that he has faithfully fulfilled the demands of the Jewish law, observing particular rites of washing, certain ways of eating and dressing, and special rhythms of activity and rest. These outward practices shaping his routine have served as a constant reminder of his relationship with God and his Jewish identity. Meanwhile, Anna has also been faithful in outward ways, constantly at the Temple, worshipping there night and day, praying and fasting. Luke's description of Simeon and Anna reminds us that every time we attend worship or say our prayers, our attentiveness to God is being nurtured.

The inward dimension

But that's not all that has been preparing them for this moment. Second, Simeon and Anna's attentiveness to God is sustained by their deep interior life. Each is inwardly open and sensitive to the movement of the Holy Spirit. Simeon, Luke says, is devout: a man of prayer with a strong sense of the presence of God. Luke mentions the action of the Holy Spirit three times in relation to him in the space of as many verses. Anna also has a great openness to the Holy Spirit. In describing her as a prophetess, Luke tells us that she had a divinely inspired gift of speaking.

How open are we to the inward prompting of the Holy Spirit? Perhaps we often imagine that we are most open to God when we experience great joy or profound longing, or a sense of being inspired to do something. Everyday moments too – when we're taking the dog for a walk, or gazing at something beautiful – can offer opportunities to be aware of God's presence. Yet times of vulnerability, of grief or sickness, when our defences are laid bare, can also be profound opportunities to be more open to God. Instead of cutting ourselves off from God at such times, we can grow more attentive to the Spirit's prompting by seeking God's presence at the heart of our experience.

Inward and outward dimensions together

It is striking that both outward and inward elements of spiritual attentiveness come together at the moment when Simeon and Anna recognize the identity of the child Jesus. Outwardly, they are there in the Temple, faithful in the practices of worship. Inwardly, they are open to the Spirit, having spent a lifetime in prayerful hoping and waiting.

Everything that has happened before has been building to this moment. Standing now in the presence of the child and his parents and also in the presence of the eternal God, Simeon's vision is confirmed. In this child, past, present and future fuse together as God's promises come to fulfilment. Simeon can now depart in peace in the knowledge that God's new future is breaking in. Anna, equally, has the inner conviction that the liberation of Jerusalem is coming. Her years of prayerfulness suddenly bear fruit in this moment as her attentiveness to God overflows into her relationships with others. She just can't help but tell everyone about the child.

If we ever wonder how we might grow in our relationship with God, Simeon and Anna have much to teach us. To grow in faith and discernment we need to be attentive in both the outward and inward dimensions. They belong together. Such attentiveness does not come overnight. But as, year on year, we offer ourselves to God, we will be led – as were Simeon and Anna – into extraordinary moments of insight, wonder and praise.

Mary Cotes

Hymn suggestions

As the deer pants for the water; One thing I ask, one thing I seek; Prayer is the soul's sincere desire; Focus my eyes on you, O Lord.

St Joseph of Nazareth   20 March (transferred)
Mary and Joseph: Models of Costly Obedience
2 Sam. 7.4–16; Ps. 89.26–36; Rom. 4.13–18; **Matt. 1.18–end**

When life doesn't go according to plan

Gabriel the archangel had come to Mary; human face to angelic features. For Joseph, it was in a dream that an angel came. Millennia before, God had spoken to Joseph's namesake, to the dreamer who went from slave to overseeing the whole of Egypt for Pharaoh.

Now, centuries later, Joseph of Nazareth was betrothed to Mary a young woman from the neighbourhood. Joseph must have hoped that their families had chosen wisely, that he and Mary would be compatible, sharing similar values, capable of creating a peaceful home together. He probably wondered about how life would unfold and imagined their life together. Maybe he had some questions too: would he be able to provide for Mary and any children they might have? Would his work as a craftsman sustain them? Would he be able to ensure their shelter, their food, their safety? Would he be a good husband? A good father?

And then, Matthew tells us, Mary was 'found to be with child'. Just a few words, yet what human drama and turmoil they hint at.

Joseph is caught up in one of those life-changing flashes in time, when the predictable, the comfortable, the expected is overturned. From this moment, whatever future he had imagined looks radically different, no matter what he does. The world is a much more uncertain place than it was yesterday. There is an urgent decision to be made and perhaps lots of 'helpful' advice given. What should he do now? Could Joseph possibly marry her, knowing that he is not the father of the child Mary was carrying? Should he expose her to the shame which no doubt she deserved?

Joseph was a 'good man', we are told, a 'righteous man'. Finally, he comes to a resolution that brings some calm to his heart, something that will not unduly punish Mary but which will appease his own pain and his family's honour. Matthew tells us that Joseph, 'unwilling to expose her to public disgrace, planned to dismiss her quietly'.

What a precarious, and all the more precious, moment this is. Joseph could have insisted that Mary, and with her the unborn child, be stoned to death. Instead, he stayed his hand and extended compassion. This prayerful, well-reasoned decision seems to have given Joseph enough inner peace to sleep and, in this more relaxed state of sleep, to dream. Joseph's dream takes him beyond even his 'reasonable' decision and sets him off on a life course involving tremendous risk and responsibility.

A twin 'yes' to God

The angel reminds Joseph of his spiritual heritage. This 'Son of David' is invited to own his present life story in relation to the generations past and to generations to come. We don't hear Joseph's voice in the gospel accounts, but we do see his response to God in action. He plans, he resolves, he dreams, he hears and significantly he changes his mind and obeys. His decisions, his actions, would have tremendous consequences. I wonder when we last changed course in obedience to what we have discerned from God?

We rightly rejoice in Mary's 'yes' to God. Today we also give thanks for the determined obedience of Joseph, who wakes ready to do as God commands. Obedience is probably an undervalued virtue today, yet Joseph is not passive. Rather, he paid attention to God (and 'paying' attention can indeed be costly) and he ventured to risk. Though his dreaming and adventuring drew little attention or glory to Joseph himself, the impact would be world-changing.

Joseph and Jesus

The child whom Mary brought forth, whom Joseph sheltered, would grow in obedience and compassion himself. Joseph had been unwilling to turn Mary over to public disgrace, even public execution; years later an angry group of men would drag a woman in front of Joseph's foster son, ready to stone her for alleged sexual misconduct. Like his foster father before him, Jesus paused, and when he responded it was with thoughtful mercy and daring compassion. Later Jesus himself would be exposed to public disgrace and condemnation, in his path of obedience. Even then his compassion and mercy would extend to his torturers and those who hung beside him. He was the Father's Son, and dare we imagine that he was his foster father's son too?

Joseph knew both fear and hope. And when the angel came, he chose hope. Hope for himself, for Mary, for his family, for his people – hope for the world. He chose the hope that comes from attending to God, from committing to another person and to a community, from choosing to trust and care and to love even in the face of the world's nagging doubts. He knew the hope that comes from trying to be a good person, God's person, in the small unnoticed things as well as the big ones.

Tricia Hillas

Hymn suggestions

O Jesus, I have promised; When Joseph was an old man (Cherry Tree Carol); Hail, holy Joseph, hail; For all the saints.

Annunciation of Our Lord to the Blessed Virgin Mary   25 March
Announcing the Kingdom of God
Isa. 7.10–14; Ps. 40.5–11; Heb. 10.4–10; **Luke 1.26–38**

'What's to be done about Mary?'

'What's to be done about Mary?' sings Graham Kendrick in one of his Christmas songs. It's a question that has haunted the Church for centuries. For some, she is the symbol of meekness, for others of strength. She is the God-bearer for the devout, a sign of Christian irrationality for those who don't believe. Romanticized on cards and in nativities, confined to a stable by those who want to avoid some difficult questions, stored away with the rest of the nativity scene at the end of Christmas. What's to be done about her?

Although in various works of art and theology, Mary is Queen of Heaven, in Luke's story of her encounter with the angel, Mary seems, at first sight, to be nobody special. We find out about her relationships with men before we find out even her name. She's a virgin, Luke tells us twice, and she's engaged. It's a sign of those times and these that most women's significance is gauged in relation to men. To God, however, Mary is favoured. The Lord is with her before she is asked to bear God's son, and before she agrees.

Mary stops to think

How easily we skip over Luke's words here. Mary stops to think what the angel might mean. Some images of Mary have her reading, as in Robert Campin's triptych from the 1400s. As a faithful Jew,

302

Mary knew what it meant to be favoured by God – including the fact that it wasn't always easy. No wonder she stopped to think. Legend even has it that Mary was not the first to be approached by God with this request. She knew what the consequence might be – shame on her family, disgrace for her. She might be thrown out of the village, become 'damaged goods', unwanted as a prospective wife, at a time where women needed either father or husband. And she must have wondered at the angel's confidence that she would bear a son at a time when one in three babies died at or before birth. No wonder she stopped to think.

As a faithful Jew, Mary also knew about the promised Messiah, the coming kingdom. Did she connect what she knew with what was happening? The angel's description must have rung some bells in her mind. Imagine the enormity of the moment – an angel appearing to an insignificant woman, and asking her to birth the Messiah, to bring to flesh the kingdom of God through her own body.

In four scenes, the annunciation to Mary goes something like this:

- An angel appears and tells her that she is favoured by God.
- Mary is puzzled and stops to think.
- The angel asks her to bear the Son of God.
- Mary asks what will happen and consents.

The final scene

The good news is this. The invitation has been extended. Each of us has been given an invitation to birth the kingdom of God in our own world. 'What does it avail me that the birth is always happening, if it does not happen to me?' asked Meister Eckhart, a German theologian and mystic. In other words, the annunciation to Mary makes no difference unless we too join in the birthing of God's kingdom. Meister Eckhart went on to say, 'And what good is it to me if Mary is full of grace if I am not also full of grace?'

In answer to the question we began with, 'What's to be done about Mary?', I want to suggest that we take her out of the box in which we store our nativity set, dust off the veneer of mildness and inconsequence, and dwell on what we can learn from her.

The Angelus is a traditional prayer often offered at points throughout the day. You may not feel comfortable with all of its words, but it is a reminder of what we can learn from Mary and the annunciation. This is how it goes:

The angel of the Lord declared unto Mary,
And she conceived of the Holy Spirit.
Hail Mary, full of grace, the Lord is with thee;
Blessed art thou among women,
and blessed is the fruit of thy womb, Jesus.
Holy Mary, Mother of God,
pray for us sinners,
now and at the hour of our death. Amen.
Behold the handmaid of the Lord.
Be it done unto me according to thy word.
And the Word was made flesh.
And dwelt among us.

May it be our prayer that the Word continues to be made flesh as
we follow Mary's example.

Liz Shercliff

Hymn suggestions

*What's to be done about Mary? Sing of Mary pure and lowly; Ye
who claim the faith of Jesus; In my life, Lord, be glorified.*

St Mark the Evangelist   25 April
Principal Service   **And Immediately …**
Prov. 15.28–end, *or* Acts 15.35–end; Ps. 119.9–16; Eph. 4.7–16;
Mark 13.5–13

Easter feasts

Several feast days in our calendar fall very close to Easter. Three
in particular: St George, SS Philip and James, and today's feast, St
Mark. Depending on where Easter falls, they can either get rather
swallowed up in our Easter celebrations or shunted about so they
end up being celebrated in a great big pile, miles away from their
actual day. This year, happily, Easter fell on 9 April, and so we
get to celebrate the feast of St Mark on its proper day and do him
justice.

Mark is pretty much always a feast that falls in Eastertide. And
isn't it appropriate to celebrate this most curious of Gospel writers
amid the flowers and decorations of Easter?

Pop quiz!

It would be quite easy to do a 'pop quiz' on St Mark's Gospel, perhaps as part of a school assembly, or even as part of the sermon! I don't propose to test you all now, but how would you do, I wonder, if we had a quiz right now, and these were some of the questions?

- Is Mark's Gospel the longest, the shortest or 'medium length' compared to the other Gospels?
- Did Mark borrow from Matthew or vice versa?
- How many chapters does Mark's Gospel contain?
- Does Mark include an account of Christmas?
- Does Mark contain a resurrection account?
- What was Mark's job?
- Who did Mark write his Gospel for?
- Did Mark know Jesus?
- What word does Mark use 46 times in his Gospel?

Discovering Mark

How do you think you might do? We know almost nothing about Mark, of course. But he is the writer of almost certainly the oldest, the earliest, of the four canonical Gospels. It's very honest as a work, pointing out the apostles' weaknesses fairly frequently, containing odd little snippets not found elsewhere, such as the man running off naked from the Garden of Gethsemane leaving his loincloth in the hands of the soldier. Could this be the author himself? Some people think so.

And the whole Gospel is hurried. It's breathless. He uses the word 'immediately' 46 times. Everything is a rush; everything is a little bit frenetic. And everything is a secret. The 'messianic secret', as theologians and biblical scholars call it. This is about the fact that some people knew who Jesus was, and others didn't, and that there was something deliberate about that. The world was waiting, God was waiting, Christ was waiting for the moment. These are the birth pangs of a new age, the age of the kingdom.

Leaving us hanging

Mark doesn't contain a Christmas story. Interestingly, he doesn't include a resurrection appearance either. Even at the very end of the Gospel, he leaves us hanging, poised, as it were, after the moment on Easter morning when the candle is lit, but before the cry of 'Alleluia!' The final words in Mark's Gospel are, the women 'went out and fled from the tomb, for terror and amazement had seized them; and they said nothing to anyone, for they were afraid'. Full of realism to the end, that's where the account stops. We know something has happened, we are captivated and confused by it, and we have then to spend the rest of our lives working out what it means to us, and to the world. Feel familiar? It does to me. I love the Gospel of Mark because it feels as if it's written by someone as excited but confused and inadequate at being a disciple as I am. Someone who, like me on my better days, has grabbed hold of the beginning of the truth, which will do me until the rest becomes clear. Mark, the mysterious author of the first Gospel, breathless and hectic, leaves us there, where most of us find ourselves from time to time, I suspect, seized with amazement at the fact that love might have found us.

Tom Clammer

Hymn suggestions

The saint who first found grace to pen; We have a gospel to proclaim; Thanks to God, whose word was spoken; Now the green blade riseth.

SS Philip and James, Apostles   1 May
Are We There Yet?
Isa. 30.15–21; Ps. 119.1–8; Eph. 1.3–10; **John 14.1–14**

Are we there yet?

Anyone who has been on a journey with children would, no doubt, have been subjected to their incessant questioning about various and often unrelated issues. One constant, however, is the metronomic repetition of the tiresome refrain, 'Are we there yet?'

To ask 'Are we there yet?' is to recognize that journeys are not aimless wanderings, but find their fulfilment not merely in departures but also in arrivals. To ask 'Are we there yet?' is an implicit recognition of the tension of transitions, the frustration of being held in the in-between spaces.

This is not the preserve of children, but an experience that we all go through, especially when life does not turn out as expected. In those instances, it may sometimes feel as if the natural course of life is interrupted, suspended in a murky mess between where we have been and where we are longing to be. This is often a place of discomfort, disruption and dislocation.

This in-between place is sometimes referred to as liminal space, a space that is not necessarily entered intentionally, but an unfamiliar space into which one is transported. Liminal places can be disorienting and profoundly disruptive, but they can also become places that afford us the urgent opportunity of reorientation and transformation.

It is in one such liminal space that the disciples – Philip and James among them – find themselves, confronted with a sense of disorientation, but soon allowed reorientation and transformation. 'Are we there yet?' seems to be the question preoccupying both Thomas and Philip, and, with them, countless generations of Christians struggling to make sense of the place of complex transition they find themselves in.

We're getting there

In these liminal places, anxiety tends to manifest through a need to know, to have clarity. So, like Philip, James, Thomas and countless other disciples, we tend to seek information and knowledge in the hope that it will give us the comfort and reassurance we long for.

Furthermore, this search for knowledge often seeks to diffuse the mist of unknowing that leads to a place of vulnerability and dependency. It feeds off our existential need for control and mastery. It titillates our aspiration to subjugate and determine the direction of our circumstances.

The perplexed disciples want to know. And yet, their quest for certainty is met with an invitation to reframe, reassess, both their experience and their relationships with Jesus. Might it be that the gift of liminality is not solely found in our quest for knowledge, but in realizing the opportunity to transform knowledge into understanding, facts into relational capital?

Jesus' confident and uncompromising statements, 'I am the way and the truth and the life' and 'Anyone who has seen me has seen the Father', do not attempt to offer easy formulaic answers to the deep existential questions of the disciples. Instead, they invite a pause, an interruption of our course of thoughts, and compel the one questioning to sit and pay attention. In his response, Jesus seems to signpost towards the truth that the essence of journeys is not in departures and arrivals, but that the journey itself is a pedagogue.

Indeed, journeying with Jesus gives us insights into the essence of God, and helps us negotiate the anxiety of different arrival, or delayed journey. In Jesus, we discover not merely the fullness of God, but we are afforded an insight into our own particular stories, our own identity.

We've been there all along

And yet, the journey is not static, but dynamic. It seems that in this liminal space, the way forward can only be found in the disciples' capacity to resist the temptation to rush forward and explain tensions and paradoxes away, and with a commitment to linger with the question. Like the old spiritual practice of equanimity, followers of Christ are invited to lean into the discomfort and disruption, to sit with the question, and to do that together with others. As we develop these habits and practices, we become able to potentially reorient our lives and our stories for and towards the new normal we find ourselves in. From that place, we may also start to create and imagine new pathways towards a potentially life-giving and life-affirming future, thus establishing a creative balance between outward movement and inner work.

And still, the question is asked: 'Are we there yet?' Otherwise formulated, it raises the challenge of how we face and contend with the disruption and dislocation of our circumstances. How do we confront the risk of disintegration of hope and fragmentation of community?

Asking the question, 'Are *we* there yet?' reminds us that this venture is not a solitary pursuit aimed at satisfying individual longings. It only makes sense when framed through a collective dynamic, so it's good to celebrate two disciples today. 'Are we there yet?' is an invitation to reassess and reframe relational dynamics within the fellowship of faith. It is about reassessing and reorienting our collective stories so that they intersect with the story of Jesus to the extent that we too may be able to state with confidence that those in whose company we journey give us an insight into God's kingdom. Those who journey with us will see insights into God.

Lusa Nsenga Ngoy

308

Hymn suggestions

Alleluia! Sing to Jesus; And can it be; Behold the Lamb; Love divine, all loves excelling.

St Matthias the Apostle 15 May
(transferred from 14 May)
Cast!

Isa. 22.15–end, *or* **Acts 1.15–end**; Ps. 15; Acts 1.15–end
(*if the Acts reading is used instead of the Old Testament reading, the New Testament reading is 1 Cor. 4.1–7*); John 15.9–17

It all happened by casting lots! The disciples needing to replace Judas chose two possible candidates, Matthias and Justus. Then they voted. They cast lots to decide their new colleague and apostle – and the lot fell to Matthias. We know so little about him – just those brief verses that we heard read from the Acts of the Apostles. It feels a bit alien to make decisions by casting lots – especially to us in the Church where appointments are increasingly decided through interview, presentation and selection. But it's worth remembering that the Church in many places in the world elects its leaders. And of course, in a democracy, we vote for those we wish to represent us in government.

Into the limelight

I imagine that the meeting to elect a new apostle was a difficult one for Peter to chair. The disciples would have been very conscious of what had happened to Judas – how he had come to a sorry end and hanged himself, because of his betrayal. How easily Peter might have been in Judas' shoes. There's not much difference between denying your master and betraying him. There but for the grace of God might Peter have gone – into the grave – rather than emerging as the leader of the infant Church.

The meeting chose a successor for Judas. They selected Matthias. Who was he? We don't hear about him in the Gospels before this episode. We don't hear of him again after this episode. We know nothing of his ministry. We do know that he was a follower of Jesus from the time of John the Baptist to the ascension. But Jesus didn't choose him to be one of the original Twelve.

I wonder how Matthias felt when Peter was selected to be an apostle. Peter was impetuous and always got things wrong. And what about Thomas, who doubted? How did Matthias feel when he saw Judas called by Jesus? How did he feel when the risen Christ appeared first to Mary Magdalene? Matthias was always there, but never part of the inner circle.

If you've ever been passed over for a task you felt should be yours, you'll know how hard that can be! How did you react? Did you sulk? Did you fret? Did you rebel? Did you turn your back on the whole enterprise – try to rubbish it – feeling unloved and therefore unsupportive.

Serving backstage

Matthias continued with the Christian company although he wasn't chosen as one of the Twelve by Jesus. He was faithful, though he was never in the limelight. He got on with the task of being a follower of Jesus with no thought of reward. He was loyal and dependable: available when the time came. Matthias was faithful. He had patience and humility. He could be relied upon. He didn't need to be the centre of attention. What an excellent role model for us as Christians today.

Matthias would have been there when Jesus spoke the words to the disciples recorded in John's Gospel. He would have heard himself called to love those around him and to be prepared to sacrifice himself for them. He would have heard that he belonged to Jesus and thus to God. He would have heard himself called a friend of Jesus and chosen by him. He would have heard himself appointed to go and bear fruit, spreading the good news to others. He would know that he was called to bear witness to the truth – come what may – however dangerous.

He was serving alongside all the followers of Jesus and he didn't need to be one of the Twelve to do it. And then suddenly he found himself elected to take the place of Judas. How might that have felt? Did he want to be placed in that position? Perhaps he preferred serving backstage.

Our part

And the message for us today? We are called to be faithful, to use the opportunities that come our way, to be patient, to do things well without expecting recognition. We are to avoid the self-destructiveness of empty ambition. But God calls all of us and we don't need a special label or badge – other than our baptism – for the Holy Spirit to use us in God's service to the world. Some are called into particular positions with significant responsibilities. For some that can be an uncomfortable place to be.

This week, let's try to do some hidden things – some good that only God sees. Let's do it simply because we belong to God, the Spirit dwells within us, and Jesus calls us to be his friends and together makes us his body. God chooses us to be bearers of light and hope within our community whether we receive human recognition or not. We don't have to be voted in to do good!

In the limelight or backstage, we all have a part to play.

Catherine Williams

Hymn suggestions

Brother, sister, let me serve you; God has chosen me; I, the Lord of seas and sky; Will you come and follow me.

Visit of the Blessed Virgin Mary to Elizabeth 31 May
Charged with Expectation
Zeph. 3.14–18; Ps. 113; Rom. 12.9–16; **Luke 1.39–49 [50–56]**

Some stories are so deeply embedded in our cultural imaginations, even in these seemingly post-Christian times, that one can feel one has nothing valuable to say. I've met many preachers, ordained and lay, who feel that way about Christmas or Good Friday or Easter Day. If the visit of the Blessed Virgin Mary to Elizabeth has not been mined quite so deeply as Christmas, Easter or even the annunciation, my imagination is filled with famous images of Mary's meeting with her cousin Elizabeth. I can picture their encounter in part because western art has painted it so very often – sometimes sentimentally, sometimes startlingly, always as a potent encounter between two iconic women. Equally, Mary's Magnificat has been set so often by great composers and is said so often in worship (at Evening Prayer in particular) that one becomes almost inured to its power.

The divine drama

My own reaction to this encounter is increasingly coloured both by my sense of identification with Mary and Elizabeth – as examples of women facing extraordinary circumstances through friendship and solidarity – and my sense of alienation from them.

Alienation? Well, Mary and Elizabeth are mothers-to-be and the fact is I shall never be one. In a society that still over-praises motherhood as a vocation for women, it is easy to lionize Mary, the young mum-to-be, and Elizabeth, the barren woman who is redeemed from failure by late motherhood. Though I am mostly at peace with the fact I shall not be a mum, in a persistently patriarchal world I feel the cut of being unable to be a mother (in a conventional sense).

Of course, what we witness in the encounter between Mary and Elizabeth is the 'cosmic' meeting the 'intimate'. These are women caught up in a divine drama. Their lives have become entangled in Love's redeeming work. When they meet each other, they greet each other as cousins; as women; as part of a sisterhood of those who are expecting children. They also greet each other as those who recognize the mutual grace they inhabit: their worlds have been transformed by the world of the Holy Spirit. They are physically expecting, but that is matched by their hopeful expectation.

Intimate and profound

I am deeply moved by this intersection of intimacy with the profound. While Elizabeth and Mary's places in God's story are key and dramatic ones – they are, after all, the mothers of John the Baptist and Jesus, respectively – their stories invite us to be alert to the Spirit's movement in our lives. We too are ordinary people called into God's drama. Our seemingly everyday stories are charged with love and hope and can be charged with expectation.

Elizabeth and Mary's lives are no grander than ours. If Elizabeth had *de jure* status as the wife of a priest, the fact that she had no children would likely have damaged her public standing in her community. Mary is little more than a child herself and a girl at that, easily ignored and dismissed. These are ordinary lives: that of a young woman in a no-note province of the Roman Empire and that of an older woman who had given up on the prospect of ever being a mother. Through the work of God, they become charged with the divine promise. This is a calling that the 'great and the good' – the powerful in their community – might only dream of.

People of expectation

While none of us is called to be the mother of Jesus like Mary or even the mother of a great prophet like Elizabeth, I sense that we, in our everyday and ordinary lives, are being invited to step into the promise and grace they knew. When Mary sings, 'He has scattered the proud in the thoughts of their hearts. He has brought down the powerful from their thrones, and lifted up the lowly,' I think she is inviting us to recognize that we too are participants in the divine work. We are called to make a difference. We are called to make hope and love practical horizons of our lives.

I think that Mary and Elizabeth show us how to participate in God's kingdom and make a practical difference: it is through solidarity with one another and with all who are not centre stage (which is pretty much all of us).

Because of all the art and music which has accrued around an event like the visitation, we think of Mary and Elizabeth as main actors in the drama. In God's economy that is true, but the meeting of these women took place away from the sight of great men and history's stage. However, that does not make their faithfulness, obedience and sense of expectation valueless. Indeed, it is their openness to God – shown in their mutual recognition and delight in what God is up to in them and in the world – that means that together and individually they will make all the difference in the world. What they do will change the world for ever. We too can be agents of such change.

Rachel Mann

Hymn suggestions

Tell out my soul; My soul proclaims the greatness (Farrell); Take my life and let it be; Trust and obey.

Day of Thanksgiving for the Institution of the Holy Communion (Corpus Christi) 8 June
We Are What We Eat!
Gen. 14.18–20; Ps. 116.10–end; 1 Cor. 11.23–26;
John 6.51–58

I really enjoy my food. And from time to time, I have to take myself in hand and shed those extra pounds. What we eat can affect the shape we become. Or, as it's said, 'We are what we eat!'

The context of John 6

The Gospel for today, the festival of Corpus Christi, is only part of a long discourse (the whole of John 6) on the 'bread of life'. The chapter begins with the miraculous feeding of the 5,000, after which Jesus tells the crowd, 'I am the bread of life.' This theme is then developed further, with Jesus making a link between eating his flesh and drinking his blood and the gift of eternal life.

Some biblical scholars are convinced that this chapter grew out of the context of eucharistic worship in the early Church. The words 'those who eat my flesh and drink my blood' take us well beyond a miracle in which bread satisfies a crowd's physical hunger into the realm of sacramental feeding on Christ himself. The words themselves are shocking. The notion of eating human flesh and drinking human blood is abhorrent. So, what's going on, and what might we make of it? How do we approach the consecrated bread and wine of Holy Communion? For they are given to us with the words, 'the body of Christ' and 'the blood of Christ'.

Eucharistic presence and memorial

Down the centuries, theologians have wrestled with what Jesus might have meant. Does the bread and wine of communion become Jesus' flesh and blood? The answer, as with many things in the realm of faith, is 'perhaps, yes and no'. But exactly how it might be 'yes' and 'no' has never been agreed by all Christians. The sacrament – intended as a sign of the unity of God's people – has become a source of deep division.

At one end of the spectrum are those who hold that the bread and wine of the Eucharist are none other than the body and blood of Christ, physically present. For them, the words 'this is my body/

this is my blood' are absolute. During the Eucharistic Prayer, the substance of the bread and wine changes and the communicant receives the body and blood of Christ.

At the other extreme are those who see the Eucharist purely as a memorial of Jesus and, specifically, a memorial of his death. This view takes seriously Jesus' command to 'do this in remembrance' of him – to the extent that remembrance becomes the focus.

A middle way

Between a 'Catholic real presence' and a 'Protestant memorial' lie other views which aim to balance the truths from both ends of the spectrum. A helpful middle way is found in Richard Crashaw's version of one of Thomas Aquinas' great hymns:

> O dear memorial of that death
> Which lives still and allows us breath.[11]

This is 'both/and' theology. It affirms that the Eucharist is a memorial of Christ, but not a dead memorial – like a tombstone which points to the past – but a living memorial: still alive, reminding us not only of Jesus' death but also his resurrection and, through that, our own hope of eternal life.

The Anglican 39 Articles of Religion speak of 'the Body of Christ [being] given, taken and eaten ... after an heavenly and spiritual manner. And the means whereby the Body of Christ is received and eaten in the Supper is Faith.' In other words, when the bread and wine of the Eucharist are received with faith, we receive Christ's body and blood in an utterly real but spiritual sense.

Draw near with faith

If we eat the bread of the Eucharist expecting only a piece of bread given in memory, then we will receive nothing more and very little will happen as a result. If, however, we 'draw near *with faith*' and expect to receive none other than Christ himself, then we will receive nothing less, and we shall be changed by that encounter. The faithful eating and drinking of the body and blood of Christ is a part of our 'abiding in Christ', and through this we are transformed into the people God calls us to become. 'We are what we eat.'

But this is God's doing. The Eucharist is a sacrament: a divine gift. No amount of trying on our part, or liturgical precision, can conjure up an authentic real presence in the sacrament. Christ's body and blood are his gift to us and can be received by faith alone.

> We need not now go up to heaven,
> To bring the long-sought Saviour down;
> Thou art to all already given,
> Thou dost ev'n now thy banquet crown:
> To every faithful soul appear,
> And show thy real presence here![12]

Peter Moger

Hymn suggestions

Glory, love and praise and honour; Here, O my Lord, I see thee face to face; Let all mortal flesh keep silence; Victim divine, thy grace we claim.

St Barnabas the Apostle
11 June (or transferred to 12th)
'Send Barnabas!'
Job 29.11–16, *or* Acts 11.19–end; Ps. 112; **Acts 11.19–end**
(*if the Acts reading is used instead of the Old Testament reading, the New Testament reading is* Gal. 2.1–10); John 15.12–17

Barnabas, the good'n

The first thing we hear of Barnabas is that he did what he was told. The church in Jerusalem sent him to a group of 'Hellenists' and he went. My guess is that he wanted to go; that he was persuaded of the breadth of the gospel; that he was excited that others were receiving Jesus Christ into their lives. But even if he went begrudgingly, he still went.

> *Lord, help us go when we are called.*

Next, Barnabas recognized the grace of God. That is a big compliment to pay someone. We can recognize many things in the world – problems, opportunities, change – but the grace of God, that needs particular eyes. More than that, Barnabas rejoiced in God's grace.

Lord, help us be those who recognize your grace and delight in it.

Barnabas not only recognized God's grace but could see it in other people – people not normally expected to be grace receivers. I wonder if we often find it easier to see good in people similar to us, rather than those most unlike us. The gospel says something different. God's grace can show up, and so often does, in the places and people most unexpected to us.

Lord, help us see you at work in others, even those in whom we least expect it.

Barnabas, it also seems, was an exhorter. Was he an especially skilled orator? Who knows? Was he convicted enough by the good news of Jesus Christ to want others to understand it? Yes, definitely. He likewise knew that he needed to encourage these new Christ-followers to endure – to remain faithful.

Lord, help us be ready to give an account of the gospel.
Help us too to encourage each other in the journey of faith.

The list of Barnabas' qualities keeps coming: 'he was a good man, full of the Holy Spirit and of faith.' This is high praise. I'm sure Barnabas had his faults. I'm sure he too needed grace, just as much as we do. Nevertheless, he was a 'good'n'. To be described as 'good', the quality of his character must have been excellent. How wonderful to be known as one such as this!

Lord, we know this is big, but help us be found as 'good'.

It's not such a surprise that Barnabas was 'full of the Holy Spirit'. To be full of the Spirit is to have received God's personal presence; to have received what the prophet Joel had prophesied – God coming to be with 'all flesh'. To be full of the Spirit is to be grafted into the gathering of people from many nations and cultures, just as those gathered at Pentecost were. To be full of the Spirit is to know the source of life, the joy of God's presence, the intimacy of God's love.

It's likewise not so surprising that Barnabas went to these Hellenists, knowing the Spirit as he did. Receiving the Spirit is a beautiful thing; it is as if every bit of our body and mind comes alive. But it's also a mission thing. The Spirit fills us and leads us out into the world.

Spirit of God, fill us and send us out!

317

Called to be us

There is more we could say of Barnabas, his faith, his on-and-off friendship with Paul, but we would be at risk of feeling woefully inadequate compared to him if we carried on! We might instead want to remember who Barnabas attributed all this to: to Christ, the Messiah, the Saviour of Israel, but more than that, the saviour of all human beings. Barnabas could see God's grace in all people because he knew God's grace had reached him.

We needn't copy Barnabas, then, wonderful saint that he is. We would do well to serve his master; to serve Jesus, the one in whom goodness is personified, the one who encourages, affirms and challenges us with such authority that we are changed, renewed and made alive.

What we have seen in Barnabas is remarkable – the grace of God at work in the world. But God is not calling us to be another Barnabas. No, we are called to be us, with all our quirks, graces, weaknesses and gifts. And really, that is a fine thing.

Lord, help me not to become like Barnabas, but to become who you are calling me to be in you and for the renewal of the world. Help us, as the community of the beloved, become who you want us to be for your kingdom, now, and for ever. Amen.

Mark Amos

Hymn suggestions

When I needed a neighbour; Spirit of the living God, fall afresh on me; O for a thousand tongues; This little light of mine.

Birth of John the Baptist   24 June
John is His Name
Isa. 40.1–11; Ps. 85.7–end; Acts 13.14b–26, *or* Gal. 3.23–end; **Luke 1.57–66, 80**

I don't know about you, but I am used to thinking about John the Baptist in the Advent season when we recall the adult John, the prophet who prepares the way for the coming Christ. Thus, he has a unique role in salvation history. In Luke's Gospel, he is destined for this role from before his birth. The story of his parents is peculiar to that Gospel. Today's reading reminds us of John's birth, his naming and the gossip that arose about him at that time.

That birth

The story of his conception and birth has clear parallels to the story of Isaac (and of other Old Testament notables, born to barren or ageing women) and to that of Jesus. The unusual events surrounding his birth indicate that this child will be of future significance. Yet, the account of the expected child's birth takes up just one brief sentence (it's an announcement that could have been tweeted!).

Elizabeth's expected, awaited son has been born. Her family and her neighbours rejoice with her. Gabriel's (God's) promise to her has been fulfilled. The Lord has shown his mercy to her, removing the stigma of barrenness.

What's in a name?

As the story unfolds, Luke goes into greater detail in recounting a naming or circumcision ritual for the child, which occurs on the eighth day. This is a curious ceremony: in the Old Testament the name would be given to a child at birth, so this linking of a naming ceremony to the rite of circumcision would appear to be a new practice (corroborating a reference which is not found until eighth-century Jewish writings). In the occupied state in which John was born, perhaps it was modelled on Roman custom (where a boy-child would be named on the ninth day) or on Greek practice (a naming ceremony would take place on the seventh or the tenth day). It seems that we should not rule out the possibility of the dynamic nature of contemporary Jewish culture embracing new customs.

We're told that those present for the ceremony were minded to name the baby Zechariah after his father, though this would have been unusual in Jewish culture of the time (where a son would be identified as 'X the son of Y'). Father and son would tend to bear different names (however, as in many cultures today, the recurrence of familial given names might honour previous generations).

Elizabeth effectively vetoed the suggestion, stating, emphatically, 'No; he is to be called John.' The supporters must have wondered where on earth she got that idea from and so appealed to Zechariah to make the final decision! (Can you imagine the poor priest waiting patiently for the issue to be resolved?) Zechariah, who had been struck dumb because of his lack of faith that Elizabeth would bear a child, asked for a tablet upon which to write and thereon reiterated the name she had stated. By writing and accepting for his son the name that the angel had told to him, 'John', that is 'YHWH is gracious', Zechariah made a statement of faith. His son is the living and so-named proof of that faith.

What does your name mean? Do you bear as portentous a name as John? As I baptize children today, I sometimes wonder whether we have lost sight of the significance and meaning of names. (I can recall an infant whose name was that of a motorway exit that had caught the imagination of the expectant parents as they drove south.) Remember, names can be prescriptively formative! John had a lot to live up to.

The whispers begin ...

Suddenly freed to speak, the previously mute Zechariah is enabled to praise God. The onlookers are amazed and, perchance, awestruck. Then, Luke says, the witnesses began to talk. I'd like to think that this was not just idle gossip about Zechariah, Elizabeth and baby John, but that they did seriously 'ponder', reflecting theologically and considering the implications of what they had witnessed. Were they filled with a sense of awe, acknowledging the hand of God upon John? What might this child become? Did they dare to hope for a new Elijah, a great prophet who would speak to and for God's stricken, subjugated people?

Our reading did not include the Benedictus, Zechariah's hymn that foretells John's prophetic significance. However, it did conclude with the verse that says, 'The child grew and became strong in spirit, and he was in the wilderness until the day he appeared publicly to Israel.' The whispered-about child will return from the wilderness, that traditional place of spiritual and prophetic inspiration (where there is speculation that he may have been raised by or encountered the Essenes with whom the Dead Sea Scrolls have been linked). The verse effectively bridges Luke's unique account of John's birth and naming and the (parallel) accounts in all the Gospels of his later ministry.

John will fulfil his calling to preach repentance and make way for the Lord. Who are we, I wonder, and what are we called to be and do?

Wendy Kilworth-Mason

Hymn suggestions

For the healing of the nations; God has spoken by his prophets; In Christ, there is no east or west; On Jordan's bank the Baptist's cry.

SS Peter and Paul, Apostles 29 June
Lives Transformed

Zech. 4.1–6a, 10b–end, *or* Acts 12.1–11; Ps. 125; Acts 12.1–11 *(if the Acts reading is used instead of the Old Testament reading, the New Testament reading is 2 Tim. 4.6–8, 17–18)*; **Matt. 16.13–19**

The oil of baptism

I do a lot of work in schools, and every year I have the opportunity to re-enact a baptism with year one at a local primary school. The children volunteer to take the parts of parent and godparent, and we have a large candle and a bowl of water and a doll (and me). But there is something that I have noticed every year that happens without exception as we go through the baptism service. When I anoint the doll's head with the sign of the cross with holy oil, the children are spellbound and go completely silent. It happens every time. It is as if they know that something sacred and special is happening. It captivates me, that in an age of play stations, mobile phones and the internet, anointing a doll with oil can provoke such a response in 5-year-olds.

Milk before or after?

The world can be divided in many different ways, one of which is whether you take your tea with milk added to the cup before pouring or add it after. Similarly, some feel this feast day should be reserved just for St Peter, and some for whom St Peter and St Paul jointly celebrated is more important. Being Anglican, the choice is given to us. Whatever you decide, there is no doubt that both individuals' lives were utterly transformed by their relationship with God in Jesus in a pretty dramatic way. Both witness to the fact that if we are in Christ we shall be changed, transformed and called to do things that we never imagined we would do.

Doors

I am really quite slow to work some things out, and it only occurred to me recently that what makes a door a door is its hinges. Without hinges, it ceases to be a door. Hinges need oil to keep them working, and oil is featured quite a lot in today's readings: both in Zechariah and in Matthew's Gospel. The Hebrew title 'Messiah' ('Christ' in Greek) means 'anointed'. Oil comes to us, like wine, through things that are crushed and broken; to bring us something inherent within them that gives joy and life. To be a follower of Christ is to open the door of our hearts to God, and that door needs well-oiled hinges.

Priesthood

Today is evocative for many who are ordained, for it is now common practice in the Church of England to be ordained at Petertide. It is now also more common than it used to be for a deacon to be anointed when they are ordained priest by the bishop. Jesus says some very powerful words to Peter in today's Gospel about the keys to the kingdom, which he gives to Peter, and the terms 'bind' and 'loose' are judicial terms for 'forbid' and 'permit'.

Opening prison gates

If we are truthful with ourselves, there will be things that we are imprisoned by in our lives – be it our need for others, things, approval, status or achievement. As time has gone on, I have come to realize ever more deeply the incredible power of ordained ministry to open things up and also to close things down. Every so often, by God's grace, conversations and pastoral encounters have opened the lid on a treasure trove that is a person's inner life, and I have been given the privilege of seeing something of what God is doing in that person's soul. The sacred story of Paul and Peter, of lives transformed, like many sacred stories, is messy and full of mistakes and failure. But they are also stories of liberation. Stories of being set free. They are stories of the gates of imprisonment being flung open both literally and metaphorically.

Setting others free

The invitation that comes from this experience and from Jesus is to help set others free. Both Peter and Paul, like the olives that are crushed and broken to produce oil, had to be broken to bear fruit. They had to die to old beliefs and grow in a living faith that changed them and others. They had to learn the hard reality of being forgiven when they had so publicly made mistakes. But through all this they learned to be free: to know the reality of being loved sinners. It is only when we know that reality that we can do the same for others. Whether you are a just-Peter or a Peter-and-Paul type of Christian, the reality is the same: transformed lives transform others. That is what we celebrate today and every day.

Jonathan Lawson

Hymn suggestions

And can it be; Amazing grace; God forgave my sin; Let us build a house.

St Thomas the Apostle   3 July
Thomas, Jesus and Scars
Hab. 2.1–4; Ps. 31.1–6; Eph. 2.19–end; **John 20.24–29**

Facing our doubts

A few years ago I went, with my family, to a restaurant run by a TV chef. The food was amazing, the atmosphere refined. Just before coffee was served, I left the table to go to the bathroom. When I returned there were smiles on everyone's face. Something had happened to them that had not happened to me. The well-known chef had come out to talk to them. I had missed out. I wasn't there.

Something similar happens to Thomas in today's Gospel reading. He wasn't there when one of the greatest events in history took place. We don't know why he wasn't there. We don't know whether he had been absent the whole time or whether he had popped out for a moment. Whatever the reason, Thomas missed it. The expressions on his friends' faces would have told him something had happened. But what had happened was so extraordinary, so unlikely, that Thomas wondered. In fact, he doubted. Thomas doubted that a person who he knew had been crucified and certified dead by expert executioners has simply dropped in. And so, he demanded evidence. He wanted to see it for himself. A pre-Enlightenment, Enlightenment apostle, you might think.

And then a week passes.

What a difference a week makes

From other stories about Thomas in John's Gospel, we know that he is an analyst. When Jesus sets off to Bethany to Martha and Mary whose brother Lazarus has died, Thomas intervenes. The other disciples try to persuade Jesus not to go through Judaea because people there have recently tried to kill him. Thomas weighs the evidence and concludes, 'Let's go too so that we might die with Jesus.' Thomas is not faithless. He is a faithful thinker.

Maybe during the week that passes after Jesus' appearance to the others, Thomas has been weighing the evidence, remembering things Jesus said. At the start of the week, he had demanded physical evidence – 'I need to touch him myself.' But when Jesus appears, Thomas merely bows in adoration, 'My Lord and my God!' Thomas is a model of constructive scepticism rather than corrosive cynicism. A model of positive scepticism rather than blind faith.

Most people, I guess, have heard of Galileo and Steve Jobs. Galileo discovered that objects, no matter their size or weight or shape, accelerate towards the earth at the same rate. Steve Jobs revolutionized computing. But why? Because Galileo was sceptical about Aristotle's theories, and Steve Jobs was sceptical about the received wisdom in the computer industry. In both cases, scepticism led to greater insight. It's that kind of thinking that we see in Thomas. Not corrosive cynicism, but positive scepticism. Scepticism in its original meaning – inquiring, investigating, looking around.

In the week between the two parts of our story, I imagine Thomas looking around – in his memory, at what he had heard and seen Jesus do. He has a week to be the kind of sceptic that Galileo and Steve Jobs were, to question the accepted wisdom of his religion, and begin to see things differently.

From seeing to understanding

Thomas' scepticism, over a week, leads him from the simple declaration his friends made, 'We have seen the Lord', to his own deeply theological confession, 'My Lord and my God!'

In response, Jesus asks, 'Have you believed because you have seen me?' We never hear Thomas' reply – it could be 'no'. 'Blessed are those who have not seen and yet have come to believe.' Perhaps Jesus is not talking here about those of us who at one time or another committed to follow Jesus, but those who have struggled with faith, who have come through dark times and doubting times, and arrived at the deep kind of faith displayed by Thomas. And Greek being Greek, with tenses that are so different from English, perhaps Jesus is also saying, 'Blessed are those who are constantly coming to believe, who wrestle over and over with questions.'

So what do we learn from Thomas?

We do not need to fear asking questions of our faith. We do not need to fear times of doubt. Embracing them can lead to deeper understanding of the one who is both Lord and God. Ignoring our questions does not deal with them, it simply pushes them into the further recesses of our minds until a moment of weakness allows them to burst to the fore. How many, I wonder, have left the Church and even the faith because their questions were never answered. Thomas provides an example of honestly facing things.

C. H. Spurgeon, who is sometimes known as the 'Prince of Preachers', said this:

> The highest science, the loftiest speculation, the mightiest philosophy, which can ever engage the attention of a child of God, is the name, the nature, the person, the work, the doings, and the existence of that great God.[13]

May God bless you both in your thinking and your encounter with the One who is our Lord and God.

Liz Shercliff

Hymn suggestions

The Church's one foundation; O sons and daughters of the King; Jesus, stand among us; We walk by faith and not by sight.

St Mary Magdalene 22 July
I Have Seen the Lord
S. of Sol. 3.1–4; Ps. 42.1–10; 2 Cor. 5.14–17;
John 20.1–2, 11–18

A roller-coaster ride

Wasn't it exciting, that first time you were allowed out after lock-down – the moment you could see, even if not hug, your family or friends, when it felt, for a moment at least, as though the isolation and fear and threat of the pandemic had receded? I remember the first eerily silent days of the first lockdown. Almost no cars moved. The roads were so quiet that in an effort to distance themselves from others, walkers occupied the space usually reserved for traffic. Gradually we got used to it. We waved to people from across the street, or contacted friends and family online. Excitement built as a promised relaxation of the rules came closer. Then, the promise was withdrawn and it was back to fearing the worst again. The pandemic, and subsequent lockdowns, brought a roller coaster of emotion for many of us, I suspect. Perhaps as I describe them now, you can sense some of those emotions rising within you.

Mary Magdalene must have felt similarly turbulent emotions as she went through the ups and downs of Jesus' final week – the apparent triumph of Jesus' arrival in Jerusalem, through his trial, Pilates' offer of executing an alternative, and finally the death that brought her to the tomb, on this morning, to be close to her dead friend, perhaps to say a final goodbye.

Finding the tomb empty must have been just one more emotional tumble to endure. She went to tell the others, who came – and went. No wonder she stood and wept. Sometimes standing and weeping is the only appropriate response. Notice that the angels don't pop out of the tomb to let Mary know everything is OK. They wait until she is ready to look in and see them.

Looking into the darkness

Eventually, Mary does look into the tomb. 'Just one more time, just in case,' she thought, perhaps. Maybe the hope she had in Jesus simply refused to die. Again, the angels don't interrupt Mary with a solution. They ask her what's wrong. 'They have taken away my Lord,' she tells them. I wonder how often we try to fix things rather than asking others what's wrong and then listening to what they say. Circumstances or troubles can seem to take away our Lord, and we need to be honest about that. Distress, discomfort or doubt can seem to take Jesus from us. Maybe it's easier to focus our gaze on the darkness of the tomb. But in the middle of that darkness, when our eyes adjust, there is hope. And when Mary steps away from the darkness, although she does not yet recognize him, Jesus is there with her.

He too asks a question – more specific this time. Not, 'Why are you weeping?' but 'For whom are you looking?'

Then there is that poignant exchange of names.

'Mary.'

'Teacher.'

No further explanation necessary amid the mutual recognition.

For Mary, there is no disembodied voice, no reassuring doctrinal proposition. Jesus is there for her. At first, no words are required.

Who was Mary?

Some areas of the Church remember Mary as a bad woman come good. This telling of her story does not come from the Gospel writers or the early Church. It was in the sixth century that Pope Gregory denounced her in an Easter sermon as a prostitute. What the Gospel writers actually tell us is that she was a faithful disciple. All four Gospel writers place Mary Magdalene at the cross of Jesus, witnessing his death. John also has her at the empty tomb. Mary was a faithful disciple, a lover of Jesus who witnessed his death and went to his empty tomb. A woman who was the first to meet Jesus face to face after his resurrection. A woman who was the apostle to the apostles.

'Have you seen him too?'

Just as the religious and political powers collaborated to silence Jesus, so over the centuries they have silenced Mary. Mary is troublesome – in John's account she realized first what had happened. Mary is inconvenient – church history would have it that the apostles were male. Mary is disturbing – there she stands, at the mouth of an empty tomb, speaking with the risen Jesus. Mary is perturbing – there she goes, to tell the disciples that she has seen the Lord. And Mary is challenging too. For today, as we commemorate her and read her story, here she stands, before us, telling us that she has seen the Lord. Perhaps she is also asking, 'Have you seen him too?'

Liz Shercliff

Hymn suggestions

Mary to her Saviour's tomb; Take my life and let it be; A woman in a world of men; Now the green blade riseth.

St James the Apostle 25 July
The Journey of True Greatness

Jer. 45.1–5, *or* Acts 11.27—12.2; Ps. 126; Acts 11.27—12.2
(if the Acts reading is used instead of the Old Testament reading, the New Testament reading is 2 Cor. 4.7–15); **Matt. 20.20–28**

The journey to Jerusalem

Jesus was travelling to Jerusalem for the most important festival of the Jewish people – Passover – the story of their liberation from slavery. Celebrating such a story in an occupied nation means that Rome was going to be on full alert for any hint of trouble. Jesus knew that continuing to teach and live out his subversive message of God's love to the whole world would get him into trouble, not just with the religious authorities but also with Rome.

So, Jesus is quite honest with his disciples. His mission is to enable God's values of justice, righteousness, equality and love to be revealed in such a way that it will change the world. That will have its cost not just for him but for those who will carry on the work of the mission of God – to enable it to come about on earth as it is in heaven.

James and John and their mum miss the point, assuming that Jesus is come to enable the world's values to come about in heaven as it is on earth. So, when you get through this revolution, their mum says, when you're in charge instead of Rome, can you make sure that my boys get the top jobs? Make sure that there is some reward for them to make it all worthwhile.

Jesus says, have you heard a word I told you, about what might happen? Yes, we heard, we'll be there right by your side, don't worry. We just want to make sure that in the end there is something in it for us when we have drunk from that deep bitter cup. And Jesus reminds them that what God brings out of this will be for everyone, not just for the chosen, privileged few.

Of course, the rest of the gang hear what James and John's mum has asked, and they are not happy at all. Their displeasure stems from the wrong reasons. Not because they understand it any better, but because they think the top jobs might already have gone.

The journey beyond Jerusalem

Well, we know what happened to Jesus. But what of James and John? Acts records that James, son of Zebedee, was beheaded by Herod Agrippa, the first of the disciples to be martyred. Ironically, he becomes known as James the Greater and became the patron saint of Spain. According to legend, his remains were buried in Santiago de Compostela in Galicia. The traditional pilgrimage to his supposed grave, known as the 'Way of St James', has been the most popular pilgrimage for Western European Catholics from the early Middle Ages.

His brother John was possibly the only one of the Twelve to die of old age. Tradition says that he was also the beloved disciple who looked after Mary following the crucifixion; that he was the author of the Gospel of John and of Revelation – although scholars will go on arguing about this for years to come.

I wonder what their mum thought about it all afterwards. They certainly became well known, her boys. And one of them, the one whose feast day it is today, has churches named after him, St James the Greater! And people walk pilgrimages to find themselves and something greater than the ordinary, whatever their faith tradition may be. After the crucifixion and the resurrection, did she remember that walk to Jerusalem when Jesus subverted every human category in a moment and said, 'Whoever wishes to be great among you must be your servant, and whoever wishes to be first among you must be your slave'?

The journey of the Church

Do we still baulk at those reminders – the audacious subversive nature of the gospel of Christ? Or do we forget it? When we look at the hierarchy of world status, even in the Church, do we forget what Jesus told them again and again? Do we still hunger for greatness, self-importance? The churches are full of plaques that state how important people are, what roles and positions they have held, what great benefactors they have been. Did they not learn what Christ meant?

Do we too crave greatness by the world's standards, wanting our acts of service to have the recognition we think we deserve, for our sacrifices to be rewarded appropriately? Do we believe that through long service we earn a right to manipulate or control?

Do we, the Church that bears Christ's name, still covet those thrones on the left and the right, forgetting that the one whose kingdom we serve subverted the customs of his day in a radical retelling of God's grace? Jesus' own mother sang a song when he was in the womb that told of bringing the mighty down from their thrones and exalting the humble. She watched her son become the servant of all, all the way to the cross and grave. She drank the bitterest cup.

Perhaps she shared that with another mother who understandably wanted something more than suffering for her sons. Those two women stood at the cross together. Perhaps on resurrection morning, they understood the life and love that broke through it all to reveal true greatness.

Carey Saleh

Hymn suggestions

What kind of greatness can this be; From heaven you came; Beauty for brokenness; Great God, your love has called us here.

Transfiguration of Our Lord   6 August
(*or* transferred to 7 August)
Recognizing Jesus in the Everyday
Dan. 7.9–10, 13–14; Ps. 97; 2 Peter 1.16–19; **Luke 9.28–36**

Come up the mountain ...

Come with me up the mountain. It's the only peak around here, rising from the plain. It's only a couple of miles' walk but from the top, you'll see right across Galilee to the sea. Come with me, and with Peter, James and John. Look down on the land where Jesus has been journeying for many months. Jesus said that we have come up here to pray. Perhaps Mount Tabor feels closer to God than the surrounding land.

The sun is bright, beating down on us as we look across the Megiddo valley, mentioned by the prophet Zechariah as a place of great mourning. As we reach the summit you lift your eyes from the valley below. You are dazzled by the brightness of the sun. For a moment you see nothing. You are blinded by an almost burning, dazzling light. As your eyes adjust you realize that this light isn't coming from the sun. It's all around us. It's coming from Jesus. Not from his clothes, or his skin. It isn't surface light. It seems to shine out of him, from his very being. As though he is the source of it all.

Your eyes are glued to Jesus. He *is* the Jesus you know. But he is more than that. You look around. The people you came with are there – the same slightly sweaty walkers you arrived with. But then – surely that's Moses and Elijah? Finally, a voice from heaven: 'This is my Son, my Chosen.' It's like meeting YHWH in person, the light, the voice, Moses, Elijah – and you.

You can't store the moment up, you can't build a tent and stay here.

This moment, like all moments, passes.

What does this moment mean?

There is symbolism in the story of course. Moses and Elijah are there, the Law and the Prophets both fulfilled in Jesus. The valley over which the disciples looked is called Megiddo, Armageddon. In the Hebrew Bible it's where false gods are dethroned, and for some Christians it is also synonymous with the end of the world. Jesus' transfiguration is perhaps forward-looking as well as backward. He fulfils the Law and the Prophets but he is also true God among false ones, and Lord of the future.

Years later, Peter writes of this experience not in terms of doctrine or teaching but in terms of encounter: 'We ourselves heard it.' We know the truth of Jesus not because we have learnt it, but because we have seen it. God is often revealed not in teaching, maybe not even in liturgy or worship, but in an encounter. When, as on the mountain, the veil of the humdrum is lifted, or when the mists of busyness part and we glimpse beneath it the divine presence; when we realize that Jesus is at the heart of our every day, that the whole world is filled with his glory, then we encounter him. It is never the case that God is absent, only that our attention has wandered. It is right to seek God, of course. But sometimes it is also right to simply

331

give our consent to be where we already are, to accept that God is already here and to uncover the treasure of Jesus' presence.

Peter probably understood this moment of transfiguration retrospectively, rather than at the time. As the full truth of Jesus' resurrection began to dawn, day by day, month by month, perhaps Peter looked back and began to work out what the bright light, the voice, the presence of Moses and Elijah meant. Later he must have wondered what his own presence there meant too. As you seek an encounter with God this week, notice where you are; realize the depth of the moment, and wonder what you are doing there. What might Jesus be calling you to?

Recognizing Jesus' presence

Recognizing Jesus' presence as we go about our daily chores is one way of realizing his presence and his call. I would like to finish with a poem written during a very heavy storm when I realized God's presence with me:

> Weather Bomb
> Along the lakeside
> the storm bellows
> waves break
> wind howls
> feet splash
> through endless, edgeless puddles.
> Along the lakeside
> my heart is stilled
> and I find You.
> Along the lakeside
> the storm bellows
> emails to answer
> papers to read
> sermons to prepare
> tasks to complete
> feet splash
> through endless, edgeless puddles.
> Along the lakeside
> my mind is stilled
> and I find You.
> © Liz Shercliff 2017

Liz Shercliff

Hymn suggestions

New every morning is the love; Crown him with many crowns: Rejoice, the Lord is King; O worship the King.

The Blessed Virgin Mary   15 August
Magnificat!
Isa. 61.10–end, *or* Rev. 11.19—12.6, 10; Ps. 45.10–end;
Gal. 4.4–7; **Luke 1.46–55**

Magnificat!

The Magnificat: repeated often in worship, familiar words, such that they can become part of our internal repertoire to draw upon in times of joy, trouble, anger, when in need of comfort. The Magnificat – 'My soul magnifies the Lord' – words that have resonated down the centuries and continue to inspire the imagination of our hearts, just as God inspired Mary, the Mother of God, chosen to become the mother of the Son of God, Jesus Christ our Lord.

But 'magnify'?

There is a puzzling ambivalence, though, in that word 'magnify'. In Latin, it means 'make greater'. But how can we, do we, magnify the Lord? What did Mary mean by 'My soul magnifies the Lord'? How can we make the Lord greater?

We can't: the Lord God is greater than anything that humanity can conceive or imagine. The Lord God is greater than anything. Indeed, because God is no thing, but being itself, God is greater than all there is, seen and unseen. So how can the soul of a simple, pure girl magnify God? Or we, singing her words? There is nothing that can be added to God.

The greatness of love

But to stop there is to miss something vital about God. For God came to a humble girl and chose her to be the mother of the incarnation. God begins with a relationship – an ongoing relationship with the created order and humanity from the beginning of time. God is not above all that there is, with no connection, no interrelation. God's greatness is a greatness of love. A love that forever empties itself into the world, into creation, into humanity, into that young woman Mary. A love in which we participate when we come to worship. And because of this, when we respond in love, we do indeed magnify the Lord.

God doesn't need us. But God's love is such that it requires a response.

The response of 'Yes!'

Mary's response, all those centuries ago, was a yes – a yes that came from the heart of all she was. It was utterly profound as it offered God all she had. Her spirit rejoiced in God her saviour. And yes, since then, all generations have called her blessed.

Mary shows us how to understand the nature of God's love, and how to respond. God's love is not far distant, with a great gulf between God and created humanity, such that we have to earn our right to receive the blessings of God's grace. We don't have to win God's love; it is not conditional upon our response. Rather God's love is there, around us, sustaining all that is, infused in everything. God's love is everywhere – fundamentally different from the things of the world. God's love is the ground of all there is, a love in which we participate, by which we become real.

Mary's 'Yes!' is her soul magnifying the Lord that draws us to the truth that God's active love is the element in which we love and move and have our being. Like the fish of the sea, the birds of the air, we are at home in God's love.

'Yes!' or 'No ...'

To participate in God is our choice. We can turn away from our full humanity in God. We can diminish ourselves, shrinking away into death and oblivion, utter darkness and forgetfulness. Or we can face towards the light and brightness, the warmth of the fire of God's love, and live.

So, Mary chose. She chose to recognize the love in which she participated and to say, 'Yes!' And so, as she magnified the Lord, as she sang of God's overwhelming greatness, so her soul grew in fullness.

The fullness of God

The fullness in which we participate – the fullness of God, the fullness of love – has a deep significance to how we understand our lives and purpose. In the fullness of time, God sent his Son. In Jesus, the fullness of God is come to be; it is already realized. It is a fullness that is beyond our comprehension; a love that passes our understanding.

We see it all around us: in acts of kindness and generosity. In self-giving and forgiveness that Jesus teaches us. In moments and glimpses of glory. In that deep sense of peace that can come in anxiety or grief. Such moments remind us of the realm of God's constant glory and eternal love. Where our restless hearts find their rest in the reality of love that is our true home, where we belong now and for all eternity. In the love of God which is the fullness that makes us whole. In which we are magnified.

We sing with Mary, allowing our souls to magnify the Lord. For then we are magnified with her by God's love, and we grow into the fullness of God, in which is our true belonging, in which we are all God calls us to be.

Frances Ward

Hymn suggestions

Tell out my soul; Lord, Jesus Christ, you have come to us; Blest are the pure in heart; For Mary, mother of our Lord.

St Bartholomew the Apostle   24 August
What's in a Name?
Isa. 43.8–13, *or* Acts 5.12–16; Ps. 145.1–7; Acts 5.12–16
(*if the Acts reading is used instead of the Old Testament reading, the New Testament reading is 1 Cor. 4.9–15*); **Luke 22.24–30**

Bartholomew: who was he?

I served my curacy in a market town in Lancashire, which, in medieval times, long gone past, had been the location of the abattoir that served the surrounding area. It was no surprise, then, that the Church took its patronage from a saint who is the patron saint of tanners and butchers. You'll see him depicted carrying a large butcher's knife, and often carrying his skin over his arm: St Bartholomew. Martyred in Armenia by being flayed alive.

In the Gospels, there's not much to be gleaned about Bartholomew. He is often identified as the same person as Nathanael in St John's Gospel, for he is the constant companion of Philip. But he doesn't really emerge from the text with anything significant or personal about him – no anecdote or story.

His legacy sanctifies the ordinary

Over the centuries those sorts of associations enrich our lives and our culture, sometimes in strange and rather weird ways. We don't know very much about St Bartholomew, but hospitals, schools, churches and squares have been named after him. He gives his name and it triggers our imaginations into remembrance of the Christian heritage.

Bartholomew's name is a strange reverse of the presence of the unknown soldier, represented by statues in many town squares, who recalls our thoughts to those who paid the ultimate price but who remain nameless. Their personal details are lost to us, but their contribution lives on, challenging us to acknowledge and commemorate our debt to them. Our present lives are built on the past: we remember all those who have worked, fought and suffered for our safety and security. Our ordinary lives are blessed by them, whether they have names or not.

Bartholomew's name leaves a rich associative history and culture, attached to particular places that take on significance and meaning. Like any patron saint, he sanctifies the ordinary: for example, he also gives a sense of God's presence as animals are slaughtered by butchers who take seriously their patron saint, or as surgeons sharpen their knives in his name. Patron saints are there to protect, to bless, to intercede for us. They give a sense of connection with the divine, a sanctification of the everyday. By their names, they remind us of how God creates and sustains the everyday, ordinary world in love and blessing. Everything is in God's hands – whether we give it a name or not. We honour the nameless people of the past who suffered martyrdom to witness to God, to express the greater love. We acknowledge with appreciation our inheritance from them, recalling their patronage as we attend to the holy in the ordinary actions of life.

Standing by Jesus in his trials

The fate of those first disciples and apostles was not nice. Matthew, killed in Ethiopia by the sword. Mark, dragged by horses through the streets of Alexandria until he died. Luke, hanged on an olive tree in Greece. St John of the Revelation, survived boiling in oil and was the only apostle to die peacefully. Peter, crucified upside down. James, thrown from the Temple in Jerusalem and then beaten to death. James the Greater, beheaded. Andrew, crucified. Thomas, stabbed with a spear. Jude, killed with arrows. Matthias, who replaced Judas, stoned and beheaded.

There are many suffering real martyrdom in the world today. You need only to see images of churches destroyed – ancient churches, some dating back to St Bartholomew's time, on fire, wrecked and demolished. Christians suffer from the growing divisions of the world, in many places.

Surrounded by a great cloud

In worship today, imagine yourself surrounded by a great cloud of witnesses, the saints and martyrs of all times, including our own, who witness to Christ today in the face of death and terror. Pray for them. Pledge yourself to be alongside them, to suffer with them in your minds and hearts. For we may not know their names, but they need our prayer. And do give to charities dedicated to bringing humanitarian aid to those who are persecuted, or are forced to leave their homes with nothing, of whatever creed or culture.

St Bartholomew reminds us of the Christian way to follow Jesus who is the way, the truth and the life. He received God's grace to believe and preach the Word, and it led him to India, to Armenia. It led him on a way of self-sacrifice. What more can we do, to be self-sacrificial for the sake of others? For the sake of Christians, throughout the world, who suffer today? We can give thanks for the ordinary things we receive from God's hands, remembering the saints of all ages who sanctify the world with God's presence.

Frances Ward

Hymn suggestions

Will you come and follow me? Saints of old! Lo, Jesu's people; For all thy saints, O Lord; Ye watchers and ye holy ones.

Holy Cross Day   14 September
The Scandalous Cross
Num. 21.4–9; Ps. 22.23–28; Phil. 2.6–11; **John 3.13–17**

'When I survey the wondrous cross, on which the Prince of glory died ...'

These famous opening lines from Isaac Watts' classic hymn takes us to the heart of a paradox. In Christianity, no symbol has been more lionized than the cross. It is a site of wonder and promise; it is the signal of sacrificial redemption ... and yet ... there is something extraordinary and disconcerting about the fact that our faith has transformed a device designed to torture, humiliate and, ultimately, kill criminals in the vilest way into a sign of hope.

Scandalous power

The feast of the Holy Cross or Holy Cross Day is, then, a little unsettling. It is sufficiently so that it is tempting simply to rush on past it, just as some Christians long to get past the trauma of Good Friday, Holy Saturday and get to Easter Day as quickly as possible. To skip Holy Cross Day, as it were, is I think a mistake. Whatever one thinks or feels about the cross of Christ it is non-negotiable, it is a still point at the heart of our stories of faith.

There is something scandalous about the cross. Crucifixion was used as a means of torture and humiliation reserved for criminals and rebels. Yet, as we know – and as we celebrate on Holy Cross Day – the cross is for Christians a sign and means of salvation. Yet it is also scandal in its earliest sense: a stumbling block or tripwire. It can be experienced as a block to faith.

Perhaps part of the strange beauty of the cross of Christ is its ironic power. It is surely impossible to celebrate an instrument of violence in and of itself. However, as St John's words indicate, ironically, his way of death becomes the route to salvation: 'And just as Moses lifted up the serpent in the wilderness, so must the Son of Man be lifted up, that whoever believes in him may have eternal life.'

Lift high the cross

The language here has an exquisite ambiguity: 'lifted up' can mean 'exalted' or raised high, as a sovereign is raised up on a throne dais.

John is alert to this connotation. Jesus, the Son of Man, is to be lifted up high so that all may see his majesty and, in faith, receive the life of God – eternal life.

At the same time, we who know the facts of Jesus' story also know that the way he was 'lifted up' was on a cross. As Jesus is lifted up physically on an instrument of torture he is also lifted up symbolically. The point of his humiliation is the moment when he is raised up for all people to see him in glory.

For those of us who have given our lives to Christ, it can be really challenging to appreciate just how much of a stumbling block it can be when we treat Jesus' humiliation as a moment of glory. For example, in orthodox Islamic thought, Jesus is a prophet, second only to Muhammad. As such, Jesus cannot be permitted to die on the cross. In Islamic thought, it is commonly held that at the point of crucifixion Jesus was substituted for a criminal who dies in his place. Jesus, the prophet, ascends to heaven in glory.

Given the horror of the cross, I think I do understand the response of Muslims, even as I disagree with their analysis. To meditate seriously on the holy cross is to be stopped short. For to accept that an instrument of torture can be a site of holiness and glory is quite extraordinary. Indeed, it took centuries for it to be accepted as the primary symbol of Christianity. For early Christians, close as they were to persecution and violence, the Good Shepherd was a more powerful image of Christ.

Set apart/joined together

One of the meanings of 'holy' is 'set apart'. The holy cross sets Christ apart, but all of us are called to find our salvation in him. While I could see how some might read the cross as, in effect, a glorification of violence and suffering in which we are invited to almost revel in Christ's willingness to be punished on our behalf, such a reading works less and less for me. Increasingly I see in Christ's taking on himself the violence of the world – ours and others – as a savage indictment of our capacity to make of God our victim. I see an invitation to live another way: the way of reconciliation and promise. That's why the cross without the resurrection is ugly and nihilistic. The other side of the cross is resurrection and its invitation to live a life of reconciliation with all our violence exposed for the empty path it is. The cross is holy, but not simply because it is a cross. The cross takes us into the depths of who we really are and invites us to live Christ's risen, loving life. As Watts finishes his hymn:

Love so amazing, so divine
Demands my soul, my life, my all.

Rachel Mann

Hymn suggestions

When I survey the wondrous cross; Lift high the cross; The old rugged cross; Be still my soul.

St Matthew, Apostle and Evangelist 21 September
Our Wealth is Christ

Prov. 3.13–18; Ps. 119.65–72; 2 Cor. 4.1–6; **Matt. 9.9–13**

The problem of money

Tax-collectors have never been popular. True today. True in the time of Jesus. So, when he picks up this man called Matthew sitting at his tax booth, Jesus put a veritable cat among the pigeons. How could he possibly sully his little band of followers, and, more importantly, his pure message of salvation, with the presence of someone so despicable?

Money is not easy to deal with. Think of Matthew 6.24: 'No one can serve two masters ... You cannot serve God and wealth.' Or Timothy: 'For the love of money is a root of all kinds of evil ...' Money, wealth: a distraction from the real spiritual business of God.

How should we, as followers of Jesus Christ today, contribute to debates about money? Those debates are all around us. How much the living wage should be. The growing differential between the very rich and the very poor. The future of capital in the twenty-first century. Big questions. Is our relationship with God separate from the Monday–Saturday lives we lead?

Christian concern with politics and economics

As Christians, we should be fundamentally concerned with how society works. It becomes destabilized when the gap between the rich and the poor grows. Many economists and philosophers are increasingly concerned that when economic inequality becomes extreme, social stability is threatened. We have a duty of care for those who struggle without enough. The teaching of Jesus is a constant jolt to our conscience. So today, when we celebrate St Matthew, what helps us to think more deeply about wealth and poverty?

The place of wealth

There's nothing wrong with wealth: it is at the heart of a healthy, strong society. The problems come when wealth becomes a master. When people become greedy; too concerned with security, comfort and luxury, or success. We can be so seduced by money and making money that we lose perspective on the real riches that make life worth living: friendship, love, kindness, generosity. Money can't buy happiness. Christian faith can help us think about our gifts and talents, and about the responsibility of wealth.

Matthew the tax-collector

That Jesus chose a tax-collector is significant. It brings money, tax, right into the heart of the gospel. In his day, tax collection was doubly unpopular because Matthew collected from Jewish people for the Romans, the occupying force. To survive, he would have creamed off what he could into his own pockets. A sinner and a tax-collector. The words went together.

Paying tax, generous wages and philanthropy

We tend to bemoan the taxes we pay. It's a universal gripe. But taxation is essential to things we take for granted – education, health, the transport infrastructure; defence, social care, research and development, overseas aid – that make us into society. Aspects of our life together, our common good, that make us civilized. That give opportunities through education; a chance to survive illness. Society enables us to help others at times of crisis, war or famine. Taxation is a good thing. Should we pay more? Particularly as the rich have become very rich over recent decades in the West. Capital, left to its own market forces, does not regulate itself but accumulates wealth on wealth. How to harness this for the good of all? Especially in times of crisis, when society threatens to break down. Progressive taxation to redistribute wealth back into society could be the answer.

Others have different solutions. Some billionaires argue that if everyone is paid a generous wage then the markets benefit; if poor people have more to spend, they become socially mobile. There's the example of Henry Ford: he paid his workers well enough so they could buy the cars they made. A different way of tackling inequality. Closer to the idea of the living wage.

Another way is philanthropy. Those well off give generously in a spirit of care and love of fellow human beings, with community foundations in each country to encourage philanthropy.

The good news of Christ: our wealth lies with him

Jesus chose Matthew and he challenges us to think about wealth and poverty. We should be merciful, mindful of those in need. If we are wealthy, we should be always grateful for what we have. It does not give happiness or security, but the opportunity to respond to God with generous hearts. We should pay tax with willing spirits. Be positive about the redistribution of wealth, that those in need might live life more abundantly.

To give reflects the outpouring love of God, which overflows with an income that is better than silver, revenue that is better than gold. We are stewards, not owners: all we have comes from God and of his own do we give. When we follow Jesus, we are immeasurably rich. St Matthew found that out as he left his tax booth: his wealth was Jesus Christ.

Frances Ward

Hymn suggestions

There's a wideness in God's mercy; Teach me, my God and King; Lord, for the years; For all the saints who from their labours rest.

St Michael and All Angels   29 September
Protectors of Truth

Gen. 28.10–17, or Rev. 12.7–12; Ps. 103.19–end; Rev. 12.7–12
(if the Revelation reading is used instead of the Old Testament
reading, the New Testament reading is Heb. 1.5–end);
John 1.47–end

Michaelmas

Time-travelling back a century or so, to this day – Michaelmas – we
would witness the end of the financial year. It was a day for settling
accounts and hiring new labourers. It was a time when the Church
prayed for protection from Michael and All Angels for the coming
longer nights when dark forces were thought to be lurking.

Angels are messengers of God. Michael the Archangel is the
messenger who protects and delivers God's people. In the book
of Revelation Michael leads the armies of angels in their defeat of
the 'dragon'. The dragon is a symbol for Satan, the fallen angel
'Lucifer' – the most beautiful of all the archangels. Satan in Hebrew
theology is 'the deceiver', the one who leads people astray. Lucifer
was banished from heaven for trying to usurp God's place, thinking
himself more beautiful even than God. Putting himself first led to
Lucifer's downfall.

And so the battle in heaven between Michael and Satan is not so
much a battle between good and evil as between truth and deceit.
Michael fights for that which is true; he is the protector of truth.

No deceit

When Jesus sees Nathanael under the fig tree, he sees one in whom
there is no deceit. Nathanael is truth-filled, and Jesus spots him a
mile off. Nathanael sticks out because he is without deceit.

As Christians, we are called to be people of truth, those like
Nathanael, without deceit. A person of truth has integrity. The
life of a person of truth holds together and is all of a piece. Not
someone who says one thing and does another. Not someone who
breaks promises, or hides parts of themselves, or is living a lie. The
one who is without deceit will be open, honest and real. That's
quite unusual in our world of fake news, where it's hard to discern
where truth lies.

343

To get to truth-filled places we often have to struggle, and doubt, and ask many questions on the way. We have to let things go and dare to think and try new things. We have to be curious explorers, who ponder and take risks.

Finding truth

I'm not good at Maths but I do know that if the answer is 7, the question could be what is 4+3, but it could be what is 6+1, or what is 21 divided by 3, or how many days in the week are there? So many ways to arrive at the truth of the number 7, and all the questions that lead to that answer are valid.

There are many and varied questions and routes that lead to the truth of God, and we need to be open to them, both in ourselves and in others. If we are people who search for truth, we will be used to finding it in unexpected and surprising places.

That's what happened to Jacob, asleep on the ground on his way to Haran, miles from the Temple. He awakes to realize that he has found holy ground: 'Surely the LORD is in this place and I did not know it.' A vision of heaven and a promise from God makes him realize God is with him. He has stumbled upon truth and he wasn't even awake when it happened.

Jesus said, 'I am the way, and the truth and the life', and if we are to be people of truth then we will be those who are close to Jesus. When Jesus looks on us, is he able to say, 'Here is a person in whom there is no deceit'? Though we often hide things from one another, we can hide nothing from God who knows us through and through.

Open-handed

We have to work at becoming people of truth. Following Christ means changing and growing throughout our Christian pilgrimage – being prepared to experience and find God in the most surprising and new ways. It means acknowledging that God is a God of all time and eternity whom we are to proclaim afresh to each generation.

We are to be open-handed, generous and sacrificial with the truth we bear – just as Jesus was open-handed for the world on the cross. Such generosity led Christ and the world to new life: to resurrection and restoration.

Our questing to be God's people – the people of Jesus who journey, those filled with the courage and passion of the Holy Spirit – should make us stand up for the rights of others, speak out on

344

community issues, pursue justice for those who can't do it for themselves, defend and support the poor, strive to serve our neighbours both here and in the wider world. If we do these things, we, like Nathanael, will stand out a mile and people will be drawn to the lively and committed faith they see us practising.

So, let's remember and give thanks for St Michael who protects us from both the deceit of others and the deceit that lies within ourselves. Michael and the angels are protecting the truth within each one of us, as they protect the truth of Jesus Christ for the world. The angels ascend and descend to defend the truth of the Son of Man – Jesus. We are called to join with Michael and all the angels to be truth bearers, truth proclaimers, truth protectors as we declare together:

Holy holy holy,
the Lord God Almighty,
   who was and is and is to come.

Catherine Williams

Hymn suggestions

Ye watchers and ye holy ones; Holy, holy, holy is the Lord; Angel voices ever singing; How shall I sing that majesty.

St Luke the Evangelist   18 October
On Being Comfortable with Serendipity
Isa. 35.3–6, *or* Acts 16.6–12a; Ps. 147.1–7; 2 Tim. 4.5–17; Luke 10.1–9

Hope that perches in the soul

I wonder what words you would use to describe your relationship with this thing called hope. Perhaps you are someone whose life has been defined by dashed hopes or defined by fulfilled hopes. Perhaps you are the sort of person who is hope-full, or hope-less. Perhaps you have hope. Perhaps you simply hold on to hope, or hold on to hope for others – or someone else holds on to hope for you. Perhaps you have lost hope or found hope. I wonder if your relationship with this thing called hope has changed through the years or remained constant.

Hope is a well-used word. Hope is perhaps one of those things that 'perches in our souls', to quote Emily Dickinson, more than one of those things we can pin down with definitions. That doesn't mean that we should stop trying to understand hope. After all, it plays such a big part in what it means to be human that to explore it, play with its meanings and twiddle with the edges of its implications can be a profound experience.

The big stuff

Our reading from Isaiah 35 is big stuff; it's no wonder that it forms some of the first part of Handel's *Messiah*. It is poetic language that gives us the big picture of what we are hoping for in dramatic terms. We get the message in glorious 3D, HD, blue-ray or, for those of us who still operate in old money, technicolour – that creation will be transformed, and humanity will be transformed. And literally, as well as symbolically, central to this tale of transformation is the presence of God. There are ten verses in this passage and in the second half of verse 4 a shout goes up, 'Here is your God.' It would be very easy to pause at this point and read off a very simple message that we can, and should, be hopeful people. It's simply a matter of passive, confident belief in a brighter future.

However, this big-picture description of the transformation of creation and humanity follows hard on the heels of an equally dramatic description of God's judgement and vengeance on the nations in the preceding chapter. This paints such a horrible picture of the future that if it were on the radio or television news the newsreader would be giving out that warning about it including material some people might find disturbing. Read together you get whiplash. We are brought face to face, I think, with the reality that the presence of God – 'Here is your God!' – can be as disturbing and frightening as it can be comforting and encouraging.

Hanging on

Today is the feast of Luke the evangelist. Modern scholars aren't sure if the Gospel of Luke was actually written by Luke the physician, travelling companion of Paul and evangelist, but the text as we have it today is at the very least a remembering in his name, something which catches his character and priorities. And Luke was all about looking at the big picture and hanging on to hope. Luke primarily wrote a narrative, a story, 'an orderly account', to quote his own words. Luke included the speeches and sayings that others left out. 'Here is your God,' he indicates, in particular events which tell of pleasure, comfort and transformation. And 'Here is your God' too in events of absolute fear and disturbance. 'This is what it all means,' he says as he puts words and sentences into accounts of speeches. Hang on, in the flow of the story, God is ultimately faithful and longs to bring salvation to everyone. In the context of the persecution of the first Christians, it is not too much of a stretch to imagine copies of Luke's orderly account acting as transitional objects providing security, strength and certainty.

Getting comfy

There's a lot about hope that we can't pin down with words, not because it's simply an internal feeling but because there's so much about hope that is simply a mystery. What is hopeful to cling on to when what you are experiencing is terrifying or disturbing? And yet we often do hope at those times, because we believe in a narrative or because sometimes, if we are honest, habit. Central to Christian belief is the image of the empty tomb – not the symbol of the absence of God but the symbol of the presence of God, always slightly ahead of us on the road, leaving a faint trace behind or casting a long shadow back. That's 'the tune without words that never stops at all', to quote Dickinson again. That's the plot of the story. To live as people comfortable with the mysterious side of hope, to wait for the big picture to emerge as the writer(s) of Luke's Gospel did, would give us all permission to be a bit more open to the opportunities and sheer joy of serendipity and a bit more absorbed by goodness.

Esther Elliott

Hymn suggestions

All my hope on God is founded; We lay our broken world; St Luke, beloved physician; Lord of all hopefulness.

SS Simon and Jude, Apostles 28 October
Lost Causes?

Isa. 28.14–16; **Ps. 119.89–96**; Eph. 2.19–end; John 15.17–end

Some years ago, my wife and I were walking along one of the beaches on Iona. It was windy, and the wind was blowing sand into our faces. Heather got some sand in her eye and took out her contact lens to clean it. Along came another gust of wind, and the lens was gone. We were miles from anywhere with no replacement lens, and no glasses either! We began to search.

Looking for a contact lens on a beach is frustrating, to say the least. Forty-five minutes later, we were still searching. It seemed a totally lost cause. And so we decided to seek the help of St Jude, the patron saint of lost causes. In a few minutes, we found the missing lens, sitting innocently on the sand.

Simon and Jude

Today is the feast of Simon and Jude – two of Jesus' 12 apostles. Simon was known as the Zealot, presumably because he belonged to a resistance movement opposing the Roman occupying forces. Jude (or Judas) is probably the same person as Thaddaeus. They are remembered together, because of a tradition that they both evangelized in Mesopotamia.

Because Jude's name is similar to that of Judas Iscariot, historically Christians tended not to pray through him. It seems likely that he became something of a 'last resort' for prayer; hence the patron saint of lost causes. But is there really such a thing as a lost cause?

All part of God's plan?

Christians sometimes say, when things don't work out, 'It's all part of God's plan.' I find this annoying. Most of us have situations in our lives when things don't turn out as we hope (or expect) they will. Sometimes, looking back, we realize that, in the end, there was a different outcome which turned out to be better. Hindsight is a wonderful thing! But did God really *plan* it like that? Are our lives mapped out to the nth degree, and is our job as faithful Christians to try and stick absolutely to God's plan – whatever that might be – making sure we don't put a foot wrong?

In the film *About Time*, Tim, a young man, can travel back in time and relive episodes in his past – altering the past to improve his own future and that of others. The plot centres on his relationship with Mary: by continually revisiting encounters from the past, he can engineer events so that they end up together. It's good entertainment – but it does beg several questions:

- Is there really a single right path?
- If we 'go wrong' – can we put things right, or are we a lost cause?
- And what might God have to do with it?

In the Bible, there are two distinct strands of thinking. On the one hand is an all-seeing and all-knowing God – God with a plan. On the other is the metaphor of walking faithfully with God, using imagery of paths and ways. This was picked up by the first Christians who spoke of their faith as 'the Way'.

So, does God have a plan for us? The danger of swallowing this wholesale is that we can easily be convinced that if we depart from it, everything becomes a lost cause, and ultimately *we* become a lost cause too. This can drive us either to excessive caution or bleak despair; or resignation that everything happens 'because it's God's will'.

Free will and responsibility

As Christians, we hold that God gives us free will. Although we might know exactly what we should do, we are free to choose to do otherwise. We leave undone those things which we ought to do; and we do those things which we ought not to do. Free will is a divine gift and is one of the marks of humanity that stems from the fact that we bear God's image. God expects us to use our free will sensibly: to think about our actions, but above all to walk continually with God. God has less a plan than a *purpose* for us: that we keep walking in the Way. As we walk, we are to pray that we will stick close to God.

Sometimes we're good at this, at other times we're more like the proverbial sheep who go astray. But when we stray from the Way, all is not lost – we are never a lost cause. God is still there, because Jesus – through whom we know God – is *himself* the Way. Our faith is fundamentally personal and relational. St Jude once asked Jesus the question: 'Lord, how is it that you will reveal yourself to us ...?' Jesus replied, 'Those who love me will keep my word, and

349

my Father will love them, and we will come to them and make our home with them.'

Peter Moger

Hymn suggestions

O God, you search me and you know me; O for a closer walk with God; There is no moment of my life; We have a gospel to proclaim.

All Saints' Day   1 November (*or* 5 November)
Remembering the Saints
Rev. 7.9–end; Ps. 34.1–10; 1 John 3.1–3; **Matt. 5.1–12**

Legacy of saints

Since my father's death in 2021, All Saints' Day has taken on a more significant meaning in my life. For his funeral in Nigeria, I had the task of writing his obituary. The process of writing the highlights of my father's legacy to our family and all those touched by his life was both a gift and a burden. My father, a man who dedicated his life to Christ and gave his life to the service of humanity, is indeed one of the many saints who shaped my life. Today's Gospel is the Beatitudes, where Jesus offers a description of a life blessed by God. We are reminded that whoever lives out the Beatitudes fully will indeed become a saint. The Beatitudes speak to our relationship with God and our relationship with our neighbour.

When a person we love dies, the relationship that continues is significant when understood as an embodiment of history and memory which lives on through those left behind. Similarly, the saints of our Scriptures play a role in communicating the links between tradition, remembering and the gospel. There is a sense in which we participate in collaborative work with the saints, past and present day, as we contribute to the missional work of the gospel.

Blessed are the poor in spirit

One thing I find reassuring about the saints is that they are far from perfect, just like you and me. To illustrate, even though St Peter left everything to follow Christ and witnessed incredible miracles performed by Jesus, at certain points his faith failed him to the point of denying Christ not once but three times. Nonetheless, God never lets go of Peter and he became one of the great builders of the Church.

'Blessed are the poor in spirit, for theirs is the kingdom of heaven,' says Jesus. Put another way, we are being reminded, blessed are those who know their need of God and also know their need for God's love, help, strength, guidance and forgiveness. The saints reflect this paradox of being poor in spirit and yet knowing the goodness of God. They relied fully on God, trusting the divine for renewed vision, purpose and hope in the face of life's challenges. They turned to God for the infilling of the fruits of the Spirit: love, joy, peace, patience, kindness, goodness, faithfulness and self-control. Because, as Psalm 34 reminds us, 'I sought the LORD, and he answered me, and delivered me from all my fears.' We are told that the kingdom of heaven belongs to such people: those who realize that they are nothing and God is everything.

Living in the footsteps of the saints

The stories of the saints encourage and inspire us in our service to God. Their lives and testimonies point us to God's kingdom values and reveal what kingdom life is like. The saints in their living out the Beatitudes offer us a study in faith, perseverance and service.

The Beatitudes are less about actions and more about relationships. They are less about what we do, and more about how we do, and who we are as followers of Christ. To live the Beatitudes is to live a life of generous compassion and radical love for God and our neighbour. We live the Beatitudes as a response to God's abundance and provision in our lives.

We are called every day to love God more by leaning into our Creator in prayer, word and fellowship. Jesus longs for us to learn from him so that we can live lives in the footsteps of the saints whom we remember today, lives which bless others.

Catherine Okoronkwo

Hymn suggestions

Blessed are the poorest ones (The Beatitudes, Hillsong); Come, let us join our friends above; The Church's one foundation; For all the saints, who from their labours rest.

Commemoration of the Faithful Departed
(All Souls' Day)   2 November
The Darkness and the Light
Lam. 3.17–26, 31–33, or Wisd. 3.1–9; Ps. 23, or Ps. 27.1–6,
16–end; Rom. 5.5–11, or 1 Peter 1.3–9; John 5.19–25,
or **John 6.37–40**

The darkness and the light

In almost all of the great works of fantasy or adventure, there is a
juxtaposition between darkness and light. Think of any epic poem,
story, film or novel – anything with 'goodies and baddies', and we
are likely to find that the breaking through of light into somewhere
dark is a powerful symbol of hope or joy or peace breaking into
a place of fear, isolation or dread. Whether you're thinking of an
historic work of fiction or the most recent superhero movie, the
theme is hard to miss. And of course, the theme is front and centre
in the Bible itself.

There is a link between the light and the darkness, the glory and
the shadow. We are called, of course, to look into the light, but the
light causes shadows, the darkness must be recognized and wrestled
with, because it belongs to us, like our shadow on a bright and
sunny day. It is hard to miss.

Feeling the darkness

And that is not a new thought, of course. Christian theologians,
philosophers and poets have struggled with the relationship
between the light and the darkness since the beginning. And we
feel it, in particular, in two places in our annual journey through
the Christian year – on Good Friday, and here, amid these two
special days which come one after another, and indeed are often
kept together in parish churches: All Saints' and All Souls'.

Yesterday, in a blaze of gold, white and light, probably with
hymns of joy and triumph, we gave thanks to God 'For all the
saints who from their labours rest'. For all those countless people,
young and old who have been lights on the way, heralds of the
kingdom and witnesses to the Lord. Great ones: prophets, kings,
priests, evangelists, missionaries, teachers, nurses, lovers of people
and servants of God. We gave thanks for the great host, vested in

the panoply of God, who surround our steps, aid our prayers and worship before God in his nearer presence.

Grieving our own saints

Today, muted, quieter and with a rather different tone, we acknowledge the shadow which comes with this light. The shadow in the lives of the saints, the shadow which streams from you and me when we meet here this evening, is grief. Is loss. St Matthew was someone's son. So was John Chrysostom. Mary Magdalene was someone's daughter, someone's friend, was special to someone. So were each of the saints to whom our local churches are dedicated. The saints pump faith and light into the bloodstream of the praying community, but they are also grieved and missed – some of them by entire continents, entire churches. Most of them by families, and some of them perhaps by just one or two people. But they are grieved and missed because they were people. Loved, missed and grieved.

The people we remember today, on All Souls' Day, whether their names are read out loud in church or cried out in prayer from the depths of our hearts, are those who have been saints to us, our local saints, if you like – those who have spoken to us, encouraged us, whose lives have met with ours – possibly just kissing our life for a few brief weeks or months, possibly absolutely intertwined with ours for decades. People with whom we have laughed and argued and fallen out. People who have left handprints on our hearts.

And though in many cases we will be full of thankfulness for their lives, still we walk in the shadow that their death casts over us. And here, on this day, we can acknowledge that, and pray through it, and wait in the stillness for God to speak and to offer his arms of consolation, that we might rest in them.

Hearing the 'Alleluia' build

And we offer it all up to the God who knows about the darkness – the God who sank into the depths on Good Friday when a whole society drove him over the edge and into the grave. But the God, also, whose grave-clothes were folded three days later, and whose tomb stood empty: a confident assertion of the victory of the light, no matter how dark the shadows might sometimes become. Because today's promise is the same as yesterday's. The tomb is empty – the dark place where we thought we had to go alone is not empty at all,

353

because God is there, in our shadows as in our light, and there is an 'Alleluia' building in the deep,

And when the strife is fierce, the warfare long,
Steals on the ear the distant triumph song,
And hearts are brave, again, and arms are strong.
Alleluia, Alleluia!

Tom Clammer

Hymn suggestions

Going home, moving on; Go, silent friend; In our day of thanksgiving, one psalm let us offer; Now is eternal life.

St Andrew the Apostle 30 November
Follow Me
Isa. 52.7–10; Ps. 19.1–6; Rom. 10.12–18; **Matt. 4.18–22**

Some celebrities can boast hundreds of thousands of Twitter followers. [Name a few with their statistics.]

In today's Gospel reading, Jesus appears to start with just four followers: Simon Peter, Andrew, James and John. We don't know why these first followers left their nets and followed him or why James and John did, but their father, who was in the boat with them at the same time, didn't. John's Gospel tells us that Andrew, whose feast we celebrate today, was a disciple of John the Baptist. So, perhaps the men knew of Jesus by reputation already, or maybe they met him on a previous occasion. But follow Jesus they did, and it is because of their faith and the faith of others like them that we find ourselves here today. Our call to follow Jesus is similar to theirs.

Journeying with Jesus

Following an itinerant preacher like Jesus meant that life was never going to be static. They were always going to be on something like a journey for the rest of their lives. There was, of course, the initial decision to follow Jesus, followed by the actions (and upheaval) that would inevitably entail. The disciples did not know where it would lead them or the joy and hardships to come, but they followed Jesus. They embarked on their journeys, drawn by the attraction of Jesus: who he was and what he said and did.

And as they went on this journey with Jesus, their knowledge and experience of him journeyed too. It deepened and developed; it did not remain static. They discovered new things about him, sometimes radical and shocking, as they began to understand what his presence in their lives and the world meant: the real meaning of his incarnation with its demands and challenges.

In the same way, Jesus invites us as his followers on that same journey. He invites us to come to know more and more about him and his relevance for us and our world as we walk with him on the journey of our lives. And in the same way, our understanding of him and our spiritual lives cannot remain static; our faith should develop from our early insights as we follow him. We should expect to learn more and more about Jesus.

Leaving their nets behind

Almost by definition, if you're on a journey, you can't take everything with you. Just like the disciples, who left their nets behind, we too may be asked to leave some things behind as we journey with Jesus, sometimes the very things that give us security and some degree of comfort. Moving on implies leaving some things behind.

Part of that leaving behind is contained in the vital message Jesus gives to all who would seek to follow him. Repent. Turn (back) to God because the kingdom of heaven is near at hand. Coming close to God so God can come close to us is about turning around and turning to God. Turning away and leaving the things that separate us from God, and turning to the things that draw us closer to him. Being active and involved in extending his kingdom.

Jesus calls us as his followers to be fishers of people. To go and tell the good news of his kingdom, the good news of justice, peace and equality for all so that others may come to be his followers too. He calls us too to speak up and step up.

Like the early disciples, we may not know what we are being called to next. Like them, we may not, in the first instance, have witnessed miracles of healing or supernatural activity. But like those early fishermen, we are called to leave our nets – those things that give us earthly security – and follow him.

Nets will never be the same again

From the Gospel account, we know that these fishermen-disciples did, from time to time, go back to their nets. But when they did, they did so with a different outlook. Jesus the Messiah – not their earthly skills or possessions – was their security. The risen Jesus met them where they first began, but so much had happened that things could never be the same again.

Likewise, we are free to go back to our nets, but after encountering the risen Jesus we will never see things in the same light again. Those things that once held us back can, in the light of the transforming power of the resurrection, be instruments of the kingdom. Things can never be the same again for those who have met the risen Christ.

Come, follow me, says Jesus. The invitation is his; the response, like St Andrew, is ours.

Paul Williams

Hymn suggestions

Jesus calls us, o'er the tumult; Will you come and follow me; When Christ our Lord to Andrew cried; Go forth and tell.

Harvest Festival
The Harvest of the Sea
Deut. 8.7–18, *or* Deut. 28.1–14; **Ps. 65**; 2 Cor. 9.6–end; **Luke 12.16–30**, *or* Luke 17.11–19

The pull of the sea

> I must go down to the seas again, to the lonely sea and the sky …
> To the gull's way and the whale's way where the wind's like a whetted knife.

The sea is an ever-present reality in the UK – only a couple of hours away, even if you live in Lichfield, which at 84 miles is the farthest from the sea in any direction. Yet the tidal rhythms are never far from mind; or from reality, as the rivers snake inland. John Masefield's poem expresses the yearning for the grey mist on the sea's face; the grey dawn breaking.

The Psalmist prays to the God of our salvation, who is 'the hope of all the ends of the earth and of the farthest seas', who silences 'the roaring of the seas, the roaring of their waves, the tumult of the peoples'.

Land ... and sea

So often, at harvest festival, we focus on the work of farmers – and yes, thanks are due for all farmers do to ensure this nation is fed. But what of the sea? The fishermen who catch our fish and chips (well, not the chips, obviously). Who brave the seas to draw out what God so generously provides, who harvest the living things both small and great.

Fishing remains the most dangerous peacetime occupation in the UK. Death and serious injury are often the true cost of the fish we enjoy. Retired fishermen and their families struggle with poverty and chronic ill health following life at sea. The Marine Accident Investigation Branch offers a litany of loss of life and vessel – shocking to read. The Fishermen's Mission[14] is as busy as ever, watching out for active fishermen working out of many different ports, inlets and harbours and caring for retired colleagues and families. There is a true cost of our fish and chips; and the reality behind the statistics are the families, children, loved ones, friends and grief-stricken communities left behind.

Costs and responsibilities

The costs are not only human – in all our farming and fishing. Thousands of tons of debris are discarded each year, with a severe cost to wildlife. Seabirds become entangled in the 'ghost' fishing nets that drift through the sea, abandoned by trawlers. Leviathan, that wonderful and ancient word for the whale, created by God to sport in the sea – and what a sight that is; to watch whales playing, singing, their enormous, awesome bulk at home in the waves. But now whales, dolphins and porpoises die with digestive tracts full of plastic packaging and shopping bags.

Whether fisher or farmer, whether consumer or tourist, we need to know, far more responsibly, the costs of our needs and desires. Today we give thanks, but we also turn to God, the Creator and giver of all good things, and we say sorry. Harvest is the time to promise reverence for the natural world. Deuteronomy expresses God's call to humanity not to be greedy but to act responsibly in creation, as stewards of the beautiful world God has made, which is everywhere described in the Bible. For from the rich gifts of creation, humanity is satisfied. Fish, meat, vegetables, wine, oil, bread. What more could humanity need?

God, the Creator of this planet earth, with humanity – given responsibility for the created order, not the right to exploit. We know this is complex: the pressures of an ever-changing political scene, where uncertainty about the future and anxiety are real, where times are hard. But we must make changes to our lifestyles. As consumers we can bring pressure, as we buy our fish, our meat and vegetables – to reduce plastic, to enhance environmentally friendly policies.

Giving thanks, changing lifestyles

Christians bring deep thinking to commend hope in God in the faith that inspires people to change. We can and should take and use only what we need; training our appetites, away from greed and selfishness. And we should use the power we have as consumers, heeding the warning to the rich man with his larger barns. It is our richness towards God that matters, not our all-too-affluent lifestyles.

As we give thanks today, let us also repent and change, and live differently on this planet, with the intense current pressures it faces. Let's act, fully aware of the damage we do to the natural environment. The natural world that provides so much needs us to care for it, not turn it into a rubbish tip. So, the God-given Leviathan, the birds and the fish, can sport without danger, and numbers grow in God-given abundance.

Frances Ward

Hymn suggestions

There's a wideness in God's mercy; All creatures of our God and king; Eternal Father, strong to save; For the beauty of the earth.

All-Age Services

Advent All-Age

The Jesse Tree

This service can be used on any of the Sundays of Advent. Choose appropriate readings from those set for the Sundays in Advent (Year A).

Props

- A large branch planted in a pot, or a large house plant – that can hold decorations.
- The following decorations – pictures, models etc. (use your imagination!) of apples, rainbows, tents, rolled-up hymns, tablets of stone, question marks, arrows, hammers, hearts, strips of cloth.
- Handheld microphone.

Script: Christmas trees

Wander about the congregation with the microphone asking these questions:

Who has put their Christmas tree up already?
Where have you put it?
What does it look like?
What have you put on it?
Who has homemade decorations on their tree?
Who made them?

Feedback and develop as appropriate.

Did you know Christmas trees are quite new in the UK? They were introduced from Germany by Prince Albert in the nineteenth century. However, we used to have a tradition in this country called the Jesse Tree and that dates from the eleventh century – so nearly 1,000 years ago.

The Jesse Tree

Throughout Advent the Jesse Tree was decorated with symbols. It was a way of using stories from the Bible to remind people of their roots in faith.

It's called the Jesse Tree because in the Bible it says the Messiah will come from the house of David. In Isaiah, it says: 'A shoot shall come out from the stump of Jesse, and a branch shall grow out of his roots.' Jesse was King David's father, and Jesus was indeed related to King David. That's why Mary and Joseph went to Bethlehem to register during the census.

Here's our Jesse Tree and we're going to cover it today with decorations that remind us of people in the Bible – our ancestors in faith. I'll describe an event in the Bible and the sort of person that relates to, and if that sounds like you, I'd like you to come and hang a decoration on the tree. It's for all ages – all of us. You don't have to hang a decoration and you can hang more than one if you like.

Decorating the Jesse Tree

1 At the very beginning of the Bible we learn that God is our Creator. God makes all things, the universe and everything in it. Adam and Eve are the first people God creates. They live in the Garden of Eden but they disobey God and their friendship with God is broken.

   If you are someone who loves creation – and cares about the natural world and if you long to see things made whole and restored – then come and hang an **apple** on the tree.

2 Noah was a very faithful man at a time when the world wasn't much interested in God. God kept Noah and his family and two of every animal safe during the great flood. God promised to keep loving people and being their God for ever. The rainbow is a symbol of God's promise.

   If you are someone who trusts in God's promises and who recognizes that God's love never ends, and everyone is included in that love – then come and hang a **rainbow** on the tree.

3 Abraham and Sarah left their home to go where God led them and together founded a new nation. Abraham and Sarah welcomed angels into their tent in the desert and were blessed by God.

If you are someone who is faithful to God by opening your home and sharing lots of hospitality, and if you regularly have friends in to play or for meals – then come and hang a **tent** on the tree.

4 David was an unimportant shepherd boy who became a great king. God often does amazing things with the small and the least. David worshipped God with music and wrote many songs which we still use today.

If you are someone who feels close to God through music, or if you express your love for God by making music, or you love singing – then come and hang a **hymn** on the tree.

5 Moses led God's people out of Israel to freedom. God gave Moses the Ten Commandments so that we could learn to live our lives under God's laws.

If you are someone who longs for others to be free, or who finds yourself leading people or teaching them – then come and hang **tablets of stone** on the tree.

6 Jeremiah was a prophet who struggled with God. He was often depressed and angry and couldn't understand what God was doing. Jeremiah's ordinary human weakness helped people grow in faith.

If you are someone who struggles with God and who asks 'Why?' a lot and finds it hard to make sense of what God is doing – then come and hang a **question mark** on our tree.

7 John the Baptist prepared the way for the Messiah – for Jesus. He called people to turn their lives around and start fresh with God.

If you are someone who tries to point the way to Jesus, and who helps others change direction to find God – then come and hang an **arrow** on the tree.

8 Joseph was a carpenter who found himself caught up in God's plan and wasn't sure what to do. But he was loyal and trusted Mary and was a good dad for Jesus.

If you are someone who expresses your faith through practical things, doing things for God, or you are working hard to be a good and loyal parent – then come and hang a **hammer** on the tree.

9 Mary was a brave woman, who did what God wanted even though it brought scandal. She was a woman who dared to do life differently. She carried the Messiah Jesus inside her and so was perhaps closer to God than anyone has ever been.

   If you are someone who is making a place for Jesus in your heart this Christmas and you long to be closer to God – then come and hang a **heart** on the tree.

10 Advent is the time of year when we remember that God came into our world in Jesus, that God is with us now in the Holy Spirit and that Jesus has promised to come again.

   If you are someone wanting to get ready for Jesus, if you are waiting and watching for him – then come and tie a **strip of cloth** to the tree, your gift to prepare the manger.

So that's a Jesse Tree – thank you for your help. When you decorate your Christmas tree think about what your decorations could mean – and perhaps make some new ones too to reflect your faith. Remember that you are decorating your house in celebration and preparation for Jesus, who is coming very soon. As you prepare your house, prepare your heart too to receive Jesus.

Catherine Williams

Hymn suggestions

Make way, make way; Long ago, prophets knew; All I once held dear; O come, O come, Emmanuel.

Christmas
The Gift of Jesus
Isa. 9.2–7; Titus 2.11–14; **Luke 2.1–14 [15–20]**

Preparation

Paul and I often preach together for all-age worship. We find a variety of voices, conversational dialogue and congregation participation keeps people of all ages attentive and engaged. This sermon could be adapted for a single voice, but it's good to collaborate with others if you can.

Props

You will need a large carton of wrapped sweets (Celebrations, Heroes, Lindors etc.) wrapped in shiny red/gold Christmas paper, tied in gold ribbon with a couple of stick-on ribbon bows, and a large wastepaper basket.

Script

Voice 1: Happy Christmas! I hope Father Christmas has visited you, and some exciting gifts have appeared in your house to help you celebrate the birthday of Jesus.

Voice 2: I've got a gift here for you – from me.

Voice 1: Ooo! How exciting! Thank you! It looks beautiful. Did you wrap it yourself?

Voice 2: Well, almost – I had a little help!

Voice 1: It's lovely! Look! Two beautiful bows – I must keep them – they'll make perfect accessories for my stole!
(*Stick the ribbon bows on to stole/preaching scarf etc.*)
And look at this lovely gold ribbon – it will make a fabulous bracelet.
(*Tie ribbon around wrist and display to the congregation.*)
The paper is rather wonderful too – if I smooth it out I could keep it and use it again.
(*Unwrap present and smooth out the paper.*)

Voice 2: It will make a great seasonal super-frontal for the altar (hanging for the pulpit/lectern etc.)!
(*Pin the wrapping paper to the altar, or hang from the pulpit/lectern etc. and admire.*)

Voice 1:   Great box too – I don't need the contents – where's the bin?
(*Pour chocolates into the wastepaper basket.*) That's all just rubbish. But the box will make an excellent vase – I'll pop it here on the altar.
(*Place the carton on the altar and admire.*)

Voice 2:   Actually, the contents aren't rubbish – look at these lovely shiny bits of paper – I'm sure we could use these for something.
(*Unwrap a sweet each – throw the sweets in the bin and look thoughtfully at the sweet wrapper – hold it up to the light and ponder.*)

Voice 2:   I know!

Voices 1 and 2 together: A stained-glass window!

Voice 1:   Thanks for such a great gift – much appreciated.

Voice 1:   Sadly, some people treat the celebration of Christmas a bit like that. They get very excited about the trappings, the decorations, the shopping, the food, the television, the parties – all the outside bits – but they forget the inner importance, the reason for the season. The true gift is Jesus, God born among us, as one of us – come to save us.

Voice 2:   Jesus is the perfect gift. He holds his value for all eternity. He's a gift that keeps on giving, a gift that never expires. There's no use-by date on Jesus. He won't go bad or spoil. You'll never have to throw him out. He doesn't even go out of fashion. Whatever age you are, he's right for you! Every generation needs a Saviour, someone to walk alongside them, rescue them and make them right with God.

Voice 1:   I'm not sure I've been good enough to deserve such a special gift!

Voice 2:   That's the best part of all. You don't have to earn the gift of Jesus – he's a free gift, available to everyone, whoever you are and whatever you've done. When Jesus was born, the shepherds weren't special people – they didn't go to the Temple and some thought they were bad people, but the angels brought them the good news about the birth of Jesus. The shepherds were able to go and see the baby and thank God for the gift. Their lives changed because of the gift of Jesus.

Voice 1:   It's very important that we use the gift of Jesus – and not forget about him or keep him for special days and celebrations. Our faith needs to grow, to be nourished and nurtured – just like the baby Jesus – so that we can grow up into the full stature of Christ, and become more and more like Jesus in our words and actions. The gift of Jesus is for each of us, and for us to give away to others too.

Voice 2:   How can you use the gift of Jesus this Christmas? Our world is a really troubled and hurting place at the moment. How could you use the gift of Jesus to make the world a better place? Some of the names used by the prophet Isaiah help us here.

Voice 1:   Jesus is a Wonderful Counsellor – someone who walks alongside and listens, and guides people. Where can you do that for another? Jesus is described as Mighty God – where can you lend your strength to help another? How can you point someone to God …?

Voice 2:   Jesus comes from the everlasting Father. Where can you bring hope to someone – belief that things in the future will improve and be bright, belief that God holds on to us come what may and will never let us go. Keeping hope alive is a very Christ-shaped activity. Jesus is the Prince of Peace – our world really needs peace, between nations, in our communities and homes and relationships. Being a person of peace means going the extra mile in our relationships, working hard to bring about reconciliation so that we can move forward together.

Voice 1:   This Christmas, resolve to use the gift of Jesus given to you. Share him with others. Be a person of faith, integrity, peace, strength, hope and goodness. Go out from here and resolve to change the world because of the great gift of Jesus you've been given. 'For a child has been born for us, a son given to us … and he is named Wonderful Counsellor, Mighty God, Everlasting Father, Prince of Peace.'

Catherine and Paul Williams

Hymn suggestions

While shepherds watched; Joy to the world; Hark! the herald angels sing; Mary's boy child.

Mothering Sunday   19 March
Star Mums!

Ex. 2.1–10, *or* 1 Sam. 1.20–end; Ps. 34.11–20, *or* Ps. 127.1–4;
2 Cor. 1.3–7, *or* Col. 3.12–17; Luke 2.33–35, *or* John 19.25b–27

Props

- Eight giant fluorescent stars. Each one with a name written on it (Eve, Sarah, Elizabeth, Naomi, Hannah, Rachel, Deborah, Mary).
- Sufficient small fluorescent stars for everyone in the congregation (give these out beforehand).
- Pens for everyone.
- Handheld microphone.

NB Depending on your context, you might want to use terms such as 'carer' as well as 'mum'.

Script

Mothering Sunday. Today's the day we remember and give thanks for our mum. It's also a day to give thanks for our 'mother church' – so that's both our church here and our cathedral. It's also a time when we remember that God is like a mother to us – loving and caring for us.

Star mums in church

Hands up if you have ever had a mother?
That's everyone! All of us were born – we've all had a mother at some point in our lives.
Hands up if you think your mum is a 'star' – who's got a 'star mum?'
(*Walk around with microphone asking: 'Why is your mum a star?' Feedback and develop as appropriate.*)
There are lots of star mums here today.

Star mums in the Bible

There are lots of star mums in the Bible too. I thought we'd have a quiz this morning and see if we can name some star mums in the Bible.

(As each correct answer is given, ask the person to come up and place the large star with the appropriate name on it somewhere where everyone can see it – e.g., in front of the altar or somewhere central.)

- This mum was the very first mum of all – and it's a hard job doing things for the first time so she didn't always get it right (*Eve*).
- This mum left her home when she was very old and travelled with her husband Abraham to a new place. She found out she was pregnant when she was about 80 years old and she was so surprised she laughed (*Sarah*).
- This person was the mum of John of the Baptist (*Elizabeth*).
- This mum in the Old Testament was the mother-in-law of Ruth – her name begins with N (*Naomi*).
- This mum wanted a baby so badly she prayed and prayed to God, and when she had a son, she called him Samuel and gave him back to God and he was brought up in the Temple (*Hannah*).
- This was the mum of Joseph and Benjamin in the Old Testament. She was very beautiful and she and her sister Leah were both married to Jacob (*Rachel*).
- This mum was a judge. She ruled over all the land and she was called the mother of Israel – her name begins with D (*Deborah*).
- This is an easy one – this mum had a baby at Christmas (*Mary*).

Lots of star mums – some old, some young. Some had lots of children, some had a few. None of them were perfect but they were all loved by their families and by God. And they were faithful to God and brought up their children to love, worship and serve God, even when that was very difficult or dangerous. One of the most important things that a Christian mum can do is to pass on her faith in Jesus Christ to her family and teach her children through her own example to love God.

Thanking God

We've got some star mums here by the altar (*point to the large stars*) but it would be good to have some more too. You should have all been given a small star when you came in. I'd like you to write the name of your mum on the star, or the name of someone who is like a mum to you. I've written the name of my mum on my star even though she's in heaven – because she's alive in God and I can still remember her and say 'thank you' for her even though she's no longer here with me.

When you've written the name, come and place your star on the altar.

(*Place stars on the altar – if you are presiding, place the corporeal over the stars so that you are presiding on top of all the names.*)

Let's pray:
Thank you, God, for our star mums.
For all the love and care they've given us over the years.
Keep each of us faithful to Jesus
and help us to grow more and more into your family.
In the name of Jesus and through the power of the Holy Spirit,
we pray. Amen.

Catherine Williams

Hymn suggestions

For the beauty of the earth; For Mary, mother of our Lord, He's got the whole world in his hands; Jesus put this song into our hearts.

Notes

1 See https://www.merriam-webster.com/dictionary/Pollyanna, accessed 11.05.2021.
2 A. A. Milne, *The House at Pooh Corner* (London: Methuen and Co. Ltd, 1926).
3 Julian of Norwich, *Revelations of Divine Love* (Harmondsworth: Penguin, 1966), p. 103.
4 For Judas' betrayal, see Matthew 26.14–16, 47–50; Mark 14.10–11, 43–45; Luke 22.1–6, 47–48; John 13.21–30; 18.2–3. For Peter's denial, see Matthew 26.69–75; Mark 14.66–72; Luke 22.54–62; John 18.15–18, 25–27.
5 Matthew 26.36–46; 14.32–42; Luke 22.39–46.
6 W. Brueggemann, *The Message of the Psalms: A Theological Commentary* (Minneapolis, MN: Augsburg, 1984); *Finally Comes the Poet: Daring Speech for Proclamation* (Minneapolis, MN: Fortress Press, 1989); *Cadences of Home: Preaching among Exiles* (Louisville, KY: Westminster John Knox Press, 1997); *Spirituality of the Psalms* (Minneapolis, MN: Fortress Press, 2002).
7 The prayer used after the laying-on of hands and anointing, *Common Worship: Wholeness and Healing*, www.churchofengland.org/prayer-and-worship/worship-texts-and-resources/common-worship/wholeness-and-healing/wholeness-and#mm091, accessed 11.01.2022.
8 From George Herbert, 'The Call'.
9 Quoted in M. Jagessar and A. Reddie, *Black Theology in Britain: A Reader* (London: Equinox, 2007), p. 50.
10 John L. Bell © 1995 Iona Community admin. GIA Publications Inc., https://hymnary.org/text/take_o_take_me_as_i_am, accessed 11.01.2022.
11 Richard Crashaw (c. 1612–49), *Adoro te: Hymn in Adoration of the Blessed Sacrament*, after Thomas Aquinas (c. 1225–74).
12 Charles Wesley (1707–88), 'Victim divine, thy grace we claim', in *Hymns on the Lord's Supper* (Bristol, 1745).
13 C. H. Spurgeon, from a sermon preached on 7 January 1855, cited in J. I. Parker, *Knowing God* (London: Hodder and Stoughton, 1973), p. 13.
14 See www.fishermensmission.org.uk/, accessed 11.02.2022.